EXAMINING
HEISEI JAPAN

EXAMINING HEISEI JAPAN

POLITICS

Supervised by
KITAOKA Shinichi

Edited by
IIO Jun

VOL. II

Japan Publishing Industry Foundation for Culture

Publisher's Note
This book follows the Hepburn system of romanization, with long vowels indicated by macrons. The tradition of placing the family name first has been followed for Japanese, Chinese, and Korean names. All essays featured in this compilation are from academic sources and were written between the years 1989 and 2019. With permission, adjustments have been made to each essay for purposes of style and readability.

Examining Heisei Japan, Vol. II: Politics
Supervised by Kitaoka Shinichi. Edited by Iio Jun.

Published by
Japan Publishing Industry Foundation for Culture (JPIC)
2-2-30 Kanda-Jinbocho, Chiyoda-ku, Tokyo 101-0051, Japan

First edition: November 2023

This publication is the result of a collaborative effort between the Japan Institute of International Affairs (JIIA) and Japan Publishing Industry Foundation for Culture (JPIC).

Book design: Miki Kazuhiko, Ampersand Works

Printed in Japan
hardcover ISBN 978-4-86658-247-4
ebook (ePub) ISBN 978-4-86658-171-2
https://www.jpicinternational.com/

CONTENTS

FOREWORD

This volume is based on a suggestion made by Dr. Kitaoka Shinichi, special advisor to the president of the Japan International Cooperation Agency (JICA) and a member of the steering committee for the territory, sovereignty, and history studies project that the Japan Institute of International Affairs (JIIA) undertook under a contract with the Japanese government.

Compiled here are English articles published during the Heisei years (1989–2019) by leading scholars and academic figures in various fields. This publication is intended, through these articles, to reexamine the features characterizing the Heisei era that extended over three decades of postwar Japanese history, and to make their insights more broadly available to the world.

The Heisei era, which started in 1989, was a period of turmoil both in Japan and internationally, contrary to the meaning of its name. Up until its end in 2019, the era was consistently characterized by unpredictability. By examining the writings of the leading scholars of the time, we can come to know how they regarded the era they lived through and, by sharing their thoughts in English with a global readership, we can provide important insights to better understand the Heisei era and to chart Japan's future path as we move forward in the Reiwa era.

Previously published volumes in the series addressed foreign and security policies and the economy during the Heisei years. This volume looks back on the shifts in the Japanese political environment of the time. Edited by Professor Iio Jun of the National Graduate Institute for Policy Studies (GRIPS), it brings together essays by leading researchers, political analysts, and practitioners. By presenting both contemporaneous and retrospective analyses, it aims to provide a multifaceted understanding of the complex political changes of Heisei Japan. The forthcoming final volume in the series will look back on the culture and society of this era.

In closing, I would like to express my profound gratitude to Dr. Kitaoka who suggested this program and guided it through to fruition; to our editor Professor Iio; the outstanding scholars who supported the project's objective and so generously donated their time, insights, and writings; and all those who contributed so much to make this publication possible.

Sasae Kenichiro
President, JIIA
November 2023

PREFACE

Iio Jun

Heisei is the Japanese era name assigned to the period when Emperor Akihito occupied the throne, from 1989 to 2019. It is, accordingly, a historical demarcation with no inherent political significance. As it happened, however, the Heisei era began as the Cold War was drawing to a close and ended just before the COVID-19 pandemic, a time of great social ferment. The intervening thirty years witnessed considerable upheaval in Japan and significant shifts in the political landscape. In the following, I provide a brief overview of the political history of the Heisei era as background for the essays collected here.

At the start of the Heisei era, the Japanese government was headed by Prime Minister Takeshita Noboru, president of the long-ruling Liberal Democratic Party (LDP). Backed by the LDP's most powerful faction, the Takeshita cabinet had succeeded in instituting a national consumption tax, a challenge that had defeated two previous administrations. But the Recruit scandal seriously eroded support for the Takeshita cabinet, and it resigned en masse in June 1989. Under Takeshita's successor, Prime Minister Uno Sōsuke, the LDP suffered a massive defeat in the 1989 House of Councillors election, losing the upper house majority it had held for many years. This election was a prelude to the political volatility that characterized Heisei-era Japan almost from the beginning, after the relative stability of the late Shōwa era.

The next LDP president and prime minister was the reform-minded Kaifu Toshiki. While the Kaifu cabinet managed to navigate the challenges of the Gulf War, it was unable to push through the political reforms needed to restore the public's confidence in government, and it stepped down in 1991.

Leadership then passed to the cabinet of Prime Minister Miyazawa Kiichi, which had its hands full controlling the damage from the collapse of the "bubble economy." In 1992, amid mounting cross-partisan calls for political reform, the stability of the LDP was eroded by internecine strife, which split the powerful Takeshita faction. In June 1993, the power struggle within the LDP climaxed as party dissidents joined with the opposition to pass a motion of no-confidence against the Miyazawa cabinet. Miyazawa responded by dissolving the House of Representatives and calling a general election, with the result that the LDP lost its majority in the lower house.

In the wake of this historic defeat, an anti-LDP coalition emerged from a diverse assemblage of parties, including the Social Democratic Party of Japan, or SDPJ (the new English name of the Japan Socialist Party), and two new breakaway parties formed by LDP defectors. In August 1993, the first non-LDP cabinet in almost 38 years was formed under Prime Minister Hosokawa Morihiro. In March 1994, the Hosokawa cabinet managed to enact sweeping reform legislation revamping the lower house electoral system and regulating political finances. The electoral reforms fundamentally altered the dynamics of House of Representatives elections with huge repercussions for Japanese politics in the Heisei era. But Hosokawa, unable to hold the alliance together, stepped down in April 1994.

When the SDPJ withdrew from the coalition, Hosokawa's successor, Hata Tsutomu, was obliged to form a minority cabinet. The Hata cabinet resigned just two months later, in June 1994. After a bout of furious maneuvering, the LDP managed to assemble a lower house majority by forging a coalition with the Social Democrats (longtime antagonists), tapping SDPJ leader Murayama Tomiichi as prime minister. The former members of Hata's coalition then coalesced into the New Frontier Party (NFP), laying the groundwork for a two-party setup.

The Murayama cabinet struggled with an ailing financial sector and a stagnant economy, while dogged by revelations of corruption in the bureaucracy. In January 1995, the Great Hanshin-Awaji Earthquake struck the Kobe area, and the government came under criticism for its slow response. Then came the Tokyo subway sarin attack of March 1995, which shocked the nation and fueled a growing sense of social malaise. The embattled Murayama cabinet stepped down in January 1996.

Upon Murayama's resignation, LDP president Hashimoto Ryūtarō became prime minister and formed another coalition cabinet. In the general election of October 1996, the LDP faced a new challenge as the coalition lost members to the newly formed Democratic Party of Japan (DPJ). Nonetheless, it came out ahead of the NFP, the leading opposition party. The second Hashimoto cabinet launched a crusade for "six great reforms," including the restructuring of government finances. Of particular significance for Heisei politics was Hashimoto's reorganization of the administrative apparatus, the first large-scale attempt by politicians to rein in Japan's powerful central bureaucracy. The Hashimoto cabinet also reached a key agreement with the US government on the return and relocation of various military facilities in Okinawa. But support for the administration slipped as the East Asian financial crisis triggered another economic downturn.

The NFP had splintered in late 1997, but much of the fragmented opposition united in the spring of 1998 to form the new DPJ, which made dramatic gains in the July 1998 House of Councillors election. The LDP government was left without an upper house majority, and Hashimoto resigned to take responsibility.

Under Hashimoto's successor, Obuchi Keizō, the LDP was obliged to compromise with opposition leaders on financial reform and other legislation, having lost control of the House of Councillors. At the same time, the Obuchi cabinet was working to strengthen the ruling party's position in the House of Councillors through coalition building. After enlisting the Liberal Party (LP) in late 1998, it brought Kōmeitō into the fold and formed an LDP-LP-Kōmeitō coalition cabinet in 1999. But Obuchi's tenure was cut short in April 2000 by disease. His successor, Mori Yoshirō, formed a coalition cabinet with Kōmeitō and the small Conservative Party (an offshoot of the LP, which had left the coalition). This laid the foundation for an enduring LDP-Kōmeitō partnership.

In the April 2001 LDP presidential election, dark horse candidate Koizumi Junichirō, a charismatic maverick, prevailed over former prime minister Hashimoto after vowing to "destroy the LDP" from within. He was designated prime minister and formed a cabinet the same month. Prime Minister Koizumi was a hit with the public, and his popularity translated into big gains for the LDP-led coalition in the July 2001 House of Councillors election. By leveraging his personal popularity and taking advantage of administrative reforms set in motion under Prime Minister Hashimoto, Koizumi was able to build a strong top-down policymaking apparatus and remain in office for almost five and a half years, despite his relatively weak power base within the LDP. As a prime minister who relied on popular support to consolidate political control, he was cited as an example of the "presidentialization" of parliamentary party politics, a trending international topic. At the same time, Koizumi was a controversial figure at home, criticized for his use of catchy sound bites and slogans to rally knee-jerk public support on complex issues. As a result, while his cabinet's approval ratings were outstanding, disapproval was relatively high as well.

Under the Koizumi cabinet, the government managed to resolve the problem of nonperforming loans that had weighed on the financial sector since the bubble's collapse. It also implemented the Trinity Reform of local public finances—an integrated readjustment of local taxes, national subsidies, and local allocation tax grants. In the arena of foreign policy, Koizumi adopted a newly assertive and proactive brand of diplomacy.

His secretly planned, abruptly announced visit to Pyongyang led to a breakthrough in Japan–North Korea negotiations. Koizumi expressed his unqualified support for the US-led operation in Iraq in March 2003, and he subsequently sent Self-Defense Force troops to the region. While postponing plans to privatize the Japan Highway Public Corporation, he forged ahead with the privatization of the postal system in the face of fierce opposition.

The Koizumi cabinet's high approval ratings notwithstanding, potential electoral challenges loomed for the LDP. In 2003, the LP merged with the DPJ to create an opposition force numerically worthy of a two-party system. Around the same time, Japan's political parties began to adopt the practice of issuing manifestos before each election, systematically setting forth their policy goals and ways to achieve them. This sharpened the focus on policy choices during election campaigns and encouraged voters to think twice about which party they wanted to support. It was in this uncertain context that Koizumi dissolved the House of Representatives and called a snap election in September 2005. The purpose was clear: to break the deadlock over the prime minister's postal privatization bill, which had failed in the upper house owing to resistance from within his own party. In the runup to the 2005 general election, seen as a referendum on postal privatization, Koizumi led a drama-filled campaign, fielding "assassin candidates" to unseat recalcitrant LDP politicians. The strategy was a success, and the LDP won the election by a landslide, buoyed by Koizumi's legion of devoted fans. In spite of such electoral triumphs, Koizumi opted to step down in the fall of 2006, citing LDP term limits.

Prime Minister Abe Shinzō formed his first cabinet in September 2006. Having inherited a strong majority in both chambers of the Diet, he moved quickly to advance his policy agenda, including a major revision of the Basic Act on Education. Unfortunately, Abe made a number of strategic and tactical errors, and his cabinet quickly lost support amid a series of government scandals. In the July 2007 House of Councillors election, the DPJ posted big gains and overtook the LDP as the largest party in the upper house.

Abe, who was suffering from poor health, stepped down the following September.

The cabinet of Prime Minister Fukuda Yasuo, formed in September 2007, faced the challenge of governing amid the legislative gridlock of a "twisted" Diet (divided bicameralism). With the opposition-controlled House of Councillors blocking one bill after another, the Fukuda cabinet's hands were tied. Asō Tarō took over as prime minister in September 2008, around the height of the US subprime mortgage crisis. As Japan sank deeper into recession, the LDP government had no chance of rebuilding the voters' confidence.

In the historic general election of August 2009, the DPJ secured a majority of seats in the House of Representatives and replaced the LDP as the party in power. This dramatic outcome spoke to the high hopes invested in the untried DPJ after three disappointing LDP cabinets. The first DPJ cabinet was headed by Prime Minister Hatoyama Yukio. Despite his lack of cabinet experience, Hatoyama hastily instituted new decision-making mechanisms, and he blundered badly with a rash pledge to move Marine Corps Air Station Futenma outside of Okinawa, backtracking on a key agreement with Washington. Revelations of political funding irregularities compounded his woes. Having vowed to transfer power from the bureaucracy to elected politicians, the DPJ leadership took steps to exclude civil servants from the decision-making arenas, depriving the cabinet of much-needed support. The government also had difficulty unifying the ruling parties behind its policies. With support for the cabinet collapsing, Hatoyama resigned in June 2010 and was replaced by a new DPJ leader, Kan Naoto.

The Kan cabinet was barely a month old when the DPJ government found itself without an upper house majority after an unexpectedly poor performance in the July 2010 House of Councillors election. The following year, the government came under intense criticism for its response to the nuclear accident triggered by the Great East Japan Earthquake of March 2011. With forces inside and outside the DPJ clamoring for Kan's resignation, Noda Yoshihiko took the reins. Prime Minister Noda's base of power was weak, but by cleaving to a policy of cooperation and compromise with the LDP and Kōmeitō, his cabinet was able to make some progress, including the enactment of "integrated reform of the tax and social security systems." But that controversial measure, which mandated a 5-point hike in the consumption tax, triggered an exodus of politicians from the DPJ. In December 2012, Noda dissolved the House of Representatives and called a general election.

In the general election of December 2012, the LDP scored a landslide victory, aided by fierce competition between the DPJ and the newly formed Japan Restoration Party, which split the anti-LDP vote. As president of the LDP, Abe Shinzō again assumed the office of prime minister. From the outset, Abe's LDP-Kōmeitō coalition cabinet functioned smoothly, thanks to carefully thought-out personnel appointments and seamless cooperation among the administration's key figures. In the July 2013 House of Councillors election, the LDP-led coalition secured a majority in the upper house, placing the administration on a firm footing.

Aided by the strategic timing of general elections and the opposition's disarray, the LDP enjoyed a string of electoral successes, with the result that the second Abe administration was notable for its longevity. The Abe cabinet's public approval rating fell sharply in 2015, when it pushed through controversial security legislation in the face of fierce resistance from the opposition. After that, however, Abe maintained an adequate level of popular support by skirting the hot-button issues. He twice postponed a scheduled increase in the consumption tax and stepped back from his long-standing pledge to amend the Constitution. In the diplomatic arena, Abe emerged as a familiar and forceful presence in international negotiations. Under his leadership, Japan spearheaded such successful diplomatic initiatives as the Quadrilateral (Japan-US-Australia-India) Security Dialogue.

In the summer of 2016, Emperor Akihito created a stir by announcing his wish to abdicate in a televised speech. Because Japanese law made no provision for abdication of the emperor, there was considerable debate about how to proceed.

In the end, the ruling and opposition parties came together to enact special legislation permitting Emperor Akihito to step down. The emperor abdicated in favor of his son, Crown Prince Naruhito, on April 30, 2019, and the Heisei era came to an end. (Prime Minister Abe continued in office through the first phase of the COVID-19 pandemic, becoming the longest-serving prime minister in Japanese history, before finally stepping down for reasons of poor health in September 2020.)

The compilation of essays for this volume was constrained by the availability of published English translations, the quantity of which has fluctuated over time. The pieces originally selected for publication in English did not invariably cover all the key issues and themes occupying Japanese scholars and journalists at the time. Moreover, much political commentary is centered around short-term predictions and sheds little light on the era after the fact. In our selection of essays, we have leaned toward scholarly or semi-scholarly pieces that analyze major developments retrospectively, as opposed to columns commenting on the latest events. We have also prioritized balance in our selection, presenting authors with diverse viewpoints while striving for fairly even coverage of the entire three-decade period.

Political Reform and
the Anti-LDP Coalitions

In the early years of the Heisei era, as the Cold War drew to a close, Japan entered a period of political upheaval. Escalating power struggles within the ruling Liberal Democratic Party (LDP) eventually led to a split, and the LDP's long-standing monopoly on government power came to an end with the rise of a non-LDP coalition under Prime Minister Hosokawa Morihiro. While internecine strife was the immediate cause of the LDP's downfall, an important underlying factor was the cross-partisan drive for "political reform," an issue in which the public took a deep interest. The ostensible purpose of that movement was to address the root causes of political dysfunction by revamping the House of Representatives election system and reforming political funding, though the perceived scope and purpose expanded as the conversation gathered momentum.

Part I of this book features a selection of commentary and analysis from the early Heisei era on the overlapping themes of reform and regime change. In the 1989 piece "The Day the Mountains Moved," political scientist Shinohara Hajime describes the LDP's defeat in the recent House of Councillors election as a watershed event and renews his call for the opposition to unite and replace what he characterizes as a decayed and dysfunctional regime. Kitaoka Shinichi, one of Japan's leading political thinkers during the Heisei era, was among the first to examine the connections between Japan's political ferment and the global transition to a post–Cold War order, a theme explored in "Beyond the Politics of Saying No." In "Following Through on Electoral Reform," journalist Yayama Tarō argues for a mixed electoral system centered on single-seat districts as the key to revitalizing Japanese politics.

Back in the real world, the coalition of reformists had proved unstable, leading to the resignation of two non-LDP cabinets (under Prime Ministers Hosokawa Morihiro and Hata Tsutomu) in less than a year. Inoguchi Takashi, whose work appears prominently in English-language publications of the period, offers a comparative analysis of the two non-LDP coalition cabinets in "The Rise and Fall of 'Reformist Governments.'"

The Day the Mountains Moved

Shinohara Hajime
Japan Echo, 1989

Doi Takako, chairwoman of the Japan Socialist Party (JSP), called it "the day the mountains moved," a phrase from the prewar poet Yosano Akiko. In the Tokyo Metropolitan Assembly elections of July 2, the number of seats held by the ruling Liberal Democratic Party (LDP) dropped from 63 to 43 (out of a total of 128), and Socialist or Socialist-backed candidates won 36 seats, exactly three times the number they held before the election. In terms of vote share, the LDP and JSP were neck and neck with 30.4 and 29.3 percent, respectively. One-third of the winning JSP candidates were women, an indication of the rapid transformation underway in Japan's traditionally male-dominated society. The results pointed to a dramatic shift in the political climate of this stable, advanced capitalist nation.

The Tokyo election was seen as a prelude to the July 23 national election for the House of Councillors, the less powerful chamber of the bicameral National Diet. And the outcome of this latter vote is particularly significant, since it may be considered a proxy for a House of Representatives election, which the opposition has demanded but the LDP administration has deferred.

The House of Councillors poll dealt the LDP an even greater upset than the Tokyo election. Of the 126 seats up for election (half the membership of the upper house), the Socialists won 46, more than twice the 22 they had held before the election: combined with the 20 held by Socialist incumbents with unexpired terms, this gave the JSP a total of 67 seats. The LDP won only 36 seats, barely half their pre-election 69; even after adding the 73 held by LDP incumbents, the ruling party found itself with just 109 of the 252 seats in the chamber, less than a majority. In the aftermath, Prime Minister Uno Sōsuke and his cabinet were obliged to resign after a mere two months in office.

The upper house election results effectively silenced those who had called the earlier vote a fluke. The turnout for the two elections was nearly identical, and in the ballot for the nationwide proportional representation seats, in which votes are cast for a party, the Socialists and their allies won as much support from Tokyo voters as they had in the metropolitan assembly balloting, while the vote for the LDP dropped much lower. The daily *Asahi Shimbun* has estimated that at this rate the JSP could win 217 seats in the 512-member House of Representatives at the next general election provided it manages to field enough candidates.

In addition to the JSP's triumph, the two July elections saw striking advances by women. In the Tokyo assembly their number rose from 9 to 17, or 13 percent of the total. And in the House of Councillors, they won 22, or 17 percent, of the seats up for election.

End of an Era?

Some have ascribed the recent shift in patterns of support to no more than a passing mood, predicting a return to business as usual after the public vents its anger at the LDP. Much analysis of political events in the past few months was in this vein, though many commentators modified their views after seeing the July election results. If politics is the art of the possible, we must recognize the possibility of a variety of future courses. It now seems reasonable, however, to conclude that we are witnessing a period of systemic transformation, that is, structural change.

The LDP has held power continuously since its creation through the merger of conservative political forces in 1955. Under this extended one-party rule, referred to as the "1955 setup," Japan has had a multiparty system in form only; in fact, the LDP has monopolized power. The uninterrupted rule of the conservatives has encouraged collusion between the political and business worlds, a cozy arrangement that has left room for the economy to develop but has stifled innovation in politics, education, and culture. If we are correct in judging the magnitude of the political change now underway, we can expect to see the demise of this system of one-party dominance.

In a situation where two major parties have been contending for power, it matters little if this bipolar setup gives way to one in which a few smaller parties vie with one another. But when a single party has ruled for over thirty years, the switch to a system of smaller parties makes a great difference indeed; in fact it represents a systemic change. Such a shift will meet stiff resistance among those who have benefited from the status quo. This sort of resistance was seen in the efforts of the LDP and business leaders to persuade voters in the recent election that they were choosing between "freedom" (continued LDP rule) and "socialism" (a term that in Japan is often used as a synonym for communism). Another point to note about this sort of systemic change is that it requires the opposition forces to alter their own attitudes and mobilize a vast amount of energy. The members of the opposition should recognize the far-reaching nature of the transformation that they are attempting. The task they face is that of replacing one system with another.

What form is this systemic change taking? In what follows, I will address this question by analyzing specific features of the present system now in the process of collapse and by examining the shifts in public attitudes that are at once a cause and an effect of this collapse.

Political Patronage and Corruption

The advanced age of the 1955 setup has made its blemishes increasingly difficult to conceal. One problem is a laxity in the handling of political funds encouraged by the unnaturally close relations between business and the LDP leadership. Another is a political insensitivity to the gross inequities of representation between urban and rural areas. Just as aging aircraft are subject to metal fatigue, the political setup has begun to show systemic fatigue, even systemic decay.

Three years ago, when elections were held simultaneously for the two houses of the Diet, then prime minister Nakasone Yasuhiro deliberately circumvented a divisive issue by promising not to enact a general sales tax. This contributed to the landslide victory of the LDP, which captured 304 of the 512 seats in the House of Representatives. Nakasone and his brain trust proclaimed the birth of a "1986 setup," boasting that the LDP's hold on power had achieved complete stability, surpassing even that which it had enjoyed under the 1955 setup. In retrospect, however, it appears that the years since then have been a period not of stability but of decay, marking what may be called the terminal phase of the 1955 setup. Whether the setup will actually collapse depends greatly on the power that the opposition is able to muster. But the fact that the old setup has started to crumble is beyond denial.

The decay of the system can be addressed from many angles, but I will limit my discussion to three major aspects, beginning with the problem of structural corruption in the ruling party. The 1955 setup has served as a fertile breeding ground for graft, leading periodically to major scandals. Part of the problem is the fact that the LDP's monopoly of power has naturally caused the flow of political funds to turn in its direction. But there is another more fundamental problem in the background. This is the practice of patronage, which is deeply rooted in postwar Japanese politics. It is a system in which money and all manner of other benefits flow from patrons at the center of political power to their clients on the periphery, in return for which the latter reward the former with their support. In Japan this structure comprises multiple levels: the big patrons, today's equivalent of the daimyo, or feudal lords, protect their vassal clients, who are patrons in turn to lesser clients, and so on down the line.

Tanaka Kakuei, prime minister from 1972 to 1974, is the classic example of a big patron, but patronage did not fade from the picture along with Tanaka's political power. Prime Minister Takeshita Noboru was also a devoted practitioner, as suggested by the fact that during his administration (1987–89), Tanaka's home ground of Niigata yielded to Takeshita's native Shimane as the prefecture receiving the largest amount of national subsidies per capita. Of course, patronage is not the only factor at work in the politics of contemporary Japan, which is after all one of the world's most advanced capitalist nations. It is nevertheless a fact that the principle permeates conservative politics from the grassroots level up.

In the years following 1973, as economic growth slowed, there emerged a neoconservatism embodied in the work of various government reform commissions. This movement gave precedence to market principles even in areas like welfare, advocating small government for economic efficiency; it thus stood in apparent opposition to political patronage. But the two approaches shared an emphasis on material gain. To borrow Erich Fromm's terminology, they both stood for *having* as opposed to *being*. Instead of curbing patronage, therefore, the neoconservative movement actually amplified its effect, so that the impulse toward "having" came to dominate Japanese society to an abnormal degree. "Having" money and social standing reigned as the dominant and unquestioned value of the age. It reached the point where even among high school students, more than half professed interest in money games.

In this sort of culture, the spread of corruption among politicians seeking to acquire money and status was inevitable. This tendency, which was already strong in the LDP, received additional impetus from the influence-peddling activities of Ezoe Hiromasa, founder of the Recruit group of companies, which made huge profits in the information and real estate industries, as well as from stock transactions. With society dominated by the ethics of "having," criticism of unethical political conduct was muted, and political decay penetrated ever deeper into the tissue of government. The Recruit scandal revealed just how deeply the decay had eaten into the 1955 setup.

Back-Scratching among the Factions

The second major aspect of the decay of Japan's present political setup is the breakdown of its self-corrective mechanism. Obviously the persistence of LDP rule for more than three decades indicates that the system had incorporated some sort of adaptive machinery allowing its self-perpetuation. In fact, the innovative impetus that political scientists expect the leading opposition party to provide has, in Japan's case, been supplied instead by the ruling party's internal subgroups. As is frequently noted, the 1955 setup replaced the transfer of power between political parties with a somewhat similar transfer among the leaders of different LDP factions. For example, in 1960, after heated domestic confrontation over conclusion of a new Japan-US security treaty, Ikeda Hayato replaced Kishi Nobusuke as prime minister, setting a softer tone and defusing the animosity with his income-doubling plan. In 1974, when the corruption of the Tanaka administration emerged as a major political issue, Miki Takeo ("Mr. Clean") provided a breath of fresh air. And in 1982, after two years with the lackluster Suzuki Zenkō at the helm, leadership was assumed by Nakasone, who offered a sharply contrasting style with his forcefulness and love of the limelight. In this way the ruling party demonstrated its adaptability to changing conditions. Each new administration was generally able to win back some of the support lost by its predecessor, thereby reinforcing the stability of LDP rule.

Since the collapse of the Takeshita administration in June this year, however, the political process has taken a different turn. Despite, or perhaps because of, the massive majority held by the LDP in the Diet since 1986, rivalry among the parties' factions has abated, creating what is in effect a single mainstream camp. Since the transfer of leadership among the factions has been based on cooperation rather than competition, the party has become far less responsive to external change, and the timeliness of the transfers has suffered. Part of the reason for the delay in picking new leaders is the dearth of suitable candidates now that a lack of interfactional competition has allowed corruption to spread unchecked. This is not the only problem, however; it is also evident that mutual back-scratching among the factions has allowed the LDP to turn increasingly inward, widening the gap between rulers and ruled.

Uno, who was finally settled on as Takeshita's replacement, led what was nothing more than a puppet administration acting out a scenario written by his predecessor. One might consider the creation of this administration a triumph of factional aesthetics but certainly not a transfer of power. Support for the new cabinet fell short of 30 percent from the start and soon sank below 20 percent, nearly matching the unpopularity of the Takeshita administration just before the latter's fall.

The July rout at the polls has presented the LDP with one of the most serious crises in its history at a time when the 1955 setup has manifestly ceased to function. The party is completely incapable of effecting the sort of interfactional power transfer that it formerly carried out when its fortunes were low. And the more the party tries to operate as if the old setup were still functioning, the faster the system heads toward collapse.

A Leadership Drought

The third factor promoting the system's decay is an absence of leadership. Takeshita thought his administration was built on a solid foundation, but its fall and the prompt demise of the Uno cabinet in its wake showed how thoroughly the very core of the political establishment had degenerated. This decay resembles the meltdown of a nuclear reactor's core: as it disintegrates, it releases deadly wastes into the environment.

During Diet deliberation on the budget for fiscal 1989 (April 1989 to March 1990), Takeshita—known for his skill at achieving legislative consensus—failed to win over the opposition: for the first time in Japanese history the budget passed the Diet solely on the strength of the ruling party's majority. Clearly, Takeshita had lost his magic touch. That he was able to remain in office even after his support ratings fell below 10 percent is testimony, perhaps, to the strength of his control over the LDP. But it is also an indication of the depths to which parliamentary democracy had sunk. The nation's leadership was concerned not with the will of the people but only with the will of the legislature—and

ultimately only with the will of the ruling party itself. With his base of power thus narrowed, Takeshita proved surprisingly vulnerable when it was revealed that he had received a ¥50 million loan from the Recruit group, even though this was a relatively minor peccadillo in the context of the scandal as a whole. His supposedly solid administration came tumbling down.

Much remains unclear about the complex drama that followed Takeshita's resignation announcement. Politicians are normally a power-hungry lot; the absence of contenders for the highest office and the fact that at least one to whom it was offered declined the invitation were nothing short of extraordinary, particularly within a party that enjoys a huge legislative majority. The situation revealed a virtual leadership vacuum. The Recruit scandal had disqualified all the senior candidates for the prime minister's office, and no one suitable emerged from among the ranks of younger party members.

Then, as if from nowhere, Uno surfaced as a man who suited the requirements of traditional factional politics and would allow Takeshita to continue wielding influence from behind the scenes. But this sort of factional maneuvering, predicated on the assumptions of the 1955 setup, worked against Takeshita and the party as a whole in the context of the old system's decline. One could hardly expect courageous leadership from a new prime minister who had no views of his own on political reform—the most crucial issue of the day—and who had not put his personal affairs in order before assuming the post for the simple reason that he never expected to be named to it. Lacking authenticity to begin with, Uno's authority evaporated when his involvement in a sex scandal came to light. During the House of Councillors election campaign, he was not even allowed to stump for LDP candidates.

The weakness of leadership under Uno was unparalleled in the annals of modern Japanese politics. To make matters worse, there was no one to replace him even after the sex scandal had made his position untenable. And at this stage it is impossible to see any light at the end of the tunnel. If this is not a meltdown of the system, what is?

New Patterns in Voter Support

The decay of the old system in respect to leadership and organization, as examined above, parallels changes in the attitudes of the public at large. The meltdown of the 1955 setup should be viewed as concomitant with the maturation of Japan's civil society. This progressive maturation has led to a corresponding evolution of political and social attitudes, which I would like to examine from three angles. First, the public has demonstrated, more strongly than ever before, a clear desire to see the reins of power transferred from the LDP to another party. In Western democracies, it is taken for granted that in due time the party in power will lose an election and the opposition will take over. In this sense, Japan's system since 1955 could only be called semi-democratic.

Japan's political evolution has differed from that of the major established democracies. The difference stems in part from the fact that it underwent a barrage of reforms in the period immediately after World War II. One way of measuring the changes since then is by observing the movement of the "political volatility index," an indicator developed by Danish political scientist Mogens N. Pedersen to quantify the variability of popular support for parties. In Scandinavia, this index has been on the rise since about 1970. In Japan's case, the index was high from 1945 to 1955; then it dropped, and it has been more or less flat since 1970. If, however, trends in abstentions are counted along with those in the vote for particular parties, volatility appears to have been on the rise since the 1970s.

What seems to have happened in this period is that voters expressed their displeasure with some blunder by the ruling party by staying away from the polls, sometimes with the result that the party failed to win a legislative majority—though it always managed to hold on to power, most often by drafting conservative independents. Opinion polls showed periodic dips in LDP support, but no corresponding rise in support for the opposition. The votes that the LDP lost turned into abstentions sinking vertically, as it were, to below the surface instead of shifting horizontally to other parties.

This pattern persisted until the Recruit scandal and the consumption tax triggered a major change. Both in the polls and at the ballot box, the LDP's support base has been shrinking and the JSP's expanding. This time, in other words, votes are being transferred horizontally. This cannot be explained merely as the result of technical fumbling by the LDP, nor can it be attributed to some special charm exerted by the Socialists. In gubernatorial elections where the JSP was unable to put up a candidate, anti-LDP votes turned not into abstentions but into protest votes for Japanese Communist Party (JCP) candidates, demonstrating the strength of the electorate's desire to see power change hands.

Is this horizontal shift of votes a passing phenomenon? Commentators whose outlook is conditioned by the 1955 setup expected voters to revert to form in a couple of months, once they had gotten over their pique. But several months have passed without any sign that the winds of change are subsiding.

To the contrary, there are signs that public disaffection with the Liberal Democrats runs deep indeed. The party now leads in the "never would vote for" ratings, a dubious honor traditionally held by the Communists, with the Kōmeitō (Clean Government Party) in second place. According to a poll by the daily *Yomiuri Shimbun* published on June 5, the JCP and Kōmeitō continue to labor under high negative ratings of 31.6 and 19.2 percent, respectively (compared to only 4.7 percent who say they would never vote for the Socialists), but the LDP tops the list at 31.9 percent. With negative sentiment running this high, voter support will not readily drift back to the LDP. Especially now that the core of the party's authority has suffered a meltdown, recovery will be no easy matter.

A giant abyss has opened in front of the LDP. Few of the disaffected voters are likely to be satisfied with the drubbing they gave the ruling party in the July election. Rather, now that the upper house poll has shown that the once-unthinkable dethroning of the LDP is actually within reach, the prevailing impulse is to try to turn this possibility into a reality in the next House of Representatives election.

A final point that should be addressed in connection with political attitudes is the shift in voting patterns among young people and women—a factor, incidentally, in François Mitterrand's Socialist victory in France. In the 1986 elections for both houses of the Diet, two out of three young people voted for the LDP. But in a survey by the *Nihon Keizai Shimbun*, carried in the paper's July 11 evening issue, only 12.2 percent of those in their early twenties said they support the LDP—exactly the same share as support the JSP. And among the 56.4 percent of this age group who declared support for no party, only 12.8 percent named the LDP when asked what party they were favorably disposed toward, and almost twice as many, 22.0 percent, named the JSP.

Among those in their early forties, meanwhile, 26.0 percent of the women polled said that they support or are favorably disposed toward the Socialists, significantly more than the 20.6 percent who support or lean toward the LDP. This trend sets them clearly apart from their male contemporaries, among whom almost 30 percent support or favor the ruling party. Previously observers had noted an increasing trend toward conservatism among young people and a tendency for many women to be politically apathetic. But recent developments give the lie to such conventional wisdom and lend support to the view that the shift in support patterns is no transitory phenomenon.

The Taxpayers' Revolt

The second major harbinger of change in the national political consciousness is to be seen in the public's attitudes toward the consumption tax introduced this past April. In a recent survey by NHK (Japan Broadcasting Corporation), only 4 percent of those polled said that they regard the new tax as acceptable in its present form. Ruling party ideologues brand this phenomenon as mass hysteria. Their irritation with the public outcry is understandable, inasmuch as it forced the party to consider revising the tax less than three months after it had come into effect. But this is a democracy, after all, and such indignation is only natural after the ruling party rammed the measure through the Diet despite the obvious strength of public sentiment against it.

In July 1986 the LDP won a great election victory partly on the strength of a commitment by Nakasone and other LDP candidates not to enact a major indirect tax against the will of the people. A review of the candidates' campaign statements and their replies to questionnaires reveals that 250 of the 304 LDP candidates elected to the House of Representatives and 40 of the party's 74 successful upper house candidates had voiced their opposition to such a tax. Yet three years later, with no intervening election to determine the popular will, the ruling party railroaded the consumption tax through the Diet. And as noted above, the party even went so far as to force through the budget for fiscal 1989, basing it on revenue estimates that included income from the new tax, on the strength of its majority alone.

Not only did the tax's passage mock the democratic process, but the revenue assumptions on which it was based were flawed. The Ministry of Finance underestimated the natural growth in revenues from existing taxes, which has actually come to considerably more than the amount the consumption tax is expected to bring in (these underestimates are in fact a perennial feature of the ministry's forecasts). This natural growth largely invalidates the LDP's case for a new tax. Unlike family budgets, where income is a given and spending must be planned accordingly, a national budget should first establish the level of necessary expenditures and then arrange for sufficient revenues; if the government finds itself taking in more money than it needs, as is the case now, it has mismanaged its fiscal affairs. Meanwhile, even as the administration was claiming that the purpose of the new tax was to fund the future welfare costs of Japan's aging society, it went ahead and hiked mandatory contributions to the public pension system by two percentage points. And it further alienated the people's trust by designing the income tax cuts that accompanied introduction of the new tax along neoconservative lines, giving the biggest breaks to those in the highest brackets.

A step like the introduction of the consumption tax, which is bound to cause taxpayer resentment, needs to be preceded by serious efforts to correct gross inequities in the existing tax system and to win popular recognition of the necessity of the new tax. But the LDP neglected this groundwork, confident in the might of its huge legislative majority and eager to take advantage of that majority to push the tax through. The party seems to have thought, based on previous experience, that the initial outburst of popular resentment would quickly die down. In general, the Japanese have meekly submitted to laws once they are passed, considering it pointless to protest a fait accompli. Revision or repeal of a recently adopted piece of legislation has proved virtually impossible. In this case, however, opposition to the new tax increased after its enactment.

This development should probably be taken as another sign of transformation in Japan's culture. What we are witnessing is not "mass hysteria," as the ruling party's apologists claim, but the emergence among the people of an acute consciousness of their role as taxpayers. Though it is naturally a nuisance from the viewpoint of those in power, taxpayer resentment is an important lever of citizens' politics. It must not be forgotten that many of history's rebellions and revolutions have been triggered by popular resistance to taxation. This is the sort of backlash that the government now faces.

Behind the cultural transformation lies a change in Japan's social class structure. This is a topic that requires academic study, and space does not permit me to examine it fully here. But it is worthwhile to note some of the indicators of this change, namely, the widening of income differentials in Japan's "affluent" society, the yawning gap in financial assets between those in a position to play the stock market and those who are not, and of course the great divide between those who owned real estate before the dizzying land-price spiral and those who remain landless. This gradual widening of wealth differentials, reflecting the "success" of neoconservative policies, has been evident in the statistics since 1985.

Such gaps in affluence foster strong feelings of injustice and could prove a major problem for Japan as the nation's civil society matures. Perceptions of inequity have fueled not only resentment of the consumption tax but also anger at those involved in the Recruit scandal ("Some people get rich without lifting a finger") and opposition to liberalization of agricultural imports ("Why should we farmers, who produce what people really need, have to suffer on account of big-business exporters?"). People's attitudes are changing.

The Advent of "Woman Power"

The third change in national consciousness has to do with the relationship between women and politics. As I mentioned above, women made a significant sally into Japanese politics with their advances in the Tokyo Metropolitan Assembly and House of Councillors elections. Early signs of this development were apparent in the major urban regions two years ago when local elections were held across Japan. At that time observers called it a passing trend. But this year the feminist tide spread across the nation, as signaled by the victory of a female JSP candidate in the February House of Councillors by-election in Niigata Prefecture, normally an LDP stronghold. The July elections have confirmed this trend. The next question is whether the Socialists and their allies can elect at least 10 women to the House of Representatives in the upcoming contest (there are currently only two female JSP members in the lower house).

Here, however, I wish to focus not on the growing number of women in politics but on the emergence of male-female relationships as a political issue. One of the things that make politics so interesting is the manner in which sudden, unforeseen developments can change the course of events. Prime Minister Uno's involvement in a sex scandal is a case in point. The scandal broke because the managing editor of the weekly *Sunday Mainichi* decided that the time had come for this sort of news to be laid on the table in Japan. It was a perceptive judgment. But Japanese politics is still a man's world. It took foreign interest to bring the issue to a head. The foreign press picked up the *Sunday Mainichi*'s story, and then the Japanese media started reporting the overseas coverage. "No punches below the belt"—one of the unwritten rules of Japanese political reporting—was finally struck from the journalistic code.

Even more revealing than the *Sunday Mainichi*'s initial exposé of the scandal were the reactions that the magazine elicited from Japanese commentators. Men and women shied away from the issue with equal discomfort. Commentators offered a uniformly tame response, suggesting that it was vulgar even to raise such an issue, or that the woman involved in the affair was equally to blame, or that one had to question her motives in speaking to the media.

When ordinary women got the chance to air their views, however, they pulled no punches, seizing the occasion to tell the country's politicians that they had better clean up their act if they hoped to move up in the world and making it clear that not even the prime minister had the privilege of hiding behind a wall of privacy.

The strength of this new reaction was apparent in the results of a *Nihon Keizai Shimbun* survey published in the paper's July 12 evening edition. Asked what response was appropriate from a legislator revealed to have committed sexual indiscretions, 39.7 percent of women in their early twenties called for resignation, significantly more than the 26.6 percent who felt it was a personal matter requiring no action: another 28.5 percent thought a public apology would suffice (among men of this age group, those calling for resignation and for no action were equally balanced at 29.6 percent each). The attitude of women in their early forties was even more critical: 52.4 percent favored resignation, as against 27.3 percent who demanded no action and only 12.7 percent who called for a public apology. The men of this age group were also quite critical, with 47.2 percent, or almost half, calling for resignation. It would seem that Japanese attitudes on this sort of question are converging with the Western norm—one of a number of respects, as we have seen, in which Japanese society is maturing, or at least changing.

Overcoming Outmoded Attitudes

In the foregoing we have seen how the 1955 setup has been decaying and how, at the same time, Japanese civil society has been maturing. Further progress along these lines should make it possible to transform Japan from a semi-democratic nation into a full-fledged democracy with a number of moderate political parties grouped around two major ones. But even if current trends are leading in this direction, it must be remembered that residual attitudes could seriously hinder the conversion to a new system.

This residue of old thinking is to be found at various levels. It is especially conspicuous in the behavior of LDP politicians, notably their extramarital relationships and stage-whisper questioning of Chairwoman Doi's political qualifications on the grounds of her sex or her celibacy. Nor are their antiquated attitudes limited to matters involving women: LDP leaders regularly come out with embarrassing statements on any number of topics, remarking, for example, that farmers are manual laborers incapable of office work. The Socialists are not without their faults either, as seen in the case of the JSP candidate in the July upper house election who had a *shinkansen* bullet train make an unscheduled stop in a town where he was to speak. The failings of the JSP are bound to grow increasingly conspicuous with each step the party takes toward assuming power. The Socialists must plan carefully so that they can respond quickly to minor crises like the bullet train incident that betray a lack of civic mindedness.

Outdated mindsets also persist among the public at large. Even as we stand on the brink of political transformation, there are always some people who insist, in TV interviews and similar forums, that nothing will change regardless of who takes over. That may have been true while the LDP held a monopoly on power, but what these people seem to overlook is that the LDP monopoly is precisely what made the party so corrupt and cavalier about its policy. To illustrate another example of rigid thinking, a recent letter to the editor of a major newspaper stated that power should not be given to people without the proper qualifications, just as someone without a driver's license should not be allowed to drive. There is still considerable hesitancy about putting a new party into power. This view is obviously a holdover from the days when people had virtually forgotten that it was possible for power to change hands. However unfounded, it will obstruct the incipient transformation.

The responsibility of those who seek to change the system is all the greater for that reason. In the months to come, they will confront the challenging task of leading the search for new directions while struggling to overcome the grip of old attitudes. The reformers face two major tasks. The first is to marshal their own forces instead of waiting with arms crossed for the old system to collapse. Numbers definitely matter in politics, and in order to change the system, the reform camp must win as many seats as possible in the next House of Representatives election.

The second task is for the Socialists to present a coherent set of policies; this is essential if the public is to form a positive image of the potential new administration. Detailed policy formulation is not needed at election time, however; all that is required is the broad outlines. In this context, the functioning of the JSP's policymaking apparatus and its approach to cabinet formation are of the essence. The Socialists must also work with other opposition parties to present credible plans for a coalition government. By providing the public with a reasonably concrete image of what will take place after power changes hands, the opposition can dispel the psychological residue of the 1955 setup.

It is not enough simply to wait for the mountains to move. Much progress has been made; in the short time that remains before the next election, the opposition must redouble its efforts to close the gap between the existing political system and the nation's emerging civic consciousness. A harsh judgment will fall on the reformers if they fail now, within sight of the goal.

Courtesy of Japan Echo.

English version originally published in *Japan Echo* 16, no. 4 (1989): 14–22. Translated from "Shisutemu no henkan wa kanō ka," in *Sekai* (September 1989): 10–21 (courtesy of Iwanami Shoten).

I-(2) Beyond the Politics of Saying No

Kitaoka Shinichi
Japan Echo, 1991

The House of Representatives election of February 1990 resulted in an unexpectedly large victory for the ruling Liberal Democratic Party (LDP). Many have complained that the election was bought, and those complaints cannot be totally ignored. But elections cannot be won by the power of money alone. The two that were held while Tanaka Kakuei was prime minister, one for the lower house in 1972 and the other for the upper house in 1974, both achieved notoriety as money-driven events, but the ruling party was unable to increase its number of seats in either. The LDP's success last February was made possible not so much by major infusions of cash as by the fact that its popular support had recovered to close to the level of the 1986 joint election for the two houses of the National Diet.

The dramatic turnaround from the LDP's rout in the July 1989 House of Councillors election offers an extremely interesting topic for academic research, and doubtless it will be the object of numerous full-fledged studies. While it is still rather early for a rigorous analysis, in what follows I will offer some historical and intellectual observations and suggest what the outcome tells us about the state of Japanese politics.

The "Abolish the Consumption Tax" Canard

I was struck by the interviews with successful candidates after the votes were counted in February. To be sure, perhaps we cannot expect polished statements at such a busy time from people whose excitement is at a peak. But the responses of the victorious opposition candidates to the customary questions about their aspirations had a particularly hollow ring this time. They talked of immediately undertaking to abolish the consumption tax, but they hardly appeared to believe that they had any chance of actually doing so. From their statements, one got no sense of what abolishing the consumption tax would mean or what purpose it would serve. Perhaps if they had spoken of creating a more prosperous Japan and a more just society and had explained how repealing this tax was necessary for these greater goals, one could have understood their position. But they made no attempt to put the consumption tax issue into that sort of broader perspective.

The lower house election has been called a victory for both the LDP and the Japan Socialist Party (JSP), the largest opposition force. In terms of the issues on which the campaign was fought, though, it can only be interpreted as a defeat for the opposition as a whole, which had trounced the LDP in the July 1989 upper house election on a platform calling for repeal of the consumption tax and had continued to harp on that issue in the months leading up to the lower house poll. The opposition parties failed to win the majority necessary to take over from the Liberal Democrats, and the reason for their failure was the fact that they took repeal of the tax as the banner under which to campaign.

On the few occasions in the past when the opposition has been able to take over the reins of power by winning a majority in the lower house, it has been by banding together to fight on a serious issue. In 1924, for example, three opposition parties won by campaigning on a platform of universal male suffrage. And back in 1898, a coalition of forces opposed to higher land taxes emerged victorious. The tax at the time was already a steep 2.5 percent of the value of land,

26

and it was to be raised to an even more punitive 4.0 percent. For the people of the period, this represented a burden to which today's 3 percent consumption tax does not begin to compare.

In the months between the upper and lower house elections, a number of important developments occurred. The yen dropped sharply against the dollar, Japan and the United States entered into a highly significant round of trade talks, and a series of genuine revolutions unfolded in Eastern Europe. Against this backdrop, the consumption tax issue hardly appeared to be of prime significance.

The Will of the People

After their victory in the House of Councillors, the opposition cried out that repealing the consumption tax was the will of the people. Was this a fair assessment? In order to answer this question, we should consider what "the will of the people" means.

Concealed within the concept of the public will is the premise that each person in the nation has an individual will. When it comes to specifics, however, individuals do not necessarily have clear views. We sometimes cannot even decide what to wear or what to eat on a particular day. Needless to say, clearly formed opinions are even less frequent on complex political and social issues.

Joseph Schumpeter focused on this point in his criticism of the classical view of democracy as a system in which politicians loyally represent and implement the will of voters (*Capitalism, Socialism and Democracy*, 1942). The mandate of the people is created by a process in which politicians present a range of alternatives and compete with each other in presenting them to the people; it is not something that exists a priori. In pointing this out, Schumpeter argued that the essence of democracy consists of free competition among political parties.

Let us take a few examples from Japan's history. If an election had been held in September 1905, those who denounced the Treaty of Portsmouth would have received overwhelming support, and the Russo-Japanese War would have dragged on, probably ending with a crushing defeat for Japan instead of a victory. If a public

opinion poll had been conducted after the attack on Pearl Harbor in December 1941, it would probably have revealed close to 100 percent support for Tōjō Hideki's administration. And if a national referendum had been held just prior to August 15, 1945, the people would have indicated their absolute opposition to the Potsdam Declaration and their willingness to carry on the war, which would have brought about even more tragic consequences.

Unless the full range of possible alternatives, along with the merits and demerits of each, is made clear to the people, the opinion of the majority should not be considered the popular will. While the voice of the majority is important, it should not be fawned on. Professional politicians must dig deeper to find what the true will of the people is.

The will that was manifested in the 1989 upper house election was not actually a call for abolition of the consumption tax. As many have pointed out, opposition to the tax just happened to be the form in which people expressed the frustrations that had built up over the long years of LDP rule. In fact, the steep rise in land prices from 1986 to 1988 was sufficient grounds for accusing the Liberal Democratic administration of gross incompetence. There was no need for the opposition parties to harp on the consumption tax alone; they might also have focused their campaign on, for example, a call to drive the money-tainted LDP out of office. If the Socialists had promised not to change the country's basic diplomatic and defense policies until receiving a popular mandate to do so in a subsequent election, they might have been able to lead the opposition to victory on such a platform; they had a golden opportunity, but they threw it away.

To be sure, the anti-tax sentiment was strong, and it allowed the JSP to make significant gains even in the lower house election. But it was not enough to defeat the LDP. The modern era is one of rapid change. The issue that brought victory to the opposition in July 1989 did not have the same power to sway voters half a year later. The opposition failed to look beyond the voice of the majority and discover the genuine popular will.

A Choice between Regimes?

The LDP, meanwhile, claimed that the lower house election offered voters "a choice between regimes," but this was also a peculiar issue on which to base a campaign. If we understand the "regime" referred to as the domestic political structure and its ideological foundations, the usual meaning of the term, the upheaval in Eastern Europe had produced a clear winner well before the election, and in any event, none of the opposition parties was advocating a change from liberal democracy to socialism. But in the course of the campaign the LDP shifted the sense of "regime" to refer to Japan's external political and economic policies.

The LDP's strategy, as is evident from its campaign literature, was to put down the Socialists for their lack of experience in foreign affairs. And this ploy was successful. For one thing, there was a heightened sense of tension in Japan-US relations: In May 1989 Washington included Japan on a list of unfair trading partners under the Super 301 provision of the 1988 Omnibus Trade Act, and in September the two countries embarked on the Structural Impediments Initiative, a tough round of economic negotiations. At the same time, the feeling that the Cold War was over deepened concern that Japan would be left isolated within the international community. Under circumstances like these, people were prone to doubt the JSP's ability to handle diplomacy successfully.

In 1936, immediately after the attempted coup d'état of February 26, Foreign Minister Hirota Kōki, a career diplomat, was appointed prime minister. As the foreign affairs expert Kiyosawa Kiyoshi observed, this was an interesting development. The failed putsch itself was not directly related to foreign affairs, but many people evidently felt that the forces behind the incident represented a threat to the country's external relations, and so they were reassured to have a diplomat take the helm. The period leading up to this year's election probably left many people with a similar sense of danger looming in the diplomatic arena. This would explain why Prime Minister Kaifu Toshiki enjoyed a higher level of support for his conduct of foreign policy than in other areas—despite his lack of diplomatic experience.

The JSP did, to be sure, try to adjust its foreign policy stance. It proclaimed its readiness to cooperate with the United States and softened its unfriendly position toward South Korea. But the absence of malice is not a sufficient basis for a cooperative relationship. Furthermore, Japan is not a nation living in quiet isolation in some remote corner of the world. Its gross national product accounts for 15 percent of the global total, it has economic ties that extend all around the world, and its actions have a tremendous impact on other countries. In order to survive, Japan must conduct a constant process of self-examination and self-reform. The Socialists' gesture of modifying their approach to relations with Washington and Seoul leaves a lot of ground uncovered.

Let us think for a moment about a hypothetical farming family growing rice in the suburbs of Tokyo. The family receives subsidies from the government and is guaranteed a high price for its rice, which results in high prices for consumers. It pays much lower property taxes than other landowners, and its reluctance to part with the farmland fans the rise in land prices, hampering solutions to the housing problem and making it harder for foreign firms to set up shop in Japan. And the farm's output deprives rice growers in other countries of the chance to export to Japan. In today's world, farming families like this one are actually malefactors, though they would probably never think of themselves as such.

In its foreign policy stance the JSP exhibited the same sort of smug naiveté as our farming family. It is only natural that this should have made many people feel uneasy. But the external policies espoused by the Liberal Democrats during the course of the campaign were not very good either—their insistence, for example, that "not a single grain of rice" would be let in from abroad. All in all, the victory that the LDP won was an expression not so much of active popular support for its external policies as of misgivings about those of its rivals. Its lower house win was based on a negative appeal: "Don't let them change the regime." In this sense it was similar to the opposition's victory the previous summer in the upper house election, which was also won on a negative call: "Repeal the consumption tax." The ruling party should realize that this sort of support may prove highly evanescent.

Getting the Party Chiefs Together

The elections of 1989 and 1990 gave the opposition a majority in the House of Councillors but left the LDP in control of the House of Representatives. Given this split, no major reforms can be implemented unless the ruling and opposition parties overcome their rigid adversarial relationship. They will have to create a new framework, as LDP secretary-general Ozawa Ichirō suggested at the beginning of the lower house election campaign.

Up until now, the government and the LDP have worked together to prepare new legislation and have left little room for amendment of the bills they submit to the Diet: they have generally managed to get them enacted in their original form either with steamrolling tactics or by making deals with the opposition. The opposition delegates have frequently criticized shortcomings in proposed legislation, but they have not concentrated their efforts on rewriting the bills.

Now that the opposition controls the upper house, however, this approach will not work. Since the LDP can no longer force bills through the legislature, it will have to allow for the incorporation of other parties' views. Rather than have bills amended substantially after they are submitted to the Diet, which may not be practical, the ruling party needs to consult with the opposition during the course of the drafting process.

The LDP, not the government, should seek these consultations with the other parties. The idea should be for the parties to deal with each other as equals, breaking away from the ossified relationship that has pitted the government against the opposition. And the call for talks should come from the LDP's topmost leader, its president (who is also the nation's prime minister), rather than from its secretary-general or the chair of its Policy Research Council. As in summit meetings between countries, the people at the top with ultimate responsibility should take part in talks aimed at settling the most important issues.

One of the issues that might well be addressed by a summit of party heads is the high land prices. Other summits or interparty councils might tackle the removal of structural barriers to imports and the preparation of legislation related to the Uruguay Round of multilateral trade talks. Consultations should be held to consider not individual bills but the whole range of legislative action required to deal with particular issues. At the same time, however, they should focus on definite objectives and operate within fixed time frames.

The process of conducting such consultations may sound complicated, but it is something that every coalition government does. A similar sort of interparty dialogue is seen in the bipartisan approach taken for important problems in the United States. Our own history offers an interesting example of this approach, namely, the advisory council on foreign relations, made up of party heads and other influential people, which operated from 1917 to 1922. While this council was not entirely successful, it did enable the various parties to affect the conduct of foreign policy to a certain extent even when the Diet was not in session; it also permitted the government to count on support from the parties on matters for which it had secured commitments from them.

Even if a framework for interparty consultations is established, however, it is impossible to say whether the JSP can be drawn into it. The party's activists still consist largely of ideologues, and Chairwoman Doi Takako herself is not a realistic policy expert. Moreover, the party's recent victories at the polls have brought a large number of newcomers into its contingent of lawmakers. These people tend to hold strictly to what they see as right and to reject compromise. And some are single-issue activists who campaigned on causes like abolition of the consumption tax or protection of the environment. Doubts remain as to whether they will be able to take part in the formation of comprehensive and realistic policies.

It bears noting that when the above-mentioned advisory council was formed in 1917, the Kenseikai (Constitutional Association), the number-two party at the time, refused to participate. This was because the party's leader, Katō Takaaki, who was something of a stickler for principle, thought that the council was an unconstitutional institution that infringed upon the responsibilities of the cabinet, and also because the Kenseikai, like today's JSP, included many newcomers to the political stage who espoused a rigid line. This inflexible stance kept the party out of power for a number of years thereafter.

The JSP may end up taking a similar stance. In that case it can expect to continue to be supported by the 20 to 30 percent of the public that is highly dissatisfied with the political status quo, but it may fail to develop into a responsible party capable of ruling the nation. The task of instilling realism into the JSP is no easy one.

The Politics of Vision

Carl Schmitt, in his *Die geistesgeschichtliche Lage des heutigen Parlamentarismus* (1924; translated into English as *The Crisis of Parliamentary Politics*), emphasized the differences in the principles underlying parliamentary politics and those underlying democracy and argued that mass democracy was creating a crisis for the parliamentary system. According to Schmitt, open debate in the legislature is the essence of parliamentarism and serves as the means of discovering the national interest; the essence of democracy, meanwhile, is unity between the leader and the masses. By permitting the rise of leaders fanatically supported by the masses, democracy, in his view, was interfering with the normal conduct of parliamentary politics. Underlying his position was the emergence of the forces of communism and fascism.

Ideology was a major actor in democracy as defined by Schmitt. But today it has reached a dead end. Communism has collapsed, and as a result anticommunism has also lost its appeal. Religious and nationalistic ideologies may continue to hold sway in some small and medium-sized countries, but in the major industrial nations the politics of ideology is on the wane.

Even where no powerful ideologies exert a pull, however, parliamentary politics has deteriorated. In order to win as many votes as possible, political parties have come to seek support from a variety of groups, such as farm organizations, labor unions, and supporters' associations for individual politicians. The LDP in particular has cast its nets wide; it has turned into a "catchall"

party, and its politicians' activities center on brokering between the interests of the various support groups. The web of special interests has spread to every nook and cranny of society, hobbling political activity. It is absolutely impossible for the ruling party to carry through bold reforms while it attempts to reconcile the interests of all of its supporters—farmers, small shopkeepers, the construction industry, large corporations, and urban consumers.

In *The New Realities* (1989), Peter Drucker notes the decline of ideology as a political force and the paralysis of politics by special interests, or single-cause pressure groups, as he calls them. The task of political leadership from now on, he suggests, is to build a consensus on the ends to be achieved and to work doggedly toward their achievement. He emphasizes the need for clear goals and vision. Though Drucker does not go into the details of how "vision" politics should operate, I see it as a process of working toward medium- and long-term objectives. It lacks the driving force of ideology, but unlike interest brokering, it does not try to deal with the problems at hand on an ad hoc basis but sets goals and strives to achieve them.

The issue of liberalizing rice imports, which I touched on above, is one area where the politics of vision could well be brought to bear. Another is the problem of land and housing. Thus far the government has responded after the fact to the spiraling cost of real estate with steps like expansion of the system of public financing for people purchasing homes and enlargement of the districts subject to land-price monitoring. Vision politics would instead establish a goal first—for example, to enable the average salaried worker in Tokyo to acquire a reasonably sized home, maybe 160 square meters, within a commuting time of fifty minutes—and then consider the strategy for achieving this objective. Even the idea of moving the capital out of Tokyo should be contemplated.

Major problems of great complexity require strategic thinking of ambitious scale, for which purpose we must first come up with grand objectives. And in order to achieve this politics of vision, open debate between the parties is essential. New life must be breathed back into the Diet.

The Problem of a Multiseat Constituency System

Above I cited Schumpeter to point out that competition between political parties is needed as a means of clarifying the issues and elucidating the will of the people. There is another reason I welcome such competition. As Max Weber stated repeatedly in "Parlament und Regierung im neugeordneten Deutschland" (1917; translated into English as "Parliament and Government in a Reconstructed Germany") and elsewhere, the primary virtue of parliamentary politics—party politics, in other words—is that it breeds leaders competent in the field of foreign affairs. Those who emerge at the helm of government have successfully led their parties in competition with other parties, and as such they can be expected to be capable of leading their countries to victory in international competition.

In the September 1989 issue of *Chūō Kōron*, I wrote an article pointing out how ineffective Japan's legislature is as a forum for effective competition between parties, stressing the negative effects on our country's ability to conduct foreign policy. I would add here that I was surprised by the lack of punch in the ruling party's interpellations in the autumn 1989 House of Councillors deliberations on abolishing the consumption tax. This I would attribute to the fact that the upper house has traditionally lacked real debate. The LDP has faced even less interparty competition there than in the House of Representatives.

In order to enhance competition between parties, there is a need for reform outside of the Diet as well. The first requirement is an overhaul of the electoral system, a process that should take as its primary goal the fostering of competition rather than the usually advanced goal of reducing inflated campaign costs.

The current system of "medium-sized" electoral districts (mostly with three to five seats) for the lower house makes it possible for a party to get a fair number of its candidates elected by merely going after one seat in each district. This means that it can campaign on a platform that reveals only what it opposes, ducking the issue of what program it would pursue if it took power. The difficulty of fielding more than one candidate per district was in fact one of the major stumbling blocks for the JSP in the 1990 lower house election. But the problem presented by the multiseat districts is not limited to the Socialists: All incumbents, who are more interested in their own reelection than in victory for their party, seek votes by opposing what the public opposes rather than by endorsing what some voters may dislike. The existing setup is an institutional impediment to positive campaign messages.

To be sure, the multiseat districts have served some useful purposes, perhaps the most important being their contribution to political stability during an age of fierce ideological confrontation. But in the light of the system's demerits, the time has come for it to be replaced.

Two other types of reform should be undertaken concomitantly. One is the decentralization of administrative power. In Japan, the largest industrial democracy that does not have a federal system, excessive demands are placed on politics and government at the national level. Without bold moves to transfer authority to the regions, we are unlikely to see the emergence of an effective political decision-making process. The other reform is the introduction of primaries for the selection of the major parties' candidates for the Diet. Once the multiseat districts have given way to the proposed single-seat constituencies, primaries will be needed to ensure that political bosses do not dominate the nomination process. The combination of these reforms would allow the candidates in the single-seat districts to reveal positive stances—to stop saying no so much and start saying yes more often.

Changing No to Yes

In 1989 the word *no* seemed to be in the air. Ishihara Shintarō and Morita Akio published their *"No" to ieru Nihon* (*The Japan That Can Say No*). JSP chairwoman Doi Takako went around proclaiming, "What won't do, won't do" (a reference to the consumption tax in particular). And criticism of sexual harassment came to the fore—a no hurled by women at the male-dominated corporate world.

The last phenomenon was, I believe, a sign that the rising level of education of women has begun to exert a far-reaching influence on society as a whole. Allow me to refer to some developments I have noted in my own work. At the law faculty of Rikkyo University where I teach, the share of women students has risen from about 10 percent a decade ago to about 30 percent now. Of the top ten students in the 1990 graduating class, nine were female. The overwhelming majority of those going on to graduate school were women, including all five of the students who were accepted at graduate schools affiliated with universities other than Rikkyo. Also, two-thirds of those sent to study abroad by the university were women.

Many have carped at women's achievements. Female students have been criticized for merely having good attendance records, for being grade-grubbers, for lacking creativity, for tending to select easy classes, and for wanting to go to graduate school or abroad with little serious motivation. But the figures cited above deprive these complaints of their cogency. Women are now packing even seminars like mine that (by reputation, at least) are tough.

Though today's young women may outperform men in college, once they graduate and take jobs they can expect to encounter visible and invisible types of unpleasantness in the workplace. Since they are unlikely to feel fettered by the same unseen chains as their male colleagues, however, they will probably not hesitate to say no when they want to. Older women too can be expected to imitate this assertiveness, leaving the men wondering why they alone must put up with all the demands placed on them.

It may be that the increased readiness to say no means people have become more spoiled and irresponsible and have adopted shorter time horizons. This could produce a negative effect on public policy. Still, if people do not begin to assert their own interests clearly, it will be difficult to initiate constructive debate. It is the responsibility of politicians to channel people's negative sentiments in a positive direction—to convert the politics of no to the politics of yes.

Courtesy of Japan Echo.

English version originally published in *Japan Echo* 18, Special Issue (1991): 62–68. Translated from "Hitei no seiji o koete," in *Bungei Shunjū* (May 1990): 110–20; slightly abridged (courtesy of Bungeishunjū).

I-(3) Following Through on Electoral Reform

Yayama Tarō
Japan Echo, 1991

People around the world see Japan as a country incapable of reforming itself without outside pressure. Why is it that the Japanese seem unable to decide on changes unassisted? The answer is simple enough. A powerful network of entrenched interests sees to it that disadvantageous changes are either turned back or at least watered down. This network comprises bureaucrats, politicians, and industrialists. Their tripartite alliance represents a formidable obstacle to any meaningful reform.

The Glue in the Tripartite Alliance

One of Japan's goals today is to internationalize, bringing the country's institutions and practices into line with global norms. But such a goal is anathema to the old guard, with its vested interest in the status quo. And as long as the moves to internationalize are stymied, we can expect friction with other countries to mount, leading to more Japan bashing.

The glue that holds the tripartite alliance together comes in part from the electoral system, especially the "medium-sized" districts of three to five seats for the powerful House of Representatives. Because of the multiseat districts, the ruling Liberal Democratic Party (LDP) must run two or more candidates in many districts to capture a majority of the seats in the lower house. Engaging in hard-fought contests against members of their own party, these candidates need vast sums of money. They raise it by lining up corporate supporters, and once in office they return the favor by looking after their supporters' interests. Within the National Diet the LDP legislators tied to specific industries band together in *zoku*, or "tribes," to enhance their influence, and they also forge ties with the responsible

bureaucrats. Since the bureaucrats are constantly struggling to protect their turf, they readily join forces with the *zoku* legislators and the industrialists behind them.

Strong political leadership is essential in order to implement the radical reforms now needed. Japan's politicians are incapable of such leadership, however. In collusion with the bureaucracy and business circles, they are devoting their time to obstructing reform efforts. They have in effect paralyzed the political system, preventing an appropriate response to the changes on the international scene.

In April 1990 Prime Minister Kaifu Toshiki promised to push through a bold reform of the electoral system. Due to resistance within the LDP, however, no agreement was reached on a system to replace the multiseat districts until the end of the year. Since the details are still being worked out, a bill will not be drafted until April or May this year. If Kaifu is serious about getting the bill passed before his tenure as LDP president expires in October, he will have to convene a Diet session in June or July to deliberate the legislation. And at that point the LDP will have to lock horns with the opposition.

The LDP's plan, based on an April 1990 report of the government's Election System Council, is to use a dual system of small, single-member constituencies and larger, proportional-representation districts in place of the multiseat system. Each voter would receive two ballots, one to pick a candidate for the local constituency and the other to select a party for proportional representation. The parties would prepare slates of proportional-representation candidates beforehand, and a number of candidates corresponding to each party's

33

share of the second ballots would take office. The council recommended that the size of the House of Representatives be cut from its present 512 members to 501, of whom 301 would be elected from the single-seat districts and 200 from the proportional-representation districts. The LDP's proposal goes further, shrinking the lower house to 471 seats—the size prescribed for this chamber long ago by law—of which 300 would be in the small constituencies and 171 in the larger districts. These numbers may change, however, during negotiations with the opposition parties.

None of the opposition parties, including the biggest, the Social Democratic Party of Japan (SDPJ, as the Japan Socialist Party, or JSP, has recently renamed itself in English), likes the design of this reform. Their complaint is not with the proportional-representation part of the plan, which would secure some seats even for small parties, but with the single-seat districts, where the big parties, the LDP in particular, would have a decisive advantage. If a change is to be made, the opposition would prefer an arrangement where the two parts of the dual system are tied together, retaining the single-member districts but adjusting the total seat shares to match more closely each party's vote share. Given the fact that the LDP currently does not have a majority in the House of Councillors, there is little chance for quick passage of the dual system as presently envisioned. But the debate over it is likely to heat up soon, when the bill-drafting work leads to concrete proposals on district boundaries and seats.

Redrawing the Electoral Map

SDPJ chairwoman Doi Takako says that before thinking about the dual system, reforms should be implemented to clean politics up and reapportion the multiseat districts. But reapportionment is in itself a tricky business. A radical redistricting initiative would entail adjusting the boundary lines or the number of seats in probably 80 percent or more of the existing 130 districts. And as Doi should know from her own experience when her district almost lost a seat several years back, politicians get quite hysterical when their power base is endangered.

The Supreme Court has ruled that malapportionment is not unconstitutional as long as the number of people per representative in any one district does not exceed three times the number in any other district, or as it is often expressed, as long as no vote weighs more than three times any other. Taking advantage of this lenient guideline, the Diet thus far has contented itself with occasionally adding a seat here and subtracting a seat there. And since subtractions tend to meet stiff resistance, most of the adjustments have been additions, swelling the lower house bit by bit to its present 512 members. Due to the inadequacies of this piecemeal approach, there are fifteen prefectures today that have a bigger population than another prefecture and yet elect fewer representatives, and the same is true of fifty-three electoral districts. And even using the 3:1 ratio, eight districts now need reapportionment.

Everyone agrees that the malapportionment is too serious to be condoned. The Diet itself adopted a resolution in 1986 calling for a radical reapportionment, and in June last year the Election System Council recommended that the discrepancy in vote weights be brought within a ratio of 2:1. This 2:1 ratio is favored by the academic community, and indeed probably nobody would say it is too strict. But if we define the radical reapportionment needed as one that meets the 2:1 criterion and trims the lower house to the originally intended 471 seats—a definition that none of the ruling and opposition parties rejects—we find that practically the whole house must be redistricted. In a plan drawn up by Kumamoto governor Fukushima Jōji, a former LDP labor minister, it was found that boundaries would have to be redrawn or seats reallocated in 115 of the 130 districts.

While the Social Democrats accuse the ruling party of dragging its feet on reapportionment, they also are to blame for the lack of action. The SDPJ, after all, voted in favor of the 1986 Diet resolution, and if it is dissatisfied with the LDP proposal for discarding the multiseat districts, it should take the lead by showing how they can be reasonably redistricted. But this is probably asking too much of an opposition party that never does anything more than gripe about LDP initiatives.

What will happen if nothing is done? The administration contends that it can dissolve the Diet and hold a general election at any time even though the vote weights in eight districts currently exceed the 3:1 ceiling. But if an election is held, the Supreme Court is liable to rule it unconstitutional, invalidating the results. So reapportionment must be carried out before the next election, and since the current term of the lower house members runs out in February 1994, that is the ultimate deadline for reform. Before that time there must be either some stopgap measures, a radical overhaul of the multiseat constituencies, or the implementation of the LDP's dual system.

If the opposition parties fail to produce a reform proposal of their own, there will be no choice but to consider the merits of the LDP proposal. And if the opposition then confines itself to negative comments about the dual system, the electorate will eventually turn against it for not taking a constructive approach to a serious problem. Thus while the LDP plan may have only a slim chance of passing through both chambers of the Diet in the near future, over the long run its prospects are better.

A Record of Expedient Reforms

Japan is the only industrial country that has a system of medium-sized electoral districts. Even in Japan, moreover, other district configurations have been used. When Japan's first general election was held in 1890, single-seat districts were the rule. These small constituencies were retained until the 1902 election, when a shift was made to large, multiseat districts. The single-seat constituencies were then reinstated in the 1920 election. Not until 1928, when the first election under universal male suffrage was held, did medium-sized districts with three to five seats make their appearance. The first election following World War II again employed a large-constituency system, but a reform in 1947 restored the medium-sized districts.

The difficulty of holding a closely supervised election in a war-devastated country was what prompted the authorities to turn to large constituencies in 1946. Why did they then opt for the medium-sized districts a year later? According to people who have researched this question, the Diet, under orders from the Allied occupation authorities to stage another lower house election as well as the country's first upper house election in April 1947, when local elections were also held, simply dusted off the old system of medium-sized districts to get the electoral machinery ready in time. Today's districts, in other words, were put into place for no better reason than that a plan was already available.

Research by Furuya Keigi, a former member of the House of Councillors, also throws light on the scrapping of the single-member districts in the 1900 reform of the election law. In those days political parties were beginning to mature, and they posed a threat to the clannish rule by the powerful domains that had engineered the Meiji Restoration of 1868. The Meiji oligarchy wanted to hold the parties in check, and it selected the large districts as a tool for this purpose. A document of the Privy Council on electoral reform stated the case as follows: "The system of small districts tends to strengthen the parties pointlessly and to augment their vigor. The switch to large districts would not crush the parties, but it would have the effect of stopping their expansion and even causing their contraction."

For such reasons the single-seat districts were thrown out, but the multiseat districts, in which voters each selected a single candidate, also proved to be problematical. When they were discarded in the 1919 reform of the election law, the home minister deemed them to be an obstacle to the improvement of political ethics and the development of the parties. "The problem is the in-fighting among candidates from the same party. . . . The politicians build support bases [in these large districts] and turn them into private fiefs. . . . Party comrades do their best to steal votes from each other." In their configuration, these large districts were not unlike today's medium-sized districts, and evidently they caused similar problems.

The single-seat districts then made a brief comeback, only to be scrapped again in the electoral reform of 1925. And again the choice of a replacement, the world's only system of districts with three to five seats, was based on political expediency. There were three major political parties at the time—the Kenseikai (Constitutional Association), Kakushin Kurabu (Reform Club), and Rikken Seiyūkai (Constitutional Political Friends Association)—and they ran the country together in coalition governments. The three-seat districts gave them a way to cooperate in elections, running one member from each party in every district. The four- and five-seat districts were created, according to Furuya, merely to give the smaller opposition parties a few seats in the legislature.

Some people argue that the medium-sized districts are perfect for Japan's political climate, but this sentiment may simply be the result of the fact that the Japanese have grown used to them. There is no evidence that this electoral system, born from a cozy agreement among three prewar parties, is intrinsically superior to other systems.

A System that Breeds Corruption

Just two years after the medium-sized constituencies were hastily brought back in 1947, a government advisory committee was established to offer ideas on possible improvements. In 1951 the panel recommended that the country return to single-member constituencies, and in 1956, during the administration of Hatoyama Ichirō, a reform bill based on this plan was submitted to the Diet. This bill went down to defeat, but the problems it was meant to address, notably the collusion between politicians and business leaders in a shipbuilding scandal, remained unremedied. About once every decade since then a major scandal has emerged, such as the Lockheed payoffs scandal of the mid-1970s and the Recruit stocks-for-favors scandal of the late 1980s, but subsequent attempts at reform have always stopped short of overhauling the electoral system. One bid was made to adopt the single-seat system in 1972, under Prime Minister Tanaka Kakuei, but it was also turned back.

After the Recruit scandal surfaced in 1988, a group of junior LDP legislators made public a study on just how expensive politics has become. According to the report, on the average each of these politicians spends the staggering sum of ¥120 million a year. This money goes for things like mailing postcards to constituents—this alone can cost more than ¥10 million—and running local offices. Representatives from geographically large districts try to keep as many as ten to fifteen offices open the year round.

The reason these ruling-party legislators cultivate their constituents so aggressively is, of course, because they must guard against the encroachment of rivals from their own party. To win a majority of 257 in the 512-member lower house, the LDP must field multiple candidates in nearly every district. And these candidates end up attacking each other to gain a larger share of the same conservative vote. The case of lower house member Gotōda Masaharu is typical. His Tokushima constituency has five seats, which are now held by two Liberal Democrats, two Social Democrats, and one member of the Kōmeitō (Clean Government Party). "I don't pick up any extra votes if I attack the SDPJ, and I even lose some votes if I say bad things about the Kōmeitō. My real rivals, in short, are other LDP candidates." Since opposition parties generally field only one candidate in the districts they decide to contest, their politicians can campaign on party platforms and hold their expenses much lower.

In the mid-1970s Prime Minister Miki Takeo tried to put an end to money politics by tightening the Political Funds Control Law, but this did not reach to the core of the problem. Politicians simply found ways of raising money that were not covered by the new law, such as by selling exorbitantly priced tickets to fund-raising parties. And when these parties became too conspicuous and people called for self-restraint, even more subtle methods were contrived, including stock and real-estate transactions. If nothing else, the Recruit scandal served to demonstrate where politicians are now looking for money. The next step may well be a ban on dealing in stocks and real estate, but this will only lead to new fund-raising schemes. No amount of lecturing on ethics will cure the problems as long as the electoral system compels politicians to raise huge sums to keep their jobs.

The fundraising needs have forced each LDP Diet member to organize a personal support group. These groups, which play a far greater role than the counterpart organizations in other countries, bring the politicians together with wealthy local constituents and lessen their reliance on the party. Various other problems arise from the operation of these groups, but they cannot be disbanded as long as the multiseat districts exist.

Another attendant evil of the multiseat system is the rampant factionalism within the ruling party. Anybody who sets out to become an LDP Diet member must first locate a friendly faction boss who will furnish the ¥300 million to ¥500 million needed to launch a career in national politics. This money, which goes for the fostering of a personal support group, becomes the first of the bonds tying the rank and file to faction leaders. Not wishing to get dragged into factional politics, many talented individuals with large followings opt for other careers. One way of getting around this initial investment is to inherit a support group. Of the LDP candidates elected to the lower house for the first time in recent elections, one-third inherited their seats from a relative, usually their father. Increasingly, the new entrants to the LDP are people like these, who move into a ready-made base, or people who have amassed a personal fortune.

Disregarding the Will of the Majority

Data from past elections shows that in a three-seat district, a candidate needs to win only 25 percent of the votes cast to get elected, and in a five-seat district the percentage drops to 15 percent. Directing one's campaign efforts at the general public is not the most efficient way to win 15 to 25 percent of the ballots cast. It is far more effective to cater to special-interest groups in exchange for their support. Having bridges and roads built in the district can also help, even though by rights this sort of work should be carried out under the purview of the prefectural authorities rather than in response to prodding from national legislators.

In single-member constituencies, by contrast, one needs a majority to win. Naturally one cannot woo 51 percent of the electorate with a style of politics that benefits only some 15 percent. Those hoping to be reelected must back legislation and advocate policies designed to serve voters in general. In the last general election, which

was supposed to cleanse politics of the Recruit mess, almost all the implicated politicians were reelected. The results would have been vastly different if a single-seat system had been in place.

Industries now exert inordinate influence on politics by lavishing funds on individual politicians, the factions, and the parties, nurturing the *zoku*, or tribes, which then work on their behalf. Although a political party is supposed to formulate policies from an impartial and broad perspective, the LDP's policies have been warped by its numerous *zoku* members. Together with bureaucrats interested in preserving their powers, they are blocking Japan's internationalization.

It is time that we woke up to the fact that the electoral system is one of the main obstacles to Japan's integration into the global community. There is no question that single-seat constituencies would force the parties to shape up. They would have to begin looking beyond free-spending industries and vocal regional minorities, addressing the concerns of the general public.

One argument that is sometimes dragged out against the small constituencies is that they would lead to more "dead" votes, that is, ballots cast for candidates who lose, thus leaving the voters who cast them with no voice in government. But this is not necessarily so. Any candidate who wins in a close contest is in danger of losing in the next election. Thus, though up to 49 percent of the votes may initially appear to have been wasted, the winner will still strive to serve this minority in order to stay in office.

Again, some Social Democrats argue that fiddling with the electoral system to remedy weaknesses in the LDP is putting the cart before the horse. But this thinking ignores the fact that corruption within the government party is a byproduct of the electoral system. If the SDPJ were to move into power, its politicians would soon be organizing their own personal support groups and stabbing each other in the back, just like LDP members. More than that, the single-seat system would do much to improve the SDPJ. It would force this opposition party to formulate policies appealing to a wide audience, not just the unions and groups that have been its principal supporters. The party would have to stop contenting itself with about half the numerical strength of the Liberal Democrats and with a posture of only saying no to LDP initiatives. The naysaying of the SDPJ, in fact, is another byproduct of the multiseat system. It derives from the party's complacency with a share of the vote sufficient to elect one candidate in each of the three- to five-seat districts. The way to turn the party into a serious contender for power is to force its candidates into races where they must attract at least half the votes.

The LDP in all likelihood would walk away the overwhelming winner in the first few elections held under a dual system of single-seat contests and proportional representation. But after several big losses, the Social Democrats would scrap their unrealistic policies, and in a decade or so they might finally be ready for a successful showdown with the ruling conservatives. If, however, the SDPJ insists on maintaining the multiseat system, it can be sure that it will never manage to grab the reins of government.

Debunking the Critics' Assumptions

The dual system, the critics complain, might give the LDP 70 or 80 percent of the lower house seats with only 40 percent of the vote. It is true that an electoral system should be designed to reflect the will of the public in seat shares, but it should also be designed to install a responsible administration. A pure proportional-representation system would indeed reflect the nuances in the public's will, but it might not put any single party in charge. There would be an inherent tendency toward coalition governments formed by minority parties.

The electoral system used in Germany, like that proposed for Japan, is a mixed system of single-member constituencies and proportional-representation districts. But because the allocation of the overall seats is linked to each party's share of the vote, in practice the system works like straight proportional representation. The present government is a coalition between the biggest party, the Christian Democratic Union (CDU), and the Free Democratic Party, which ranks third. Thus although the CDU may have won the largest share of votes, it cannot disregard the wishes of the Free Democrats in its policies.

Italy also employs proportional representation: its large districts have twenty seats on the average. There the number one Christian Democracy has teamed up with the parties ranked from third to fifth, excluding the number two Democratic Party of the Left, the former Italian Communist Party. The fate of the coalition often lies in the hands of the smaller parties, and it is not unusual for one of their leaders to head the government. In this system, where the top party is obliged to please two or more coalition partners, it is by no means clear that the will of the public is reflected faithfully in government. The question of who to credit or blame for policies is often ambiguous, and coalition deals are often brokered behind closed doors, not in the voting booth.

Britain, by contrast, uses single-member districts. They have served to foster what is basically a two-party system. Because the party holding the greatest number of seats forms the government, the responsibility for policy decisions is seldom in doubt.

We must also question the common assumption that the dual system would only strengthen the LDP's position as the perennial government party. In the July 1989 election for the House of Councillors, the LDP suffered a humiliating defeat. Had the same votes been cast in a lower house election under the dual system, one calculation shows that the LDP would have captured a mere 123 seats to the opposition's 378. Although many Japanese take the LDP's rule for granted, overlooking its policy blunders and financial scandals, another bungle like the Recruit flap would, in a single-seat system, send the Liberal Democrats hobbling to the sidelines. And the fear of this prospect should prompt the ruling party to be more careful about its policy responsibilities and political ethics.

Some argue that a system of small constituencies, in each of which the LDP would put up only a single candidate, would place too much power in the hands of the party's top executives. Their say over who was to be the party's choice would, it is suggested, turn them into dictators. Others assert that the system would work to block outsiders, stemming the flow of new blood into the party. But these concerns, even if they do transpire, would not be attributable to the electoral system; they would merely represent shortcomings in the way the party is managed. Witness, for example, how Britain's Conservative Party selects new candidates. It invites applications from around the country, and the applicants are interviewed by the party's national and regional leaders on policies, political convictions, and ambitions. Those who pass the screening process receive the party's support when they stand for office. Former prime minister Margaret Thatcher won approval to be a candidate when she was twenty-nine years old and ran successfully for a seat in the House of Commons when she was thirty-three. It was the party's impartiality in screening candidates that allowed her to enter politics regardless of family background or wealth and to sit at the nation's helm for more than eleven years.

A pure system of single-member districts has the virtue of magnifying the will of the largest segments of the public, generally assuring that just one party forms the government and can be held accountable for its policies. Were such a system to be introduced in Japan, however, it could very well reduce the playing field to just the LDP and the SDPJ, squeezing out such opposition forces as the Kōmeitō, Democratic Socialist Party, and Japanese Communist Party. Since they represent important minority views, it is desirable that they continue to have a voice in the political arena. It is for this reason that the Election System Council recommended choosing two-fifths of the lower house seats through proportional representation and that the LDP, though reducing the ratio of these seats, went along with the idea of a dual system of this sort.

There is, of course, no perfect system of selecting legislators. But the multiseat system we have today is badly flawed. At a time when Japan is being called upon to bring its institutions and practices into line with international norms, this setup is preventing politicians from rising above the narrow interests of the bureaucracy and the business world to carry out sweeping reforms. If Japan is to join the international community, it must remodel its electoral system.

Courtesy of Japan Echo.

English version originally published in *Japan Echo* 18, no. 2 (1991): 29–34. Translated from "'Seiji kaikaku' wa doko e itta?" in *Shokun* (April 1991): 228–37; abridged by about one-third (courtesy of Bungeishunjū).

The Rise and Fall of "Reformist Governments"
Hosokawa and Hata, 1993–1994

I-(4)

Inoguchi Takashi
Asian Journal of Political Science, 1994

Introduction

On June 18, 1993, in front of Prime Minister Miyazawa Kiichi, a no-confidence bill was passed by a vote of 255 to 220 in the House of Representatives. It was not the first time an incumbent prime minister received a no-confidence vote in the National Diet. In this case, however, the incumbent party lost its majority in the House of Representatives in the general election of July 18, 1993. In the election's aftermath, the Liberal Democratic Party (LDP), still the largest party, opted to step down without inquiring too deeply into the possibility of forming a coalition government. The LDP was in fact outmaneuvered by a coalition consisting of the Japan New Party and the New Party Sakigake. In August they formed a coalition government with all the other opposition parties, except for the Japanese Communist Party (JCP). It put an end to thirty-eight uninterrupted years of the LDP as the ruling party.[1]

The new coalition government consisted of the Social Democratic Party of Japan (SDPJ), the Democratic Socialist Party, the Kōmeitō (Clean Government Party), the Japan Renewal Party (JRP), the Japan New Party, and the New Party Sakigake. The last three were composed largely of those ex-LDP members who left the party out of their commitment to "reform" the 1955 system (Tanaka 1994).

Both sets of politicians found the reformist movement most convenient to serve their purposes. First, those activists of the Takeshita Noboru faction who had to distance themselves from the allegedly corrupt LDP politics formed the JRP. Second, those LDP politicians whose careers had been circumscribed by the excessively large and bureaucratized party organization formed the Japan New Party and the New Party Sakigake (Inoguchi and Iwai 1987). They were largely backbenchers. They were joined by totally new politicians who wanted to become parliamentary members ex nihilo by jumping on the bandwagon of reformism. Both groups were supported by the electorate, whose distrust in LDP politicians reached new heights (Kabashima 1994). This can be considered reformism from the bottom up in the sense that reformist sentiments of the electorate were siphoned by these two kinds of politicians most successfully (Takabatake 1994).

"Reform," in fact, meant a number of different things. First, it was purported that the Japanese political system is too prone to scandal and should be reformed (Tanaka 1994). This has been especially evident since 1989, when the Recruit scandal was revealed during the legislative efforts to enact a consumption tax bill. Second, the sentiment was strong that the Japanese economic system had gone wrong and that disentangling it and deregulating it may be the wave of the future, especially amidst the longest recession since the collapse of the bubble economy (Nakatani 1993). Third, the view was gaining some support that the Japanese state should be able to act in a much more resolute fashion and that Japan should play a more positive role in the world (Kitaoka 1992). This sentiment has grown especially since the Gulf Crisis of 1990–1991, when Japan's reluctant and limited (mostly financial) participation in the war was severely criticized (Inoguchi 1991b).

Whether the self-claimed reformers are real reformers or not is something that is not a concern here. But the kinds of things they advocate reveal a number of layered dimensions in Japanese politics. Understanding these dimensions also enables one to understand how the "reformist" government of Hosokawa Morihiro was abandoned by the Social Democrats and Sakigake in spring 1994, leaving the Japan Renewal Party, the Japan New Party, and the Kōmeitō maintaining a minority coalition government with Hata Tsutomu heading it, and further how Hata lost power in June 1994 and was in turn replaced by the coalition government of the Social Democrats, the LDP, and Sakigake.

In less than a year, the prime minister changed three times. The way in which the prime ministers changed has prompted this author to coin the term "karaoke democracy" to characterize Japanese politics of 1993–1994 (Inoguchi 1994e, 1994f).[2] By that I mean the kind of democratic politics with two major components: (1) like karaoke, everyone can take a turn at the microphone and sing songs to the karaoke orchestra, and yet one can treat the whole thing with indifference; and (2) like karaoke, everyone can sing songs reasonably well with the support of karaoke equipment, that is, melodies coming from the CD and words of songs appearing on the TV in front of the singer's eyes. In other words, (1) everyone is almost persuaded that he or she can become a prime minister, and (2) everyone can perform reasonably well, supported by the bureaucrats orchestrating policy legislation and implementation.

In what follows, I will explain how the reformist governments rose and fell under "karaoke democracy." Lastly, I will touch on the prospects for Japanese democratic politics.

Three Dimensions of Reformist Politics

It is my contention that the major symbols of the self-claimed reformers lay bare the key dimensions of Japanese politics in 1993–1994. They are: (1) political ethics, (2) the free market mechanism, and (3) a "normal" state.

Political ethics

It is very important that the reformist movement started as a reaction to the revelations of political scandals enveloping the LDP, especially its largest faction, the Takeshita faction, in 1992.

The Takeshita faction was virtually run by its deputy, Kanemaru Shin, since Takeshita Noboru,

its leader, was forced to resign as prime minister because of the passage of the consumption tax law and subsequently quit the LDP because of the Recruit scandal in 1989–1990. It was a time when business boomed, but the cost of living rose as well. The occurrence of politicians taking bribes with such ease and legislating a tax hike infuriated a large number of the electorate.

But Kanemaru was himself hit hard by the revelation of the Sagawa Kyūbin scandal of 1992 and forced to quit politics. Since the bubble economy had deflated and people were badly out of pocket, the scandals were sufficient to make the electorate feel negatively about LDP politics.

The task confronting LDP members in general and Takeshita faction members in particular was how to project a clean image and uphold political ethics when the pervasive distrust in politicians was expressed daily in the mass media. When the de facto leader was arrested, many Takeshita faction members had to distance themselves from the taint of corruption. Hence the formation in spring 1993 of the Japan Renewal Party, whose members were largely from the Takeshita faction and among the most active in running the Takeshita-led or Kanemaru-led LDP politics in the late 1980s and early 1990s.

Given the strong record in Japanese politics that those parties whose politicians were tainted by big scandals tend to be punished in the succeeding election fairly substantially (Reed 1994), it is no wonder the de facto leader is Ozawa Ichirō, a protégé of Kanemaru until his fall in 1992 and of Takeshita until his fall in 1989. Similarly many LDP politicians felt the same way as Japan Renewal Party members. Especially those LDP members whose electoral power bases in their respective districts were not so strong felt acute anxiety as to their reelection prospects. Already in late 1992 the LDP was putting forward the idea of revising the Public Offices Election Law from the system whereby two to five persons are elected in one district with one nontransferable vote (the medium-sized system) to the system whereby one person is elected in one district with one vote (the Anglo-American system).

The reasoning is that with the medium-sized system, the LDP fields plural candidates among whom competition does not reflect policy differences but the extent to which personal and district needs are satisfied by LDP candidates, thus fostering the climate for higher corruption. Yet many LDP politicians not so confident in his or her reelection possibility felt all the more anxiety about losing their seats given the prospect of competing with fellow LDP candidates in the same district with only one candidate to be elected.

The LDP's proposed reform package in 1992 prompted all the opposition parties to push the counter-scheme of choosing candidates by proportional representation of parties in addition to the Anglo-American system. The opposition parties were all smaller than the incumbent party. Therefore their apprehension is that if only one person is to be elected in one district, the LDP might capture most of the districts. The opposition parties were joined by some LDP politicians who were not so confident about their electoral prospects once the Anglo-American system was adopted.

But once Prime Minister Miyazawa sought to make some concessions toward accommodating those resisting the adoption of the Anglo-American system, opposition within the LDP to the prime minister became intense for being too appeasing toward the opposition parties. Thus the prime minister's position was undermined from both within and without the LDP and thus led to the no-confidence bill in June 1993.

What emerges from this summary is the great significance of electoral uncertainty associated with the impact of the Sagawa Kyūbin scandal and the related electoral system reform prospects on politicians' realignment patterns (Kōno 1994). In other words, reform became everyone's slogan amidst the pervasive distrust of LDP politics. It resembled in a sense the Chinese Red Guard's style of waving the Red Flag in order to oppose the Red Flag. Everyone became a reformist waving the reformist flag, however different their underlying motives and concerns were.

Free market mechanism

The logic of this key symbol is as follows. Corruption takes place in large part because of the close business-government relationship cemented over years of LDP rule. Consequently, deregulating government control and setting the market free from political regulation will alleviate the maladies of corruption. The so-called *zoku* politicians who favor business firms and bureaucratic agencies in return for political donations from the former and legislative support from the latter were notorious for their propensity to take bribes. Public opinion critical of *zoku* politicians welcomed this line of logic as well (Inoguchi and Iwai 1987).

Furthermore, the logic was accepted because the collapse of the bubble economy and the consequent prolonged recession were due in large part to the insufficiently deregulated financial system's overlending. The acceptance of the logic was made easier by the visible loss of competitiveness of the Japanese manufacturing and financial sectors. Many manufacturing firms have to go abroad for direct investment because of the high costs of production at home, while the financial system does not attract foreign capital because of too many regulations. Market liberalization and bureaucratic deregulation became everyone's buzzwords (Nakatani 1993).

In addition to these two political and economic factors, an additional international factor was important (Inoguchi 1993d). Market liberalization had been advocated by the US government for years. But the advent of the Democratic administration of Bill Clinton in the winter of 1993 heralded a much tougher attitude toward the snail's pace of Japan's market liberalization in a number of key sectors. The constituents of the Democratic Party and the end of the Cold War accentuated this tough attitude of the US government on the market liberalization efforts of foreign countries.

The US government's logic is as follows: the huge trade deficit vis-à-vis Japan is caused in a fairly large part by the Japanese government's unjustifiable regulation of its economy. Since the Japanese government has vested interests in keeping a number of key sectors largely regulated, the best policy is to make consumers conscious of the benefits of market liberalization. For that purpose, courting and mobilizing the consumers-cum-voters and even the opposition parties for the support of market liberalization should be vigorously pursued.

Amongst the opposition parties, the Japan New Party and the Japan Renewal Party portrayed themselves as a party of market liberalization. The US government gave moral support and encouragement to them on a number of public occasions, most notably when President Clinton visited Tokyo in spring 1993. President Clinton met in a most cordial and intimate fashion with some opposition party leaders, like Hosokawa Morihiro of the Japan New Party and Ozawa Ichirō of the Japan Renewal Party, while his meeting with Prime Minister Miyazawa Kiichi was conducted in a very chilly atmosphere.

Of all the opposition politicians it was Ozawa who expressed the free market philosophy most lucidly (Ozawa 1993).[3] The publication of his book into English and the high-level attention paid to it in Washington, DC, was clear evidence of what he had in mind. Recognizing the need to enhance his and the Japan Renewal Party's position and power, he tried to make the best use of the sympathy of the US government by appealing to its two major concerns vis-à-vis Japan: market liberalization and the political role of Japan in the world. He played up these two themes along with that of political ethics. His own previous engagements with the US government in economic and security matters during Japan-US trade and economic negotiations and in Japan's cooperation and participation in the Gulf Crisis no doubt shaped his own philosophy on Japan's policy on market liberalization and security cooperation. What is important to note is that he believes in what he says and in what that means to the LDP government and the US government from the viewpoint of enhancing his power and position.

The LDP government was cornered in a sense in the game of market liberalization politics by this two-pronged assault: one prong being the US government and the other Ozawa Ichirō.

All these factors lent support to reformist politicians in 1993–1994.

A "normal" state

The impact of the Gulf Crisis of 1990–1991 on Japanese thinking about international peace and security opened up the question of whether Japan should become "normal" or not (Inoguchi 1992, 1993c). "Normal" here is understood to mean that Japan can participate in international security efforts like any sovereign state. This debate entailed the controversy about whether the Constitution should be revised or not. The Constitution explicitly renounces the use of military force for the resolution of international disputes. The controversy has been enlivened by the perceived lack of strong political leadership in Japan's diplomatic conduct, not only in the Gulf Crisis but also in the Japan-US economic talks. The issue of political leadership in crisis management, be it security-related or economic, was linked with the issue of political reform by reformists. What was portrayed by US, international, and Japanese media of Prime Minister Kaifu Toshiki's handling of the Gulf Crisis and cooperation with the United States and Prime Minister Miyazawa's handling of economic negotiations with the United States led many voters to believe that political leadership would be enhanced by restructuring the Japanese state through a series of reforms. The vocabulary of democracy like accountability and responsibility was stressed.

Reformists presented a number of schemes towards that goal. They included enhancing the powers of the Prime Minister's Office and reducing the authority of the central government bureaucracy. The Japanese prime minister does not have a large staff of his own, and staff members are mostly recruited from the central government bureaucracy. The result is that the prime minister is more than usually constrained by bureaucrats. The prime minister does not enjoy independent sources of information and independent assistance for policy assessment and judgment. Moreover, the prime minister and elected politicians are perennially handicapped by bureaucrats when the Cabinet Legislative Bureau and the Finance Ministry's Budget Bureau require the bill's consistency with existing laws and the feasibility of budgeting, since only bureaucrats fully have such expertise and information.

To remedy this imbalance of power, the reformists proposed appointing many elected politicians to the position of vice minister, appointing the prime minister's staff independent of bureaucratic recruitment, and increasing the staff and the budget of the Prime Minister's Office (*Asahi Shimbun* 1994).

The reform package dealing with political ethics includes four laws pertaining to political donations, the electoral system, subsidies for political parties, and reshaping of House of Representatives districts according to the changed electoral system. These laws have thus some elements that were argued by reformists to be conducive to greater exercise of political leadership.

The reform package restricted political donations to individual politicians, rather than to political parties, giving party headquarters more leverage over party members, as they could control the allocation of such money. Political parties of center-right persuasions have tended to be grassroots-oriented, with the headquarters' powers being significantly curtailed by intensely district-oriented politicians.

The changed electoral system is also regarded as conducive to greater exercise of political leadership. House of Representatives elections are to be conducted under the Anglo-American system of choosing one person in one district. This encourages the creation of a two-party system, it is argued, because the system enables party headquarters to have greater leverage over the selection of a candidate in a district.

Subsidies to political parties in proportion to their parliamentary size and their expenditure are also seen as conducive to the exercise of greater authority by party headquarters.

In the area of foreign relations, the issues of UN peacekeeping operations and Japan's aspiration to become a permanent member of the UN Security Council kept the debate alive throughout 1993–1994. Japan's participation in the UN Transitional Authority in Cambodia (UNTAC) in running a free election and forming a democratically elected government was seen as a step forward, even if some interpreted it as being accompanied by a timid half step backward (Inoguchi, forthcoming). Prime Minister Miyazawa's speech in the UN General Assembly in 1992, noting Japan's aspiration-cum-determination to become

the Security Council's next permanent member, subsequently helped the reformists' plea for a normal state.

Yet all these do not seem to have created a normal state. Rather, the issue of a normal state seems to have been raised in order to shake the LDP government, whose position had been undermined by its Cold War-era mentality of relying on the United States for security and global market access but resisting its demands to revise its often parochial outlook on world affairs.

Two Steps Forward, One Step Backward

Thus the reformists scored a triumph in 1993 by making the best use of three key terms: political ethics, market liberalization, and a normal state. The next question is: how did they collapse so abruptly in spring 1994 after the passage of political reform legislation?

Basically, the reformists moved two steps forward in a fashion that aroused anxiety in many parliamentarians, and in order to counter the two steps forward the opponents moved one step backward.

It was in late 1993 that the political reform package was legislated. This represents two steps forward. Yet anxiety was also aroused. The Hosokawa government was perennially plagued by revelations of further divisions within the coalition as to what is to be done next and what is to be the general direction of policy.

Then rumors circulated that Prime Minister Hosokawa was tainted by potential scandal. Furthermore, the prime minister clearly said no to the US government in early spring of 1994 during economic negotiations, not bowing to US demands to set numerical targets for market liberalization in a number of sectors. And most importantly, Ozawa Ichirō's influence was felt by some coalition partners to be unduly large.

In April 1994 the Social Democrats abruptly declared its withdrawal from the coalition government, as did Sakigake. A minority coalition government headed by Hata Tsutomu of the JRP was formed shortly after that. The frustration of the SDPJ and Sakigake was that their voices were not well reflected in the Hosokawa government's policy. Once the reform package was legislated, they quit the coalition. The LDP, the largest party, adopted a wait-and-see attitude. Thus a minority coalition government consisting of the Japan Renewal Party, the Kōmeitō, and the Japan New Party was formed. But it was only a matter of time before the Hata government fell. It remained in power for two months.

By this time it was very clear that the SDPJ was worried about the other two key terms: market liberalization and a normal state, which were lucidly promoted by Ozawa Ichirō of the Japan Renewal Party. The SDPJ was frightened by the prospect of remaining in the coalition government, and it thus went out first. Then it discovered that the LDP was not particularly unhappy about the possibility of forming a coalition with the Social Democrats. After all, they are the largest two parties in the Diet and, most importantly, the two parties that worked together for thirty-eight years as the ruling and biggest opposition parties. The thirty-eight years largely coincided with the Cold War era and, more importantly, the era of Japan's "peace and prosperity in one country."[4]

On the two key terms, the positions of the LDP and the SDPJ turned out to be not very different. Both wanted to see market liberalization to move slowly and one step at a time. Also, both wanted to see the Japanese state remain a civilian power, rather than a normal state shouldering too much risk and responsibility.

The discovery of the same policy inclination on these economic and security agendas made the parties natural allies. The government led by an SDPJ prime minister was born out of this understanding in June 1994.

Although somewhat confusing and bewildering, it should not be very difficult to see the contrasts:

Hosokawa said no to the bilateral protectionism suggested by the US government in 1994. After all, the reformist coalition government was for market liberalization. On the other hand, both Miyazawa and SDPJ prime minister Murayama Tomiichi concluded agreements with the US government in 1993 and 1994, respectively. They both agreed with the US government in working out bilateral deals, if not in advancing outright bilateral protectionism.

International security efforts were addressed under Miyazawa and Murayama for Cambodia and Rwanda despite their respective constituencies' much more inward-looking pacifist policy preferences. A few hundred Self-Defense Force officers and soldiers were sent to Cambodia and Rwanda, respectively, against all kinds of warnings against the dispatch. Under Hosokawa and Hata, no new major change was seen in this policy realm in the more outward looking and activist line, perhaps except for the more straightforward apologies expressed for Japan's actions in World War II and for the unconditional extension of the Non-Proliferation Treaty.

Reformism from the Inside Out

If the reformist governments of Hosokawa and Hata represent two steps forward and one step backward in terms of political reform legislation, then a less reformist government under Murayama represents reformism from the inside out. By this I mean the outlook that sees policy tasks from the inside, although those tasks are intended to cope with and adapt to the basic external forces confronting Japan.

The following two tasks are regarded as most important: (1) optimal taxation in the light of the growing need to adapt to the steadily aging society and its proportionately increasing demand for medical and welfare expenditures; and (2) optimal institutional division of labor between central and local governments.

Optimal taxation is not easy to determine. The frustration of the electorate over one of the longest recessions since the first oil crisis of 1973–1974, together with Murayama's need to please the public, has led the government to reduce the income tax for the next three years. The Finance Ministry is not necessarily happy about a tax reduction when it is not accompanied by tax hike schemes to meet demands for the steady increase in expenditures. Yet in the longer term one needs to satisfy the electorate's preferences at least at first. Otherwise, whatever tax hike schemes might be conjured up would not be sustainable politically.

Thus even if the direction of taxation looks at first contrary to the prospect for rapidly growing expenditures, it is because the current coalition looks at policy tasks from the inside out.

The optimal division of labor between central and local governments is not easy to determine as well. Political pressure on administrative reform, that is, bureaucratic deregulation and decentralization combined, has not died out yet. Deregulation and decentralization are designed to go together. Deregulation at the central level is bound to proceed. Market liberalization and globalization have led most countries to adapt to these forces. Japan is not an exception. Along with economic liberalization, a lot of bureaucratic regulation has to go. Hence there is a need to substantially curtail the growth of the central bureaucracy in the longer term.

Yet bureaucratic reduction cannot be implemented unless there are institutions that can accommodate some surplus personnel at the central level—namely, the local bureaucracy, especially at the prefectural level. Hence deregulation has to proceed in tandem with bureaucratic decentralization. In other words, bureaucratic decentralization is necessary from the viewpoint of alleviating the overload of the central bureaucracy as well.

Those policy areas suited to bureaucratic decentralization include education, welfare, construction, and transportation. While the former two areas take up two large expenditure items in the central government, the latter two areas where the bulk of public works projects fall are indispensable to keep local economies alive and well.

At the central government, such policy tasks as (1) diplomacy and defense; (2) money and finance and macroeconomic management; and (3) intelligence and coordination will be accentuated. These are intended to meet the challenges of market liberalization and globalization and enmeshment of national and international security.

Thus even if administrative reform means the reduction of personnel at the central level, it would mean a stronger focus on a number of policy areas with which the central government grapples and the wider-scale shouldering of a number of policy tasks at the local government level. In the longer term this direction represents institutional reform to be conducted without much fanfare.[5]

When reformism from the inside out is shared more or less by the two largest parties, then the reformist governments driven by the key concepts of political ethics, market liberalization, and a normal state have to go. It was reformism from the bottom up in the sense that it was driven by the electorate's pervasive distrust of politicians. Once the reformism from the bottom up achieved its minimum task of appeasing the electorate and achieving the minimum legislative task of political reform, then reformism from the inside out ushered in the dramatic change of coalitions.

When one compares European and Japanese socialist parties, one can see immediately the great emphasis placed on foreign and defense policy in Japan compared to Europe, where emphasis is primarily on social and economic policy. Thus the impact of the end of the Cold War was most tangible among Japanese socialists. They lost their cause célèbre. Prime Minister Murayama represents this most eloquently. He was one of the most left-leaning members of the socialist party, building his career on his strong opposition to the Japan-US Security Treaty. With the end of the Cold War, the Japanese socialists have become not so different from other parties.

Prospect for Japanese Democratic Politics

Frightened by electoral uncertainty amidst the electorate's pervasive distrust of politicians since the Sagawa Kyūbin scandal of 1992, Japanese politicians of all stripes rode the bandwagon of reformism. The three key terms were political ethics, market liberalization, and a normal state.

It was reformism from the bottom up. The self-proclaimed reformists rode the bandwagon of reformist sentiments of the electorate and took new initiatives in taking two steps forward in legislating the political reform package. But once the political reform legislation was completed the electorate's reformist sentiments substantially subsided. The disarray within the coalition manifested itself more strongly. Plagued by the much larger divisions in policy preferences over the key symbols of market liberalization and a normal state among coalition partners than with the LDP, the Social Democrats and Sakigake quit the reformist coalition, leaving the Japan

Renewal Party, the Japan New Party, and the Kōmeitō in the minority government, which fell within two months.

The two largest opposition parties, the LDP and the SDPJ, found it more comfortable to form a coalition together in terms of parliamentary size and policy preferences. In other words, on the basis of the newly found policy quasi-convergence in relation to the much more ideologically purist Japan Renewal Party on such issues as market liberalization and a normal state, they found a formula to assure political stability. This led to the coalition government of the LDP, the SDPJ, and Sakigake in June 1994 with Murayama, a socialist, as prime minister.

The key actor in this was the SDPJ. Stripped of its pet cause of anti-Americanism with the end of the Cold War, the Social Democrats found themselves quite akin to the LDP's policy preferences in terms of market liberalization and a normal state. Both were cautious and moderate on these issues. Murayama announced that the government would pursue "gentle politics." By that he meant the government would proceed to liberalize the economy and to enhance Japan's global role in a prudent and orderly fashion. He does not want to see a shock-therapy-like style of market liberalization. Nor does he like to see the Japanese state become a normal state in the sense of making Japan an active state deploying military force for the settlement of international disputes. On both policy issues, the LDP and the SDPJ are not far apart.

The somewhat opportunistic but bold policy lines of the Japan Renewal Party heralded the advent of Japan's reformist era in 1993–1994. But once it came down to the real tough issues of the speed and nature of market liberalization and the adaptation-cum-transformation of the Japanese state, then the majority favored the coalition of the LDP and SDPJ in terms of policy preference.

Japanese electoral politics seems to unfold in a somewhat dialectic fashion like the reformist politics of two steps forward, one step backward. It looks as if the backward step is permanent at the moment. But the global forces pertaining to security configuration, market forces, and human

values will steadily lead the Japanese government to move in the direction that the reformist governments of Hosokawa and Hata proclaimed.

The following three factors will lead Japanese electoral politics to proceed roughly as follows:

First, the SDPJ will shrink in parliamentary size. The steady convergence of policy preferences of the center-right parties makes it hard for the SDPJ to maintain party identity. The Anglo-American system will further knock it down in the forthcoming general election. Second, the LDP will come back even if it may not achieve a parliamentary majority as it has had for most of the past thirty-eight years. Third, a new party that is expected to be founded with the Japan Renewal Party, the Kōmeitō, the New Japan Party and some other small parties as founding partners will establish a substantial parliamentary influence.

But more important beyond the prospects for electoral politics are the three basic factors that continue to shape Japanese democratic politics: first, the increasingly visible convergence of the electorate into center-right ideological preferences; second, the perennial need for politicians to cope with bureaucratic power; and third, the perennial need for center-right parties to have a united candidate at the district level.

First, the electorate's preferences will increasingly converge into center-right positions (Kabashima 1994). All the public opinion poll data attest to this. Second, Japanese politicians have been plagued by the soft power of Japanese bureaucrats since 1890 when the Imperial Diet was convened for the first time (Inoguchi 1994b, 1994d). To cope with the power of bureaucrats in policy formation and implementation, center-right parties will start to think that they have to be a predominant party of a large size and to stay in power for a long time in order to let bureaucrats know that they cannot straitjacket politicians. Third, two of the empirical regularities in Japanese electoral politics are that the smaller the district size, the more united the candidates and that the more local level at which the election is held, the more united the candidates (Reed 1993). Since the district size will become much smaller than the previous district size in terms of the electorate from the next general election onward, these empirical regularities will hold in stronger form.

Given all these conditions, I suspect that after three to five general elections, that is, in three to ten years, Japan might give birth to a new predominant party with a new set of policy priorities, given the rapidly changing policy environments confronting Japan. The spirit of that possible transformation is to retain the merits of "karaoke democracy" in terms of ensuring wide political participation and political efficacy at the same time but to remold it in a way that enables Japan more adroitly to adapt to changing environments in a more astute fashion than before (Inoguchi 1994g).

English version originally published in *Asian Journal of Political Science* 2, no. 2 (1994): 73–88.

Notes

1. The heyday of LDP rule has been analyzed in terms of policy function and reaction function in Inoguchi 1983. See also Inoguchi 1990. LDP politics toward the end of one-party dominance in 1993 was analyzed in Inoguchi 1993b.

2. "Karaoke democracy" was commented on in the *Economist* (July 2, 1994), 23–24, and the *Far Eastern Economic Review* (July 14, 1994), 11.

3. See also my comparative analysis of Ozawa's and Hashimoto Ryūtarō's books, Inoguchi 1994c.

4. As to Japan's foreign policy, see Inoguchi and Okimoto 1988; Inoguchi 1991a, 1993a. The nature of global change is fully analyzed in Inoguchi 1994a.

5. Prime Minister Murayama has been shifting his focus from bureaucratic deregulation to bureaucratic decentralization.

References

Asahi Shimbun. 1994. "Seikan ryōmen kara Shushō Kantei kyōka" [Enhancing the Prime Minister's Office from Both Sides of Politicians and Bureaucrats]. October 9, 1994.

Inoguchi Takashi and Daniel Okimoto, eds. 1988. *The Political Economy of Japan Vol. 2: The Changing International Context*. Stanford: Stanford University Press.

Inoguchi Takashi and Iwai Tomoaki. 1987. *Zoku-giin no kenkyū* [A Study of Policy Tribes]. Tokyo: Nihon Keizai Shimbunsha.

Inoguchi Takashi. 1983. *Gendai Nihon seiji keizai no kōzu* [Contemporary Japanese Political Economy]. Tokyo: Tōyō Keizai Shimpōsha.

———. 1990. "The Political Economy of Conservative Resurgence under Recession: Public Policies and Political Support in Japan, 1977–1986." In *Uncommon Democracies: The One-Party Dominant Regimes*, edited by T. J. Pempel, 189–225. Ithaca: Cornell University Press.

———. 1991a. *Japan's International Relations*. London: Pinter Publisher / Boulder: Westview Press.

———. 1991b. "Japan's Response to the Gulf Crisis: An Analytic Overview." *The Journal of Japanese Studies* 17 (2): 257–273.

———. 1992. "Japan's Role in International Affairs." *Survival* 34 (2): 71–87.

———. 1993a. *Japan's Foreign Policy in an Era of Global Change*. London: Pinter Publisher.

———. 1993b. *Nihon: Keizai taikoku no seiji un'ei* [Japan: The Governing of an Economic Superpower]. Tokyo: University of Tokyo Press.

———. 1993c. "Japan in Search of a Normal Role." *Adelphi Paper*, no. 275, 58–68.

———. 1993d. "Japanese Politics in Transition: A Theoretical Review." *Government and Opposition* 28 (4): 445–455.

———. 1994a. *Sekai hendō no mikata* [How to Analyze Global Changes]. Tokyo: Chikuma Shobō.

———. 1994b. "Shin zoku giin taibō ron" [New Policy Tribes Be Born]. *Chūō Kōron* 109, no. 3 (February): 45–56.

———. 1994c. "Futatsu no seisaku pakkeiji: 'Nihon kaizō keikaku' to 'Vision of Japan'" [Two Policy Packages: 'The Plan to Reform Japan' and 'The Vision of Japan']. *Yomu* [Reading] (March 1994): 28–29.

———. 1994d. "The Pragmatic Evolution of Japanese Democratic Politics." Paper presented at the conference on Democracy and Democratization in Asia, Lovain-la-Neuve, Belgium, May 30–June 1, 1994.

———. 1994e. "Nihon seiji no mikata" [How to Analyze Japanese Politics]. *Shiten* [Viewpoint], NHK TV Program Channel 3, 10:00 p.m.–10:10 p.m., June 30, 1994.

———. 1994f. "Ronten" [My Argument]. *Yomiuri Shimbun*, July 2, 1994.

———. 1994g. "Global Forces and Democratic Politics in Pacific Asia." Paper presented at the World

Congress of the International Political Science Association, Berlin, August 24–28, 1994.

———. Forthcoming. "Japan and United Nations Peace Keeping Operations." *International Journal*. [Published as "Japan's United Nations Peace Keeping and Other Operations" in 1995, *International Journal* 50, no. 2 (Spring): 325–342—Ed.]

Kabashima Ikuo. 1994. "Shin hoshu jidai no makuake" [Opening of a New Conservative Era]. *Mainichi Shimbun,* July 20, 1994.

Kitaoka Shinichi. 1991. *Nichi-Bei kankei no riarizumu* [Realism in Japan-US Relations]. Tokyo: Chūōkōronsha.

Kōno Masaru. 1994. *Japan's Postwar Party Politics: A Microanalytic Reassessment*. Unpublished dissertation, Stanford University. August 1994.

Nakatani Iwao. 1994. *Nihon keizai kasseika no jōken* [Conditions for the Revitalization of the Japanese Economy]. Tokyo: Tōyō Keizai Shimpōsha.

Ozawa Ichirō. 1993. *Nihon kaizō keikaku* [The Plan to Reform Japan]. Tokyo: Kōdansha.

Reed, Steven R. 1993. *Making Common Sense of Japanese Politics*. Pittsburgh: University of Pittsburgh Press.

———. 1994. "Scandals and Elections in Japanese Politics." Paper presented at the World Congress of the International Political Science Association, Berlin, August 24–28.

Takabatake Michitoshi. 1994. *Nihon seiji no kōzō tenkan* [Structural Transformation of Japanese Politics]. Tokyo: San'ichi Shobō.

Tanaka Naoki. 1994. *Nihon seiji no kōsō* [Envisioning Japanese Politics]. Tokyo: Nihon Keizai Shimbunsha.

Partisan Realignment and Institutional Reform

In the mid-1990s, amid ongoing political instability and shifting partisan alignments, the public's sense of security was deeply shaken by two tragic events: the Great Hanshin-Awaji Earthquake that struck the Kobe area in January 1995 and the Tokyo subway sarin gas attack carried out by the Aum Shinrikyō cult two months later. These disasters fueled a surge in commentary and criticism on the need for better emergency management and stronger political leadership. Sassa Atsuyuki, a former government official specializing in crisis management, leads off this section with "Fault Lines in Our Emergency Management System," which critiques the government's disaster response and examines the political dimensions of emergency management.

During the same period, the nation was grappling with an ailing post-bubble economy and a crisis of confidence in the bureaucracy, while successive coalition governments—from the diverse cabinet formed by Hosokawa Morihiro after the fall of the long-ruling Liberal Democratic Party (LDP) to the unlikely union between the LDP and the Social Democratic Party of Japan—were developing new decision-making processes through trial and error. Shinoda Tomohito's "Japan's Decision-Making under the Coalition Governments" is an early example of a comparative approach, a departure from the prevalent practice of critiquing a particular government in isolation.

The 1990s were a time of wide-ranging institutional reform, from the adoption of a new electoral system to the reorganization of the central bureaucracy under Prime Minister Hashimoto Ryūtarō. As an introductory survey of these developments, which received surprisingly little attention overseas, we have included Nakano Minoru's "National Political Reform in the 1990s."

Another conspicuous trend of the period, accompanying the succession of coalition cabinets, was the ongoing partisan realignment of anti-LDP forces. With a plethora of new parties forming, merging, and splitting in rapid succession, a growing number of voters began identifying as independents, unaffiliated with any party. Tanaka Aiji shares his research into this and other aspects of Japanese voter behavior in the section's final offering, "Two Faces of the Japanese Electorate."

Fault Lines in Our Emergency Management System

Sassa Atsuyuki
Japan Echo, 1995

On January 20, during a plenary session of the House of Representatives, Prime Minister Murayama Tomiichi frankly acknowledged his administration's failure to mobilize relief efforts in timely fashion following the catastrophic Kobe earthquake of January 17, explaining, "The event was a first."

This initial public statement from the man at the top of the government's crisis-management system was surprisingly well received by the Japanese people, who tend to view Murayama's artlessness as a virtue. After all, the prime minister heads the Social Democratic Party of Japan, which for thirty-eight years had played the role of the political opposition. How could he be expected to perform like a seasoned leader? The public seemed prepared to accept the prime minister's ingenuous plea.

Until the January disaster, Murayama may not have realized what a lonely and isolated position the prime minister occupies. Only recently, it seems, has it dawned on him that even in our information-inundated society, the office where the prime minister works is all too easily stifled by bureaucratic constraints and shut off from the data it needs to act independently—and furthermore, that without capable and trustworthy staff, the nation's top leader is soon exposed to the world as an emperor with no clothes. Be that as it may, in public-relations terms, Murayama acquitted himself well on that occasion as commander-in-chief of the government's crisis-management operations.

Likewise, on January 19, at a press conference held upon his return from a tour of the disaster area, he came across as sincerely sympathetic. "It was awful," he said, "worse than I had expected." Murayama spoke of shifting authority over the national disaster-relief efforts from the National Land Agency (NLA) to an "emergency disaster countermeasures headquarters" organ directly under himself. On this occasion, too, the prime minister struck the right note.

I have always maintained that one of the most important qualities for a top leader is the ability to find the right words to deal with a crisis. Just as words are a weapon to be used in battle, they are a tool for restoring peace. A choice turn of phrase may be all it takes to rouse the bureaucracy from inertia for the sake of the stricken area, and it can surely help calm the apprehensions of the residents. In a situation where the toll of dead, injured, and homeless is mounting daily and the victims and their families are seized with grief, anguish, and resentment, the country's top leader can do much to assuage their feelings by speaking in a manner that conveys sincerity and empathy—or, conversely, exacerbate those feelings by saying the wrong thing. The initial statement following a disaster must therefore be formulated with a clear realization of its potential impact. If it impresses the public as heartfelt and honest, subsequent words of condolence and encouragement to the victims are more likely to be regarded as sincere.

On the evening of January 19, however, the prime minister amended his earlier statement, explaining "When I said 'emergency disaster countermeasures headquarters,' I meant 'emergency countermeasures headquarters.' Under the Disaster Countermeasures Basic Act, emergency disaster countermeasures headquarters would have the power to curtail private rights, as in a national state of emergency. Since there has been no rioting, we see no need to go that far. Instead, we'll deal with the situation by setting up emergency countermeasures headquarters comprising the heads of the ministries and agencies that oversee economic affairs."

To the average listener, this bit of obfuscation may have merited little more than a confused shrug of the shoulders, but to people versed in such matters, it was obvious that this seemingly trivial semantic distinction concealed an about-face. The presence or absence of the word *disaster* makes all the difference in terms of the organ's legal powers. Emergency countermeasures headquarters, unlike emergency disaster countermeasures headquarters, constitute nothing more than a liaison committee to coordinate relief efforts by different government agencies and have no power to impose price controls, secure supplies of goods, or in any other way limit private rights. Nor can such an organ consolidate command over the separate, uncoordinated relief efforts of the Ground, Air, and Maritime Self-Defense Forces (SDF); police riot squads; the Fire Defense Agency; and the Maritime Safety Agency. This was nothing more than an attempt to paper over matters with deceptive rhetoric.

In either case, by January 20, it was already too late to save the situation. The prime minister's leadership was critical during the first seventy-two hours after the quake struck, when hundreds of people were trapped under the rubble, and a life was being lost with each passing minute. It was then that a real difference could have been made by controlling the spread of fires, providing refuge to the thousands wandering about without shelter or transportation after buildings and roads collapsed, giving emergency treatment to the seriously wounded, and controlling traffic so that rescue teams and supplies could get through. This is the stage at which Kobe demanded the decisive and courageous command that only the top political leader can provide.

By January 20, establishing a new administrative entity—whether emergency disaster countermeasures headquarters or the more politically innocuous emergency countermeasures headquarters—was like calling the doctor after the patient had died; it was a domestic version of the Gulf War debacle, when Tokyo's offers of assistance

amounted to too little, too late. Moreover, unlike the Gulf War, in which the Japanese suffered no casualties, the Kobe earthquake took some 5,400 lives here in Japan. The present cabinet bears a grave responsibility for its failure to act at the early stage of rescue efforts.

Defending the Bureaucrats

The Diet interpellation on January 23 was the first following the Kobe earthquake. It was led off by former prime minister Kaifu Toshiki, who heads the largest opposition force, the New Frontier Party (Shinshintō in Japanese). The thrust of Kaifu's questioning was whether the prime minister's office had responded in an appropriate and effective manner to an unprecedented catastrophe that had left more than 5,400 dead, upwards of 27,000 injured, some 300,000 at least temporarily homeless, and over 100,000 buildings destroyed or damaged. This time, Murayama unequivocally defended the government's actions. "We moved as quickly as possible to set the [Land Agency's] Headquarters for Major Disaster Countermeasures in motion and to establish a cooperative relationship with prefectural and municipal authorities. I have also appointed a minister in charge of quake-relief efforts," Murayama asserted. "I can tell you with assurance that we have taken the best possible steps within the present system." Kaifu also asked a question with profound repercussions for the Murayama cabinet: whether the government should not establish emergency disaster countermeasures headquarters directly under the prime minister, giving him sweeping powers to deal with the emergency in Kobe. Murayama let it be known he was not contemplating the creation of such a body.

From the television broadcast of these proceedings, it was obvious that the prime minister was reading mechanically from materials prepared by other administrative officials. It was a bungled reply, communicating none of the empathy that the public has a right to expect from Murayama as a prime minister who claims to be the champion of "people-friendly politics."

Having spent twelve years in the inner circles of the national government—nine in the

Japan Defense Agency and three in the Cabinet Secretariat—I have a good idea of how the prime minister's responses to Diet interpellation are formulated. Each question, submitted in advance, is handed to the relevant ministry or agency. Officials in the bureau or division concerned produce a draft and hand it over to the counselor in the Cabinet Secretariat, the backbone of the prime minister's support staff. Aides and assistants in the secretariat review, amend, and revise the draft and return it to the ministry or agency. The draft response then goes back and forth between the ministry and the prime minister's official residence, often until late into the night or even the early morning hours, as content and wording is adjusted and fine-tuned. When this process is completed, the cabinet counselor reports the result to the deputy chief cabinet secretary in charge of administrative affairs (who may review the responses himself) and then submits the entire bundle to the chief cabinet secretary. The prime minister is briefed the next morning, just before the Diet convenes.

Murayama's reply on January 23 was clearly drafted by agency bureaucrats, but it cannot have reached the floor of the Diet without the approval of the chief cabinet secretary and others surrounding the prime minister. The contrast with Murayama's straightforward answer of a few days before—"The event was a first"—is illuminating. The earlier statement was doubtless the prime minister's spontaneous response, unvetted by his staff. Members of this staff, along with the bureaucrats who populate the offices of Kasumigaseki, were aghast at his remark because it implied a lapse on their part. Joining forces, they pressured Murayama to read directly from the script they had prepared. The prime minister's insistence that he had taken "the best possible steps" was in fact the bureaucracy speaking in its own defense.

The prime minister, for his part, should have put his foot down. He should have cried, "More than five thousand dead, and you want me to say we did the best that could be done? I refuse to be the bureaucrats' mouthpiece." Murayama should never have delivered a reply so certain to provoke indignation among the quake's victims and relatives of the dead, and his staff was wrong to let him.

In the days immediately following the quake, the victims of the disaster showed astonishing calm, fortitude, and respect for the law as they coped with the crisis. There was scarcely a sign of panic and no rioting or looting. Citizens formed long, orderly lines outside of convenience stores and patiently waited their turn. People from all around the world praised the residents of Kobe for the dignity with which they handled themselves in this extreme situation. Their quiet heroism became the government's excuse for not taking decisive action. Responding to the question of why the administration did not establish emergency disaster countermeasures headquarters or convene the Cabinet Security Council, Ishihara Nobuo, deputy chief cabinet secretary in charge of administrative affairs, stated, "Establishing such headquarters could make people think terrible things are in the offing, resulting in unnecessary fear and confusion. Our judgment was that we were not facing that sort of situation. And I still believe that was the correct judgment." He underscored the point, saying, "It's true that the casualty count was climbing, but there were no reports of civil disturbances. In our judgment, there was no need to convene the Cabinet Security Council." He added, "In terms of effective crisis management, I doubt that it's a good idea to overreact. In crisis management, a flashy response isn't necessarily a better response. The important thing is to respond in the manner most appropriate to the circumstances" (*Mainichi Shimbun*, January 29, 1995).

The absence of civil disturbances following the earthquake is not something for which the prime minister's staff can take credit. It is a testament to the character of the Japanese people. Although the feature in the daily *Mainichi Shimbun* that presented Ishihara's comments invoked in its headlines the need for major reform in the system by which information is channeled to the prime minister and in legislation governing disaster relief, the theme pervading his piece from beginning to end was denial of any responsibility on the part of the prime minister's office. For example, regarding the SDF's slow mobilization, he blames the Defense Agency. He notes that he admonished the chief of the agency's Bureau of Defense Policy for passively awaiting a formal request from the governor of Hyōgo Prefecture and "urged him to take the initiative in asking if there was something the SDF could do to help." In another newspaper article, he commented, "The SDF should have mobilized relief efforts on their own initiative instead of waiting for a request from the governor," drawing an angry protest from the Defense Agency. Ishihara blames the National Land Agency for the fact that the prime minister was slow to learn of the quake, saying, "All information regarding natural disasters is funneled to the NLA's Disaster Prevention Bureau, which is supposed to report anything serious to the prime minister's office. This is the established procedure, but this time the source [the Disaster Prevention Bureau] wasn't functioning."

In the *Mainichi* piece, Ishihara also slams my suggestion that the minister of home affairs should have been put in charge of the headquarters, insisting that "the Disaster Countermeasures Basic Act is under the jurisdiction of the NLA, so the minister in charge is the director general of that agency. It doesn't make sense to put the home affairs minister in charge." If the director general of the NLA is the only person legally qualified to head relief efforts, why did they later shift responsibility from NLA director general Ozawa Kiyoshi to Ozato Sadatoshi, hastily appointed to the ad hoc position of "state minister in charge of disaster relief"?

On the basis of the foregoing, it should be obvious who set the tone for the prime minister's January 23 statement, with its bureaucratic mentality and total lack of empathy for the victims. I have mentioned empathy several times because I believe this human capacity is indispensable not only to great writers and performers but also to political leaders. For Murayama to give a statement that causes people to question his capacity for empathy is tantamount to publicly repudiating the "people-friendly politics" on which he claims his government is founded. It is, in a word, political suicide.

This disaster may well have been a "first" for Murayama, but it was not the first time the disaster-handling authorities of the Cabinet Secretariat and the NLA had faced such a situation. Least

of all was it a first for Deputy Chief Cabinet Secretary Ishihara, who has served under seven prime ministers and occupied this important post for more than eight years—a period that witnessed both the disastrous 1991 eruption of Mount Unzen on Kyushu and the tidal wave that ravaged Okushiri Island off Hokkaido in 1993. Ishihara cannot be unaware that these earlier calamities were marked by similar problems: delays in apprising the prime minister's office of the situation, the absence of a top commander coordinating rescue efforts, and confusion in the chain of command. Our government officials do not seem to understand that there is more to gathering information than reading the standardized bureaucratic memos that make their way up from the lower levels of the administrative apparatus to the top through rigidly prescribed channels. A glance at the live news coverage that appeared on television screens all over the country should have sufficed to impress on the prime minister's staff the gravity of the situation.

The worst part of the administration's failure in crisis management was that it "struck out" without even swinging at the ball. Nothing could be more shameful than the inaction, indecision, and inertia that characterized the initial response to the disaster. To hit home runs, one has to swing the bat, even if it may not connect with the ball. Using the excuse that "a flashy response isn't necessarily a better response," our government officials waited passively like mandarins for information to filter in before taking action, insisting on a formal request from the governor before mobilizing the SDF (in accordance with the Self-Defense Forces Law), whittling away at specific items in appeals for help, and concentrating more on the approval process than on getting things done. The result of this bureaucratic approach was more deaths and more homes destroyed by fire.

The prime minister's response of January 23 bespoke a truly mandarin mindset. The administration chose to take the view that in the case of an "act of nature beyond our control," a sin of omission was preferable to the risk of being held responsible for any untoward consequences resulting from commission, that is, decisive command based on a judgment arrived at after actively gathering the necessary data.

Protectors of the People

In the wake of the Kobe earthquake, it became clear that the cabinet secretariat has a surfeit of mandarins and a deficit of people who could be described as "consuls." In the ancient Roman republic, a consul was a chief magistrate charged with protecting the rights of the plebeians, as an act of noblesse oblige. (Today the English word *consul* is applied to officials of a country's foreign service whose task is to protect the rights and interests of that country's citizens overseas.) Before World War II, the bureaucrats in the Home Ministry were instilled with a consul's sense of duty. On September 2, 1923, the day after the Great Kantō Earthquake struck, Prime Minister Yamamoto Gonnohyōe declared martial law, and approximately one-third of the country's army and naval troops were dispatched to Tokyo. To aid the homeless, maintain calm, and preserve law and order, the government immediately set up a Special Executive Office of Earthquake Relief Aid. Prime Minister Yamamoto himself headed the office, and Home Minister Gotō Shinpei was appointed second in command, while participants included the administrative vice-ministers of each ministry, the director general of the Home Ministry's Social Bureau, the superintendent-general of the Metropolitan Police, the governor of Tokyo Prefecture, and the mayor of Tokyo. Altogether, the office consisted of about 700 people, directly responsible to the prime minister, working tirelessly day and night to hammer out, implement, and coordinate relief measures. Because the offices of the Home Ministry were destroyed by fire, a temporary administrative center was set up in the official residence of the home minister, which had been spared. Civil servants worked from dawn to dusk, many of them in tents erected on the lawn; some fell victim to the waves of disease that were spreading through the city and died at their posts. Such is the dedication of officials who take seriously their duty to protect the people.

This time the bureaucrats were operating on an as-usual footing. In the first forty-eight hours after the Kobe earthquake struck—the most crucial period in terms of controlling fires and saving lives—the government did not even bother to ask the Air Self-Defense Force (ASDF) for the use of its RF Phantom surveillance craft to help assess the extent of the damage with aerial photographs. And there was no one in charge to reach a decision and give the necessary orders to deploy firefighting helicopters, even though their use to control fires at an early stage by spraying extinguishing agents has become standard practice throughout the world.

As sanctioned by the Constitution, the Fire Service Law allows for the destruction of property to control the spread of fire, providing the owner is compensated. Again, no one gave the order. The mobilization of SDF troops was too little, too late. The prime minister's staff did not even bother to have Murayama appear on television to address the nation, console the victims, or send messages of encouragement to bolster the morale of those directly involved in rescue and relief efforts: the employees of city and prefectural offices, as well as the SDF, police force, fire department, and Maritime Safety Agency. These are gestures that almost any nation would expect of its chief executive under the circumstances.

The most important job of a country's political and administrative leaders is to protect the lives, physical well-being, and property of the people in times of emergency. If our government officials were instilled with a sense of duty toward the people they serve, the moment they saw those first televised images of the earthquake—people trapped beneath collapsed buildings or fleeing in confusion from the flames—every ministry would have immediately rallied around the prime minister's office and set about getting things done.

In November 1986, when Mount Mihara erupted on the island of Ōshima and a lava flow threatened the lives of 13,000 residents and tourists on the island, the government response was much the same as that seen after the Kobe earthquake. Information was late in reaching the prime minister's office. Long meetings were held, but nothing was accomplished because no one was clearly in charge. At 6:00 p.m. the NLA's switchboard closed as usual, and there was no one on duty either there or at the prime minister's official residence—just as during the Kobe earthquake. The major difference was the presence of several veteran political and administrative leaders who had served in the prewar Home Ministry and continued to carry on its tradition of dutifully protecting the people: Prime Minister Nakasone Yasuhiro, Chief Cabinet Secretary Gotōda Masaharu, Deputy Chief Cabinet Secretary Fujimori Shōichi (director of the General Affairs Division in the Mie prefectural government during the typhoon that devastated that area in 1959), Tokyo governor Suzuki Shunichi, and Tokyo vice-governor Yokota Masatsugu.

Chief Cabinet Secretary Gotōda, seeing that the meeting of NLA officials was dragging on and fearing that residents would not be evacuated in time, announced that he would take personal responsibility. Broadly interpreting the chief cabinet secretary's role as cabinet mediator and coordinator, as stipulated in Article 12 of the Cabinet Law, he convened a meeting of the chiefs of all the agencies and bureaus that commanded rescue or relief field units, including the chief of the Defense Agency's Bureau of Defense Policy, the chief of the National Police Agency's Security Bureau, the director general of the Fire Defense Agency, and the director general of the Maritime Safety Agency. With the help of Hashimoto Ryūtarō, who was minister of transport at the time, thirty-seven boats were mobilized within two hours to ferry evacuees, including escort ships of the Maritime Self-Defense Force (MSDF), patrol boats of the Maritime Safety Agency, and commercial ferries. By 3:00 a.m. they had succeeded in evacuating 13,000 islanders to the Tokyo mainland without a single casualty.

The Kobe earthquake not only destroyed a major city; it also wrecked the nation's confidence in the central government's ability to cope with crises. The state's crisis management system has been shown to be deeply flawed. We have seen that communication and coordination between the politicians and administrators is inadequate and the gears do not intermesh; we have seen also that in administration of disaster measures, the division of labor between central and local government is blurred.

A Crisis in Crisis Management

Until the Kobe earthquake, prefectural governments have generally been able to handle any disaster that came along. That is why, since the passage of the Disaster Countermeasures Basic Act thirty-four years ago, no one has felt compelled to reform this fundamentally flawed framework. But it is obviously unrealistic to make the same prefectures that have sustained the damage responsible for primary relief measures.

In the wake of Japan's worst disaster since World War II, not a single official resigned either at the local or at the national level. The fact of the matter is that no one can take responsibility for the failures of the government's disaster relief efforts because no one was in charge, no one was in a position to give orders. This frightening state of affairs has persisted for decades now.

Disaster relief is broadly divided into two phases. The first encompasses the initial mobilization of efforts during the first seventy-two hours—or, some would say, ninety-six hours—after the disaster strikes. These involve mobilizing and managing forces from the SDF, police and fire departments, and Maritime Safety Agency to handle rescue efforts, firefighting, evacuation, traffic control, emergency medical treatment, and delivery of emergency relief supplies and so limit damage as much as possible—the fundamental goal of crisis management. This is dangerous work requiring cooperative efforts on the part of those four agencies best trained for crisis management, whose employees are sworn to perform their duty in times of emergency without regard for their own lives: the SDF, the National Police Agency, the Fire Defense Agency, and the Maritime Safety Agency. As far as possible, these agencies should carry out early operations under a unified command and should regularly participate in joint drills so that they are able to coordinate their activities during this critical phase.

The second stage involves, first, the rehabilitation efforts that begin after the fires are extinguished and the buried have been dug out (general relief for the displaced, repair of roads, and so forth) and, second, policies geared to long-range reconstruction, including unemployment measures, housing, and urban planning. The NLA is the government office best equipped to supervise this phase, and it has an excellent track record in this area, having formulated many a fine plan for rehabilitation and reconstruction. The problem lies with the country's misguided policy of putting the NLA in charge of both phases, despite the very different nature of the work involved.

The NLA is fundamentally an economic agency, with its top bureaucrat appointed from within the Ministry of Finance. It has no emergency field unit under its direction and no one on duty after regular office hours. Yet under the Disaster Countermeasures Act, this agency is given oversight of first-stage rescue and relief operations. This was a mistake when the law was enacted in 1961, and it remains a mistake today, thirty-four years later.

It would have been far more sensible to assign the task of coordinating and commanding first-stage rescue and relief efforts to the Ministry of Home Affairs. Home Affairs has jurisdiction over the local governments that have de jure responsibility for disaster relief, as well as over the Fire Defense Agency, an external organ of the ministry. Further, the home affairs minister traditionally doubles as chairman of the National Public Safety Commission. Unfortunately, at the time the 1961 disaster-relief legislation was being deliberated, the government was pressured by vociferous demands for stronger, more independent local government and by a general concern that giving too much authority to the Home Affairs Ministry would resurrect the fearsome power wielded by the Home Ministry (Naimushō) before and during the war. In the end, the NLA was chosen as a less controversial locus of authority. Nonetheless, the Disaster Countermeasures Act does not insist that the headquarters in charge of disaster relief be headed by the director general of this agency. It does stipulate that the headquarters be run by a state minister, which is why the government made Ozato Sadatoshi "state minister in charge of disaster relief" when it shifted responsibility to him from NLA director general Ozawa a few days after the quake. My question was why they did not give the authority instead to Home Affairs Minister Nonaka Hiromu, who has the ability to get things done.

Article 107 of the Disaster Countermeasures Act provides for the establishment of the aforementioned emergency disaster countermeasures headquarters directly under the command of the prime minister when a national emergency is declared under Article 105. Unfortunately the government, after a false start, did an about-face and refused to take advantage of this useful provision, citing constitutional protections of private rights and arguing that nothing so drastic as a state of economic emergency was required as long as no one was rioting or looting.

The role of the SDF in relief efforts is another serious problem. In almost any other country in the world, the military forms the backbone of rescue and relief operations. The SDF are able to function without the support of other agencies and organs; they have land, sea, and air quick-response capabilities; they are extremely well equipped and provisioned; and they are trained to function effectively as a group. Together with the police and fire departments, they should naturally be part of the initial relief force.

The problem is that when the Self-Defense Forces Law passed the Diet in 1954, it did so despite the opposition of a substantial segment of the population, which believed that the Constitution prohibited Japan from possessing such forces, and it did so amidst a wave of popular sentiment favoring a shift of power to the local governments. This political climate made it necessary to include, under Article 83, a stipulation that in principle SDF troops cannot be dispatched to deal with local situations unless the prefectural governor makes a formal request for troops (paragraph 1), who can then assist relief efforts in a secondary capacity. Paragraph 2 permits the SDF to dispatch units autonomously under exceptional circumstances, while paragraph 3 allows for units that happen to be in the vicinity of a disaster site to be put into action. Paragraph 2 has never been invoked.

Article 94 of the same law clearly restricts the authority of SDF troops mobilized for disaster relief. They are granted only a small fraction of the authority given to police under the Law on the Performance of Police Duties—and that only if no police officers are present: They may evacuate residents and they may enter buildings, but they may not—even if they arrive long before other personnel—take charge of any other functions, such as traffic control, firefighting, or recovering bodies. The reason for including these restrictions, clearly, was the concern that if the SDF were given the same authority as local or national police when stationed within local entities, it would amount to the enforcement of martial law or the dispatch of government troops to quell civil unrest.

Some have suggested that the SDF should have dispatched troops independently under paragraph 2. It is convenient to say after the fact that things would have worked out better that way, but it is also a gross error. For armed forces like the SDF to move without waiting for either a request from the governor or an order from the prime minister would be a violation of the all-important principle of civilian control of the military. The problem is the practical one of how, in future situations, we can arrange to dispatch SDF troops legally for the purpose of saving human lives if a request from the governor is not forthcoming or is delayed. The answer—especially now that the Cold War is over—is for the Japanese to get over their military allergy and accord the SDF a primary role in all major disaster relief operations. Article 3 of the Self-Defense Forces Law should be amended to reflect this new post–Cold War role, along with that of international peacekeeping. As for Article 83, paragraph 3 could be expanded to provide for the prime minister to dispatch SDF troops to a disaster site within a specified time for the purpose of saving lives. The government should also consider revising Article 94 to allow SDF troops to perform the same functions as police officers.

Improvements also need to be made in the area of equipment. In the 1970s, the Maritime Self-Defense Force experimentally modified the US-1 four-turboprop amphibian craft to enhance its fire-fighting capabilities, fitting it with a fifteen-ton water tank. The program should be revived, since craft of this sort could be indispensable for extinguishing urban fires—especially blazes of the "towering inferno" type breaking out in high-rise buildings—in the event that water supplies were cut off. Other important items include chemical fire extinguishing bombs, mobile water-purification equipment, helicopter-mounted remote video cameras, and a shared transmitting frequency for command of land, sea, and air units. In addition, amendment of the Self-Defense Forces Law should include establishment of the order of succession for commander-in-chief of the armed forces in the event that the prime minister is unable to carry out those duties much as the US Constitution does vis-à-vis the presidency. This precaution is especially important in view of the possibility of Tokyo being hit by a major earthquake.

A Stopgap Solution

Since the Kobe earthquake there has been much talk of restructuring Japan's crisis-management apparatus with such steps as revision of the legal framework and establishment of an office like the United States' Federal Emergency Management Agency. But all of these are long-range plans requiring new appropriations of funds, and thus fail to address the problem of what to do if another major disaster strikes tomorrow. What we need immediately is a practicable system that is easily implemented and requires no new legislation or special budgetary provisions.

What can be done to create a new national crisis-management system under the current administrative and legislative framework is to establish, by cabinet decision, a crisis management commission comprised of high-level bureaucrats from each of the concerned ministries and agencies to act as an ad hoc disaster countermeasures headquarters. The legal basis for such a decision can be found in Article 12 of the Cabinet Law, which outlines the coordinating and mediating powers of the chief cabinet secretary. A precedent exists in the decision of October 4, 1977, to establish within the Cabinet Secretariat a commission that was named Headquarters to Counter Hijacking and Similar Inhumane Crimes of Violence.

This "Hijack Headquarters" was absorbed into the Cabinet Security Affairs Office in July 1986, when that office and four others were set up under the Cabinet Secretariat at the same time that a law was passed replacing the National Defense Council with the Security Council. Interestingly, one of the duties assigned to the Cabinet Security Affairs Office was to deal with the aftermath of a devastating earthquake accompanied by a breakdown of law and order. But with the NLA technically heading relief operations, it remained unclear who would be in charge of what in such an event. This murky division of labor is a fundamental problem that needs to be addressed.

I recommend a dual command structure to cope with the two phases of disaster relief. In the first ninety-six hours, when early rescue and relief efforts are carried out, the ad hoc crisis-management commission would aid the prime minister in the command of those operations. During the rehabilitation and reconstruction phase, the commission would dissolve, and the NLA could take over. When Chief Cabinet Secretary Gotōda took over management of evacuation operations during the eruption of Mount Mihara in 1986, he was working from basically the same concept. I propose putting this crisis-management system in place as an interim measure while more thoroughgoing reforms are carefully deliberated over the course of the next year or so. (One important task, of course, is to improve the information-gathering functions of the prime minister's office. The government is on the right track here with its plan to make more effective use of the Cabinet Information Research Office and add a disaster-relief officer to its staff.)

I would propose that the commission follow the precedent of the hijack commission in putting its general affairs in the hands of the Cabinet Security Affairs Office. (As for the location of the ad hoc commission's offices, an ideal place would be the so-called C3I (command, control, communications, and information) center of the Security Affairs Office, slated to occupy about 500 square meters of the new prime minister's official residence. Until construction is completed, however, I suggest the commission make use of one of the dining rooms in the prime minister's official residence.) Should the disaster escalate into a serious emergency situation involving a breakdown of law and order threatening the nation's security, authority would automatically shift from the NLA, which is responsible for implementation of the Disaster Countermeasures Act, to the

Security Council, which is under the administrative aegis of the Cabinet Security Affairs Office and chaired by the prime minister. With this in mind, the Cabinet Security Affairs Office should be observing and cooperating in the NLA's ongoing disaster-relief efforts.

To be sure, the prime minister and his staff are generally uncomfortable about involving the Cabinet Security Affairs Office, which includes SDF brass. Even during the Gulf War crisis, they expressed their aversion to seeing military uniforms in the prime minister's residence and complained that it created a crisis atmosphere. This military allergy is one of the major factors behind the inaction that allowed the death toll from the Kobe earthquake to climb to 5,400. If the government feels any sense of responsibility for what happened, it should overcome this irrational aversion once and for all and apply itself diligently to putting in place a workable crisis-management system to ensure that such a tragedy never happens again.

Courtesy of Japan Echo.

English version originally published in *Japan Echo* 22, no. 2 (1995): 20–27. Translated from "'Gominkan' ga inakatta sōri kantei," in *Chūō Kōron* (April 1995): 62–73; slightly abridged (courtesy of Chūōkōronsha).

Japan's Decision-Making under the Coalition Governments

Shinoda Tomohito
Asian Survey, 1998

Analysts predict that the July 1998 House of Councillors election will put Prime Minister Hashimoto Ryūtarō and the Liberal Democratic Party (LDP) back in position to run a single-party majority government after a five-year period of working in coalitions.[1] The Japanese political scene has witnessed a series of drastic changes since the end of the LDP's thirty-eight-year reign in 1993. Four coalition governments have led the country since that watershed year: the eight-party, non-LDP coalition led by Hosokawa Morihiro; the short-lived minority government under Hata Tsutomu; and the LDP–Japan Socialist Party (JSP)–New Party Sakigake coalitions under first JSP leader Murayama Tomiichi and then LDP president Hashimoto. These changes have created a new political environment that has had a significant impact on Japan's policymaking mechanisms. This article examines how policy-making has been transformed under the coalition governments since 1993.

Many scholars have described Japan's policy-making system under the LDP's long reign as one in which the nonelected civil service played an influential role. A gradual structural change took place during this period. Some LDP Diet members accumulated knowledge and experience in specific policy areas and became identified as *zoku*, or policy "tribes." Those who earned the *zoku* label became the ultimate arbiters of political power over specific issues and increased their influence vis-à-vis bureaucrats in those policy fields. As a result, the members of the LDP's Policy Research Council (Seichō-kai) and its divisions (*bukai*) became instrumental in policymaking.

The shift in power from the bureaucracy to the LDP policy committees became more apparent after the two oil shocks of the 1970s. During the era of high-speed growth (the 1950s and 1960s), government revenue increased significantly each year, and a majority of policy decisions involved the allocation of extra revenues to a variety of programs. However, after the oil shocks, slower economic growth reduced government revenue and thus decreased the money available to such programs. With funding limited, bureaucratic officials became more dependent on the media-tion and political decisions of members of the ruling party when seeking to reallocate funds among administrative programs (see Nakamura 1984). It became part of the official process for bureaucrats to seek approval from the relevant *zoku* members before submitting budget propos-als and other policy initiatives to the cabinet.

These *zoku* members formed what may be termed subgovernments based in the LDP's policy committees. The party had seventeen *bukai* and thirty commissions. Commissions were designed to deal with broader issues rather than specific legislation, while the *bukai* corresponded to administrative ministries. They were used by the LDP to influence policy decisions and budget formation in each policy area. The prime minister delegated considerable policymaking authority over specific issues to these specialists within the party organization while he concentrated on broader issues. These subgovernments often became serious obstacles to the implementation of broader government policy initiatives under the long LDP reign. This system continued through the early 1990s but was totally revamped with the end of the one-party dominant system in 1993.

The Hosokawa Cabinet

In June 1993, the House of Representatives (the Diet's lower house) passed a no-confidence resolution against the LDP government headed by Miyazawa Kiichi, effectively putting an end to the LDP's long reign subsequently sealed by the July general election. This was followed by the establishment of a non-LDP coalition government in August. The prime minister that emerged was Hosokawa Morihiro of the Japan New Party (JNP). He had to tackle difficult political issues, including the conclusion of the GATT (General Agreement on Tariffs and Trade) Uruguay Round of trade negotiations abroad and political reform at home, while trying to lead an unprecedented coalition of eight political groups with a wide range of conflicting political ideas.[2]

To maintain the vulnerable coalition, Hosokawa introduced a new decision-making mechanism outside of the cabinet: the Council of Representatives of the Coalition Parties (Yotō Daihyōsha Kaigi). The council was composed of the secretaries-general (second in command) of each party in the coalition; under its banner, they would meet and discuss major political issues. In his writings before becoming premier, Hosokawa had warned repeatedly that the rigidity of the Japanese bureaucracy causes problems in society. An example of this is the so-called "vertical administration" or sectionalism within the government. This was not the only reason why the new government introduced a new decision-making system. In an interview with the author, Hosokawa (November 15, 1996) confided about the difficult situation in which he found himself: "Under the coalition government with eight different political parties, the centralization of policymaking was the only choice. It was impossible to have issue-specific committees."

Under the Council of Representatives, Hosokawa also formed the Policy Adjustment Council to discuss policy matters among the coalition parties. Excepting members of the Japan Renewal Party (JRP) and Sakigake, however, the coalition parties had no prior experience of running a government and thus little background in practical policy formulation. Without the old system with its influential LDP *zoku* members,

bureaucratic officials were able to play an even more important role in the decision-making process than under the LDP governments (see Ishihara 1998, 49–50).[3] Major policy issues, however, were brought up in the council where the political actors made political decisions. This centralized decision-making institution shaped Hosokawa's major policy outcomes.

Prime Minister Hosokawa personally placed the highest priority on the conclusion of the GATT Uruguay Round. To put it in his words: "Japan is in the world system, and I thought that we must show leadership by contributing to the successful conclusion of the Uruguay Round" (Hosokawa, interview by author, November 15, 1996). In order to bring about the successful conclusion of the multilateral trade agreement, Japan needed to open up its rice market regardless of the strong pressures from the politically powerful agricultural interest groups and politicians who represented rural areas. Consensus for opening the rice market had been building since the Miyazawa administration (1991–93) (see Ishihara 1995, 100–108). Japan, as the world's second largest economy and an export superpower, would not be able to maintain a position that could eventually cause it to be blamed as the reason for the Uruguay Round's failure. Years of foreign pressure, especially from the US, had created a mood favorable to the internationalization of Japan's agricultural market. But the political leaders were hesitant to make the final decision as they did not wish to invite the wrath of farmers. Hosokawa, who took office during the final round of the agricultural negotiations, had to make and announce a politically risky decision. To do so, he needed to have some degree of consensus in the Council of Representatives. Though the JSP was reluctant to give its support, Hosokawa's JNP, the JRP, Kōmeitō (Clean Government Party), and the Democratic Socialist Party (DSP) did give their backing to the prime minister's policy on the rice issue.

After an agreement was reached between Europe and the US, Hosokawa announced that his government was ready to accept a compromise on the issue of opening Japan's rice market. As expected, strong opposition came from agricultural interests and LDP politicians, who took advantage of being in the opposition to blame the Hosokawa government for damaging Japan's agriculture. To make matters worse, Hosokawa was faced with a rebellion that erupted within his fragile eight-party coalition government. The JSP, the largest of the eight and with many members elected from rural agricultural areas, threatened to leave the coalition.

Hosokawa, however, did not yield, knowing that the public was backing him. Every national poll taken in the months just prior to his announcement showed that most Japanese agreed that the time had come to import at least some rice. "It is the role of a leader to present a specified goal. If the goal was right, I believed the people would support me," said Hosokawa (interview by author, November 15, 1996), explaining what he was feeling at the time. The JSP held a 12-hour meeting to dramatize its opposition. The JSP representative at the Council of Representatives, Kubo Wataru, went back and forth between the council and JSP headquarters, negotiating and working to persuade the JSP members to comply (Ishihara Nobuo, interview in Mikuriya and Watanabe 1997, 153). In the end, the party decided that breaking with the popular prime minister and bearing the blame for the collapse of the world trade system would be much more dangerous politically than protecting rice farmers, giving Hosokawa his victory. The centralized nature of the coalition government helped in implementing Hosokawa's political decision to open the rice market. The policy subcommittee system would have given agricultural experts a stage from which to voice their opposition, making it more difficult for the prime minister to reach a final decision. In the end, Hosokawa made a predawn announcement on December 14 that Japan must accept rice imports "for our sake and the world's."

Once the market question had been dealt with, political and public interest in Japan swiftly shifted to the political reform issue that had been at the center of the country's political revolution. The reform would institute a new single-member district electoral system in the lower house. Prime Minister Hosokawa declared that he would stake

his political career on achieving this objective. The public, which had been disappointed by the failure of LDP prime ministers Kaifu Toshiki and Miyazawa Kiichi to deliver on similar promises of reform due to intraparty conflicts, strongly supported Hosokawa. His public support ratings stood at more than 70 percent.[4]

Even with this enormous popularity, it was not easy for Hosokawa to pass the reform bills, which were controversial among the politicians. Ozawa Ichiro of the JRP and Ichikawa Yūichi of Kōmeitō, two leading members of the Council of Representatives who together formed the so-called "Ichi-Ichi Line," took initiative and actively sought consensus within the coalition. Although the council accepted the political reform package, some members of the coalition parties covertly implemented a rebellious plan. On January 21, 1994, the JSP's left-wing effectively killed the political reform bills by voting against them in the upper house, thereby breaking the agreement reached among the party leaders in the council. Negotiations taking place in a joint committee of members from the upper and lower houses broke up, leaving Hosokawa with only two more days in the Diet session to achieve political reform.

The prime minister publicly restated his willingness to sacrifice his post to get the reforms passed, and he called for a meeting with President Kōno Yōhei of the opposition LDP. Behind the scenes, Ozawa had lobbied many LDP members for political reform, and some had expressed their willingness to leave the party if it blocked Hosokawa's political reform package. Ozawa then called LDP secretary-general Mori Yoshiro to set up the Hosokawa-Kōno meeting. Made aware of the threatened defections by the members themselves and fearing the possible breakup of the LDP, Mori (interview in Tahara 1997, 82–86) agreed. In the negotiations with Kōno, Hosokawa accepted the LDP's requests to change the number of electoral districts and ease the reporting requirements on political fundraising. Based on these concessions, they reached an agreement. Although many LDP members opposed the political reform, they did not want to be blamed for blocking bills that were popular with the public. This compromise enabled the Hosokawa coalition government to pass the political reform bills in both the upper and lower houses on January 29, 1994.

While the centralized decision-making mechanism helped both in implementing Hosokawa's political reform and opening the rice market, it did not work well in the case of his attempt to raise the consumption tax. The tax issue was deeply connected to the negotiations on the US-Japan Economic Framework Talks, which were ongoing during the political reform debate. In their early stages, the talks were primarily focused on Japan's macroeconomic policies. Japan was asked to present an economic stimulus package in order to increase its imports. The Hosokawa government thought that it was possible to introduce the large-scale tax cut the US government had requested if, and only if, an increase in the consumption tax would follow in a few years to make up for the income shortage that would result. Without a future tax increase, the powerful Ministry of Finance (MOF) would never agree to a tax cut. MOF officials saw this as a great opportunity to raise the existing 3 percent consumption tax, which they considered very low.

Hosokawa faced a dilemma. Time was needed for a political debate, but if a tax increase were announced, Hosokawa would fall from the political tightrope he was walking at the time over the single-member district electoral reform. He decided to keep the tax issue on the back burner until the political reform bills passed in the Diet. The Diet session lasted longer than Hosokawa expected. By the time the bills had passed both the lower and upper houses, it was already less than two weeks before Hosokawa's scheduled February 11 meeting with President Bill Clinton, at which time he planned to present an economic stimulus package that would include the future tax increase.

At the February 1 meeting of the Council of Representatives, Ozawa and Ichikawa introduced the MOF's plan to raise the consumption tax from 3 to 7 percent. The representatives took the proposal back to their own parties for review. The following afternoon, JSP leader Murayama visited the prime minister's office to discuss the tax matter with Hosokawa. However, he was made to leave the office by the Kōmeitō's

Ichikawa, who was trying to eliminate possible opposition (Takemura 1997, 336–38). This dramatic incident hardened the JSP's attitude. When the Council of Representatives met again that evening, the JSP voiced its opposition; for their part, the representatives of the JRP, the DSP, the JNP, and Sakigake announced that they would leave the final decision to the prime minister.

An emergency meeting of the party leaders of the coalition government was called at 11:00 p.m. The leaders of Sakigake, the JSP, and the DSP told Hosokawa that they could not support the abrupt announcement of the new tax plan. They complained that there had not been enough discussion on this issue. Murayama (1996), for example, told Hosokawa, "It is undemocratic to be forced to answer 'yes' or 'no' in such a short period. . . . We can never accept this." Ozawa remained silent throughout the meeting. Despite the opposition of the three coalition parties, Hosokawa held a press conference a few hours later and announced the tax package. The sudden announcement met with strong criticism from the media and the opposition LDP, as well as several of the coalition parties. The JSP demanded the withdrawal of the proposal, threatening to leave the coalition. Strong criticism was aimed at Ozawa and Ichikawa for driving the prime minister to make a hasty decision without building consensus among the coalition parties. Murayama (interview in Kanemori 1996, 31) later pinpointed Ozawa in his criticisms of the decision: "A coalition government should be operated in a democratic manner in order to reflect a wider range of opinions. Secretary-General Ozawa of the JRP did not understand this at all."

The prime minister, who previously had used public support to achieve his policies, did not make much of an effort to persuade the public over the tax issue. Hosokawa was asked at the press conference how the government had come up with the 7 percent; his answer that it was "a ballpark figure" showed that he obviously was not deeply involved in the policymaking process. Hosokawa was no longer seen as a leader who enthusiastically communicated national goals to the public. The public was disappointed to see Hosokawa acting like a servant of the very bureaucrats whose clout he had pledged to curb (Nakamoto 1994; see also Blustein 1994). To many, Hosokawa now seemed to be a puppet controlled totally by the MOF. The public resentment forced Hosokawa to retreat on the tax plan the very next day. Public support for Hosokawa continued to erode after this event, and in April 1994, he suddenly resigned amid allegations of personal financial impropriety, bringing an abrupt end to a unique period in postwar politics.

The Murayama Cabinet

Hata Tsutomu of the JRP took over the office of the prime minister in April 1994. The Hata cabinet faced political difficulty from the beginning. On the day he was elected prime minister, four of the eight coalition parties, excluding the JSP, formed a new political group within the Diet. Now the largest force in the coalition, the new group would be able to gain political advantages including the chairmanships of Diet committees that previously would have gone to the JSP. Upset by this treatment, the JSP left the coalition, leaving the new government in a vulnerable, minority status. The Hata cabinet lasted only two months, its only achievement being the passing of the 1994 budget.

The LDP, suffering from its opposition party status, contacted the JSP's Murayama regarding the possibility of a cooperative relationship between it and the JSP. The Hata government was unable to convince the JSP to return to the coalition. The minority coalition supported as the next premier candidate former prime minister Kaifu, who had defected from the LDP with thirty-four other members. In the subsequent lower house election, a new and unexpected three-party coalition was formed by the LDP, the JSP, and Sakigake. The coalition won a majority and selected Murayama as prime minister.

The new coalition was quickly criticized as a marriage of convenience. Many Japanese were doubtful that the country's new leader would be able to go against the will of numerous JSP members by supporting the US-Japan alliance and Japan's Self-Defense Forces (SDF). But Murayama's determination to back the US-Japan security alliance and the SDF was firm. In July 1994, the prime minister, in a break from the past, officially declared in the Diet that the SDF was constitutional. Two months later, the JSP approved Murayama's position and abandoned the party's traditional goal of unarmed neutrality. This historic policy shift in effect put an end to the so-called 1955 system, the political framework during the era of the LDP's long rule under which the LDP and the JSP remained ideologically split as the government and the main opposition party, respectively.

With the biggest policy gap between the JSP and the LDP now bridged, Murayama—who had opposed the undemocratic decision-making process under the Hosokawa and Hata governments—introduced a new framework to deal with policy differences within the coalition. He formed eighteen different issue-specific project teams for major policy issues in which the three government parties could exchange their views and find agreeable solutions (see Table 1). Murayama said to the author in an interview, "Clearly, policy differences existed among the three parties. In many cases, we could not reach an agreement. But through serious discussions, I believe, we developed mutual understanding and trust" (September 13, 1996).

The composition of the project teams was set almost in proportion to the numbers of Diet members affiliated with each party. In half of the eighteen teams, the number of LDP members equaled that of the JSP and Sakigake combined. On three project teams (those dealing with nonprofit organizations, Minamata disease, and information disclosure in "special," that is, public, corporations), the LDP was overrepresented, while the number of JSP and Sakigake members exceeded LDP members on the remaining six. It is worth noting that no project team was formed to discuss the National Defense Program Outline (NDPO, approved by the cabinet in November 1995). Murayama knew that the security policy differences among Diet members from the coalition parties were still too far apart to permit formulation of concrete defense policies, and so he intentionally avoided creation of an interparty project team on this issue.

Murayama also formed a policy coordination committee. Here, the policy committee chairmen

Table 1. The Composition of Project Teams under the Murayama Government

Project Team	LDP	JSP	Sakigake
Welfare	9	7	3
Administrative Reform	6	4	2
Tax Reform	10	7	3
Economic Policy	8	5	3
50th Anniversary of WWII	6	4	2
Decentralization of Government Power	5	3	2
Human Rights and Discrimination	3	3	2
New Ainu Act	3	3	2
NPO (nonprofit organization)	6	3	2
Insurance Market Access to Labor Union	6	3	2
Hanshin Earthquake	12	12	6
Disaster Relief	5	4	3
Minamata Disease	5	3	1
Information Disclosure in Special Corps.	5	2	2
Religious Corporation	5	3	2
Finance and Security	6	6	2
Forest and Greenery	4	3	1
Housing Loan Companies	10	7	3

from the three coalition parties—Katō Kōichi of the LDP, Sekiyama Nobuyuki of the JSP, and Kan Naoto of Sakigake—discussed policy matters in general. Under this committee were nineteen subcommittees divided into different fields just like the LDP's issue-specific policy *bukai*.[5] The old LDP *zoku* members regained their place and started exerting their political influence in the budget-making process in the summer of 1994, immediately after the LDP had returned to power as a part of the coalition government.

To avoid LDP dominance in policymaking, representation of the LDP, the JSP, and Sakigake was set at a 3:2:1 ratio. Prime Minister Murayama delegated most of the decision-making power to these project teams and committees, and was often criticized for not playing a leadership role as a result. Murayama told the author:

This democratic decision-making system takes time. Also, the outcomes are often products of political compromise. I received criticism for the lack of leadership on the Diet floor. But

I thought that it was important for the three parties to work hard to reach an agreement in the committees. In cases where they could not reach an agreement, I would make the final decision. I believed this was my role as prime minister. (Murayama, interview by author, September 13, 1996)

As all three parties were involved in the decision-making process, the building of a consensus became a considerably more time- and energy-consuming activity for ministry officials than it had been under the LDP government.[6]

This system worked quite well in dealing with several policy issues. One example is the Minamata disease issue, which Murayama has listed as one of his three major policy achievements (along with the enactment of the A-Bomb Victim Aid Law and his efforts regarding the "comfort women" issue). The disease, a form of mercury poisoning, had broken out in the Kyushu town of Minamata in the late 1950s. It had been revealed in 1959 that the illness was caused by an organo-mercury compound in the wastes discharged into Minamata Bay by a chemical plant. Despite this revelation and the international attention the case received, the company that owned the plant, Chisso, was allowed to continue to dump chemical waste into the bay until the plant's closing in 1969. The question of the national government's responsibility had remained an unresolved political issue through 1995. While the Kumamoto prefectural government and Chisso negotiated with the victims, the national government had refused to take any action over this issue. Murayama told the author:

The JSP brought the Minamata disease case to the Diet many times under the LDP governments. But they always turned it down. After forty years, many victims had passed away and many more didn't have much longer left to live. As prime minister from the JSP, I was determined to solve the problem immediately. Under the Hosokawa government, I proposed to the prime minister from Kumamoto [Hosokawa's home prefecture and the location of Minamata] that we act on this issue.

Mr. Hosokawa, however, could not do much due to many factors. (Murayama, interview by author, September 13, 1996)

Prime Minister Hosokawa tried to tackle the issue, but he met with strong opposition from bureaucrats in the MOF and the Environment Agency, who insisted that the liability to compensate lay totally with Chisso.

The three-party project team on Minamata disease handled this issue, and its members at the end of May 1995 found there to be a wide gap between the LDP's and the JSP's definitions of who constituted a victim of the disease. LDP zoku members supported the position of the Environment Agency: the government should accept only medical certificates issued by specified public institutions as the means of identifying victims. The JSP, on the other hand, demanded that the government also accept those certificates issued by private doctors. To bridge the gap, the leaders of the three parties first upgraded the status of the project team by appointing the policy committee chairmen of the three parties to join the original team's three representatives. On June 21, the new project team reached an agreement that called for the Kumamoto prefectural government to form a special committee that would judge a patient's status based on medical certificates from either public institutions or private doctors.

The three parties also agreed that the government would recognize its responsibility and apologize to the victims. The national government, however, was still reluctant to take responsibility. When Prime Minister Murayama issued an apology in July for the government's inability to solve this issue despite the great passage of time, a top Environment Agency official told reporters that Murayama's comment was personal and did not represent the government. After long negotiations over the amount of compensation to the victims, the government on December 15 announced its final proposal. It was accepted by the organizations of the disease victims. The national and the prefectural governments agreed to provide Chisso with ¥26 billion in loans for it to use to pay compensation to the victims. This time Murayama gave an official apology on behalf of the national

government for both having taken so long to identify the cause of disease and the delays in taking appropriate action.

Resolution of the Minamata issue was a clear case in which the tripartite coordination system helped the prime minister cope with strong opposition from the bureaucracy and its zoku sponsors. When special interest groups in the three parties agreed on the direction of policy, however, they constituted a lobbying force that was even more powerful vis-à-vis the cabinet than the LDP zoku had been under single-party rule. Under the LDP government, for example, agricultural zoku members always sought for a realistic compromise even as they called for higher rice prices to protect farmers. When the coalition government made plans to reduce the price farmers would get for their rice in fiscal 1994, though, agricultural interests within the JSP took advantage of being in government to secure their rural electoral bases. Their insistence on a higher price was much more stubborn than that of their peers from the LDP. As a result, while the rice price was kept at the same level as the previous year, the agricultural subsidy for rice farmers was nearly doubled in July 1994.

The media criticized both the revival of LDP zoku and the emergence of a new JSP equivalent. To deal with such criticisms, the coalition's three policy committee chairmen announced on September 7 that the government parties would increase the transparency of their policy process and strengthen anticorruption measures in order to curb zoku activities. But this policy had little actual impact on the decision-making process. Members representing agricultural interests in the three parties pressured the Murayama administration to increase the government subsidy to compensate farmers for the opening of Japan's rice market as called for by the World Trade Organization (WTO), which itself came out of the GATT Uruguay Round where the agreement had been reached. The MOF proposed a total amount of ¥3.5 trillion, but the zoku members were not satisfied with this figure. They threatened to kill the market-opening bills unless the figure was increased drastically (Nihon Keizai Shimbunsha 1994, 71–76). The government had to nearly double the amount of agricultural compensation, raising it to ¥6.1 trillion. This *zoku* victory marked their resurgence under the coalition government, and the LDP's *zoku* members were now in a position to increase the influence they would have under the following cabinet led by the leader of their own party.

The Hashimoto Cabinet

By January 1996, the 71-year-old Murayama Tomiichi had exhausted himself in the taxing premiership post and resigned. LDP president and minister of international trade and industry Hashimoto Ryūtarō was endorsed by the coalition to be his successor. Hashimoto promised that he would maintain the tripartite project team and policy discussion, committee decision-making system.

The new government had the immediate task of resolving the housing loan company (*jūsen*) problem. This involved the seven largest such companies that had gone bankrupt. The MOF calculated the total amount of outstanding loans from the seven at ¥13.2 trillion and identified about half of those as being unrecoverable. To liquidate these bad loans, creditors had to bear the cost. The MOF drew up its *jūsen* liquidation scheme. It called on the *jūsen*'s founding financial institutions—which included city and regional banks, life insurers, trust banks, and security firms—to give up their rights to the ¥3.5 trillion in outstanding loans to the *jūsen*. Other banks promised to do likewise, accounting for another ¥1.7 trillion of the ¥4.2 trillion remaining. The proposal also called for agricultural financial institutions, which had invested ¥5.5 trillion in the *jūsen* companies, to forfeit ¥1.1 trillion. The MOF scheme was generous to the agricultural institutions, reflecting their strong political influence. They were asked to cover just 20 percent of their investments, while the parent banks gave up 100 percent and the other banks 40 percent.

The agricultural institutions, however, rejected the request, stating that they were not able to pay that much. They lobbied LDP *zoku* politicians and successfully bargained down their payment to ¥530 billion, less than half the original request. Agricultural experts in the JSP (by this time, the

party had officially changed its name to the Social Democratic Party, or SDP, but will be referred to as the JSP for the rest of this article) also supported lessening the burden on the agricultural institutions. With the amount coming from the agricultural institutions reduced, the government rewrote the bailout plan to use ¥685 billion of public funds from the 1996 fiscal budget to make up the shortfall.

The opposition New Frontier Party (NFP, a new party created by the merger of the JRP, Kōmeitō, the JNP, and the DSP) adamantly criticized the use of public funds to bail out the *jūsen*. Its members began a sit-in that physically blocked entry to the budget committee room to protest the budget proposal. The public as a whole was critical of the government plan, but more and more people began expressing their concern for Japan's economy by the time the sit-in had gone into a third week. The Economic Planning Agency expressed concerns that a delay in approval of the budget could slow down economic recovery. More than 70 percent of the respondents to one poll said they wanted the politicians to pay more attention to prosperity and economic issues (*Nihon Keizai Shimbun*, March 12, 1996). The sit-in ended with a compromise between the ruling coalition and the NFP that assured there would be sufficient debate over the budget bills in the Diet. The Hashimoto government had managed to resolve the politically difficult *jūsen* problem.

The summer of 1996 saw the start of the last year in the lower house's four-year term. With electoral pressures growing on Diet members, Prime Minister Hashimoto and the LDP began considerations of when the best time would be to dissolve the lower house and call for elections. The moment came in September 1996 when Hashimoto took note of the rise in his cabinet's popularity that month. The election would be the first under the new electoral law that introduced single-seat districts. Under the new system, LDP candidates, even powerful incumbents, found themselves playing a completely different game. To win their seats, they needed to get a higher percentage of the total votes. For many, the pressure of the elections was much greater than ever.

In the October 20 general election, the LDP

gained 239 seats, up from 211, in the 500-seat lower house. While the result was generally seen as a victory, the LDP still came up short and was not able to win a majority. Hashimoto approached the two other government parties to maintain the same coalition. However, the election was a disaster for the LDP's coalition partners—the JSP fell from thirty to fifteen seats and Sakigake won only two seats, losing seven. The partners' participation in the coalition government with the LDP might have been the reason their liberal voters withdrew their support. The two parties decided to stay out of the cabinet to maintain their independence, but they agreed to support the LDP government to form a majority in the lower house. Thus, the second Hashimoto government began as a minority-led one.

In order to secure passage of major bills in the Diet, the Hashimoto cabinet tried to maintain the three-party project team and policy coordination committee framework. The JSP and Sakigake, however, no longer had enough legislators to maintain the seventeen project teams and the nineteen committees. The number had to be reduced. As of September 1997, the three parties had five project teams and eleven policy committees (see Table 2). This reduction in the number of committees also lessened the significance of policy coordination among the three parties. LDP divisions regained power, and most of the substantial policy discussions took place within the party. The two other parties were consulted only after such discussions had taken place and were done, in the words of an LDP politician, "just out of courtesy." Although the LDP theoretically needed approval from its informal coalition partners before introducing legislation in the Diet, the three-party consultation process became a mere ceremony. The center of decision-making shifted

to within the LDP, and that within the party became decentralized as LDP *zoku* members regained their power.

As head of the minority government, Hashimoto began to seek different partners depending on the nature of the issues on the table. In passing the 1997 budget bill, for example, Hashimoto used the same three-party coalition framework to gain support from the JSP and Sakigake. The JSP refused to cooperate with the Hashimoto government over the issue of leases for land expropriated for the US military bases in Okinawa, however. In order to secure the status of the American presence in Okinawa, Hashimoto asked the opposition NFP for support.

The issue of the US bases in Okinawa had jumped to the center of the political table following the September 1995 rape of an elementary school girl there by three US servicemen stationed on the island. The incident sparked intense protests over and criticism of US-Japan security arrangements, which forced the islands—with 1 percent of Japan's land—to bear a disproportionate burden by housing about 75 percent of all US military installations in Japan and nearly two-thirds of the 47,000 American troops stationed in the country. To satisfy Okinawan demands, Hashimoto negotiated with the Clinton administration in the US to realign and reduce American facilities in Okinawa. On the occasion of the April 1996 US-Japan summit meeting, Hashimoto and Clinton unveiled a plan to reduce eleven US bases on Okinawa over several years' time. The plan's highlight was the reversion of the US Marine Corps' Futenma Air Station, a major source of frequent complaints from local residents because of its location in a densely populated area.

This plan, however, did not totally satisfy the people in Okinawa. Some landowners continued

Table 2. The LDP-JSP-Sakigake Project Teams and Committees under the Second Hashimoto Cabinet

Project Teams	Policy Coordination Committees	
Hanshin Earthquake Disaster Relief	Defense Budget	Revision of the Civil Law
Decreasing Population	Agricultural Policy	Electoral System
Nonprofit Organizations	Ethics of Public Officials	Okinawa Issues
Revisions of the Commercial Law	Anti-Monopoly Law	US-Japan Security Guidelines
Establishing New Institution to Oversee Executive Offices	Special Corporations Reform	Medical Insurance Reform
	Tax System	

their protest and refused to renew the leases for the land on which twelve American military facilities were built. As the renewal process was not expected to be completed by the land-lease expiration date in May 1997, the Hashimoto administration proposed a revision of the 1952 Special Law Governing Land for Armed Forces Stationed in Japan. This revision would give the central government the authority to override opposition from landowners and local governments and renew the leases when those for property within US bases were to expire. As the JSP refused to cooperate with the government over this revision, Prime Minister Hashimoto contacted NFP president Ozawa, knowing that Ozawa strongly believed an American presence in Okinawa was essential for the security of Japan and the Far East. Ozawa promised to support the government's bill, and the Taiyō (Sun) Party, the recently formed Democratic Party, and Sakigake also agreed to join this coalition to secure passage of the bill in the Diet in April 1997.

The advent of cooperation between the LDP and the NFP was a major event for the coalition system. Coalition governments since the Hosokawa administration had worked to make agreements among the ruling coalition parties before approaching the opposition. Hashimoto's contact with the opposition NFP without having first made a serious effort to come to terms with the JSP was seen as the beginning of a new era, defined by parties forming different coalitions on a policy-by-policy basis. This political arrangement created a complicated situation for the LDP. Hashimoto did not have a strong power base within his own party. The LDP was split into two groups: one that supported the existing coalition with the JSP and Sakigake, and the other calling for a conservative coalition with the NFP. The political contest between the two intensified after the passage of the land-lease bill. Although Hashimoto was reappointed LDP president in September 1997 without an election, the fact remained that he had to run the government while striking a delicate balance between the two groups.

Before his term had been renewed, Hashimoto had promised to maintain the cooperative framework with the JSP and Sakigake. Once confirmed

in office, he reappointed the leaders of the LDP's pro-coalition faction in the party leadership positions they had held during the previous government. The three-party coalition framework, however, was no longer solid. This was especially true since the LDP had regained majority status in the lower house due to twelve defectors joining the ruling party. The LDP, however, still did not have a majority in the upper house and so still needed coalition partners.

Earlier that month, the Hashimoto government announced its plan to streamline the bureaucracy by reducing the number of ministries and agencies from twenty-two to thirteen by the year 2001. This plan met with heavy criticism within the LDP and from its coalition partners. The JSP and Sakigake complained that it allowed the powerful MOF to retain both fiscal and financial functions, breaking an earlier three-party agreement to separate the ministry's two major roles. In order to strengthen his power base within the LDP to pursue administrative reform, Hashimoto reshuffled his cabinet. The prime minister took a bold political gamble by naming Satō Kōko to the cabinet as head of the Management and Coordination Agency. It was a key position for Hashimoto's drive to reform Japan's unwieldy bureaucracy. The public, however, raised the red flag because of Sato's criminal involvement in the highly publicized Lockheed scandal of the 1970s.

Sensitive to public opinion, Hashimoto was hesitant at first to appoint Satō. However, former prime minister Nakasone Yasuhiro put unrelenting pressure on him to make the appointment. LDP secretary-general Katō revealed Hashimoto's agony, stating in a television discussion program, "Until the final moment, the prime minister was torn between pressure from Mr. Nakasone and public opinion." Satō's appointment was a political gift to the conservative wing of the LDP, which Nakasone led. After having reappointed the leaders of the pro-coalition faction to the LDP leadership, Hashimoto needed to offer some form of appeasement to win conservative support for the pursuit of the fiscal, administrative, and defense-related reforms on which he staked his political life. But the public reaction was much stronger than Hashimoto expected. According to a Kyōdō News poll (September 13–14), 74 percent of the respondents said that they were against Satō's appointment. Hashimoto's popularity rating dropped dramatically from 59 percent to 28 percent (*Tokyo Shimbun*, September 17, 1997). After a week of turmoil, Satō "voluntarily" resigned. At a press conference, Hashimoto bowed deeply and apologized, saying that he had not sufficiently considered public opinion.

As Hashimoto's popularity fell, LDP *zoku* members took the opportunity to attack the prime minister's administrative reform plans. They started by arguing that there was no need to respect the recommendations of the Administrative Reform Conference, which had been charged with looking for ways to streamline the bureaucracy. LDP members seeking to maintain voter support in the postal industry, for example, adamantly opposed the idea of privatizing the postal insurance service handled through Special Post Offices, which make up 80 percent of Japan's 24,600 postal outlets. Such post offices provide solid voting support for many LDP members in elections. The privatization plan and absorption of telecommunications-related activities into the newly proposed Industry Ministry would effectively dissolve the Ministry of Posts and Telecommunications (MPT). Other *zoku* members also joined the movement against Hashimoto's reform plan. The powerful construction *zoku* publicly opposed the plan to divide the responsibilities of the Ministry of Construction into two newly created ministries. In the end, although Hashimoto was able to maintain the framework of thirteen ministries and agencies, his reform plan no longer had such strong sales points as the privatization of postal services. This marked another victory for LDP *zoku* members.

In January 1998, Doi Takako was reelected to lead the JSP. She reshuffled the party leadership positions and appointed to the Policy Council chairmanship Akiba Tadatoshi, who was known to advocate the departure of his party from the governing coalition. This appointment shook the LDP leadership, especially Secretary-General Katō. Katō tactically changed the principle of the three-party policy coordination system from being based on consensus to one operating on a

majority basis (see *Yomiuri Shimbun*, March 15, 1998). The LDP could now introduce legislation without the approval of the JSP and Sakigake and did so in the case of the bill on organizational crimes introduced in mid-March. This change made it possible for the JSP to express its opposition without risking a breakup of the coalition.

Once this change in tactics had taken place, the presence of the JSP in the coalition government became even more irrelevant in the decision-making process. This was especially true with the prospect that the LDP was on its way to run a government single-handedly after the July 1998 election. With a single-party majority government, the LDP would most likely go back to the old compartmentalized division system in which *zoku* members actively pursue their sectoral interests. The prime minister would then be faced with the new challenge of pursuing governmental reform with LDP members back in their old home ground.

Conclusion

Political changes since the establishment of the Hosokawa Morihiro cabinet have brought about a series of substantial transformations to Japan's political decision-making process. The most notable characteristic of Hosokawa's term was the centralization of the decision-making process. He discontinued the issue-specific subcommittee system. In the opening of Japan's rice market, the prime minister decided behind the closed doors of the Council of the Representatives of the Coalition Parties and without disclosing information to the public to accept the GATT proposal. The political reform package was likewise passed after negotiations with the LDP president using a similar top-down decision-making style. Hosokawa's unprecedented high public support successfully contained political opposition and enabled him to achieve these goals.

This centralized decision-making system, however, was the target of heavy criticism. The JRP's Ozawa Ichirō and Kōmeitō's Ichikawa Yūichi became dominant figures as time progressed, and the council made a number of policy decisions. Leaders of the other coalition parties saw the council's decision-making process as undemocratic. In Ozawa's and his defense, Ichikawa (interview in Tahara 1997, 107) said, "Everybody became critics probably due to their long experience as opposition party members. . . . Nothing can be achieved by critics. Therefore, we [Ozawa and Ichikawa] had to take action to solve problems."

This centralized policy process, however, turned out to be inappropriate for handling the highly unpopular proposal to raise the tax rate. The nature of the tax policy required political debate where opponents could express their views on a tax increase. Media criticism painted the tax decision as the product of an undemocratic process in which a very limited number of policymakers were involved. The public felt betrayed because Hosokawa had not sought their support; without it, the prime minister—who had boasted of his high approval ratings—had to withdraw the proposal. Hosokawa's credentials and leadership capability were questioned and it eventually led to his resignation.

Murayama Tomiichi, who was critical of the autocratic nature of the Hosokawa government's decision-making style, introduced a decentralized decision-making system with issue-specific project teams and committees. The JSP leader saw his role as being that of coordinator in a democratic, bottom-up, decision-making process. This system worked in dealing with certain policy issues such as the Minamata case. At the same time, it gave LDP *zoku* members a stage on which to become politically active. New *zoku* from the JSP joined them over such issues as the setting of rice prices, the agricultural subsidies, and the *jūsen* problem, further tilting the balance of power between *zoku* and the government.

Hashimoto Ryūtarō's leadership style was different again, although he agreed to maintain the same project team and committee framework as had Murayama. Hashimoto was able to cut a deal with Ozawa to acquire the NFP's support to pass the bills covering the lease of land used for US bases in Okinawa. The approach taken was reminiscent of Hosokawa's deal with the LDP on political reform. The highly political nature of the two incidents allowed the prime ministers to exercise a top-down style of leadership.

Engaging in such a leadership style in a coalition government is possible only when the leader has succeeded in attracting public support. Such support enabled Hosokawa to open the rice market and achieve political reform, and Hashimoto to cut a deal with Ozawa. When he ignored the need to convince the public about a tax increase, however, Hosokawa failed to persuade the opposition within his governing coalition. Similarly, Hashimoto lost public support when he chose to let intraparty political considerations take precedence over the public reaction regarding the problematic appointment of Satō to the cabinet. LDP *zoku* members did not miss the opportunity to attack Hashimoto's administrative reform effort in order to protect their client industries.

In previous studies, I classified the leadership style of Japanese prime ministers into four groups depending on which informal sources of power they have and utilize: the political insider, the grandstander, the kamikaze fighter, and the peace lover (Shinoda 1994, 1996). The political insider (Satō Eisaku, Tanaka Kakuei, and Takeshita Noboru are the examples) is a leader with abundant internal sources of power who enjoys stable support within the ruling party and close ties with the bureaucracy and the opposition parties. The other three leadership styles lack such internal sources. The grandstander (such as Hosokawa and Nakasone) goes directly to the public and the media in his search for support of his policy goals to supplement his lack of internal sources of power. The kamikaze fighter (Kishi Nobusuke) tries to push through an unpopular policy by sacrificing his political leadership role, while the peace lover (Suzuki Zenkō and Kaifu Toshiki) is an indecisive leader who fails to achieve controversial policy goals because he tries to please all the actors.

The political insider has the capability to achieve unpopular policy goals without successfully gaining public support, as seen in Takeshita's tax reform of 1988. Takeshita vigorously took advantage of his status as leader of the largest LDP faction; its senior *zoku* members successfully persuaded other LDP members, their client industries, and the related ministries to support the unpopular tax reform efforts. A political insider like Takeshita, however, is the least likely type to emerge in the near future. With the breakup of the long-predominant LDP in 1993, no one faction in the ruling party is a dominant power on the political scene, and the prime minister's power base within the ruling party has been weakened.

Given this fact, any LDP prime minister under the present circumstances must attract considerable public and media support in order to maintain effectively a fractious coalition government and confront and overcome *zoku* members to achieve his policies. Under the coalition government, the JSP *zoku* members joined their LDP counterparts by taking advantage of their government party status. After an interval in the opposition, LDP *zoku* members seem even more active than in the era of single party rule. In addition, the new electoral law that has created fiercer competition over single seats has made the *zoku* members more sensitive to election pressure than to national interests and thus often more enthusiastic to please their constituencies and client industries rather than support the prime minister. To overcome opposition from such sectoral interests in a coalition environment, the prime minister needs to seek public support. As seen in the cases of Hosokawa's rice policy and political reform, a national leader without a strong power base can achieve his goals by playing the role of grandstander. Without public support, it is difficult for him to suppress the opposition of powerful *zoku* members, as seen in Hashimoto's administrative reform effort. The prime minister today must bear in mind that his will and ability to attract such support is the most critical determining factor for the successful achievement of major policy goals.

Notes

1. As this issue went to press, the LDP won only forty-six seats in the July 12 election, leaving it twenty-three seats short of a majority in the upper house. This historic loss forced Prime Minister Hashimoto to resign, and put the LDP and the new prime minister in the difficult position of having to run the government with majority control of only the lower house.

2. The eight parties were the JSP, the JRP, Kōmeitō, the JNP, Sakigake, the Democratic Socialist Party (DSP), the United Social Democratic Party, and the Democratic Reform Federation.

3. Ishihara was the deputy chief cabinet secretary who served under Prime Ministers Takeshita Noboru, Kaifu Toshiki, Miyazawa Kiichi, Hosokawa Morihiro, and Murayama Tomiichi. For the formal legislative system under the Hosokawa government, see Nakano 1997, 45–74.

4. Hosokawa's rating stood at 79 percent on September 4–5 and 75 percent on October 23–24 in two Kyōdō News polls based on 3,000-person samples from around the country.

5. The committees were (1) Legal Affairs, (2) Foreign Affairs, (3) Finance, (4) Education, (5) Welfare, (6) Agriculture and Fishery, (7) Industry, (8) Transportation, (9) Posts and Communications, (10) Labor, (11) Construction, (12) Local Governments, (13) Hokkaido Development, (14) Cabinet, (15) Defense, (16) Okinawa Development, (17) Science and Technology, (18) Environment, and (19) Budget Settlement.

6. Foreign Ministry officials, interviewed by Fukui Haruhiro, July 4, 1996, and an MITI official, interviewed by Fukui Haruhiro, July 1, 1996, both quoted in Shinoda, forthcoming. Also see Ishihara 1998, 48–50.

References

Blustein, Paul. 1994. "Japanese Leader Forced to Retreat on Taxes." *Washington Post*, February 5, 1994.

Ishihara Nobuo. 1995. *Kantei 2668 nichi* [2,668 Days at the Prime Minister's Office]. Tokyo: NHK Shuppan.

————. 1998. *Kan kakuarubeshi* [How the Bureaucrats Should Be]. Tokyo: Shōgakukan Bunko.

Mikuriya Takashi and Watanabe Akio. 1997. *Shushō kantei no ketsudan* [The Decisions of the Prime Minister's Office]. Tokyo: Chūōkōrōnsha.

Murayama Tomiichi. 1996. "Watashi no rirekisho" [My Personal History]. *Nihon Keizai Shimbun*, no. 23, August 1996.

Murayama Tomiichi and Kanemori Kazuyuki (interviewer). 1996. *Murayama Tomiichi ga kataru "tenmei" no 561 nichi* [The 561 Days of "Destiny" as Told by Murayama Tomiichi]. Tokyo: K.K. Best Sellers.

Nakamoto Michiyo. 1994. "Hosokawa Plan Has Pleased Few and Made Many Unhappy." *Financial Times*, February 4, 1994.

Nakamura Akira. 1984. "Jiyūminshutō no yottsu no kao" [The Four Faces of the LDP]. In *Nihon no seisaku katei: Jimintō, yatō, kanryō* [Policymaking in Japan: The LDP, Opposition Parties, and the Bureaucracy], edited by Nakamura Akira and Takeshita Yuzuru, 3–63. Tokyo: Azusa Shuppan.

Nakano Minoru. 1997. "The Changing Legislative Process in the Transitional Period." In *Japanese Politics Today: Beyond Karaoke Democracy?*, edited by Purnendra Jain and Takashi Inoguchi. New York: St. Martin's Press.

Nihon Keizai Shimbunsha, ed. 1994. *Renritsiu seiken no kenkyū* [Study on the Coalition Governments]. Tokyo: Nihon Keizai Shimbunsha.

Shinoda Tomohito. 1994. *Struggle to Lead: The Japanese Prime Minister's Power and His Conduct of Economic Policy*. Michigan: University Microfilm International.

———. 1996. *Kantei no kenryoku* [The Power of the Prime Minister's Office]. Tokyo: Chikuma Shobō.

———. Forthcoming. "Japan's Political Changes and Their Impacts on US-Japan Relations." In *Redefining the Partnership: The United States and Japan in East Asia*, edited by Hosoya Chihiro and Shinoda Tomohito. Lanham: University Press of America. [Published 1998—Ed.]

Tahara Sōichirō. 1997. *Atama no nai kujira: Seijigeki no shinjitsu* [A Headless Whale: The Truth of a Political Drama]. Tokyo: Asahi Shimbunsha.

Takemura Masayoshi. 1997. "Renritsu seikenka no konmei: Fukushizei tekkai sōdō no shinsō wa kōda" [The Real Story of the Controversy behind the Chaotic Withdrawal of the Welfare Tax under the Coalition Government]. *Bungei Shunjū* 75, no. 9 (July): 336–38.

II-(3) National Political Reform in the 1990s
Political Revolution from Above

Nakano Minoru
New Japanese Political Economy and Political Reform, 2002

Introduction: Basic Features of Political Reform in the 1990s

In January 1996, Hashimoto Ryūtarō succeeded Murayama Tomiichi as prime minister. The new prime minister immediately announced that his government would carry out six reforms, namely, (1) administrative reforms, (2) reforms of fiscal structures, (3) structural reforms of social security, (4) economic reforms, (5) reforms of the financial system, and (6) educational reforms. He emphasized the administrative reforms most strongly as "the third revolution" since the Meiji Restoration. Although it was not clear how much his rhetoric impressed the general public, the reforms pursued by the Hashimoto government, and then by the Obuchi Keizō government, certainly created a major trend for national political reform, along with economic liberalization and political decentralization of the late 1980s. Hashimoto and Obuchi continued the administrative and economic reforms of the financial system and economic structure. The Obuchi government also embarked on parliamentary reform, reforms of the social security system, and the reduction of the number of seats in the House of Representatives, all of which are now on the parliamentary agenda. These reforms are partly the government's response to international and domestic socioeconomic changes in the 1990s and also to public criticisms about the many recent revelations of corruption and/or incompetence among the national ministries and bureaucrats and about the systemic fatigue of the political and administrative systems dominated by bureaucrats.

There are, however, unique features in these reforms in terms of their goals, principal actors, and means if one looks closely and comprehensively at reforms in various areas of the national administration, parliament, election, economic liberalization, and decentralization. The administrative reforms of the Hashimoto and Obuchi governments were quite different from those pursued by the past Liberal Democratic Party (LDP) governments since 1955. The past attempts were mostly "slogans" without substance; even the administrative reforms of the Nakasone Yasuhiro government in the 1980s were in fact fiscal reforms, allowing the national ministries to expand. The major reorganization of the national ministries and the reinforcing of the powers of the prime minister, his office, and the cabinet were never discussed in the context of decentralization. Of political reforms, this was the first time that parliamentary reforms were included in the agenda. The Hashimoto-Obuchi administrative reforms followed the "Administrative Reforms Outline" (Gyōsei Kaikaku Taikō) adopted by the Hosokawa Morihiro government in February 1994 to a certain degree, but there was no apparent continuity with past administrative reforms, showing rather differences from the old standards and styles.

The national political reform of the 1990s, with the strongest emphasis on administrative reforms, may be characterized as follows. First, it was inspired by both international and domestic socioeconomic changes and by bureaucratic incompetence and corruption, and it was intended to transform the political and administrative system dominated by the bureaucracy and bureaucrats into the one led by political parties and politicians. It was also a "political revolution," by which the centralized political system and the bureaucrat-dominant power structure were to be reorganized into a democratic system with a decentralized system and a politician-dominant power structure. Second, it therefore included the reorganization, liberalization, and decentralization of the national ministries that had strong relevance to administrative reforms as part of the political revolution. Third, this revolution, however, was led by a group of new conservative elites within the LDP, with support from business and industry, co-opting other conservative and centrist political groups and individuals. It had a double goal of establishing a new political system with new conservatives in the center of the power structure. Fourth, the national political reform of the 1990s was only "a revolution from above" tinkering with the current election and political funding systems, without radical reforms to open the way for new party politics with new participants. And finally, the process of these reforms is also a process of nondecision-making on institutional reforms that could cause radical changes in the basic political structure and thereby threaten the support bases of the existing conservative parties and politicians. Reform programs had built-in mechanisms to suppress social and economic changes that would weaken the foundation of conservative dominance. Such suppressed institutional reforms, as well as the basic policy on social and economic changes, will be the subject of political conflict in the future.

This chapter attempts to explain in detail the nature of the national political reform of the 1990s, as briefly characterized above, with a particular focus on the administrative reforms carried out by the Hashimoto and Obuchi governments and the parliamentary reform pursued by the Obuchi government. It looks specifically at (1) political factors that prompted the major political reforms in the 1990s, (2) particular features of the administrative reforms and the built-in restraining mechanisms, and (3) the leadership of the two prime ministers—Hashimoto and Obuchi—and their political styles. Finally, the chapter suggests what political reforms are necessary for Japan to face the challenges of the twenty-first century.

1. Political Factors that Produced the Major Political Reforms

Early in the 1990s, the bubble economy burst. The Hashimoto government, formed in January 1996, faced two major policy issues of fiscal difficulty and the financial crisis. Creation of the Financial Supervisory Agency (Kin'yū Kantoku-chō) symbolized the end of the convoy system (gosō sendan hōshiki) led by the Ministry of Finance (MOF), and thus the end of MOF dominance. Reorganization of the MOF was justified in the name of troubles in the nation's financial institutions, including bad loans and bankruptcy, and also the MOF's inadequate actions. They were certainly factors to promote reforms, but they alone did not move the government and the ruling parties toward major political reforms. Although the substantial part of the ministerial reforms involved the MOF, the actual reforms were more comprehensive, including decentralization, the reinforcement of the cabinet, and parliamentary reform, which could not be explained by economic troubles alone. The reinforcement of cabinet functions also had a specific event as a major motivation: the Hanshin-Awaji earthquake of January 1995 and the government's inadequate response to it, which invited severe criticism from the general public. But, like MOF reform, it was also an issue that had been publicly debated for long; the LDP was seriously discussing the issue within the party when it was in the opposition from July 1993 to June 1994.

No matter how many environmental factors there were, the governmental reforms could not have been initiated without political leadership. It required leadership with the skills to manage the relationships with opposition parties and national ministries and also the determination to mobilize various political forces for major political reforms. The leadership styles, strategies, and tactics of Hashimoto and Obuchi will be discussed in detail in Section 3 of this chapter, "Political Leadership in National Reforms." Here I will review the political factors that had driven the major political reforms from the end of the Miyazawa Kiichi government in 1993, through the Hosokawa non-LDP coalition government, to the Obuchi government in 2000.

1.1 Generational change in conservative party leadership

The first element seems to be the accelerated generational change in the LDP that became apparent at the time of the no-confidence vote for the Miyazawa government in June 1993. The end of the Miyazawa government symbolized the end of the thirty-eight-year-long dominance of power by the LDP and of the 1955 system, but in the context of LDP internal politics, it also signified the transfer of power from the old generation to the new conservative elite. Already in 1992, the then LDP secretary-general Ozawa Ichirō strongly demonstrated the generational change by holding interviews with LDP presidential candidates of the old generation like Miyazawa. The process was accelerated by the collapse of the Miyazawa government, providing opportunities for the new conservative elite interested in major political reform, including Ozawa, Hashimoto, Obuchi, Katō Kōichi, Mori Yoshirō, Yamazaki Taku, and Kōno Yōhei. (They were all "pure" politicians [*tōjin-ha*] who began their careers in politics, except for Katō, who had a brief stint as a bureaucrat.)

1.2 The Hosokawa coalition government and the LDP in the opposition

The second element can be found in a series of events in the Hosokawa coalition government after the collapse of the Miyazawa government. The rise and fall of the Miyazawa government and the subsequent formation of the Hosokawa coalition government were the results of the surprise moves by Ozawa, a leader of the new conservatives, to leave the LDP with a group of fellow LDP members and form a new conservative party, and not of the changing balance of power between the ruling and opposition parties. The Hosokawa government therefore was a puppet of Ozawa, the real leader of the coalition. Although Ozawa intended to form a new conservative party within this coalition to rival the LDP, the coalition was actually a motley collection of seven parties and one parliamentary group with vast differences in basic policies and ideologies. It became quite unstable as the three older parties and two newer parties each formed factions and started to fight over a wide range of policies. This instability

prepared a way for the LDP to return to power soon. The LDP found another ground for hope, as the electoral reforms of the Hosokawa government were generally based on the recommendations of the Electoral System Council (Senkyo Seido Shingi-kai) during the Kaifu Toshiki government and therefore acceptable to the LDP.

Ozawa failed in his efforts to rule the Hosokawa government from behind because he made many decisions alone without consulting all the coalition partners. Especially, the incident involving a plan to raise the consumption tax rate by proposing a "national welfare tax" (*kokumin fukushi zei*) increased LDP criticism of the MOF's close cooperation with Ozawa and strengthened the LDP's determination to pursue a plan to reorganize the MOF. This incident also prompted the withdrawal of the Social Democratic Party of Japan (SDPJ) and New Party Sakigake from the ruling coalition, making it possible for the LDP to return to power by forming a coalition with them. The Hata Tsutomu non-LDP coalition government that succeeded the Hosokawa government collapsed within three months.

1.3 LDP's return to power and the birth of major administrative reforms

After Hata, the SDPJ's Murayama Tomiichi led a coalition government consisting of the LDP, SDPJ, and Sakigake. It was during his administration that specific approaches to major administrative reforms, to be later executed by Hashimoto and Obuchi, were discussed. Already in the 1980s, the third Provisional Council for Administrative Reform (Dai Sanji Rinji Gyōsei Kaikaku Suishin Shingi-kai) under the Kaifu government had proposed liberalization, reorganization of special agencies, reforms of vertically divided administration (*tatewari gyōsei*), and legislation of the Administrative Procedures Law (Gyōsei Tetsuzuki-hō). The Administrative Reform Committee (Gyōsei Kaikaku Iinkai) of the Murayama government also proposed liberalization and the legislation of the Administrative Information Disclosure Law (Jōho Kōkai-hō), among other things. They all remained as "recommendations," but concrete plans for major political reforms were steadily taking shape. The most notable move by the Murayama government was the establishment of the Committee for the Promotion of Decentralization (Chihō Bunken Suishin Iinkai, headed by Moroi Makoto), as the committee later prepared an official outline for a radical redefinition of the central-local relationship. The LDP learned new tricks while in the coalition with the SDPJ, the largest rival of the LDP for many years, and they were incorporated in Hashimoto's as well as Obuchi's style of leadership. The LDP acquired a wide range of know-how necessary for policy negotiations and cooperation with the coalition partners, while effectively controlling the Murayama government. It would have been difficult for the LDP to acknowledge Murayama's apology to Asian countries on the occasion of the fiftieth anniversary of the end of the World War II and to accept the SDPJ-initiated Atomic Bomb Survivors' Assistance Law (Hibakusha Engo-hō) if the LDP had continued to remain in power alone. The Murayama government was relatively long-lived because of the LDP's cooperative attitude.

1.4 Changes in the LDP-bureaucrat relationship

Changes were also observed in the LDP's relationship with the bureaucracy and bureaucrats while it was in the opposition. It took quite a lot of time and effort for the LDP to redefine national reform as a political initiative (*seiji shudō*), rather than being led by the bureaucrats (*kanryō shudō*), as the party had depended on bureaucrats for so long since the beginning of the 1955 system. Chronologically, the LDP-bureaucracy relationship started with (a) bureaucratic dominance, moved to (b) coexistence and integration, changed to (c) mutual restraint, and finally reached (d) competition. At stage (c), the LDP increased the power and influence of its Policy Research Council over policymaking by weaponizing a ruling party's privilege of "advance examination" (*jizen shinsa*) of bills and budgets drafted by bureaucrats. In particular areas, the Policy Research Council even dominated decision-making through the influence of policy tribes, or *zoku*. However, this relationship was still within the framework of the 1955 system, which could be described as interest group politics with the

LDP still dependent on bureaucrats. The LDP had to become an opposition party, as during the Hosokawa and Hata governments, to finally confront the bureaucracy and bureaucrats and start changing the balance of power in favor of politicians. From the bureaucrat's point of view, the Hosokawa and Hata governments were "amateur governments" that they could easily manipulate; without interference from the LDP, they hoped to revive a bureaucrat-dominant policymaking system. The abovementioned national welfare tax incident was a typical example of such bureaucratic moves. The incident, however, backfired, as it increased the LDP's distrust of the MOF and resulted in the demotion of the responsible MOF administrative vice-minister once the LDP returned to power under Murayama. The relationship with other ministries also changed while the LDP was in the opposition. One of the factors behind efforts to enact the Administrative Information Disclosure Law during the Obuchi government was reportedly the LDP's experience, while in the opposition, of not being able to access bureaucratic information as freely as when it was in power. When it lost the privilege of receiving information from bureaucrats, the LDP realized the extent to which the bureaucracy had a monopoly on information. In formulating solutions for the financial problems during the 1998 extraordinary session of the Diet, LDP members of the Diet used information acquired from private businesspeople and cooperated with members of the Democratic Party of Japan (DPJ), all the while keeping their distance from MOF officials. It was against such a background that the Obuchi government accepted the DPJ's proposal for the Financial Revitalization bill (Kin'yū Saisei-hōan). The LDP-bureaucracy relationship changed radically while the LDP was in the opposition, and this became entrenched when the LDP returned to power, making it easier for the new conservative elite to regard the breakup of the MOF and a radical reorganization of the bureaucracy in realistic terms.

1.5 Hashimoto's leadership

Hashimoto Ryūtarō and his leadership played an important role in directing these sentiments for change toward specific political reforms on a major scale and at an accelerated pace. On succeeding Murayama as prime minister, Hashimoto announced his grand vision for administrative reforms and enacted successfully the Basic Law on Central Government Reform (Chūō Shōchō-tō Kaikaku Kihon-hō). Environmental factors, such as increasing demands for liberalization and decentralization from big business, public and media criticisms about continuing bureaucratic blunders, and critical views about the bureaucracy and bureaucrats held by most of the opposition parties, certainly created a political climate favorable for reforms, but without Hashimoto's leadership, things could not have proceeded as they did. Hashimoto had a strong incentive for major political reforms. He was not wasting time while the LDP was in the opposition; he studied hard and acted vigorously as the LDP Policy Research Council chief. He instructed the council's divisions to examine policy measures for liberalization and recession and draft bills as private members' bills (*giin rippō*), even when they had no chance of passing the Diet. These actions suggested Hashimoto's plan to change the LDP's old policymaking system, which was dependent on bureaucrats, by requiring Diet members to acquire the skills needed to draft bills. It also showed Hashimoto's political passion for administrative reform, which continued to grow stronger as he became prime minister.

2. Institutional Reform from Bureaucratic Domination to Political Leadership and Its Limitations

2.1. The process of national reform and three pillars of administrative reforms

If the national political reform carried out by the Hashimoto and Obuchi governments had a dual purpose of establishing rule by a new conservative alliance while transferring decision-making power from the bureaucrats to politicians, how were these aims achieved through specific reform measures? While the reforms may look comprehensive as means of ending the bureaucratic dominance of the national political process, they also had limitations because the new conservative elite, who spearheaded the reforms, would not allow any changes that would jeopardize their political power base. In other words, the comprehensive reform measures were accompanied by mechanisms to restrain reforms that were not in the new conservatives' interests. In this section, I will examine how the specific measures for national reforms worked to serve these purposes. In particular, I will look at the administrative reform measures based on the Central Government Reform Act (Chūō Shōchō-tō Kaikaku Kanren-hō) of April 1999. The basic framework of this act had been formulated by the Hashimoto government, and Obuchi took over to successfully legislate it. I will also analyze the political reforms that were initiated in conjunction with the administrative reforms. To describe the decision-making process of the administrative reforms briefly, it started with the establishment of the Administrative Reform Conference (Gyōsei Kaikaku Kaigi) with Hashimoto as head in November 1996. The conference submitted its final recommendations in December 1997 and then was dissolved in June 1998 after fifty-five meetings in total. The final recommendations proposed various measures to reinforce the power of the prime minister and the cabinet, including the formalization under the Cabinet Law of the prime minister's right to propose a national policy program (*hatsugi-ken*) to the cabinet, the establishment of the Council on Economic and Fiscal Policy (CEFP, Keizai Zaisei Shimon Kaigi) within a newly created Cabinet Office to deal with policymaking and coordination between ministries, the appointment of special ministers within the Cabinet Office for Okinawa development and the Northern Territories issue, reductions in the number of national ministry officials, and the introduction of an independent administrative institution system (*dokuritsu gyōsei hōjin*). In December 1997, the cabinet accepted the major part of these recommendations, which were then drafted into the Basic Central Government Reform bill. In February 1998, the cabinet accepted the bill that would institutionalize the basic program to reorganize the ministries and strengthen the powers of the prime minster and the cabinet, with a view to achieving a transformation into a twenty-first century administrative system (*nijū-isseiki-gata gyōsei shisutemu*). The bill was proposed to the

Diet, and after more than ninety hours of debate, it was passed on June 9, 1998.

The Obuchi government, formed in July 1998, took over most of Hashimoto's reform policies and set up the Headquarters for the Promotion of Central Government Reform and Other Reforms (Chūō Shōchō-tō Kaikaku Suishin Honbu) to execute reforms outlined in the act. Like Hashimoto, Obuchi himself assumed the leadership of this group, with Chief Cabinet Secretary Nonaka Hiromu serving as deputy and the director general of the Management and Coordination Agency (MCA, Sōmu-chō) Ōta Seiichi as special minister in charge of administrative reform. All the other cabinet members were also involved. The existing government advisory councils, like committees on regulatory reforms (Kisei Kaikaku Iinkai), promotion of decentralization (Chihō Bunken Suishin Iinkai), and the system of public officials (Kōmuin Seido Chōsa-kai), were made answerable to the headquarters.

The Obuchi cabinet, as the headquarters for the national reform, issued an Outline for Central Government Reform (Chūō Shōchō-tō Kaikaku Taikō) to reaffirm the basic principles of the basic law in January 1999. On settling the remaining issues like the separation of budgeting and fiscal administration, the cabinet adopted the bill concerning central government and other reforms on April 27 and submitted it to the Diet on May 28. The bill consisted of seventeen acts, including amendments to the Cabinet Law and a proposal to create a new Cabinet Office—both of which were designed to institutionalize Hashimoto's basic law and Obuchi's outline—and an act to transform the Ōkura-shō into the Zaimu-shō (both called the Ministry of Finance in English). Prior to the proposal to the Diet, the headquarters issued a plan to promote central government reform (Chūō Shōchō Kaikaku no Suishin Hōshin). The bill was discussed by the Special Committee on Administrative Reform in the House of Representatives (Shūgiin Gyōsei Kaikaku Tokubetsu Iinkai), along with the comprehensive bill for decentralization (Chihō Bunken Ikkatsu-hōan), and passed by the committee with the majority support of coalition party members (LDP, Liberal Party, and Kōmeitō) on June 9 and by the lower house on the following day, to be proposed to the House of Councillors.

The national political reform of 1999 was more comprehensive than before. It called for (1) the downsizing and increased efficiency of the central bureaucracy; (2) the reinforcement of the functions of the prime minister, the prime minister's office, and the cabinet; and (3) the introduction of a policy evaluation system. In the name of simplifying and increasing administrative efficiency, the central bureaucracy's one office and twenty-two ministries were reduced to one office and twelve ministries from 2001, and it sought a 25 percent reduction in the number of bureaucrats. (In Hashimoto's basic law, the rate of reduction was set at 10 percent, but Obuchi pledged 20 percent during the LDP presidential election. The Obuchi cabinet, in the end, compromised to the Liberal Party, a coalition partner, and settled on 25 percent.) Another notable measure for downsizing was the reorganization of ninety governmental organizations into independent administrative institutions (dokuritsu gyōsei hōjin). The institutions were to be financed by the national government but given independent management control. The idea was supported by the Ministries of International Trade and Industry (MITI), Health and Welfare (MHW), and Education (MOE), but the relationship between the national ministries and such institutions was yet to be defined. There were suggestions like giving the power of licensing new institutions to a new Ministry of Management and Coordination (Sōmu-shō), or giving the power of approval over the institutions' business plans to the new MOF, all of which were criticized as efforts to force strong ministerial control over the institutions, just like the old days. Moreover, if the ministries and bureaucrats retain arbitrary decision-making power, conventionally approved by current administrative laws, new ministries like Management and Coordination (Sōmu-shō) and Land and Transport (Kokudo Kōtsū-shō) could have enormous arbitrary power, contrary to the idea of the downsizing the government.

An amendment to the National Government Organization Law (Kokka Gyōsei Soshiki-hō) will create a new section for policy evaluation in each ministry; it will also give the Ministry of Management and Coordination the general power to evaluate policies of all the ministries. It will be the first time in the history of Japanese national administration that each ministry evaluates its own policy, which is also reviewed by the Ministry of Management and Coordination from a more comprehensive point of view. This could create an opportunity to overcome the myth of bureaucratic infallibility (*mubyūsei*) and the secrecy based on arbitrary decisions. However, the evaluation is to be done internally by the ministries themselves; without impartial evaluation by third parties, its effectiveness may be limited. As mentioned early in the first part of this chapter, the real goal of the national political reform of the 1990s was to establish control over national decision-making by the new conservative parties and politicians. This was done as a "revolution from above." The reforms managed to avoid radical changes to the political structure that could threaten the support base of the conservative parties and politicians; institutional reforms were limited to the same range. Reforms that would lead to the entrenchment of control over decision-making by parties and politicians were, on the other hand, pursued vigorously, sometimes to an excessive degree. The incongruity among reform measures was therefore inevitable; in spite of the basic goal of creating a slim and efficient administration, ministerial reorganization, the independent agency system, and the policy evaluation system all have flaws, and some new ministries may even be bigger and stronger than the present ones. How effective are those reforms? What are the built-in mechanisms to restrain radical changes? And why do some reforms seem excessive? The next part will try to answer these questions by examining the specific contents of Hashimoto's basic law and Obuchi's reform laws and outline for promotion, with a particular focus on the reform of the MOF as well as the reinforcement of political leadership.

2.2 The reform of the Ministry of Finance and its restraint

The reform of the Ministry of Finance is a good example of how the conservative parties and politicians promoted institutional reforms while carefully restraining radical changes. The reorganization of the MOF started to be discussed after the economic bubble burst, against the background of public discontent over the MOF's response to the financial crisis, including bankruptcies, and over a series of MOF officials' misconduct. These events indicated the fundamental inadequacies of the MOF-centered treasury and financial system. The MOF, as the ministry of ministries, had played a central role in Japan's political economy with a firm control over both treasury and finance, but its power was undermined by the establishment of an independent Financial Supervisory Agency (Kin'yū Kantoku-chō) in 1996, taking away the monopoly of financial control from the MOF. The idea of the separation of treasury and finance was incorporated as a basic principle into the government reform program. It was considered major not only in terms of creating a slim and efficient administration and promoting liberalization and decentralization but also in terms of restructuring Japanese-style political economy, that is, from a convoy system to healthy and creative competition and the transfer of power from bureaucrats to politicians. This was why the MOF reform became a centerpiece of ministerial reform.

MOF reform would have a great impact on the future management of government treasury and finance, and also on the relationship between politicians and bureaucrats. The extent of MOF reform was a politically controversial issue, restraining the new conservative politicians within the LDP, who had advocated the breakup of MOF strongly, to search for relatively moderate reforms to avoid radical changes. Negotiations over the separation issue took place frequently between the ruling coalition and opposition parties, which agreed on the principle of separation but disagreed on how to separate, that is, whether to give a new Financial Services Agency (FSA), to be set up in July 2000, total control over financial administration, excluding the MOF from this area. The LDP, despite its initial interest, was reluctant to support such a separation, while the DPJ and Kōmeitō were strongly supportive. The three parties reached an agreement on separation, but the issue of the extent could not be solved. The Obuchi cabinet's outline for government reform (Chūō Shōchō-tō Kaikaku Taikō), issued on April 16, 1999, did not mention the details of separation. The three parties continued to negotiate in mid-April on items like jurisdiction over international finance, but failed to reach a compromise.

On April 15, however, the Kōmeitō suddenly announced that it would accept the LDP proposal of joint jurisdiction over financial administration by the MOF and the FSA, making it possible for the bill to pass the Diet. It meant that financial administration was not to be a monopoly of the FSA but done jointly with the MOF. Specifically, the FSA would have three sections—general management, inspection, and administration—for financial affairs, while the MOF would also have inspectors and divisions for financial affairs. The DPJ continued to oppose the joint jurisdiction, saying that it would break the original agreement. The issue was settled sooner than expected in spite of such opposition because the LDP's opposition to a complete separation was welcomed by bureaucrats who wanted a moderate separation (yuruyaka na bunri). In the Diet, the Liberal Party and Kōmeitō, which had opposed Hashimoto's basic law in June 1998, came around to support Obuchi's bill this time. The Kōmeitō was not satisfied with the government bill, but it decided to support the bill out of political consideration. If the passage of the bill was considerably delayed, that could prompt a move by the LDP to extend the Diet term, upon completion of which the general election might be called; the party did not want such an early general election, as it was not yet ready for an electoral campaign. This explains the Kōmeitō's sudden change of heart, only three hours after the break-up of the three-party negotiation on April 15.

2.3 The reinforcement of political leadership and its problems

The reinforcement of the powers of the prime minister, the prime minister's office, and the cabinet, that is, increasing the power at the top level, was another centerpiece not unrelated to the reorganization of the MOF, conventionally the most powerful ministry in supervising and coordinating the activities of all ministries. The reforms on this part, however, were rather substantial, sometimes to an excessive degree. The idea was conceived, like MOF reform, against the background of the inadequacy of the conventional political party system and appealed strongly to the public that started to expect strong leadership capable of responding effectively to crises, after seeing the inadequate response of the Murayama government to the Hanshin-Awaji earthquake, revelations of misconduct by central ministry officials, and the financial crisis that became serious during the Hashimoto administration. The argument for strong political leadership had surfaced to overcome international criticisms of the "faceless leadership" of Japanese politics; in the past, the "face" was represented by colorful individual politicians like Tanaka Kakuei, Nakasone Yasuhiro, and more recently, Ozawa Ichirō. Hashimoto and Obuchi were a stark contrast to those figures; Obuchi was once called a "vacuum prime minister" (shinkū sōri) by Nakasone. However, it was these two prime ministers who, riding the tide of public support, carried out institutional reforms to change the balance of power in favor of politicians and transfer decision-making powers from bureaucrats to politicians. They did that without inviting the active participation of citizens, which the DPJ advocated, but tried to reinforce the powers of the prime minister and his office as a means to guarantee rule by the conservative political elite.

For crisis management, a strong prime minister and the centralization of power in his office are not the only options. And strong political leadership can be exercised even under the current constitutional and legal provisions, as seen in the examples of Hashimoto and Obuchi, who led the administrative reforms with strong leadership. The issue of crisis management is closely related to the issue of decentralization, as it is more efficient to give local government leaders more power to deal with crises like natural disasters. On the second point of political leadership, if individuals make that much difference, that would suggest there is little institutional support for strong political leadership. If the reform of the 1990s does not remain an individual prime minister's political agenda and can successfully establish an institutional foundation for strong leadership, it may remedy the current system. It remains to be seen whether the proposed reforms will create a system in which prime ministers and the cabinet, based on Article 65 of the Constitution, which states, "Executive power shall be vested in the Cabinet," can exercise strong leadership independently from the bureaucracy and bureaucrats and also free from internal party politics.

Institutional reform measures proposed to create a strong prime minister and cabinet include, specifically, the amendment to the current Cabinet Law to clearly define the prime minister's right to propose important bills to the cabinet (*hatsugiken*) and an increase in the staff of the Cabinet Secretariat to aid the prime minister and deal with more administrative matters. Aides to the prime minister would be increased to within five, and a new post of deputy cabinet undersecretary (*kanbō fuku chōkan-ho*) would be created. These measures are all designed to establish an institution for prime-minister-centered national politics and decision-making, especially by reinforcing the function of the prime minister's office. In order to achieve that goal, it is recommended that the number of political appointees should be increased for the post of prime minister's aides, in the hopes of mobilizing professional expertise from outside the government and thus depending less on bureaucrats on secondment from the ministries.

Another measure to strengthen the prime minister's office is the reorganization of information gathering. The crisis management manual, issued by the government on April 16, 1999, indicated that in fourteen possible cases of various crises, the prime minister's office should be responsible for information gathering and analyses. The Cabinet Office, to be created in 2001, is a body to support the cabinet with the prime minister as director and the chief cabinet secretary as supervisor of routine management matters. The law to create the Cabinet Office (Naikaku-fu Secchi-hō) states that the Cabinet Law (Naikaku-hō) defines the precedence of the cabinet over other ministries and that the Cabinet Office commands the general power to coordinate between ministries. It is

designed to overcome the vertically divided structure (*tatewari kōzō*) of the national ministries and to ensure top-down decision-making in which the prime minister's policy instructions would be followed through without being overwhelmed by ministerial rivalry. In addition, the Council on Economic and Fiscal Policy (CEFP, Keizai Zaisei Shimon Kaigi), the Council for Science and Technology Policy (Sōgō Kagaku Gijutsu Kaigi), and the Council for Gender Equality (Danjo Kyōdō Sankaku Kaigi), all of which consist of the prime minister, relevant ministers, and nongovernment personnel with professional expertise on each issue, will be created as advisory councils to the cabinet to assist in policymaking, coordination, and draft legislation. The CEFP, in particular, will be given the power to formulate the basic outline of the annual budget, ensuring institutionally the precedence of decision-making by politicians. It allows politicians and nongovernmental personnel to be involved in policy areas hitherto monopolized by the MOF and also create opportunities for the prime minister to discuss important issues like crisis management and gender equality directly with the cabinet. This would lead to a change in decision-making from a bureaucrat-dominated, bottom-up process to a politician-controlled, top-down process. The legislative process in Japan conventionally started with planning by individual ministries, followed by inter-ministerial negotiation, review by the MOF and the Cabinet Legislation Bureau (Naikaku Hōsei-kyoku), discussion at a meeting of administrative vice-ministers of all ministries, cabinet approval, proposal to the Diet, and deliberation and decision in the Diet. No legislative issue reached politicians, that is, the cabinet, without going through a review by administrative vice-ministers, that is, bureaucrats. The new system is designed to revise the old bottom-up pattern and establish a top-down decision-making process, one of the goals of the national reform of the 1990s.

Hashimoto was clear from the beginning about the goal of reforming decision-making to a politician-dominated, top-down system. For example, he proposed the institutionalization of the prime minister's direct control over the ministries; he originally intended to formalize the prime minister's power to issue orders directly to ministries without consulting the relevant ministers. The Legislative Bureau of the House of Representatives (Shūgiin Hōsei-kyoku) supported the idea, but the Cabinet Legislation Bureau opposed it on the ground of possible unconstitutionality. After debate, the term "direct orders" was replaced by "right to propose" (*hatsugi ken*).

The current administrative reforms try to change the economic and fiscal systems dominated by a single ministry, establish a prime-minister-led national politics, and create a politician-dominated top-down decision-making system. In other words, they try to replace the bureaucratic monopoly of policymaking and the bureaucrat-dominated bottom-up decision making with a system of strong political leadership. If the promoters of these reforms claim that these are not done just to complete a "palace coup" but to transfer power democratically based on the legitimate principles of parliamentary democracy, they must be able to justify their actions in terms of sovereignty of the people (*kokumin shuken*) in no uncertain way. Already at the time of drafting the outline for government reform, they insisted on including the term in some way but were opposed by bureaucrats of the national ministries. Eventually, the term was included when the director general of the Management and Coordination Agency Ōta Seiichi overrode bureaucratic opposition.

Indeed, Article 65 of the Constitution clearly states that executive power lies in the cabinet and not with individual ministries or bureaucrats. The cabinet consists of ministers appointed by the prime minister, who is elected to that position by the legislative branch. These two constitutional provisions give the legislative branch the greatest importance of all three branches and place the executive branch under the legislative branch. If so, the current administrative reforms are constitutionally legitimate.

We will have to wait for developments beyond 2001 to determine whether the current administrative reforms will accomplish what they are intended for, that is, political control over the bureaucracy. There are already some doubts. For example, the Cabinet Secretariat is to assume, as part of the reinforced function, policymaking and drafting of "issues of national importance" (*kuni no jūyō seisaku*), in addition to the conventional business of general management, making the office a center of the administration. However, in this office, the number of political appointees is limited to fifteen (including the cabinet secretary), while the general staff like the prime minister's secretary are to be recruited from "competent members" (*yūshū-na jinzai*) of the ministries and experts from outside the administration. The two separate recruitment routes guarantee the bureaucracy access to the office, which might even increase ministerial influence over decision-making in the Cabinet Secretariat as its jurisdiction enhances. There may be more similar problems. The problem cannot be solved by simply increasing the number of political appointees and reducing that of bureaucrats. Ministries, due to the vertically divided jurisdiction, have tended to form human networks often called "families" that invite not only bureaucrats but also bureaucratic alumni, industry organization representatives, politicians, and governors. Such networks cannot be broken easily by tinkering at small parts. It would be necessary to advance administrative and political reforms systematically with strong political determination, as explained in detail later, in order to eliminate ministerial sectionalism (*kanchō sekushonarizumu*) based on the vertical bureaucratic structure and problems of ministerial families seeking sectional benefits from public projects and government aid. The administrative reforms of the Hashimoto and Obuchi governments are said to be the most comprehensive administrative reforms in postwar Japanese history. What are their particular features in terms of goal-setting, range, information-gathering, staffing, negotiation, persuasion, and decision-making, when compared with past reforms? The new conservative elite is deeply aware of the necessity of reforms, but the reinforcement of the prime minister and his office is not necessarily the only way. In fact, except for the breakup of the MOF and the strengthening of top-level political leadership, many reforms tend to be quite moderate or even intentionally restrained. The reforms may be only quasi-reforms to conceal the primary goal of establishing a new conservative rule of national politics by weakening bureaucratic power and strengthening the prime minister and his office. The institutional reforms with such a complicated nature could not have been implemented so efficiently and successfully without a well-thought-out plan of highly skilled new conservative politicians like Hashimoto and Obuchi. The next section will examine the political leadership style of Hashimoto and Obuchi.

3. Political Leadership in National Reforms

Ishihara Nobuo says, based on his experience as a deputy chief cabinet secretary during the Hashimoto government, that Japanese prime ministers are weak because of particular political customs rather than institutional constraints and also that the function of the prime minister's office can expand or shrink depending on the prime minister's ability. If the prime minister has the ability, the current system could work without reforms, he continues. Environmental factors such as international and domestic socioeconomic changes and political climate favorable to reforms certainly helped the reforms proceed quickly, as mentioned earlier. However, without a strong sense of purpose and an ability to take action, no one could have continued the process of reform, which had such significance, albeit with some limitations, for the future of new conservative rule. Strong leadership exercised by Hashimoto and Obuchi deserve particular mention in the success so far of the national reform of the 1990s.

3.1 Hashimoto's strategy and style

Hashimoto's leadership style was basically that of leading by example, as demonstrated in his actions to fulfill the prime minister's new roles and functions defined by the Basic Law on Central Government Reform enacted during his administration. Administrative reforms had been tried many times before but not always with success; political reforms had not even been tried. The Nakasone administrative reforms of the 1980s were basically economic reforms, which accomplished privatization of the national

railroad and telecommunication systems. Its success owed largely to Nakasone's unique political style and leadership. There are three types of prime ministers in Japan; (1) tractor, (2) mediator, and (3) puppet. Prime ministers in the early postwar years till the early 1970s like Yoshida Shigeru, Hatoyama Ichirō, Kishi Nobusuke, Satō Eisaku, and Tanaka Kakuei belong in the first group. (Tanaka's nickname was actually "computerized bulldozer.") Following the first group, Fukuda Takeo, Ōhira Masayoshi, Suzuki Zenkō, and Takeshita Noboru belong in the second, while Nakasone Yasuhiro seems to belong in the first. For a decade since Takeshita, there were nine prime ministers, most of whom were a puppet type; the prime ministerships of Uno Sōsuke and Murayama Tomiichi were criticized by the media as being mere proxies for the real sources of political power.

Hashimoto and Obuchi were considered the mediator type. Hashimoto indeed acquired bureaucratic skills and know-how to move things steadily, a perfect trait as a mediator, but he also had a strong will to promote reforms, exercising strong leadership as a "brave mediator." Obuchi, on the other hand, was initially derided as "cold pizza" by the US media and as a "vacuum prime minister" by Nakasone but continued and enhanced the range of reforms and successfully passed a series of important reform bills, sometimes exercising leadership even stronger than Hashimoto's. Obuchi may be called a "tractor with a poker face."

Looking at Hashimoto first, he basically followed the style of the Nakasone reforms of the 1980s, with additional touch of his own to implement more reforms. He wanted to avoid repeating the failures of the past prime ministers who advocated reforms without examining closely the difference between administrative and fiscal reforms; he also wanted to establish a precedent for strong political leadership. He therefore formulated a strategy to separate administrative and fiscal reforms. He linked the two in a sense that ministerial reorganization and the reduction of bureaucrats would serve the goal of fiscal reforms, but he considered that the ministerial reorganization was primarily for structural reforms of the politician-bureaucrat relationship. He therefore excluded fiscal reforms from the formal administrative reform program and dealt with it as a routine policy matter. (Hashimoto's fiscal policy was basically a retrenchment policy, which would not utilize fiscal levers to solve economic problems. However, as seen in Section 2, Hashimoto faced major financial problems like bad housing loans, bankruptcies of major financial firms like Yamaichi Securities, and bad loans accumulated by financial institutions. He abandoned the retrenchment policy and allowed government funds to be used to save troubled financial institutions.)

Second, Hashimoto preferred legislation like the basic law to set up a framework for reform over programs described in government policies (*seifu hōshin*) or outlines (*taikō*). (It was the first time in postwar history that administrative reforms were legislated.) It brought the issue and the debate over government policies to the Diet, which mobilized public interest and debate on the issue, legitimizing reform as a formal policy issue. By doing so, he successfully minimized interference from LDP *zoku* politicians, ministries, and bureaucrats in the process and prevented the reform debate from being dominated by rivalries between various organized interests. Third, in terms of organization and leadership for the promotion of administrative reforms, Hashimoto tried to set up an efficient organization for policymaking, drafting, and negotiation. He established the Administrative Reform Conference (November 28, 1996, to June 30, 1998) when he formed the second cabinet after the general election in October 1996. Unlike Nakasone, he assumed the leadership of this conference himself. Nakasone left policymaking and drafting to the second Provisional Council for Administrative Reform (Daini Rinchō), while he himself tried to put their recommendations into practice as much as possible. There was clearly a division of labor. Hashimoto, on the other hand, was involved in the conference more closely, and used a huge amount of data collected by the conference to draft the seventeen reform bills (three volumes) without delay.

Fourth, Hashimoto set up a schedule of deliberation systematically, coordinating work done by different ministries and sections of the government. It followed the example of the Daini Rinchō that stressed the importance of following procedures and schedule; it effectively prevented the process from being delayed and/or sidetracked by opposition and resistance from various sources. In major administrative reforms, opposition and resistance were expected not only from bureaucrats but also from the LDP Policy Research Council and *zoku* members of the Diet who made up "sub-governments" (*kai seifu*). The stress on procedures and schedule made it possible to cut short such opposition. Hashimoto was the chairman of the LDP Policy Research Council for fiscal and administrative affairs when the Daini Rinchō was set up; he often used advisory councils to fend off pressure from the Policy Research Council and knew well the effect of the rule of the procedure-first for the sake of scheduling.

3.2 Political strategy and style of the Obuchi cabinet

Prime Minister Obuchi followed his predecessor, using Hashimoto's strategy and style; he created the Headquarters for the Promotion of Central Government Reform and Other Reforms (Chūō Shōchō-tō Kaikaku Suishin Honbu) to follow through what Hashimoto started with the basic law and, like Hashimoto, assumed the directorship of this organization, appointing the chief cabinet secretary as the deputy and other cabinet ministers as members. Obuchi may have adopted a style similar to Hashimoto, but he also expanded the range of reforms and enhanced the perspective of administrative reforms that Hashimoto had initiated. He embarked on major reforms that included not only large-scale administrative reforms but also political reforms. The current reforms will have some impact on the institutional relationship between politicians and bureaucrats once they take effect in 2001. However, in order to achieve total structural transformation, they will have to make, at least, four changes. They are: (1) the private sector must be made, through liberalization, vigorous and autonomous enough to regain public confidence and international competitiveness; (2) local governments must be given enough authority and power, through decentralization, to take over functions previously filled by the central government; (3) the Diet must be reformed to assume the central role in national politics, as politicians are more closely involved in decision-making, unlike the time when bureaucracies were the center of national politics; and (4) the political party system, including leadership quality and recruitment within parties, must be redefined. Liberalization had already been called for by the second Provisional Council for Administrative Reform of the 1980s, but actual measures for liberalization were formulated en masse during the Hashimoto and Obuchi governments, in response to demands from business and industry for economic stimulus as a means to bring the Japanese economy out of recession. Article 4 of the Basic Law on Central Government Reform clearly defines the standards of the regulatory review. Economic reforms also advanced with policy measures like the big bang. Following the liberalization promotion plan (Kisei Kanwa Suishin Keikaku) of the 1993 Hosokawa government, 2,800 projects were listed as targets for liberalization in March 1997, to which 624 new projects were added in March 1998. Economic liberalization by the government has continued steadily, making general economic conditions from which the private sector should be able to benefit, if it is willing and able to seize the opportunity.

Decentralization started with a cabinet decision in 1990, and the Law for the Promotion of Decentralization (Chihō Bunken Suishin-hō) was enacted by the Murayama government in 1996. Three years later, the Committee for the Promotion of Decentralization (Chihō Bunken Suishin Iinkai) issued its fifth recommendation, which was incorporated into the series of bills for decentralization by the Obuchi government. The bills were passed in July 1999 by the Diet, which simultaneously passed the Central Government Reform Act. Decentralization was defined as one of the basic principle of reforms, along with liberalization, by Article 4 of the basic law. Article 51 states that ministerial reorganization and decentralization are part of the same reform program and that the committee recommendations should be respected and put into practice without delay.

All five recommendations that the committee made called for the institutionalization of new rules for the central-local relationship based on the elimination of delegated functions from the central to local governments as a primary reform toward decentralization. The Japanese administrative system had always been centralized since the Meiji Restoration, and there were substantial disparities among local governments in terms of exercising autonomy. Local governments are now expected to take advantage of changes to be created by decentralization.

Decentralization with power delegation is one of the political trends in advanced industrial countries in the 1990s. In the United States, for example, the Welfare Reform Act of 1996, dubbed a "power transfer revolution" (kengen ijō kakumei), transferred a substantial range of powers from the federal to state governments. In the United Kingdom, too, the current Labour government reexamined the centralized government relationship of the Margaret Thatcher years in the face of growing regionalism in Scotland and Wales and growing necessity for more efficient administration and decided to transfer power to the newly created legislatures of Scotland, Wales, and Northern Ireland. The decentralization trend in Japan, which also involves transfer of power to local governments, can be considered part of such a global trend. Muramatsu Michio (1999), in a paper on decentralization reforms, argues, however, that the Japanese trend is limited by built-in restraining mechanisms, pointing to the new conservatives' intentions seen in the Japanese reforms.

No matter how the central government changes and what kind of new relationship is created between the central and local governments, it is still possible for administrative and legislative processes to become even less efficient if politicians and political parties—central players in the new system—do not change accordingly. It is notable in this regard that the Obuchi government initiated political reforms focusing on parliamentary reforms. The Diet is also said to have been dominated by bureaucrats. Diet strategy politics (kokutai seiji) institutionalized under the 1955 system emphasized political negotiations and compromises (often behind closed doors), and sometimes collusion, between the ruling and opposition parties, while the formal deliberations in Diet committees and plenary sessions were mere formalities prepared and/or even performed directly by bureaucrats acting as government delegates (*seifu iin*). Obuchi embarked on Diet reform to let politicians assume a central role in formal parliamentary decision-making. There were three specific measures designed to reform the Diet, which also serve to increase the powers of the prime minister and his office: (1) reducing the number of the cabinet ministers and creating new posts like deputy ministers and parliamentary secretaries (*seimu kan*) (while abolishing the post of parliamentary vice-ministers [*seimu jikan*]); (2) replacing the government delegate system, in which bureaucrats representing the government could respond to questions, with the government representative system (*seifu setsumei-in*); and (3) setting up time for debate between leaders of ruling and opposition parties. All three measures were included in Obuchi's bill to revitalize the Diet (Kokkai Kasseika-hōan), which passed the House of Representatives on July 13, 1999. (The first two measures will be implemented from 2001.) The first two measures are supposed to work together as follows. Deputy ministers can, by the minister's orders, supervise policymaking and drafting, as well as deal with other matters and take over the minister's responsibilities when he or she is not available. There will be twenty-three deputy ministers in total, who can also represent the ministries in Diet sessions. Parliamentary secretaries (*seimu kan*) will support the minister, like the deputy ministers, mainly by supervising bureaucrats in specifically designated policy areas. It is intended to create a politician-led decision-making system by increasing the number of posts for political appointees (one deputy minister and two to six parliamentary secretaries in each ministry) and letting them be involved directly in policymaking, negotiation, and drafting. Since the deputy minister will be able to represent the ministry in Diet sessions, the government delegate system, which had allowed bureaucrats to represent ministries, will be abolished from the next Diet session, depriving bureaucrats of one of the major political

roles. It may result in significant changes in the parliamentary decision-making system. Along with ministerial reorganization, it may reduce the attractiveness of national bureaucratic positions as a dominant influence in both national politics and administration while increasing interest in the position of elected politicians.

These reforms are not without problems. If posts for parliamentary secretaries are filled by relatively young ruling-party politicians who have been reelected only two or three times and not yet fully trained in policymaking and administrative matters, they may easily become a mouthpiece of well-informed bureaucrats. Since their responsibilities are greater than those of old parliamentary vice-ministers, simply increasing the number of such posts may be problematic. It may be worthwhile to consider appointing to this post people with no government background like academics and businesspeople. It is also unclear whether the increasing number of political appointees (ministers, deputy ministers, and parliamentary secretaries) will be able to play their roles properly in the Japanese parliamentary system, in which the Diet is in session for a limited term with parliamentary committees being the major locus of policy deliberation, in contrast to the British system, where Parliament is in session throughout the year with the house floor as a major place for policy discussion.

Leaders' debate has already been put into practice. It emulates the question time in the British House of Commons, allowing the prime minister, who had only been able to answer questions from the opposition, to argue back and challenge the opposition. The Committee on Fundamental National Policies, to be created in the Diet in 2000, is to prepare procedures appropriate for the leaders' debate.

The first measure of Diet reform was officially to free cabinet ministers from too many parliamentary duties and let them engage more closely in policymaking. But in reality, it was conceived against the background of the decreasing ability and expertise of cabinet ministers who remained in their positions only for a short time due to frequent reshuffles and appointments according to factional politics within the ruling party. It was expected to break the conventional dependence on bureaucrats for responding to parliamentary questions. It should be considered an extension of the major administrative reforms of the Hashimoto and Obuchi governments. Supporting this line of reform is the Administrative Information Disclosure Law (Jōhō Kōkai-hō), proposed initially by Hashimoto in March 1998 and passed by Obuchi after modification on May 7, 1999. The law will help create an "open administration with close monitoring" (jigo kanshi-gata gyōsei), by breaking the monopoly of information by bureaucrats who used it to exercise the "arbitrary administration through advance negotiation" (jizen chōsei-teki na sairyō gyōsei). As already pointed out above, the LDP increased its criticism of the bureaucratic monopoly of information when it was in the opposition. It was typical of the Obuchi cabinet to carry out political reform in specific areas of special concern by linking it to a major program of administrative reforms.

The Obuchi cabinet successfully passed not only a series of reform-related bills but also important bills like those regarding the new National Defense Program Guidelines (Shin Gaidorain Kanren), Residential Registry (Jūmin Kihon Daichō), Interception of Communication (Tsūshin Bōju), National Flag and Anthem (Kokki Kokka), and an amendment of the Diet Law to set up a Committee for Constitutional Review (Kenpō Chōsa-kai), many of which had been unsuccessful during previous LDP cabinets. The success owed a lot to Obuchi's strong will and leadership style, which I call "a tractor with a poker face." Also important was Obuchi's style to deal with the opposition, especially since the ruling coalition did not have a majority in the House of Councillors at the time. Another important element was his skill at gathering party support for his programs.

The LDP had experienced several styles of coalition decision-making, such as a full coalition with the SDPJ and Sakigake, a policy-specific coalition (or partial coalition) with the opposition, and another full coalition, this time with the Liberal Party and Kōmeitō, and learned through these experiences to increase its legislative ability. And after a series of seemingly undisciplined

coalitions with parties of different ideologies and policies, it gradually created "a grand new conservative coalition." It was in reality a "divide and fragment" strategy toward the opposition, preventing the opposition from uniting as a major force that could threaten the LDP. In fact, many of the parties and groups that failed to ride the tide of the grand new conservative coalition have already disappeared. The Democratic Party of Japan, for example, was co-opted by the ruling coalition when the Obuchi government, in an effort to finalize the program to save troubled financial institutions, accepted the DPJ's modifications to the Financial Revitalization bill (Kin'yū Saisei-hōan); this made it easy for the ruling coalition to negotiate with the DPJ on subsequent bills for administrative reforms. On the matter of the separation of treasury and finance functions, however, the DPJ refused to compromise, and since then, the party became increasingly isolated. The LDP included the Liberal Party in the grand coalition by forming an official coalition and accepting many of its proposals for administrative and political reforms. As for the Kōmeitō, the LDP accepted its idea of regional promotion coupons (chiiki shinkō ken) as an economic stimulus measure, while successfully inducing support for the LDP proposal on the treasury-finance separation issue. Such a policy-specific coalition with the Kōmeitō led the two parties to form a full coalition later.

All these examples of the grand coalition demonstrate how irrelevant the current structure of the party system has become since the Murayama government. The Japanese Communist Party (JCP) has been the only party since then that has never joined a ruling coalition. By appealing to the opposition's policy interests and desire for power, the LDP formed cooperative relationships with them, thereby weakening their position as the opposition. This was the typical style of the Obuchi cabinet in dealing with the opposition, which may be called a "black hole" strategy of sucking in the power of the opposition.

Hashimoto and Obuchi both belonged to the LDP's biggest faction, formerly known as Keisei-kai, which had strong influence within the party. Although Hashimoto did not engage in the party's internal negotiations himself, Obuchi, with the help of Chief Cabinet Secretary Nonaka Hiromu, did go out to talk to the party himself if necessary. It was typical Diet strategy politics (*kokutai seiji*), shared by the Keisei-kai leadership, including the former prime minister Takeshita Noboru and the former deputy prime minister Kanemaru Shin. Obuchi seemed to be a leader quite skilled in this traditional style of negotiation. This section so far has reviewed the formation process of a grand coalition by the new conservative elite. There may be historic significance in the current political reforms, which are intended to transfer power and transform the decision-making system to support a new conservative politics, but they also have a number of limitations. The next section will look at such weaknesses and discuss a new frontier of national political reform.

4. The New Frontier of National Reform

The political reform carried out by Hashimoto and Obuchi in an accelerated pace contained limitations, as already mentioned in the context of the built-in restraining mechanisms reflecting the new conservative nature of reforms. Such mechanisms may have worked to help establish the grand conservative coalition, but they could also work against the coalition in the future.

4.1 Degree of decentralization

The structural reform of the national political system may be achieved by the ministerial reorganization designed to decentralize the hitherto centralized system controlled by national, career-track bureaucrats. The transformation of the power structure in favor of politicians, however, does not necessarily produce a decentralized national political system. The reform, therefore, should begin with decentralization, and then move on to the reorganization of national ministries accordingly. The new Ministry of Management and Coordination (Sōmu-shō), to be established in 2001, will be a huge ministry covering areas previously covered by the Ministry of Home Affairs (MHA, Jichi-shō), the Management and Coordination Agency (MCA, Sōmu-chō), and the Ministry of Post and Telecommunications (MPT, Yūsei-shō). The Ministry of Land and Transport (Kokudo Kōtsu-shō) will also be

huge, combining functions of the Ministries of Transport (MOT, Un'yū-shō) and Construction (MOC, Kensetsu-shō) and the Agencies of Land (NLA, Kokudo-chō) and Hokkaido Development (HDA, Hokkaido Kaihatsu-chō). The creation of such huge ministries with potential powers of controlling local governments and taking back some of the administrative powers from them can cause serious problems to further decentralization efforts. DPJ member Iwakuni Tetsundo criticizes it, saying that it would only mean "decentralization" of the central ministries, that is, a transfer of power within the bureaucracy. The Ministry of Land and Transport will also control the bulk of the budget for public construction projects, inviting criticism that such a big ministry with a virtual monopoly on the budget and power not only goes against the basic principle of the current administrative reforms but also has a danger of creating a ministry prone to large-scale grafting.

4.2 Getting rid of bureaucratic legal interpretation

The increasing power of the prime minister and his office and that of the chief cabinet secretary may result in politician-led decision-making at the national level. The Cabinet Legislation Bureau (Naikaku Hōsei-kyoku) has been so far the only body to check all the bills drafted by bureaucrats and give a seal of legal approval to them; it has even issued its own constitutional interpretations, which the Supreme Court has not dared to do, assuming responsibilities for not only regulating the legislative process but also establishing interpretations of the Constitution and other laws. It was originally just one bureau in the cabinet, yet it has monopolized legal powers that even the prime minister and the cabinet cannot challenge. If politicians rely on bureaucrats even to interpret the Constitution, they can hardly establish a politician-led decision-making system. It is imperative now to define the relationship between the prime minister and the Cabinet Legislation Bureau clearly. It may also be useful to reinforce the legislative bureaus of both houses of the Diet.

4.3 Reform of Diet conventions

The Obuchi cabinet was particularly interested in parliamentary reform to make the Diet a forum for debate between members, considering this as another means to reinforce the political leadership of the prime minister and his office. If its intention is to guarantee politician-led decision-making both in the executive and legislative branches, reform must include measures to restrain negotiations behind closed doors between the ruling and opposition parties and stimulate open debate, such as by revising the current fixed-term system to keep the Diet in session all year round and switching to a majority decision in the directors' meetings of standing committees and joint house management committee, instead of requiring a unanimous decision as currently practiced. It may also be necessary to create a body attached to the Diet to conduct national surveys and provide legislative assistance, similar to the Congressional Research Service (CRS) of the US Congress, in order to increase the number of member-sponsored bills and enhance members' legislative skills. Above all, the system of preliminary review (*jizen shinsa*) of all bills and budget-related bills by the ruling parties must be changed, as the practice of this preliminary review has robbed the Diet of the functions of issue clarification and policy deliberation, leading the Diet to be a place where the ruling and opposition parties made behind-the-scenes deals in what has come to be called Diet strategy politics.

4.4 The electoral system and reform of the House of Councillors

The above three reforms are not so contradictory to the new conservatives' intentions and may still be included in the reform agenda in the future. The most problematic limitation of the Hashimoto-Obuchi administrative reform, which is a great misfortune for voters, is that no one has explained the ideology and method of selecting the new political parties and elites suitable to the new national political system. Such issues seem to be hidden away in areas that have no relevance to administrative and political reforms. If the reform intends to change the decision-making structure, the method of selecting political parties and elites cannot be ignored. For the electoral system, the Obuchi cabinet (as of June 1999) proposed a bill to reduce the number of proportional representation

seats by fifty, in agreement with the Liberal Party. It was problematic to change the system after only one election under the system. Moreover, the bill was proposed without serious examination of its significance on general reforms of both houses and agreed on by the three coalition partners (LDP, Liberal Party, and Kōmeitō) only out of opportunistic and political considerations. Electoral reform should be discussed from a much wider perspective of how the political party system and parties should be at the time when the role of the upper house is called into question and conventional party politics is losing relevance.

The council to examine the future of the House of Councillors (Sangiin no Shōrai-zō o Kangaeru Yūshikisha Kondan-kai) issued an opinion paper for reform to upper house chairperson Saitō Jūrō on April 26, 2000. In order to make a clear distinction between the two houses, the opinion paper proposed to redefine the role of the upper house as the "house of review" (*saikō no fu*) commanding authority rather than power and to reorganize the house accordingly. Specifically, it recommended the abolishment of the upper house vote on the selection of the prime minister, change of the two-thirds rule to majority rule in the second voting in the house, and reinforcement of the powers of monitoring the administration, some of which may require a constitutional revision. The proposal was hailed as the first radical reform program of the upper house since the establishment of the 1955 system but was not received with enthusiasm by parties and politicians. This indicates that reforming the House of Councillors is difficult to achieve unless it is linked to a wider range of electoral reforms covering issues like electoral rights (voting and running for office), electoral districts, electoral campaigns, political funding, and the organization of political parties.

4.5 Door-to-door canvassing and anti-corruption law

The least adequate reform by the new conservative elite was political funding reform. The Obuchi cabinet was quite forthcoming with many reform programs except for this area. Since the lawsuit regarding political donations by Yahata

Steel in 1966, the issue of political funding from industry and other organizations has been continuously debated, yet it is not included in Obuchi's reform programs. It has not even touched the largely inadequate Political Party Subsidy Law (Seitō Joseikin-hō) enacted by the Hosokawa government in 1994. The large number of political parties that have come and gone since 1994 indicates how inadequate this law was to stabilize the political party system in Japan. It is obvious that parties would be formed only to gain the benefit of public funding if no qualifications are needed for parties to apply for the fund. And such parties are more likely to cause political corruption, as they tend to lack the sense of public duty and capacity for self-cleansing (*jijō nōryoku*). The electoral system is not the direct cause of political corruption. Regulations should be lifted for electoral campaigns to make door-to-door canvassing and campaign speeches freer—and thus generally less expensive. And for the regulation of electoral fraud and political corruption, an anti-corruption law—rather than the regulation of political funding—would be more effective. The selection of the political elite is thereby simplified but substantial, as it would increase the chances of direct contact between voters and candidates. Political parties, on the other hand, will be able to recruit candidates widely from various areas of society, utilizing the principles of equal opportunity and free competition to their advantage. The European, especially British, experience has shown that this can be the case.

4.6 Maximization of opportunities to run for election

Japanese elections in the 1990s have been characterized by voter turnout of less than 50 percent and more than 50 percent of voters saying they do not have any party they support (*shiji seitō nashi*). People have the right to vote and the right to run for election themselves. In Japan, however, the latter kind of right has not been exercised much recently, as people are discouraged by the enormous amount of money necessary for election campaigns and the exclusionary practices in candidate selection by political parties. (If the recommendation to lower the minimum age for political participation to eighteen, issued by Obuchi's private advisory council on Japan's goals in the twenty-first century [Nijū-isseiki Nihon no Kōsō Kondan-kai] in January 2000, only means the lowering of the minimum voting age, it is too simplistic a plan without close examination of Japan's reality and Europe's electoral history. The minimum voting age was lowered to eighteen in European countries because many of these countries adopted the draft system for military duties for people at the age of eighteen and had to acknowledge their voting right.)

Why has Obuchi's political reform program remained within the range of establishing the domination of decision-making by politicians only through parliamentary reforms? And why do most of the parties, while supporting the reform within this range, seem uninterested in political reforms to maximize opportunities for people to run for elections and thus to improve and modernize politicians and political parties? Such reforms, I argue, should include Diet reform (especially the upper house), electoral district reform, reforms of political funding and election campaigns, an anti-corruption law, and the voting right of non-Japanese citizens with permanent resident status. One of the reasons why the parties are reluctant to pursue such radical reforms is that they are afraid of changes to the systems of election and political funding and the organization of political parties that they are familiar with and neglect to modernize. It is no wonder that we have not seen the vision of a new political party system in the midst of the formation of a new conservative grand coalition. The current reforms have shown only the vision for change from bureaucratic control to political control of national decision-making.

4.7 From bureaucrats to politicians and then to people

As we have discussed so far, the national political reform prompted by international and domestic socioeconomic changes and the subsequent policy implementation have achieved results in terms of directing the change from bureaucratic to political control of the political power structure and the decision-making system. It still remains to be seen whether the reform measures are effectively implemented, as many of the administrative reform laws and acts will take effect in 2001. The problem, however, is that the said "political control" is likely to be exercised by the political parties and politicians, especially those of the new conservative elite who have successfully guarded their prerogatives by avoiding the expansion of political participation. It is also problematic that citizens have only a very low level of trust and expectation toward parties and politicians and weak identity with the existing political parties, according to surveys on party support and voting behavior. The lack of a close relationship between voters and political parties seems to be the result of the current election and political funding systems that tend to exclude ordinary citizens and prevent candidate recruitment from taking place in various areas of society. Interestingly, the lack of trust and expectation among people toward parties and politicians does not necessarily indicate the lack of interest in politics among them. They are rather active politically depending on issues, as seen in the recent surge of volunteer activities by nongovernmental and nonprofit organizations.

These developments point to the lack of a vision to include new actors beyond existing political parties in the current political reform, which was originally designed to protect the parties' interest. The transformation of administration and politics from centralized bureaucratic control to decentralized autonomy cannot be completed only by the revival of representative democracy based on party politics but needs more pluralistic political and administrative systems mobilizing the political resources and energy of citizens who organize grassroots activities wider in scope and more refined in organization than those of politicians. The current political reform from bureaucratic to political control, in this sense, must advance further to establish democratic governance—politics with an emphasis on citizens. Citizen participation must not be limited to indirect involvement through voting but must be expanded to direct participation as candidates and elected representatives, fixed-term appointees to bureaucratic positions, nongovernmental

members of policymaking bodies, third-party monitors of the national administration, or participants in national referendums. Chances to be candidates in elections can be increased by the liberalization of residential and other requirements for candidacy and by changes in the candidate recruitment system of political parties. Participation as fixed-term appointees to bureaucratic positions should be promoted by abolishing the career system and lifetime employment practices in the national ministries. It is only in such a system that gender becomes a legitimate and concrete political ideology, as already seen in some of the North European political systems. Citizens in this system then must be much closer to the normative "public citizens," who are urbanized and well aware of the linkage and commonalties between national, regional, international, and global politics.

Courtesy of European Press Academic Publishing.

Originally published as chapter 7 of *New Japanese Political Economy and Political Reform: Political Revolution from Above* by European Press Academic Publishing in 2002.

Bibliography

Iio Jun. 1997. "Nihon ni okeru kanmin kankei no isō" [Phases of the Government-Private Sector Relationship in Japan]. Paper presented at the Public Policy Studies Association Japan Conference, Kyoto University, Kyoto, June 1997.

Japan Association for Comparative Politics, ed. 1999. *Sekai no gyōsei kaikaku* [Administrative Reforms in the World]. Tokyo: Waseda University Press.

Keehn, Edward B. 1997. *The Mandarins of Kasumigaseki: Order and Conflict in Japan's Bureaucracy.* London: Macmillan.

Masujima Toshiyuki. 1999. "Chūō Shōchō-tō Kaikaku Kihon-hō: Gyōkaku no tokushoku to mondaiten" [The Basic Law on Central Government Reform: Features and Problems in the Administrative Reforms]. *Leviathan* 24 (Spring): 25–49.

Matsushita Keiichi. 1999. *Jichitai wa kawaruka?* [Can Local Bodies Change?]. Tokyo: Iwanami Shoten.

Muramatsu Michio. 1999. "Bunken-ka kaikaku: Takoku no keiken, Nihon no keiken" [Decentralization Reforms: Experiences in Japan and Other Countries]. *NIRA Policy Studies* 12 (2): 11–16.

Nakano Minoru. 1982. "The Electoral Cost and Campaign in Japan." In *Local Election and Campaign Financing*, edited by Chang-hyun Cho and M. Ziemen. Hanyang University and Friedrich-Naumann-Stiftung.

———. 1985. "Seiji shikin kisei no shomondai" [Problems of Political Funding Regulation]. Special issue, *Jurist* 35.

———. 1993. *Nihon no seiji rikigaku: Dare ga seisaku o kettei suru no ka?* [The Political Dynamics of Japan: Who Decides Policy?]. Tokyo: Nihon Hōsō Shuppan Kyōkai.

———. 1997a. *The Policy-making Process in Contemporary Japan*. London: Palgrave Macmillan.

———. 1997b. "The Changing Legislative Process in the Transitional Period." In *Japanese Politics Today: Beyond Karaoke Democracy?*, edited by Purnendra Jain and Inoguchi Takashi. New York: St. Martin's Press.

———. 2000. "Kyūjū-nendai Nihon no seiji keizai kiki to kokusei kaikaku: Hihan to tenbō" [The Political Economy Crisis in the 1990s and Political Reforms: Critique and Perspective]. In *Nijū-isseiki o yomitoku seijigaku* [Politics to Read the Twenty-first Century], edited by Kawakami Kazuhisa, Maruyama Naoki, and Hirano Hiroshi. Tokyo: Nihon Keizai Hyōronsha.

Sakano Tomokazu. 1998. "Chūō-chihō kankei to kiki kanri taisei" [Central-Local Relationship and Crisis Management]. *Cross-Cultural Studies Review* (Kobe University) 11: 1–30.

Tanaka Shōichi. 1999. "Igi mōshitate: Shōchō saihen koko ga mondai da" [Opposition: There Exist Problems Here]. *Weekly Tōyō Keizai*, June 13, 1999.

Ueyama Shinichi. 1999. *Gyōsei hyōka no jidai: Keiei to kokyaku no shiten kara* [The Era of Administrative Evaluation: From the Viewpoint of Management and Clients]. Tokyo: NTT Shuppan.

Two Faces of the Japanese Electorate

The Organized Voters versus the Unorganized Voters on the Process of Partisan Realignment/Dealignment

Tanaka Aiji

Waseda Political Studies, 1998

Introduction

Japanese politics has been experiencing turbulence since 1993, and its party system has been transformed since then. The so-called "1955 party system" broke down in July 1993, and since then, the Japanese party system has been in transition. However, we do not know yet what type of party system it is being transformed into. The 1955 party system was formed in 1955 when the Liberal Party and the Democratic Party merged into the Liberal Democratic Party (LDP), which was in power for thirty-eight years from 1955 to 1993. But after the LDP fell from the ruling party position, the Japanese party system has been experiencing partisan realignment or even partisan dealignment. As the percentage of those voters who do not identify with any party exceeds 50 percent, we may call this transformation of the Japanese party system "partisan dealignment" (Tanaka and Nishizawa 1997).

In the midst of the transformation of the Japanese party system, Japan changed the electoral law for House of Representatives elections. This electoral law reform brought about the single-member district system combined with the proportional representation system. The first general election under the new election system was held in October 1996. This institutional reform of the electoral law may have had an effect on the ongoing partisan transformation, but, at the same time, Japanese partisan dealignment might have taken place without electoral reform. In this paper, my analysis is too premature to answer this question fully, but as the first step to answer this question, it is necessary to capture the characteristics of the nonpartisan voters (independent voters) as well as the partisan voters in order

to determine whether partisan dealignment or realignment is taking place in Japan now. The main purpose of this paper is to characterize the nonpartisan as well as partisan voters in Japan during this turbulent period.

We conducted a two-wave panel, nationwide sample survey (called the Japan Election and Democracy Study 1996, or JEDS96) before and after the general election of 1996.[1] One purpose of this paper is to characterize the Japanese electorate to examine what kind of factors had an impact on the partisan dealignment in Japan, analyzing the rich JEDS96 data. The other purpose of this paper is to characterize the Japanese electorate by considering the meaning of the 1996 general election from the long-term perspectives. In so doing, this paper tries to utilize other opinion surveys conducted in Japan between 1972 and 1995 to compare the analyses based on JEDS96.

1. Two Faces of the Japanese Electorate: Background

The Japanese electorate has recently been divided into two groups in several ways. In the first dimension, there is the group of voters who turn out to vote and those who tend to abstain from voting. In the second dimension, one group is composed of those who have partisan attachments (identified with a party), while the other consists of those who are indifferent to political parties (independent voters). In the third dimension, one group is made up of those who are within some organizational network (organized voters), whereas the other is composed of those who are outside any organizational network (unorganized voters).

Of course, the former group in one dimension does not exactly overlap with the former group in another dimension. However, according to sociological analyses of Japanese voting behavior (Watanuki 1967; Miyake, Kinoshita, and Aiba 1967; Uchida 1974; Richardson 1974), the former group in each of the three dimensions is more likely to live in the countryside or in traditional communities, whereas the latter group in each of the three dimensions is more likely to be urban residents.

In this section, let us see how the two groups in these three dimensions are identified in the JEDS96 data and what proportion they make up of the entire electorate.

1.1 The voters versus nonvoters

The voter turnout rate for the 1996 general election was 59.7 percent, the lowest in the history of general elections for the House of the Representatives in Japan. In our JEDS96 survey, those respondents who answered that they turned out to vote were 83.6 percent. What could account for this discrepancy? One explanation is that many respondents who did not vote concealed the fact that they abstained. The other explanation is that those who generally vote and actually did vote are more likely to respond to surveys, whereas those who are not interested in voting would be much more likely to refuse survey interviews. Let us try a simple calculation based on the latter explanation. The original target sample size of the JEDS96 survey was 2,100, and we got 1,327 valid responses for the post-election wave (see note 2); of those responses, 83.6 percent (1,110) reported that they voted. This 1,110 is just 52.8 percent of the original target sample, which is lower than the actual turnout rate but is much closer to it. There seem to have been voters who refused or were not able to answer the survey interviews but voted. The probabilities of respondents lying about whether they voted or abstained seem to be a small. In the general election, about 60 percent of voters voted and 40 percent abstained. For the House of Councillors election in 1995, 44.5 percent voted and 55.5 percent did not; the percentages for 1998 were 58.4 percent and 41.4 percent, respectively.

1.2 The partisans versus the nonpartisans

The percentage of those respondents who do not have any partisanship (independent voters) exceeded 50 percent in January 1995 for the first time, according to the *Yomiuri Shimbun*'s monthly polls. Since then, the share of independent voters has stayed at the same level, except at the time of national elections, when many independent voters tend to express their vote intention as their partisanship. Figure 1 shows the longitudinal changes of percentage of partisanship in postwar Japan.[2] According to Figure 1, the most apparent and significant change was the sharp increase of political independents (or nonpartisan voters) in the 1990s. The percentage of independent voters exceeded 30 percent at some points in the 1980s as well as in 1992, but political independents sharply increased their proportion from about 33 percent in 1993 to approximately 47 percent in 1995. And after 1995, the size of the independents has remained approximately at the same level.

As Figure 1 shows, the share of independent voters was less than 10 percent throughout the 1960s, but the size doubled in the early 1970s. After that, it gradually grew to approximately 35 percent by the end of the 1980s. Independent voters quickly increased from 1993, when the LDP was split into several new conservative parties, such as the Japan Renewal Party (JRP), Japan New Party (JNP), and New Party Sakigake. Then, the size of independent voters reached about 50 percent by early 1995. Its percentage has been fluctuating a bit, but it keeps coming back to the 50 percent level up to the present time.

The LDP has managed to maintain a considerable portion of support from the electorate (about 25 to 34 percent) even after 1993, although the LDP has clearly reduced its share of support since its peak in the mid-1980s to the early 1990s, when it often enjoyed more than 50 percent of support. When the JNP emerged in 1992, new conservative parties began to expand their size, and this trend accelerated in 1993, when the JRP and Sakigake split from the LDP. But this group has not increased its size since the formation of the New Frontier Party (NFP) in late 1994, when two centrist parties (a part of Kōmeitō and the Democratic Socialist Party, or DSP) merged with the JNP and JRP into the NFP. In Figure 1, the white portion in the figure above the LDP indicates the percentages

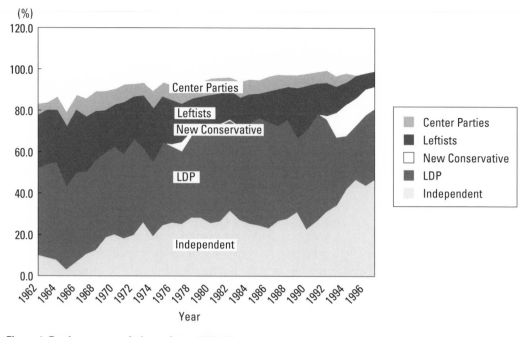

Figure 1. Partisans versus Independents, 1962–97
Source: Data from *Yomiuri Shimbun* monthly poll, January 1962 to April 1997.

of support for these new conservative parties as a whole. While this group of new conservative parties stayed about the same size from 1994 through April 1997, the leftist parties—the Japan Socialist Party (JSP) and Japanese Communist Party (JCP)—especially the JSP, saw their support base in the electorate shrink considerably, while the centrist parties diminished when both the DSP and Kōmeitō merged into the NFP in 1994. Thus, these changes in the proportion of Japanese partisan supporters are evident in the 1990s.

Of the approximately 50 percent who identify as independent, voters can be categorized into three groups: (1) the "apolitical independents" who are in accordance with the classic image of the independent voter; (2) the "politically interested independents" who are consistent with the image of the "new independents" in the 1970s of the United States (Petrocik 1974; Pomper 1975; Keith et al. 1977), and (3) the "disaffected independents" who had partisanship until around 1993 but withdrew their support during the fluctuation of the Japanese party system from 1993 on.

To figure out the approximate sizes of these three groups of independents, the data of five

nationwide surveys were utilized, as Table 1 shows. About 15 percent (16.1 percent in 1991) are "apolitical independents" who are not interested in politics at all, and about 20 percent (20.7 percent in 1991) are independent voters who are interested in politics. Therefore, (1) approximately 15 percent of the electorate are apolitical independents, and (2) about 20 percent of the electorate are those independents who are interested in politics.

The third group of independent voters are (3) the disaffected independents, who severed their partisanship after the 1955 party system collapsed with the LDP's fall from power. According to Figure 1, the percentage of independents kept increasing from approximately 35 to over 50 percent between 1993 and 1997. This suggests that the disaffected independents were about 15 percent of the electorate. This conforms with the 1995 survey data in Table 2; the size of those not having any partisanship from 1993 on, namely, (3) the "disaffected independents," was 13.7 percent—within the proximity of 15 percent.[3] Also in Table 2, the percentage of independents who stayed independent since 1995 or before was

Table 1. Changes of Types of Independents, 1976–91

	Partisans		Independents			Total Independents (1)+(2)
	Political Interest		Political Interest			
Year	Yes	No	(2)Yes	(1)No	Total	
1976	43.8%	35.2%	7.2%	13.8%	100%	20.7%
1983	40.7%	30.5%	11.8%	17.0%	100%	28.6%
1987	46.7%	17.4%	20.6%	15.3%	100%	36.0%
1991	43.4%	19.8%	20.7%	16.1%	100%	36.9%
			(2)	(1)		

Sources: Data from JABISS study, 1976; JES, 1983; Akarui Senkyo Suishin Kyōkai surveys, 1987 and 1991.

Table 2. Typology of Independents and Partisans, 1995

	Lost Partisanship	Changed Partisanship	No Change of Partisanship	Formed New Partisanship	Row Total
Independents	(3) 13.7%	11.7%	(1)+(2) 36.4%	1.5%	63.3%
Partisans	0.7%	5.9%	29.7%	0.5%	33.8%
				Grand Total	100.0%

Source: Data from nationwide telephone survey of the 1995 House of Councillors election by the Election and Democracy Research Group.[4]

36.4 percent, which is approximately the same as the size of the independent voters in 1991 (36.9 percent) in Table 1 and that in the *Yomiuri* poll data of Figure 1 (about 35 percent).

From Figure 1, it is clear and we should keep in mind that more than half of Japanese voters are without partisanship. The voting behavior of these independent voters cannot be explained by the partisan voting model. We need a new model to explain the voting behavior of the independents.

However, at least we now know that there are three groups of independent voters in Japan today. The first "traditional independents" are apolitical, while the second "politically interested independents" and the third "disaffected independents" are likely to be interested in politics. While we will have to verify this expectation, we now should treat the first group of independent voters separately from the latter two groups of independent voters.

1.3 The organized voters versus the unorganized voters

It is well known among observers of Japanese politics that many Japanese voters are affiliated

with some group or organization and that those Japanese voters are often mobilized to vote for a particular party that those groups endorse (Watanuki 1967; Uchida 1974; Richardson 1974, 1991). Recently, a more sophisticated approach to the effects of the social networks on voting behavior has been developed (Huckfeldt and Sprague 1995; Ikeda 1998). But this section will focus on the effects of the organizational (or group) membership on voting behavior, which is the traditional approach. Voters living within organizational networks and those living outside organizational networks are also two faces of the Japanese electorate. The former I call "organized voters," and the latter I call "unorganized voters."

As the first step of the analysis, it is important to identify the size of the organized and unorganized voters. According to JEDS96 data, those respondents who have membership in any organization or group accounted for 46.3 percent of total respondents. This percentage includes membership in candidate associations (*kōenkai*) but excludes membership in neighborhood or community associations, to many of which one automatically registers simply by living in a certain neighborhood, and membership in community cooperatives, to which most residents also tend to join. The figure of 46.3 percent is very close to the voter turnout for House of Councillors elections, which is 44.5 percent.

If we think about the possibility of those within organizational networks being more likely to respond to our survey interviews and those outside the networks less likely to do so, then we will have to recalculate the figure. This time, let me use the membership of all ten groups questioned about their group membership in the JEDS96 survey as well as that of the *kōenkai*. The share of those who are members of any of these eleven types of groups and organizations was 70.0 percent (929) in the JEDS96 data, while that of those who are not members of any was 30.0 percent (398). But if we use our 2,100 original target sample as the denominator to calculate these two figures, the share of organized voters (929) is 55.8 percent of the original sample, while the percentage of unorganized voters (398) is 44.2 percent. The former figure is almost the same as the turnout rate of the 1996 general election (59.6 percent) and the 1998 upper house election (58.4 percent).

While we will have to check the overlapping portion of organized voters and turned-out voters, one hypothesis is that only voters within organizational networks turn out to vote, although some of our data analyses suggest otherwise.

We have so far seen (1) 45 to 60 percent voting versus 55 to 40 percent not voting, (2) 45 percent partisans versus 50 percent independent voters, and (3) 45 to 55 percent organized voters versus 55 to 45 percent unorganized voters. We will have to see how these groups overlap with other categories and with each other.

2. Changes in Japan's Traditional Cleavages

Two traditional cleavages exist in postwar Japan. The first one is the urban-rural cleavage. And the second is the left-right ideological cleavage. Both of them are now changing in political meaning and impact on the Japanese electorate.

The traditional social cleavage of the Japanese electorate is the rural-urban cleavage (Watanuki 1967; Richardson 1974). The population shares of these two areas have been steadily changing, as

urbanization has progressed in postwar Japan from the 1950s to the present, reaching a peak in the first half of the 1970s. The proportion of the population in the thirteen largest cities is about 40 percent of Japan's entire population, and when cities with a population size of 300,000 or more are included, the urban proportion is over 50 percent. What are the sizes of these two groups in our JEDS96 data? Of the 1,452 valid responses of the pre-election study, 21.5 percent lived in the thirteen big cities of Sapporo, Sendai, Tokyo, Yokohama, Kawasaki, Chiba, Nagoya, Osaka, Kyoto, Kobe, Hiroshima, Fukuoka, and Kitakyūshū; 23.5 percent in medium-size cities; 12.1 percent in small cities; and 23.6 percent in towns and villages. These figures under-represent urban residents and over-represent rural voters. The response rate to survey interviews in rural areas is higher than in urban areas, though, and so is voter turnout. Therefore, our JEDS96 data do not necessarily misrepresent the Japanese electorate but are considered to replicate the share of turned-out voters (rather than the entire electorate) fairly closely.

Then, the next question is whether this urban-rural cleavage still has political impact. While urban residents are increasing and rural residents are decreasing, what kind of new political relationship is emerging in terms of this traditional demographic cleavage? Among the three new divisions of the Japanese electorate in recent years, the sharp increase in the percentages of independent voters and nonpartisans seems to be the most evident, if not the most important, phenomenon. Accordingly, let us look at the relationship between the urban-rural cleavage and the division between partisan and independent voters.

Opinion surveys conducted by the *Asahi Shimbun* provide some clear patterns in longitudinal changes of the relationship between the urban-rural cleavage and the partisan-independents division. Figure 2 shows the longitudinal changes in the percentage of independent voters by region. The percentage of independent voters sharply increased from 1992 on, not only in big cities but also in small and medium cities and even in towns and villages. Although the percentages for independents are consistently lower in the *Asahi* surveys than the *Yomiuri* surveys, the

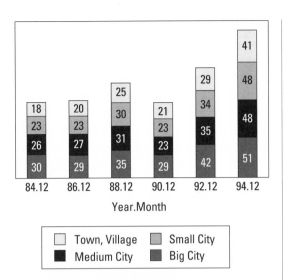

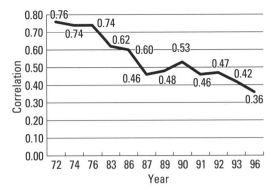

Figure 3. Changes in the Relationship between Ideology and Party Alignment, 1984–94

Sources: Data from Akarui Senkyo Suishin Kyōkai surveys, 1972–93; JABISS, 1976; JES, 1983; JEDS96, 1996.

Figure 2. Percentage of Independents in the Electorate by City Size, 1984–94

Sources: Data from *Asahi Shimbun* opinion surveys, December 1984 to December 1994.

Asahi percentage in December 1994 is very high. Thus, the Japanese electorate is clearly divided into partisans and nonpartisans (independents).

The traditional cleavage between rural and urban areas is diminishing because the percentage of independent voters is increasing even in rural area, as we have seen in Figure 2. As far as the distribution of independent voters is concerned, the rural versus urban cleavage is growing weaker. This may be due to the populations of towns and villages, which have been shrinking drastically in the last two decades. At the same time, this may also be due to the fact that political attitudes of younger voters in rural area have become similar to those of their urban counterparts, as the same media content, especially via TV broadcasting, has been viewed by all Japanese voters in the last two decades. In addition, approximately a quarter of the younger age cohorts (around forty years old or younger) in rural areas have experienced life in big cities as students or as workers. These changes in sociological and demographic conditions are considered to have had an effect on the political attitudes of younger rural voters.

The other traditional cleavage in postwar Japan has been an ideological one. The ideological cleavage dividing parties and their supporters in postwar Japanese politics has been the strongest.

The conservative camp centered on the LDP and the leftist camp centered on the JSP (Socialists) and the JCP (Communists) have confronted each other for a long time. This confrontation between the conservatives and the leftists was seen not only in the Diet but also in the electorate during elections under the 1955 party system. However, this conservative-leftist cleavage now appears to be losing its impact on the perception of voters or their cognitive map of political parties. After the Cold War ended, the ideological confrontation between the socialist and capitalist camps became much weaker in the world. Similarly, in Japan after 1990, the ideological confrontation between the socialist-oriented camp and the capitalist/business-oriented camp became weaker or even meaningless. We can see this change by looking at the longitudinal changes in relationship between ideology and partisan alignment.

Figure 3 shows the longitudinal pattern of changes in the correlation between respondents' ideological orientation and their partisanship (parties being aligned along the conservative to leftist orientation). The sharp decline of the correlation between ideology and partisan alignment is seen from 1986 to 1987, and the decline continues down to 0.36 in 1996, the lowest point. This pattern suggests that the liberal-conservative (or left-right) ideological cleavage in Japan no longer has strong explanatory power as an independent variable for partisan alignment in present-day Japan.

These changes shown in Figure 3 are considered to reflect the perceptions of Japanese voters about political parties. This means that the left-right ideological cleavage in postwar Japan lost its political meaning from the latter half of the 1980s to the mid-1990s. Now, the Japanese electorate is no longer ideologically divided between the leftist camp and the conservative camp.

This can also be verified by utilizing some multidimensional analyses, such as the principal component analyses or factor analyses, of Japanese survey data over time. Table 3 and Figure 4 show a varimax solution of a principal component analysis of feeling thermometer scales of political parties in 1983 (JES data). The configuration of the cognitive map of the Japanese electorate in 1983, as shown in Figure 4, clearly suggests that Japanese political parties were still aligned from left (JCP) to right (LDP) in 1983.

However, this configuration of the cognitive map of political parties held by the Japanese electorate has been transformed by 1996. Table 4 and Figure 5 show another principal component analysis of feeling thermometer scales of political parties in 1996 (JEDS96 data). The configuration shown in Figure 5 clearly suggests that Japanese parties in 1996 were aligned along the vertical dimension between the independent voters and the LDP. In Figure 5, the New Frontier Party led by Ozawa Ichirō is located near the LDP, while the JCP is located close to the independents. This suggests that Japanese voters in 1996 perceived independent voters and the JCP as antiparty or anti-insider politics (that is, anti-Nagatachō) and the LDP and the NFP as oriented toward political insiders (Nagatachō).

Thus, we can see that the Japanese partisan alignment has been transformed from the left-right unidimensional space in 1983 to the partisan-nonpartisan unidimensional space in

Table 3. Principal Component Analysis of Political-Party Feeling Thermometer Scales, 1983 (Varimax-Rotated Solution)

	Component 1	Component 2
LDP	0.383	-0.663
JSP	0.330	0.592
Kōmeitō	0.627	0.192
DSP	0.764	-0.134
JCP	0.244	0.784
NLC	0.828	0.103
SDL	0.796	0.286

Source: JES data in 1983.
Note: NLC, New Liberal Club; SDL, Social Democratic League.

Table 4. Principal Component Analysis of Political-Party Feeling Thermometer Scales, 1996 (Varimax-Rotated Solution)

	Component 1	Component 2
LDP	0.460	-0.663
NFP	0.528	-0.257
DPJ	0.759	-0.0008
Sakigake	0.775	0.260
SDP	0.784	0.207
JCP	0.433	0.644
Independent	0.0086	0.636

Source: JEDS96 data in 1996.

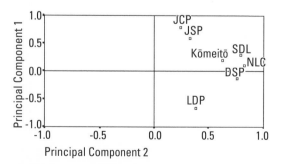

Figure 4. Cognitive Map of Political Parties in Japan, 1983

Source: JES data in 1983.

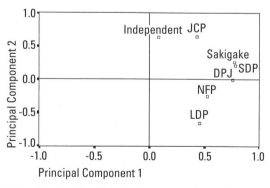

Figure 5. Cognitive Map of Political Parties in Japan, 1996

Source: JEDS96 data in 1996.

1996.[5] Now, the two opposite ends are no longer the leftist and conservative orientations but the conventional partisan (Nagatachō-type parties) and anticonventional partisan (anti-Nagatachō-type parties) orientations. This suggests that the increasingly meaningful cleavage in present-day Japanese electoral politics is the partisan-nonpartisan cleavage. Given the sharp increase in the size of independent voters in the last five years, it is logical to consider nonpartisan voters to be the more important face of the two faces of the Japanese electorate.

3. The Relationship between Nonvoters, Nonpartisans, and Unorganized Voters

Now, we should look at the degree of overlap between the two faces in the three dimensions.

First, let us take a look at how nonpartisans would vote (to see the overlap between nonpartisans and nonvoters). Table 5 shows a clear relationship between the degree of partisanship and voter turnout in 1996. The stronger the voter's partisanship, the more likely he or she was to turn out to vote. The correlation coefficient (Tau-c) shows a relatively weak relationship, but this is statistically significant.

Second, we should pay attention to the relationship between unorganized voters and voter turnout in 1996. As organizational membership increases, respondents were more likely to vote (Table 6). While the correlation coefficient (Tau-c) is rather weak (−0.09), this relationship is statistically significant.

Third, let us see the relationship between

Table 5. The Relationship between Partisan Strength and Voter Turnout, 1996

Partisan Strength	Voted	Did Not Vote	Row Total	
		Voter Turnout		
Strong Partisanship	93.5%	6.5%	100.0%	
Weak Partisanship	92.4%	7.6%	100.0%	
Leaners	81.7%	18.3%	100.0%	
Nonpartisans	72.0%	28.0%	100.0%	n=1,150
			Tau-c=0.17	

Source: JEDS96 data in 1996.

Table 6. The Relationship between Unorganized Voters and Voter Turnout, 1996

Group Membership	Voted	Did Not Vote	Row Total	
		Voter Turnout		
None	79.8%	20.2%	100.0%	
1 or 2	87.2%	12.8%	100.0%	
3 or more	94.6%	5.4%	100.0%	n=1,327
			Tau-c=-0.09	

Source: JEDS96 data in 1996.

Table 7. The Relationship between the Unorganized Voters and Partisan Strength, 1996

	Strong Partisan	Weak Partisan	Leaner	Nonpartisan	Row Total
		Partisan Strength			
Group Membership					
None	7.4%	42.7%	22.3%	27.7%	100.0%
1 or 2	18.5%	48.8%	20.0%	12.8%	100.0%
3 or more	28.2%	54.9%	8.5%	8.5%	100.0%
				Tau-c=-0.21	n=1,150

Source: JEDS96 data in 1996.

unorganized voters and the strength of partisanship. Table 7 shows that those who belong to more groups were more likely to have stronger partisanship. This relationship is statistically significant, and the correlation coefficient (Tau-c) shows a fairly clear relationship.

4. Suggestions for Further Research on Voting Behavior in Japan

Thus, unorganized voters are more likely to be the nonpartisan (independent) voters and at the same time are less likely to turn out to vote. These three groups do not perfectly overlap each other, so these types of Japanese voters have to be analyzed further. The voting behavior of those who are within an organizational network, have partisanship, and are more likely to vote has been explained (Richardson 1991, 1997).

However, when those who are unorganized and nonpartisan occasionally turn out to vote in such cases as the 1995 Tokyo gubernatorial election or the 1998 upper house election, their voting behavior seems to determine the election outcome. This is shown in Table 8, where the stronger the independent orientation, the more likely voters were to cast their ballots for a candidate with an antiparty or nonpartisan orientation. In Table 8, Aoshima Yukio was the most antipartisan candidate, and Iwakuni Tetsundo and Ōmae Kenichi were somewhat antipartisan or nonpartisan candidates; these were the candidates who attracted votes from independent voters. All the candidates with party endorsements attracted the least votes from independent voters. Therefore, now we will have to pay attention to this group of unorganized, nonpartisan, and infrequent voters in Japan.

Courtesy of Waseda University

Originally published in *Waseda Political Studies* 30 (1998): 33–51.

This article is based on an earlier paper originally prepared for delivery at the 1998 annual meeting of the American Political Science Association, Boston Marriott Copley Place and Sheraton Boston Hotel and Towers, September 3–6, 1998.

Notes

1. JEDS96 was conducted by a joint US-Japanese research team, in which the author participated. Bradley M. Richardson of Ohio State University and Uchida Mitsuru of Waseda University are the leading principal investigators of this study. The study was mainly funded by the National Science Foundation (NSF Grant No. SBR-9632113). We are grateful to the NSF and all of our colleagues on this joint research team, namely, Hayashi Fumi, Ikeda Kenichi, Kawakami Kazuhisa, Dennis Patterson, Susan Pharr, Bradley Richardson, Tanifuji Etsushi, and Uchida Mitsuru. JEDS96 has a sample size of 1,535 as a valid sample for the pre-election wave, 1,327 for the post-election wave, and 1,244 as a valid sample for both waves. JEDS96 consists of about 150 questions and over 500 variables.

2. The data for Figure 1 regarding the percentage of partisan and independent voters who support each party were obtained from the Public Opinion Office of the *Yomiuri Shimbun*, which has been publicly releasing the basic results of its monthly opinion polls since 1994. The figures used to draw the graphics in Figure 1 were calculated from the monthly figures of the *Yomiuri*'s public opinion data. We appreciate the generosity as well as the kind cooperation of the Public Opinion Office of the *Yomiuri Shimbun*.

Table 8. The Relationship between the Nonpartisan Orientation and Voting Behavior, 1995 Tokyo Gubernatorial Election

	Strength and Clearness of Nonpartisan Orientation			
	Strong	Clear	Weak or Unclear	Partisan
Aoshima	66.7%	44.9%	43.1%	19.3%
Iwakuni, Ōmae	26.3%	41.5%	37.3%	19.3%
Candidates Endorsed by Parties	7.1%	13.5%	19.6%	61.5%
Case Numbers	99%	207%	209%	135%	n=650
Column Total	100.0%	100.0%	100.0%	100.0%

Source: Data from the Election and Democracy Research Group survey on the Tokyo gubernatorial election, April 1995.

3. In the 1995 nationwide survey, we used an unconventional measure for partisanship. This new measure of partisanship was designed to tap the orientation of the respondents toward political independence or nonpartisanship (Tanaka and Weisberg 1996). Therefore, the total size of independent voters is 63.3 percent, which is much higher than the figure under conventional measures of partisanship. The presence of those who answered "changed partisanship" in the category of "independents" in Table 2 is somewhat illogical, since they are reporting that they "changed their partisanship" and yet they claim to be "independents"; this suggests that they probably felt an affinity with a particular party and loosely identified with it but still answered "independent."

4. The Election and Democracy Research Group (headed by Uchida Mitsuru) conducted a nationwide telephone survey before the House of Councillors election in July 1995. This was the first random digit dialing (RDD) nationwide telephone survey in the field of political science in Japan. The valid sample of this survey was 1,039.

5. Actually, the Japanese party system has been transformed from its alignment in the mid-1980s to the present one in the mid-1990s via various forms of partisan alignment over the decade. The dimensionality of Japan's party system has gone through three or four dimensional configurations (Tanaka and Weisberg 1996). Since these changes are too complicated to explain briefly and require a full paper, I will skip a discussion of patterns of party system change here.

Appendix

The Impact of Institutional Changes on Voter Turnout

Hurdles to go to the voting booth were relaxed to increase voter turnout in Japan. Those changes went into effect in 1998, and the upper house election of July 1998 was the first nationwide election with these relaxed voting method changes. There are three major reforms. First, the hours on election day were extended from 7:00 a.m.–6:00 p.m. to 7:00 a.m.–8:00 p.m. so that those people who went out of town on voting day can come back and vote. Second, the requirements for absentee ballots were relaxed so that voters can cast their ballots even for such reasons as a desire to play golf on election day. Third, the hours when voters can cast an absentee ballot were also extended from 8:30 a.m.–5:00 p.m. to 8:30 a.m.–8:00 p.m.

The effects of these changes can be easily measured by the aggregate data from the election management commission. The figure above shows the effects of the institutional change. Thus, the recent upper house election's higher-than-expected turnout rate was to a significant extent due to the three changes. We will thus have to analyze what type of voters would be likely to take advantage of such institutional changes.

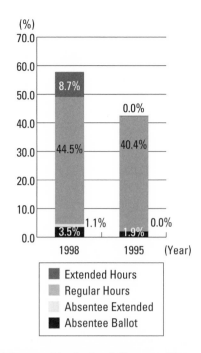

Figure 6. Impact of Institutional Change on Voter Turnout in Tokyo, 1998 versus 1995

Source: Aggregate data released by the Election Management Commission of Tokyo.

References

Huckfeldt, Robert R., and John Sprague. 1995. *Citizens, Politics, and Social Communication: Information and Influence in an Election Campaign.* Cambridge: Cambridge University Press.

Ikeda Kenichi. 1997. *Tenpen suru seiji no riariti* [Changing Political Reality]. Tokyo: Bokutakusha.

Keith, Bruce E., David B. Magleby, Candice J. Nelson, Elizabeth Orr, Mark Westlye, and Raymond Wolfinger. 1977. "The Myth of the Independent Voter." Paper presented at the 1977 annual meeting of the American Political Science Association, Washington, D.C., September 1–4, 1977.

———. 1992. *The Myth of the Independent Voter.* Berkeley: University of California Press.

Miyake Ichirō, Kinoshita Tomio, and Aiba Jūichi. 1967. *Kotonaru reberu no senkyo ni okeru tōhyō kōdō no kenkyū* [A Study of Voting Behavior at Different Levels of Elections]. Tokyo: Sōbunsha.

Petrocik, John R. 1974. "An Analysis of Intransitivities in the Index of Party Identification." *Political Methodology* 1 (3): 31–47.

Pomper, Gerald M. 1975. *Voter's Choice.* New York: Dodd, Mead.

Richardson, Bradley M. 1975. "Party Loyalties and Party Saliency in Japan." *Comparative Political Studies* 8: 32–57.

———. 1975. *The Political Culture of Japan.* Berkeley: University of California Press.

———. 1991. "Japanese Voting Behavior in Comparative Perspective." In *The Japanese Voter*, coauthored by Scott C. Flanagan, Kōhei Shinsaku, Miyake Ichirō, Bradley M. Richardson, and Watanuki Jōji. New Haven: Yale University Press.

———. 1997. *Japanese Democracy: Power, Coordination, and Performance.* New Haven: Yale University Press.

Tanaka Aiji and Herbert F. Weisberg. 1996. "Political Independence in Japan in the 1990s: Multidimensional Party Identification during the Dealignment." Paper delivered at the annual meeting of the American Political Science Association, San Francisco, August 29–September 1, 1996.

Tanaka Aiji and Nishizawa Yoshitaka. 1997. "Critical Elections of Japan in the 1990s: Does the LDP's Comeback in 1996 Mean Voter Realignment or Dealignment?" Paper delivered at the XVIIth World Congress of the International Political Science Association, Seoul, South Korea, August 17–21, 1997.

Uchida Mitsuru. 1972. *Seiii sanka to seiji katei: Gendai Nihon no seiji bunseki* [Political Participation and Political Analysis of Contemporary Japan]. Tokyo: Maeno Shoten.

Watanuki Jōji. 1967. "Patterns of Politics in Present-Day Japan." In *Party Systems and Voter Alignments: Cross-National Perspectives*, edited by Seymour M. Lipset and Stein Rokkan. New York: The Free Press.

Part III

Top-Down Leadership and a Nascent Two-Party System

Prime Minister Koizumi Junichirō's theatrical, "presidential" leadership style inspired much commentary in the early 2000s, and it seems fair in retrospect to assign his relatively long administration its own chapter in Heisei history. This section begins with a piece on a theme dear to Koizumi's heart, politics as a reflection of "the will of the people." In "Manifestoes as a Means of Reforming Japanese Politics," Sasaki Takeshi, a prolific Heisei commentator and a strong proponent of political reform, advocates the publication of concrete action plans as a tool for focusing the popular will and incorporating it in government policy.

In the second half of the 1990s, many observers had expressed disappointment with the 1994 electoral reform, given the ongoing flux and fluidity of party politics. Now, however, some were crediting that and other institutional reforms with Koizumi's rise to power and the advent of a new style of leadership. Representative of this viewpoint is Machidori Satoshi's "The 1990s Reforms Have Transformed Japanese Politics." In contrast, Yamaguchi Jirō, another prolific contributor to Heisei discourse, rejects Koizumi's neoliberal policies and calls for a social democratic "third way" in his piece, "Political Reform in Japan."

One of the most intensely debated issues of the Koizumi era was the sustainability of the pension system and the government's proposed reforms. In "The Politics of Pension Retrenchment in Japan," Shinkawa Toshimitsu offers a sweeping overview of earlier reforms and the demographic and political dynamics driving the issue.

Prime Minister Koizumi's crowning triumph was the 2005 "postal privatization election," which boosted the strength of the ruling Liberal Democratic Party while consolidating Koizumi's control of the LDP. In "Lessons from the LDP Landslide," Kabashima Ikuo and Sugawara Taku give a detailed analysis of the election results, highlighting the emergence of new voting patterns and the impact of single-seat districts. Tanaka Naoki, author of "Koizumi Ushers in the '2005 Setup,'" makes the case for the landslide as a historical watershed, opening the way for transformational policy changes and political reforms. Finally, Nonaka Naoto, training a critical eye on the ill-fated first cabinet of Prime Minister Abe Shinzō, offers his answers to the question, "What's Gone Wrong with the Abe Administration?"

Manifestoes as a Means of Reforming Japanese Politics

Sasaki Takeshi
Japan Echo, 2003

Democratic politics is a system based on the extremely clear-cut principle of one person, one vote. At the same time, however, it requires complex, refined mechanisms designed to ensure that the majority of people participate in the political process. Satisfactory results are achieved only when these mechanisms are supported by numerous official and unofficial systems. The idea that simply holding one-person-one-vote elections will make the problems inherent in democratic politics magically disappear—regardless of how badly politicians behave—does not hold water. Examining and improving the official and unofficial systems is a key task in reforming Japanese politics. Continuous, detailed examinations must be undertaken of the links between these systems and the problems of democratic politics, and specific countermeasures must be devised.

Instead of continuing politics in the same manner as before, the political world must confront the problems in its procedures and systems and act to establish public trust in politics. This undertaking is not directly related to the interests of any specific party or faction.

For several years now politicians have been preaching to the public about the need for structural reform, but there is still no clear sign of structural reform taking place in the political world itself. With a general election approaching, it is time for politicians to take decisive action to reform politics. If they are to ask voters to accept structural reform of Japan's economy and society and the sacrifices this entails, politicians must first get their own house in order. Without political self-reform, it will be impossible to carry out the tough reforms that lie ahead in other sectors, and the delays that have dogged Japan's reform efforts up to now will be repeated.

The aim of political reform is to improve the process by which parties focus the political will of voters and thereby to make Japan a politics-driven nation, meaning a nation where the government is properly controlled by duly elected political leaders. There are a variety of possible approaches to such reform, but I believe that manifestoes—preelection declarations by political parties of what they will undertake if elected to power—currently offer a chance to make a significant breakthrough. The introduction of manifestoes would inevitably bring to the surface issues that were left untouched in the last round of political reforms a decade ago.

The Difficult Task of Focusing the Popular Will

The basic problem with Japanese politics is the inability of politicians to focus the public's will. As the need to achieve such focusing has increased, this structural flaw has become ever more conspicuous. Politicians do not even appear able to accomplish this within their own camps. As a result, Japan is afflicted by a brand of party politics in which a lack of ability to pull people together and marshal their political will is almost seen as something to be proud of.

This flaw perpetuates political drift, with voters unable to evaluate which tasks politicians have started and which they have completed and parties unable to build up a record of achievements. The experiences of the past decade have exposed the scale of the economic and social costs borne by the Japanese people as a result of this drift. Policies that function effectively in other countries do not function in Japan, and this is a clear indication of these costs.

This structural flaw and the rapid rise in the number of voters with no party affiliation seen in the last decade or so are two sides of the same coin. The surge in the number of independent voters is a product of the breakdown of old-style party politics. Unlike in countries where it has served to highlight new points of convergence, however, in Japan this has acted as a brake on the process of focusing the public's political will. The failure of political parties to make any serious effort to achieve such focus and the consistently high number of independent voters have been linked in a kind of symbiotic relationship.

In a democratic political system like Japan's, which encompasses tens of millions of voters, focusing the political will of the people is no easy task. If this task is left undone, however, the elected politicians who wield power in the name of the people may draw up and implement policies as if they have been given carte blanche. Citizens, through elections, become like passengers who have bought tickets for and boarded a ship whose destination is unknown. This is the current reality in Japan. Who can claim that elections are functioning as a means for the people to pass judgment on the political establishment? In fact, elections are being held mainly for the sake of those involved in politics and have virtually nothing to do with focusing the people's political will and setting the nation's course based on their judgment.

The basic task of political reform is to fundamentally change the relationship between politicians and voters. This will not be achieved just by holding elections over and over. Focusing political will requires meticulous preparation and stage setting, tasks that, in turn, necessitate constant, concerted effort. This, ultimately, is the key to political reform.

Focusing political will is not the same as rallying people's enthusiasm or whipping up passions for no reason; it is not a form of self-satisfaction. It must be aimed at achieving a certain result and requires that support is also rallied for the route and methods used to reach this goal. For this purpose I believe we need to introduce the practice of having parties draw up manifestoes before each election. Such manifestoes would set forth each party's practical plans for government, and

as soon as the election was over, the manifesto of the victorious party would become a contract with voters specifying the tasks the new administration is to carry out. Manifestoes are a prerequisite for strong administrations and will offer political parties the chance to gain even greater support once in office by fulfilling their promises.

Manifestoes will give politics a sense of purpose and design. Since the goals an administration intends to achieve will be set out clearly in advance, political energy can be focused on the key issue of implementing the necessary measures in a deliberate manner. In politics, of course, there are always unexpected events and changes of circumstance to deal with. To argue that this uncertainty precludes conducting politics with a sense of purpose and design, however, is illogical in the extreme. It is precisely because the world of politics is susceptible to disturbance by unexpected events and by people's hunger for power that we must consciously and deliberately imbue politics with purpose and design. Otherwise, the foundation for government based on electoral responsibility will be lost. Manifestoes are a tool for giving politics, which is by its very nature unstable, a sense of purpose and design.

At the same time, manifestoes are of decisive importance in providing standards by which voters and other actors in society can judge politics. By examining the extent to which manifesto promises have been fulfilled, people will be able without great difficulty to gauge the achievements of governments and politicians. Of course, there will be debate over how strictly or leniently progress should be judged, but manifestoes will at least make the criteria for evaluating political achievements clear from the start.

By using the criteria outlined above, journalists will be able to give more specialized evaluations of politics than they do now, and this broad range of evaluations will stimulate policy debates that move forward step by step. This process will lead opposition parties to improve the quality of their own policy platforms, giving rise to the next round of policymaking and evaluation. Manifestoes are a channel through which politicians provide material to serve as the basis for voters' judgments. This will be in sharp contrast to the current situation, in which confusion reigns as to what voters should base their decisions on.

Above all, making the provision of manifestoes to voters a function of political parties will hand ultimate responsibility for policy selection and political results to the electorate. In democratic societies, even in cases where no clear manifestoes are issued, it is taken for granted that voters are responsible for the results of policies. The question is, on what clear basis and by what clear criteria should voters fulfill this responsibility? My position is that it is much fairer if voters have access to clear manifestoes than if all they are shown is lists of vague aspirations. It is surely not fair to hold elections on the basis that the victorious politicians will have carte blanche to implement whatever policies they choose and that the voters must take the blame for the consequences.

When democratic politics fails to function effectively, there is a tendency for some people to blame this on voter stupidity. But even if one supposes that voters are stupid, there is a tremendous gap between the political education they can get in a situation where their errors can be elucidated and the one they get in a situation where they cannot.

The Difference between Manifestoes and Campaign Platforms

How will manifestoes differ from the campaign platforms politicians have issued in the past? The basic difference is that they will be incomparably more specific in setting out politicians' promises and how they intend to fulfill them. Japanese election campaign platforms have tended to be masses of grand-sounding statements expressing aspirations lacking in detail. When putting together a manifesto, however, parties—providing they stick to realistic goals—will have no choice but to produce prosaic, pragmatic documents that take into account how much their proposals will cost. Campaign pledges, which are no more than temporary expedients, may offer a vehicle for politicians to set forth plans fit for Superman, but any party issuing a manifesto containing such wildly overambitious promises would be ridiculed and its credibility damaged. Politics cannot be an abstract activity and must always be concerned with practical matters, and

campaign platforms filled with abstract statements stink of self-deception.

A bigger problem with campaign pledges, however, is their looseness. There were times in the past when the breaking of campaign promises stirred controversy, and to the extent that this happened, these pledges were serving like manifestoes. The reality of politics, however, is that campaign pledges have another face. They have tended to be made just for the sake of the campaign. Such pledges are valid only during the campaign; once the election is over, they effectively expire. This results in a disconnect between the pledges made during the campaign and postelection politics. The two have effectively become independent of each other.

The total disconnection of elections from politics means that elections are transformed into mere ceremonies in which abstract messages are broadcast and candidates seek carte blanche to run things as they see fit. It is possible for campaign pledges to function as ties binding voters to politics in this situation, but they also function as tools pulling the two apart. And under certain circumstances, it is the latter function of pulling voters and politics apart that dominates.

The most important issue and the one that is easiest to understand is that of who produces campaign pledges and takes responsibility for implementing them. When the election is for an executive leader, such as a governor or mayor, the situation is very clear. The candidate is the producer of the pledges and is the only person who can be held responsible for carrying out the commitments. The situation is completely different in elections involving parties, however. Assuming a campaign platform functions as a manifesto, meaning that it consists of promises to be carried out by the postelection administration, the producer of the platform would be the person hoping to lead the administration or the group of people under his or her leadership, and this person would be responsible for fulfilling the promises. The processes by which campaign platforms are produced are many and varied, of course, but, providing there is unity between the party that wins the election and the administration it forms, the leader of the administration obviously bears ultimate responsibility.

At the same time, this implies that prior to the issuing of an election manifesto serious debate takes place within the party and that the manifesto constitutes the fruits of these deliberations. In this scenario, the task after an election is to implement the pledges that have been made, not to restart the policy debate from scratch. A manifesto is thus indivisible from a governing administration and can be seen as an expression of the collective political will of a party. Individual candidates in executive elections can issue manifestoes without going through this complex procedure, but political parties must first negotiate internal procedures and gain the approval of their membership. Considering the present state of party politics in Japan, the main issues are whether parties are capable of producing manifestoes and the extent to which the necessary procedures are in place. Until these barriers are overcome, political parties will be unable to fulfill manifesto promises. In this sense, manifestoes are inextricably linked to political parties' self-reform efforts.

If this is the status of manifestoes in party politics, is there any point in campaign platforms that do not function as manifestoes? They may serve some purpose in setting out the ideals and goals of the political party concerned, but insofar as they have no clear link with either the postelection administration or its policies, they are little more than reference material. In this context, parties may feel there is no need to undertake careful internal deliberation when producing campaign platforms and might even be tempted to leave the task to anyone with a talent for writing catchy slogans.

Campaign platforms like these have, in fact, been the norm in Japan until now. They are frequently little more than catalogs of grand-sounding aspirations with no reference to costs. These platforms are of the kind produced just for the sake of an election campaign, and the connection between the platforms and the actions of postelection administrations have always been extremely tenuous. More precisely, the looseness of these links is the only reason such platforms have been allowed to exist. If the platforms had been seen as specific and binding in the same way as a manifesto, the process by which they were produced would surely have become a major

point of contention. The lack of serious interest in such issues supports the view that the political significance of election campaign platforms has been extremely limited.

A campaign platform can also take the form of a set of pledges issued by an individual candidate for a seat in a legislative body. Given the superficial similarity between such platforms and manifestoes issued by individual candidates in executive elections, sooner or later we will probably see the term "manifesto" being applied to them also. While these platforms may have some worth in that they give voters a degree of insight into where candidates stand on certain issues, it is very hard to see what significance they can have in terms of determining the conduct of a postelection administration.

In a party political system, elections are all about the character of the resulting administration and the policies it will pursue; the ideas of individual legislators are of only secondary importance. Japanese politics is currently stuck in a severe "fallacy of composition," where the parts do not combine to produce the expected whole. People must realize that statements by candidates on their individual political views cannot take the place of party manifestoes.

A manifesto derives its importance from the fact that it is an expression of collective intent by a party, and thus the promises it contains have a good chance of being fulfilled. By contrast, while there is no guarantee whatsoever that the ideas of individual legislators will be realized, there is unlimited scope for making excuses when they are not. Confusing manifestoes and individual candidates' campaign platforms is, therefore, a fatal misjudgment. At times when voters want to know the intentions of a potential administration, expressing individual ideas whose chances of becoming reality are slim does not provide satisfactory answers.

What is at issue in elections under a system of party politics is not the ideas of individual legislators but the collective promises that a party will implement if it forms an administration. As long as these two remain confused, there will never be any improvement in the state of party politics. Indeed, any discrepancies between the opinions of individual candidates and the manifestoes of their parties can only sow the seeds of confusion among voters. All in all, campaign platforms expressing the political views of individual candidates serve little real purpose and are likely to confuse rather than inform voters.

Manifestoes as a Catalyst for Party Reform

My criticism of campaign platforms as statements of individual candidates' views in legislative elections may appear to sit uneasily with my enthusiasm for manifestoes in executive elections. It is important, however, to note the differences between local politics, which is dominated by chief executives, and national politics, which is dominated by the parties in the legislature. One key structural difference is that while in local politics the plans a specific individual has for government can immediately be turned into that person's manifesto for the postelection administration, in national politics this cannot happen.

Party politics is a world of collective, not individual, political activity, and the purpose of manifestoes in this world is to set out what a political party collectively intends to achieve, what sequence of steps it will take, and what means it will use. In other words, manifestoes are all about pinning down the intentions of a group—the party—and where responsibility lies in that group. No amount of information on what individual candidates for the legislature are trying to achieve at their own particular levels can clarify these points. If candidates in legislative elections take the same approach as candidates in executive elections, they are effectively negating the existence of their parties and setting themselves up as "parties of one." Parties must clarify where responsibility lies before issuing manifestoes. Should they fail to do so, they will be contributing to a new form of political degradation.

The point of a manifesto is not just to give more details of the policies a party intends to pursue than the kind of election pledges seen so far in Japan; it is a proposal to voters on which a party will stake its collective responsibility. This includes the responsibility to implement the proposed policies if the party wins the support of a majority of voters. This would represent a change in the procedures by which policies are decided in Japan. A manifesto would be issued as a result of preliminary deliberations by a party, including the sounding out of individual candidates' views, on the assumption that after the election the party would swiftly implement the provisions it contains. The role of the successful candidates would be to faithfully carry out those provisions. Internal deliberations would essentially be completed before the election instead of starting up again once the election is over, as they do now.

In the past, what has often happened in Japan is that parties have issued campaign platforms lacking substantive details and giving little indication as to who is responsible for fulfilling the promises, and only after the election has the party in question undertaken the task of reconciling the concrete differences of opinion among its members. One of the many disadvantages of this approach is that large amounts of time and energy have been wasted because of interference by bureaucrats and special interests. The current custom of obtaining prior approval for government policies from members of ruling parties, which has recently become the subject of some controversy, is an example of this kind of policymaking process. This mechanism may have satisfied individual lawmakers by providing them with a stage on which to strut, but it also made the policymaking process chronically slow and robbed the resulting policies of much of their freshness. It goes without saying that such flaws have had fatal consequences in the sphere of economic policy. This mechanism has fragmented and diluted political leadership in Japan and has allowed a system driven by politics to deteriorate into one driven by politicians.

The aim of introducing manifestoes to Japanese politics is to switch as much as possible from postelection to preelection policy planning. This does not mean ignoring or refusing to listen to internal party opinion. Rather, it means changing the political routine to one in which parties reconcile their internal differences before the election and, once the election is over, move swiftly to implement the measures they have proposed. It is not acceptable for parties simply to declare that their ranks "encompass a wide range of divergent opinions" and leave it at that; they should go into elections only after finalizing their manifestoes by organizing these opinions into a coherent policy platform. The system of prior policy approval by ruling parties should be applied at the manifesto-production stage, not as a means of reformulating policies after an election.

Putting manifestoes at the center of the policymaking process does not mean ignoring democratic procedures within parties; it merely means changing the positioning and timing of these procedures. Political parties only exist thanks to voters, and democracy within parties must always be aimed at a bigger goal, namely, serving the electorate. The idea that intraparty democracy is the be-all and end-all of a functioning democratic system is a threat both to parties themselves and to party politics in general.

For a variety of reasons, members of Japan's National Diet are highly sensitive to the question of when they will next face an election. If parties come to fight elections by issuing manifestoes, however, the issue of what to put into their party's manifesto will concern them at least as much as the timing of the elections. A system in which the contents of the party's policy platform were subject to preelection screening by the members of the party in the Diet would likely spark a lively internal policy debate.

It is effectively impossible for manifestoes to be issued if policy debate is continually postponed because politicians are concerned only with when the next election will be held. What is needed, of course, is an appropriate balance between interest in the timing of an election and in what kind of manifesto to issue. With a general election now said to be imminent, it is astonishing that parties are not engaged in lively internal debate over their policy pledges and in efforts to gather the disparate opinions of their members into coherent programs.

Introducing the mechanism of manifestoes to party politics would be a significant step in that it would lead to changes in policymaking procedures, accelerate the operation of the government, and make the process of government more politics driven. Manifestoes are the essence of a politics-driven system, for governing parties have a direct responsibility to voters to ensure that manifesto promises are fulfilled. The goals and lineup of the cabinet would naturally be decided in line with these promises, and, armed with the endorsement of the electorate, cabinet members could unhesitatingly exercise firm leadership over the bureaucracy.

One of the main reasons why it has been so difficult to establish a politics-driven system in Japan is that politicians have prioritized their individual campaigns over collective party activity, making it impossible to dispel the idea that politicians are the central actors in the system. Manifestoes offer a chance to clarify the links between politics-led policymaking activities and the politician-led model that has been left in place so far and to decide which of these approaches Japan will follow. As the roots of the problem are so deep, we must be careful that "manifesto" does not simply become a buzzword and the concept a fleeting fad in the political world, and that the same old problems do not simply rear their heads in a new guise.

A Means to an End

It was hoped that the political reforms undertaken a decade ago would make parties the leading actors in the policymaking process. But these hopes were subsequently dashed as parties embarked on a series of splits and mergers and failed to carry out internal reforms. The need for reform of political parties has been brought home repeatedly in the meantime, but the behavior of the parties has inevitably caused a long-term decline in the public's expectations of politics. In this context, manifestoes are a means to reform parties by using elections to involve voters in the political process and thus make politics-driven government a reality.

If the information is widely disseminated, manifestoes will also be a means to demand that parties enter elections as standard-bearers for a brand of politics characterized by clear, concrete objectives, by the ability to evaluate success or failure clearly, and by guarantees that politicians will carry out the policies they have promised. This is a political demand that any party intent on forming a government will surely find hard to refuse, for such a refusal would provoke a negative reaction among voters.

Once one party has declared that it will take

part in the manifesto mechanism, others will have no option but to join in. The mechanism will then gain its own momentum as voters and journalists become involved. This in turn will provide ample chances for the political-reform mechanism set in motion ten years ago to have a real impact.

At the same time, as the messages issued by political parties become more explicit, the weight of responsibility on voters when choosing from among those parties will become greater. Instead of just making whatever demands they feel like, voters will become acutely aware of the need to make considered judgments that take into account such aspects as the costs of proposed policies and how these would be met. This process will gradually bring home to people the idea that democratic politics is all about self-rule. Without such a realization, there is little hope of fostering the kind of cool realism Japan so desperately needs.

In my conversations with Japanese politicians, I frequently hear complaints about the unreasonable demands voters make. But instead of moaning, politicians should let voters judge what is reasonable and what is not. In this sense, while manifestoes will represent a test for political parties, we must not forget that it is in fact voters who will face the toughest test.

Japan's postwar political mechanism, in which politicians avoided forcing voters to make tough decisions under the guise of "leave it to me"–style paternalism, has already become unsustainable. There are a variety of reasons why this is so, but maintaining this mechanism will not benefit politicians or voters—much less Japan as a whole. There is now no option but to lay every aspect of the current situation on the table and have voters make hard choices about which party should govern the country. Given the current circumstances, the kind of manifestoes that will appear are unlikely to allow the masses of complacent "independents" to continue sitting on the fence.

At the same time as political parties produce manifestoes, those with no party affiliation must be prepared to leave the independent camp. Manifestoes are a means of achieving a party politics in which few games are tolerated. Sooner or later, they will bring an end to the complacency of nonaffiliated voters.

Courtesy of Japan Echo.

English version originally published in *Japan Echo* 30, no. 5 (2003): 27–31. Translated from "Seitō ni sekinin o, yūkensha ni shiren o," *Chūō Kōron* (August 2003): 140–48 (courtesy of Chūōkōron Shinsha).

The 1990s Reforms Have Transformed Japanese Politics

Machidori Satoshi
Japan Echo, 2005

It has now been almost four years since the launch of the Koizumi Junichirō administration in April 2001. Since the Liberal Democratic Party (LDP) was founded in 1955, only three of its leaders have served longer terms as prime minister than Koizumi's current record: Ikeda Hayato (1960–64), Satō Eisaku (1964–72), and Nakasone Yasuhiro (1982–87). And the only other post–World War II prime minister who served longer was Yoshida Shigeru (1946–47, 1948–54). All of these prime ministers left their mark on Japan's postwar history—Yoshida for creating the framework of modern Japanese politics, Ikeda and Satō for guiding the nation through the years of rapid economic growth, and Nakasone for embarking on reforms based on neoliberalism. In terms of longevity, Koizumi's administration is approaching the records of these past governments that blazed new trails in their time, and people will someday likely use the "Koizumi era" as a point of reference when talking about their own memories. In terms of what it has accomplished, however, assessments of the Koizumi administration at present are not very good.

Media commentators and others have severely criticized Koizumi. They complain of what they have dubbed *marunage*, his practice of "throwing things whole" to cabinet ministers and government councils, leaving it up to them to make the tough decisions about reform plans, as in the cases of the highway-related public corporations and pension system. And they drub him for failing to adequately explain his policies, as seen in his handling of the dispatch of the Self-Defense Forces to Iraq, and for excessive self-justification and political grandstanding to win the support of particular constituencies, both of which are typically represented by his insistence on visiting Yasukuni Shrine. It is also often noted that while he was swept into office as a reform candidate who said he was ready to "destroy the LDP," he has since resorted to facile compromises on difficult issues and has more than anything else contributed to preserving the party's hold on power.

One cannot say that all of these criticisms are off the mark. I think, however, that the critics are overlooking an important feature of the Koizumi administration: To put it directly, it has brought about procedural changes in the policymaking process; to put it more broadly, it has given birth to a transformation of the nation's political power structure.

The Koizumi administration has changed the shape of political leadership in Japan through the workings of two sets of reforms that were adopted in the 1990s: the overhaul of the electoral system enacted in 1994 and the administrative reforms adopted during the 1996–98 term of Prime Minister Hashimoto Ryūtarō. In short, the changes involve the establishment of a leading position for the executive, consisting of the line from the prime minister through the cabinet ministers to the ministries, over the LDP and, within the LDP, the concentration of authority in the hands of the party president (a post that Koizumi holds in addition to the premiership) and his appointed deputies. This set of changes has been causing the almost complete collapse of the traditional foundations of LDP rule. In this sense one could even say that Koizumi really has "destroyed the LDP." Another way of putting it would be to say that the Koizumi administration has transformed Japan's political system.

What interests me is the comparative political

analysis of the relationship inside the National Diet between individual legislators and the political parties. In this connection, it seems to me that discussions of the Koizumi administration so far have failed to offer appropriate assessments of the significance of the transformation that it has wrought. To be sure, there have recently been such efforts as Tatebayashi Masahiko's *Giin kōdō no seiji keizai gaku* (The Political Economy of Diet Members' Behavior; Yūhikaku Publishing, 2004), which provided a systematic analysis of the relationship between the electoral system and the activities of LDP Diet members, and Makihara Izuru's article titled "Koizumi 'Daitōryō' ga tsukuriageta shin 'Kasumigaseki'" (The New Central Government Apparatus Created by "President" Koizumi; *Shokun*, February 2005), which examines the links between the Koizumi government and the administrative reforms adopted by the Hashimoto administration. To gauge the true value of the Koizumi administration, however, it is necessary to analyze the meaning of electoral reform and administrative reform in tandem, and that is what I will attempt to do here.

The Three Pillars of LDP Politics

In order to understand the Koizumi administration's transformation of the political system, it is first necessary to grasp the characteristics of the LDP as it existed beforehand. There have been many excellent analyses of the characteristics of LDP politics since the release of *Jimintō seiken* (LDP Rule; Chūōkōronsha, 1986) by Satō Seizaburō and Matsuzaki Tetsuhisa. Though the various authors have organized their analyses differently, all of them point to the strong color of the LDP as a decentralized party dominated by Diet members. In my view, the traditional form of LDP politics had three pillars: factions, support groups, and a bottom-up approach. These three pillars functioned in large part by adapting to and mutually complementing three aspects of party functioning: electoral campaigning, organizational apparatus, and policymaking activities.

To date, the role of factions has been the largest point of contention in the debate over the nature of the LDP. While some have seen the factions as embodying premodern relationships based on patronage, others have seen them as groups providing policy coherence and continuity. I, however, believe the most important role of factions has been to serve as machinery ensuring the election of particular candidates. It is often said that a candidate needs three things to win: a support base, name recognition, and funding. The intervention of the factions in the process of selecting which candidates would receive the party's endorsement had a decisive influence on the formation of a candidate's support base, and it was the factions that provided candidates with political funds, both openly and otherwise. And once its candidates were elected, the faction would hone their skills in the policy areas in which it excelled, further strengthening their base. The fact that the number of factions gradually declined over the course of the LDP's history is probably not unrelated to the number of seats per constituency in the multiple-seat electoral districts of the House of Representatives before the 1994 overhaul. There is also a good possibility that the policy-related orientations of each of the factions became more pronounced as the result of rational choices made for the purpose of developing a power base. Seen in this light, the factions were not relics of a premodern era but were rational organizations for conducting electoral activities.

While the support groups for individual candidates of course existed to get those candidates elected, they also functioned as the units through which the LDP conducted activities directed at people in specific regions and occupational fields. To put it another way, the LDP was able to set up a network of regional organizations only by using the individual support groups of Diet members as substitutes. The best known of these support groups was Tanaka Kakuei's Etsuzankai. In addition to supporting his campaigns in the former third electoral district of Niigata, Etsuzankai connected the district's voters with Tanaka and, through him, connected the district with the LDP. But if a legislator left the LDP for another party, as happened not infrequently during the period of political realignment in the 1990s, the support group would follow the legislator, leaving the party with a gap in its organization.

The third pillar of LDP politics was its bottom-up approach to the decision-making process. Before the government submitted bills to the Diet, it would send them to the LDP, where they would be examined by the Policy Research Council and the General Council. The former in particular would make adjustments involving policy content. The Policy Research Council had policy divisions corresponding to the ministries and agencies of the central government, and the Diet members who served in a particular division for a long time and became deeply familiar with policy in that area were the prime examples of the so-called *zoku giin*, the "tribes" of legislators closely associated with a particular ministry. It was not uncommon for the leaders of policy divisions to make the final decision about proposed changes in government bills, but the junior members had plenty of opportunity to make themselves heard in the debate process. At least one of the reasons the LDP came to be described as a "free and vigorous" party was the participation of the younger legislators in these debates. The adoption of this approach led to young Diet members specializing and honing their own areas of expertise.

As Tatebayashi revealed in detail in his research, these three characteristic pillars of LDP politics were all closely related to the system of multiple-seat electoral districts. Under that system, in which most lower house districts selected from three to five Diet members, it was common for two or more LDP legislators to be elected from a single district. With the party fielding multiple candidates in the same district, merely having the party's endorsement was not enough to give an individual candidate the name recognition needed to wage a successful campaign; the candidates required assistance from a faction within the party and from a personal support group. The factions and support groups were able to justify the backing they gave to particular candidates as not being directed against other LDP candidates. Another characteristic of the multiple-seat system was that it was possible and even necessary for LDP candidates to develop areas of specialization and distinguish themselves from other candidates in their own party.

The Impact of the 1990s Reforms

The overhaul of the lower house electoral system in 1994 transformed the basic conditions on which LDP politics had been premised. The multiple-seat constituencies were replaced by a combination of single-member districts and regional proportional-representation districts. And though the proportional-representation districts send multiple members to the Diet, under this new system the LDP has sharply limited the number of candidates who are allowed to run just in a proportional-representation race; for the most part the proportional seats are assigned to people who have run but lost in single-member districts, with priority given to those who came closest to winning in their local district races. So the candidates focus overwhelmingly on winning votes in their home district.

Under the new system of single-seat districts, the key question is whether a candidate can win the exclusive endorsement of a major party. There is no longer any place for a second or third candidate from the same party, and it has also become exceedingly difficult for an independent candidate to win. The level of backing a candidate could receive from a faction or support group has paled in comparison to the importance of being the party's only officially endorsed candidate in the district. And while it was possible to win with about 20 to 30 percent of the vote under the old system, candidates now need around 50 percent; this has made expertise in a particular policy area much less useful as a campaign tool than a something-for-everyone approach of providing services to the district's constituents. In essence, factions, support groups, and the bottom-up approach based on specialization ceased to be useful tools in winning elections.

The other major set of reforms adopted in the 1990s consisted of the administrative reforms undertaken by the Hashimoto administration in 1996–97. While much of the notice paid to these reforms has concerned the name changes of the central government's ministries and agencies and the fact that their number has been reduced through consolidation, the real essence of the reforms was the increase in the power of the prime minister. In particular, whereas cabinet ministers in the past were almost always tied to a particular ministry or agency, there is now the option of naming special ministers of state to handle major areas of policy without assigning them to a particular ministry. The prime minister can also designate political appointees as special advisors. The Cabinet Office was set up as an executive staff body, including the specially designated ministers of state, advisors, and a number of policy councils, such as the newly created Council on Economic and Fiscal Policy (CEFP). These changes have created a base allowing the prime minister to make policy decisions free of the restraints that were formerly imposed by the ruling party and the ministries. This was a reform that clearly shifted the orientation of the cabinet from being a body resting on the top of the bureaucratic apparatus to being an executive organization that makes political decisions and directs the bureaucracy in line with these decisions.

Though the overhaul of the electoral system was enacted in the first half of the 1990s, it did not change the actions of politicians, political parties, and groups of supporters overnight. While research on the elections in that decade held under the new system reveals shifts in voting patterns and electoral results at a relatively early stage, it has also been noted that there was a powerful element of continuity in the actions of political parties and interest groups. Change was slow to come. What made a bigger difference was that the implementation of the Hashimoto reforms, namely, the reorganization of the administrative structure and the establishment of the Cabinet Office, did not actually happen until 2001. Up to that point, even though electoral reform had changed the structure of power within the LDP, the prime minister (and LDP president) lacked the resources to take advantage of this change. And even when the resources became available, the administration of Prime Minister Mori Yoshirō, who preceded Koizumi, seemed to lack the will to use them.

A Powerful Executive Staff

It was the Koizumi administration that converted the structural changes brought by electoral and administrative reform into a transformation of the policymaking process. From the start, Koizumi completely ignored the recommendations of faction leaders with regard to cabinet appointments, and he has since then broken with earlier practice by keeping many of his ministers in their positions for extended terms instead of rotating them frequently and by appointing relatively young people to cabinet posts. And he has also transformed the role of the LDP president. In the past, though the prime minister was also the titular head of the LDP, in practice it was rare for him to make his voice heard concerning party operations. Instead it was the LDP secretary-general who ordinarily called the shots within the party. But under Koizumi the secretary-general may either be a figure like Abe Shinzō, who served prominently as the party's "face," or one like the current incumbent, Takebe Tsutomu, who functions as a loyal subordinate of the party president; in neither case is he expected to act as an independent coordinator of party affairs. No longer are we likely to see anything like the spectacle that occurred in 1993, when LDP secretary-general Kajiyama Seiroku rejected the instructions of Miyazawa Kiichi—who was then prime minister and LDP president—to pull the party together in order to enact electoral reform legislation (a move that contributed to the fall of the Miyazawa administration, followed by a short period in which a non-LDP coalition was in power).

Koizumi has used his power to make political appointments by selecting Keio University professor Takenaka Heizō to serve in his cabinet as a state minister and naming former diplomat Okamoto Yukio as his top diplomatic advisor. He has also made good use of the CEFP. Overall, the Cabinet Office—his executive staff organ, including the political appointees and bodies like the CEFP—has begun to make its significance felt; these appointees and advisory councils have hammered out the basic plans for virtually all of the major policy agenda items that the Koizumi administration has handled since its launch.

The media has tended to focus on how the plans that emerge from the Cabinet Office under Koizumi get watered down during subsequent consultations with the LDP and on Koizumi's *marunage* habit of leaving all the specifics up to others. In fact, however, the resistance within the LDP to the administration's plans has been limited in scope, and the adjustments the party has made have been minor. Also, the prime minister is only keeping silent on the specifics to the extent that he judges the compromises with the LDP to be no more than fine-tuning. It is altogether too naive to expect the proposals of the prime minister's advisory organs and political appointees involving major policy changes to go through the process of review by the LDP totally unscathed. An appropriate standard for measuring the administration's success is whether or not the cabinet and executive staff can take the initiative to change policy and then maintain the basic direction of the proposed change until it is realized.

The fact that the prior approval of the ruling party is no longer necessarily received for every piece of legislation proposed by the cabinet is a typical example of the synergistic effect of changes in the LDP's power structure and the strengthening of the cabinet's executive function. Within the LDP the decision-making process on major policy issues has shifted from a bottom-up approach starting with the policy divisions of the Policy Research Council to a top-down model guided by the party president. While debate within the party is allowed and the necessary mechanisms to that end have been preserved, the final decision lies not with the Policy Research Council or the General Council but with the party president. The secretary-general and the party vice-president do not get involved in the consultations.

With these changes in the party, the prime minister / LDP president has lost what was formerly the prime component of the support apparatus for the process of making policy decisions. But thanks to the administrative reforms, the prime minister has the powerful support of his executive staff in the Cabinet Office. And because of the change in the electoral system, LDP legislators who want the party's endorsement for their reelection ultimately have no choice but to follow the prime minister's lead. These are the major reasons why Koizumi was able to go over the party's head on both reform of the highway-related public corporations and postal reform,

two policy issues on which he and the Cabinet Office had placed priority.

It is unclear whether Koizumi had a clear vision of this set of changes in the power structure at the time he ran for election as LDP president in 2001. His talk of "destroying the LDP" may have just been one of the bluffs that he makes from time to time. But it appears that after he took office Koizumi gradually became aware of the major changes in the institutional environment surrounding the prime minister and party president. Early in his term he apparently considered joining forces with the opposition Democratic Party of Japan (DPJ) to thwart the so-called forces of resistance within his own party. But he gradually changed course, probably because he thought that using the latent power the prime minister had been given by systemic reform removed the need to rely on the opposition or on public opinion.

In handling the situation, Koizumi has doubtless listened to advice from his political brain trust. But the important point is that he was the first prime minister to convert the groundwork laid by the reforms of the 1990s into his own personal political resources. In doing so he became not a "presidential" prime minister, as people like Makihara suggest, but rather the most "prime ministerial" of prime ministers since the formation of the LDP in 1955, one who has tapped the latent power of the parliamentary cabinet system.

Post-Koizumi Prospects for the LDP and DPJ

The changes in the process of formulating policy that have taken place under the Koizumi administration represent a change in the political structure as a whole, triggered by the systemic reforms of the 1990s. For this reason, there is little possibility that the situation will revert to its previous state after Koizumi steps down (probably upon completing his current term as LDP president in September 2006). Whether in contesting elections, serving as the LDP's regional organizations, or developing new talent, the factions and support groups no longer have much meaning. And while the divisions of the Policy Research Council will likely continue to deal with policy issues in specialized areas, being well-versed in a particular field alone will not help candidates appeal to enough voters to win election, so the significance of serving in a policy division for a long period of time is sure to weaken.

Moving in to fill the gaps left by these changes is the growing power of the executive core consisting of the cabinet and its support staff, along with a handful of senior LDP officers. In short, the LDP organizational edifice that supported postwar Japanese politics has been almost completely transformed. Following its failure even to agree on a candidate to back in last year's LDP presidential election, the party's largest faction, led by former prime minister Hashimoto, essentially collapsed. This had less to do with one-off events, such as scandals and the loss of veteran politicians due to retirement or electoral defeat, than with the fact that factions as a whole have lost their meaning. As for the support groups, though there is no doubt that they are still important to many legislators, almost all of them were put together in the days of the old multiple-seat constituencies. It seems doubtful that new candidates selected by the LDP to run in single-member districts through a process of open recruitment will be able to create and maintain such support groups. The voters that LDP candidates need to court most diligently are not the members of their own party but those who are unaffiliated and those who back the New Kōmeitō, the LDP's partner in the ruling coalition. Once Diet members decide that support groups no longer make sense, they are likely to fade away.

As Tatebayashi has noted, the directory of policy division members that used to be sold at a shop in LDP headquarters is no longer being produced. This is a profoundly symbolic development. For the average Diet member, belonging to a policy division no longer offers much in the way of voter appeal, and for the people and groups that submit petitions and carry out other political lobbying, it is clear that policy divisions are no longer the arenas where policy is decided.

The biggest problem facing the LDP is that the existing structure of political authority has collapsed and the setup that has emerged in its place allows little room for involvement by the party. If the new structure left ample space for the LDP to get involved, it would merely need to adjust its mode of operation to match the new procedures. But what has become apparent since the birth of the Koizumi administration is that it is not simply the procedures that have changed but the locus of effective decision-making power. In the past the LDP viewed the prime minister and cabinet as akin to a *mikoshi* (portable shrine)—the party had hold of the leadership and could carry it in whatever direction it wished. These days, though, it would be more apt to liken the prime minister to the driver of a car and the party members to the tires. When the driver turns the steering wheel, the tires cannot resist the change of direction, and if they try to resist, they will simply be replaced.

I view what has happened as not a mere change in the policymaking procedures but as a change in the structure of political authority, a transformation of the system. Along with everything else, this means a major opportunity awaits the DPJ, the largest opposition party. While many have noted that the LDP may have difficulty finding a suitable candidate to succeed Koizumi, in my view a more serious problem for the party is that it has been unable to adapt to the new structure of political authority. If the DPJ, by contrast, fully comprehends the decisive importance of executive authority under the new structure and lays the necessary groundwork to deal with this structure, it can probably hold on to power for a relatively long period in the event that it defeats the LDP in a post-Koizumi general election and forms a government.

More specifically, the fate of a DPJ administration will rest on its ability to secure talent to fill key executive posts, particularly as political appointees in the Cabinet Office. To this end the party must not only expand its existing staff organization but also cease the superficial and rather meaningless attacks on the bureaucracy that have been its stock in trade; it needs to create the conditions that will allow it to govern with the combined support of private-sector think tanks and the organs of the bureaucracy. This is no time for the party to content itself with hackneyed criticisms and efforts to bring down opponents by exposing scandals. The DPJ plans to establish its own in-house think tank this year; this is an appropriate move.

The same sort of requirements of course also apply to the LDP. But as long as memories of its years of success remain strong, it will not be easy for the party to rebuild its organization. And in view of voters' fatigue with the LDP's long rule, the party may find itself forced to yield power to the DPJ. It is important not to forget, however, that even though support for the LDP has been following a long-term downward trend, it still has the backing of 30 percent of the public, far more than the second-place DPJ. If it reconsiders its organizational arrangements and its relationship with the executive and manages to construct an organization suitable for the present institutional setup, the LDP should be able to make a comeback. It would not be a bad thing at all for Japanese politics to have two major parties pursuing this type of competition.

The 1990s Were Not a "Lost Decade"

In this article I have tried to show that the procedural changes in the policymaking process that have emerged under the Koizumi administration are the realization of the potential generated by the systemic reforms of the 1990s and that they reflect a transformation in the structure of political authority. They are confronting the LDP with a serious crisis and presenting the DPJ a crucial opportunity. The course of politics in the post-Koizumi era—for more than a decade, perhaps—will depend on how the two parties respond to these new circumstances. The outcome will of course also affect the policy choices that will be made. Japanese politics is approaching a fork in the road.

From this we can also see that the 1990s were not a "lost decade" for Japanese politics. The reform of the electoral system and the major overhaul of the nation's administrative organs were bound to have some impact on the policymaking process and the political power structure. The framework of Japanese politics and government in the postwar period, including the system of multiple-seat constituencies, was sturdy and had endured for a long time. It was thus unrealistic to expect that the 1990s reforms would produce an immediate transformation. While at first it may have appeared that nothing had changed and that the old system was continuing through inertia, the effects of the new system are gradually emerging. This is a much more natural way of looking at the situation. It is not appropriate to be hasty in judging the impact of a systemic transformation.

Politics is an activity that is carried out by humans, and while the human ability to learn has its limits, people do in fact learn. Even if this ability is not sufficient to advance the nature of politics itself, it can allow the people of a particular time to shape politics in a way that makes sense to them. The biggest hope of democratic politics lies in the fact that many more such people are engaged in the political process than is the case with other forms of government. This applies to Japanese democracy as well. What we see taking place today represents a change in Japanese politics based on a clearly comprehensible chain of causation. In this context it should be possible to debate the procedures and realities of policymaking on a level transcending simple questions of good or bad.

We must now free ourselves of the notion that the 1990s were a lost decade and reevaluate the present situation based on a dispassionate review of what has taken place in Japanese politics since that time. That, I strongly believe, is what is required at this juncture.

Courtesy of Japan Echo.

English version originally published in *Japan Echo* 32, no. 3 (2005): 38–43. Translated from "Koizumi chōki seiken o sasaeru seiji kaikaku no seika," *Chūō Kōron* (April 2005): 176–84 (courtesy of Chūōkōron Shinsha).

III-(3) Political Reform in Japan

Yamaguchi Jirō

Japan Review of International Affairs, 2002

In the 1990s Japan witnessed a veritable procession of reforms, which resulted, among other things, in major changes in the nation's electoral system and central administrative apparatus. Yet despite these efforts at reform, a series of scandals since the late 1990s have borne witness to ongoing corruption in both the political and administrative spheres of government. Among the most conspicuous have been the scandals in the Ministry of Foreign Affairs, which in 2001 became the object of widespread disenchantment and scorn after high-ranking officials were found to have misappropriated public funds. This year it was implicated in irregularities centering on influence peddling and bid rigging by veteran Liberal Democratic Party (LDP) politician Suzuki Muneo.

These circumstances oblige us to reassess the value of the political and administrative reforms of the 1990s. Clearly, the reform process is far from complete; in fact one is forced to conclude that the real issues have been left unaddressed. In the following, I would like to analyze the reforms and the issues driving them from a new perspective.

Input, Conversion, and Output

Needless to say, reform should not end with alterations in the electoral system or the administrative structure, since the problems to be addressed permeate the entire political system. Below I make use of David Easton's political-systems model to achieve a more comprehensive and integrated understanding of the problems afflicting Japan's political setup as a whole.

The Easton model posits an input-output cycle connecting society and government. A key stage

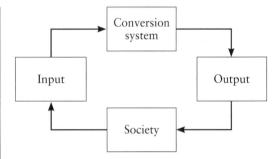

Figure 1. Easton Model of the Political System

of this cycle is conversion, the process by which output in the form of specific legislation, budgetary allocations, plans, and so forth is generated from the policy issues input into the system (Figure 1).

Input occurs through all the varied mechanisms by which the people participate directly or indirectly in the political process. Obviously, the electoral system is an extremely important component of the input system. The major issues in the early 1990s with regard to Japanese elections were unequal representation resulting from malapportionment and the predominance of pork-barrel politics, which denied voters the opportunity to choose how they wanted the government to be run and to express their policy preferences.

Unfortunately, the switch from multiseat to single-member districts combined with a system of proportional representation—the centerpiece of Japan's electoral reform—was not an effective response to these problems. To the contrary, with today's single-member districts the disparity in the value of the vote has become fixed. And given the centralized power and discretionary administration that characterize Japan's output system—which we will examine shortly—single-seat districts could only intensify the focus on protecting special interests and rewarding constituents and contributors. This is because LDP politicians, with their traditional connections to and influence on administrative government, are at an overwhelming advantage in districts that depend on allocations from the central government's budget.

But there is more to the input system than elections. The obstacles to citizen participation in setting the policy agenda led to the rise of local referendums in the second half of the 1990s. Decisions on large-scale public-works projects and policies with a major environmental impact on local areas were being made far away in legislative chambers and government offices and then presented to citizens as a fait accompli. Referendums were seen as a key strategy for breaking into this closed decision-making apparatus. Such direct-democracy movements are significant as a means of injecting into the realm of policymaking values and goals to which representative democracy has shown itself indifferent or hostile. If reform of the input system is to succeed, it is necessary to expand such opportunities for citizens to articulate their views with regard to public policy.

Let us move now to issues in the conversion system. The most important aspect of the conversion process is the formulation of specific goals from the policy issues raised in the input process and the crafting of policies to achieve those goals—in other words, policymaking. A key characteristic of Japanese government in the era since the end of World War II has been the bureaucracy's monopoly on policymaking know-how. Typically, the bureaucracy itself has led the way in acknowledging a problem and crafting policies to respond to it. In some cases, problems that the bureaucracy showed no inclination to address worsened until they provoked intense public dissatisfaction, at which point political leaders finally instructed the bureaucrats to craft countermeasures. In still other instances, foreign pressure played a key role in spurring or accelerating a policy response.

On paper, the Japanese political system gives a great deal of policymaking power to the cabinet and the ruling party. But as the years passed with no change in government, significant policy differences between the bureaucracy and ruling politicians disappeared. Indeed, each agency of the bureaucracy routinely cooperated with a corresponding division within the LDP's own policymaking apparatus to achieve the common goal of expanding its organization and securing more funds for the agency's operation. As a consequence of this close relationship, efforts to hold civil servants responsible for their failures or to limit the influence of vested interests found no place in the policymaking process. In fact, the role of political leadership in that process was not even regarded as an issue. It was only in the 1990s, when the LDP's monopoly on power was finally broken, that reformist leaders attempted to shift to a new paradigm with moves to curtail the power of the bureaucracy, force budget cuts, and eliminate collusion with vested interests. At this point, the absence of capable political leadership from the conversion process became painfully evident. At the same time, the administrative apparatus, hampered by an inefficient and sectionalist division of labor, clearly lacked the ability to undertake the kind of overarching reforms needed to cope with the dramatic changes overtaking Japan.

Against this background, the reorganization of the administrative apparatus and strengthening of cabinet functions carried out by the government of Hashimoto Ryūtarō in the late 1990s constituted an extremely important chapter in the history of political reform in postwar Japan. The explicit intent of these new policies was to transfer leadership from the administrative to the political sector, and in this sense, the Hashimoto administration demonstrated an accurate understanding of the basic problem. Unfortunately, the administrative and Diet reforms of the late 1990s did not achieve their stated goal of shifting power to elected officials. Instead, the problem has worsened, as evidenced by the failure of the country's political leaders to crack down on recent cases of corruption in the Ministry of Agriculture, Forestry, and Fisheries and the Foreign Ministry.

It is more accurate to say that the existing politicians are not capable of handling a reformed government system.

Let us now turn to output, the third basic element of Easton's model. The majority of the numerous administrative scandals to come out of Japan in the 1990s related to flaws in the output system, which the administrative branch of government is in fact charged with operating and controlling. In Japan, administrative government has two major characteristics. One is the extremely broad discretion with regard to the redistribution of wealth and the coordination of conflicting interests that is exercised by civil servants. The other is the minutely defined relationship between the central and local governments that obligates local bodies to implement national policy (the output system). These two features were responsible for many of the assorted evils that surfaced during the 1990s.

The most glaring example was corruption arising from the Ministry of Finance's discretionary power over the finance industry. Because the power wielded by government officials can have a huge impact on a bank's fortunes, the banks were at great pains to learn which way the wind was blowing at the Ministry of Finance, and this they did by courting its officials on many different fronts. Wining and dining of finance bureaucrats became routine.

However, the finance industry, while presenting some of the most egregious examples of this sort of corruption, was by no means atypical. The decade of the 1990s is awash in examples of unethical dealings between various corporate executives and the administrative officials who exercised broad powers in the granting of licenses, permits, and subsidies. This widespread phenomenon should be approached not as a sign of declining morals but as a pathology fostered by discretionary administration.

As a variation on this pattern of corruption, the decade also witnessed a nationwide epidemic of scandals involving the entertaining of central bureaucrats by local officials eager to win subsidies. This pernicious practice came to light following the enforcement of the information disclosure ordinances in many local governments, as local

civil servants came under scrutiny for such fund misappropriations as business trips not taken and lavish meals. Regarded by local bureaucrats as a necessary evil given the extreme centralization of power in Japan, the common practice of entertaining central bureaucrats caused an eruption of public outrage when it came to taxpayers' attention. Again, however, the phenomenon should be seen not as an example of moral failure but as a distillation of the evils of a centralized system in which the national government wields almost absolute power over local entities through the distribution of subsidies. The reason decentralization also emerged as a hot political topic during the 1990s was that the inefficiency of this output system had risen to an intolerable level.

A meaningful reform of the output system would include enforcement of the Administrative Procedure Act to minimize the bureaucracy's discretionary power, the enactment of the Information Disclosure Act, and steps to devolve power to the prefectures. Improving the transparency and fairness of Japan's output system through these steps is an important task facing the nation.

Why Reform Has Failed

As the foregoing suggests, in the 1990s the Japanese political system in its entirety was suffering from what one might term "system fatigue," which revealed itself in various ills of increasing severity. Unfortunately, the reforms undertaken one after another during this period were not designed to address the pervasive structural problems underlying those ills. As a result, despite the reform campaigns of the 1990s, meaningful reform of the political system remains a daunting task for Japan in the twenty-first century.

In truth, the failure of those campaigns is greater than that suggested by the foregoing statement. For by channeling the nation's political energies into superficial "quick fixes," they ensured that the underlying problems would be with us for years to come.

The fact is that "reform" during this period was first and foremost the currency with which politicians and parties sought to buy the public's support, each trying to outbid the other. Since the middle of the 1990s, the ruling coalition has held on to power not by building reform on reform in response to various problems but by waving the banner of reform as vigorously as possible and showing itself to be busily occupied with systemic change. Large-scale reforms, such as those altering the electoral system or the ministries of the state, are big issues for the politicians and bureaucrats affected and make for good political drama. They attract public notice and fuel faith in systemic reform as a silver bullet to solve all the nation's ills. The politicians who direct these efforts become a magnet for the public's hopes for positive change. Many Japanese were convinced that the problems would be solved once these systems were reformed, and no one ever bothered to audit the results or grapple seriously with the problems that persisted. This was partly because the focus of reform kept shifting.

Through the 1990s politicians and parties played "top this" with reform; first the electoral system, then the administrative apparatus, and finally the Constitution itself became the object of reformist zeal. To be sure, the electoral system and the administrative apparatus are important elements of the political system, but they have no direct bearing on the fundamental issues, namely, the clash of interests and the value distribution within our society. They are simply the internal rules governing the activities of government "professionals"—namely, politicians and bureaucrats—and the intense focus on these areas bespeaks the capabilities of Japan's politicians and political parties. Lacking the ability to take on such substantive policy challenges as reducing the fiscal deficit, restructuring the social security system, or promoting a shift in the country's economic structure, political parties instead fabricated an empty reform agenda divorced from the genuine issues of society and devoted their time to deliberating it. Their failure to address the real reform issues was one reason for the phenomenon that catapulted Koizumi Junichirō to the prime minister's seat, where for some time he enjoyed unprecedented popularity.

The Failure of the Opposition

This brings us to another reason for the failure of reform, namely, the deficiencies of the political actors whose job it was to initiate reform—particularly the opposition parties. In the 1990s Japan's political parties were continually regrouping and realigning themselves, as parties split, dissolved, and merged. Yet with all that realignment, we have yet to see the emergence of an opposition party with the wherewithal to rule. The disarray of the opposition parties today stands in stark contrast to the strength of the LDP, which remains in the driver's seat despite a series of crises in the 1990s. Epitomizing this state of affairs is the fuddled state of the Democratic Party of Japan (DPJ)—currently the largest opposition party—since Koizumi rose to power.

A number of reasons have been given for the failure of Japanese politics to produce a viable opposition force. One theory is that Japan's entrenched political machinery, built around political patronage, is basically hostile to the survival of any opposition party, and the switch to single-seat districts has made it even more so. It is certainly the case that the Liberal Democrats' traditional support base, including most of the business community, the agricultural cooperatives, and such professional organizations as the Japan Medical Association, has generally remained faithful to the LDP, while the political clout of organized labor, long the mainstay of the opposition, has waned dramatically. It could be argued that any opposition party would be hard pressed to find a support base in such an environment.

Still, in many ways the time has been ripe for the emergence of a viable, credible opposition. Public sentiment has rarely been more fluid than it is today, and voting trends in local elections indicate that the LDP's hold has been loosening. Yet the eagerly anticipated formation of a new party capable of drawing in these disaffected voters has yet to materialize.

Much of the blame for the absence of a viable alternative to the LDP today must go to the Social Democratic Party (formerly the Japan Socialist Party), for decades Japan's largest opposition force. Lacking a clear political strategy, it splintered and fell into a sharp decline in the 1990s, missing a golden opportunity to transform itself into an opposition party with the capacity to govern. The SDP's credibility as a party was fatally damaged when it reversed its long-standing position on security in order to enter into a coalition with the LDP and then tried to win back disaffected supporters with lame excuses. More fundamentally, despite its new name, the SDP never made the intellectual effort needed to shift from an outmoded socialism to a social democratic ideology suited to a changing world. In this respect, Japan's SDP stands in stark contrast to the social democratic parties of Britain and Germany, which skillfully adapted their platforms to address the phenomenon of globalization and succeeded in wresting power from their conservative rivals in the late 1990s. In Japan, no single opposition party possessed a clear vision for economic, administrative, and fiscal reform, and as a result, attempts to offer voters a viable alternative to the LDP never got farther than a patchwork alliance of anti-LDP parties.

The Koizumi Phenomenon

The inauguration of the Koizumi administration in April 2001 and the extraordinary popularity Koizumi enjoyed for about one year can be seen as a phenomenon brought about by this absence of a credible opposition. During the administration of Mori Yoshirō, support for the LDP had sunk to the point where analysts were designating it a rejected party. Support for the brash, iconoclastic Koizumi sprang from this intense backlash against the "old LDP" and the style of politics associated with it. For in fact, in his apparent determination to put an end to politics as usual, Koizumi was both more straightforward and more convincing than the DPJ. A year into his administration, the specifics of the "structural reform" he claimed to be pursuing remained unclear; nor was it clear whether structural reform was indeed a prerequisite for an economic recovery or the other way around. Still, Koizumi continued to enjoy tremendous public support simply in appreciation of his ongoing jousts with mainstream LDP leaders. And with the DPJ doing little more than shouting catcalls from the peanut gallery, Koizumi managed to look like a leader by comparison.

Japanese politics over the last ten years has been a story of reform unrealized. Despite strong public support for substantive reform, the opposition forces failed to form a political party capable of advancing such reform and so allowed the LDP to regain and maintain control of the government.

But an even more fundamental reason reform did not succeed, as we have seen, was the failure of those in power to approach it from a clear understanding of the big picture. With these general points in mind, I would like to analyze the real reform issues of the 1990s and discuss in some detail the approach by which various political forces would address them.

Successful Models of Social Democracy

Politicians, bureaucrats, and business leaders who favor deregulation and other neoliberal reforms are fond of characterizing postwar Japan's politico-economic system as "a socialist (or social democratic) success story." It seems odd to label as socialist a nation ruled almost continually by the LDP, a conservative party. The fact that many distinguished politicians and bureaucrats nevertheless describe Japan's postwar order in those terms suggests that the Japanese understanding of socialism and social democracy differs somewhat from that commonly held elsewhere in the world. It also seems to me that this tendency to speak of postwar Japan as a "socialist success story" provides a clue for understanding some of the basic features of the Japanese politico-economic system.

There are some basic features of the postwar Japanese economy on which almost everyone agrees. These are (1) that it developed at an extremely rapid pace; (2) that it is subject to much government intervention in the form of regulations, public investment, and so forth; and (3) that it created a society with a relatively small individual or regional economic disparities—a society, in effect, in which everyone belonged to the middle class. Almost all media discussions of economic policy in Japan are predicated on these shared perceptions.

It is usually the second point that receives the strongest emphasis, as commentators stress the role of Japan's regulatory regime in creating an industrial order that ensures the survival of the weakest, thus minimizing the role of competition. They note as well the tendency to concentrate public investment in the poorer rural prefectures, a policy reflecting the important place of the farm sector in the LDP's support base. These two factors are thought to have contributed greatly to the leveling of Japanese society.

The features listed above have been widely cited as ingredients in the success that Japan as a nation enjoyed in terms of economic affluence and social and political stability right up through the 1980s. In the 1990s, however, with the nation mired in a recession brought on by the bursting of the bubble economy, and global competition intensifying to boot, the aforementioned features of the Japanese system became a hindrance, suppressing economic vitality and inhibiting the attainment of greater efficiency. Within this context, advocates of reform began using the term "social democracy" in reference to the postwar Japanese system's redistribution of assets and dampening of competition. This view equated Japan's failure to adapt to the new global capitalism with the defeat of socialism in Europe and elsewhere. Thus, for the neoliberal crowd, the basic theme of reform in Japan was "a farewell to social democracy."

Of course, Japan is not a social democracy in the correct sense of the term. The percentage of the national budget devoted to welfare and social security programs is low compared with European countries. Policies to support women in the labor force are also very weak. The stable employment and relatively small income disparities for which postwar Japan was noted were not brought about by social policies implemented under pressure from organized labor as in Europe. The reason for these phenomena is that in Japan, expenditure on public fixed capital formation is unusually high as a percentage of gross domestic product (GDP). Put in concrete terms, the redistribution and equalization of assets seen in Japan has resulted primarily from policies and projects pushed by the LDP to protect and reward the construction industry, a major source of its strength, together with the local ripple effects of such projects—not from social democratic policies, as neoliberal-leaning economists and politicians have suggested. Nonetheless, by probing the circumstances that have given rise to this misconception, we can gain a better understanding of the nature of redistribution and egalitarianism within the Japanese system.

Characterizing the Socioeconomic System

We can gain a better grasp of the distinctive features of the Japanese socioeconomic system by analyzing the government's mode of involvement in society and the economy. A good way to do this is to plot a position relative to two axes—one representing the spectrum from discretionary to universal policy, and the other the spectrum from individual to socialized risk.

The discretionary-universal axis measures the fairness and uniformity of the government's involvement via policies pertaining to the regulation of industry and the distribution of profits. By the same token, it measures the degree of discretion exercised by the government agencies responsible for implementing those policies.

In terms of the distribution of benefits, a universal policy is one that aims for uniformity through the implementation or expansion of such comprehensive systems as long-term care insurance, pensions, and the like or by increasing the budget for systems like public education. In respect to the regulation of industry, a universal policy applies the rules strictly and uniformly to ensure fair competition and consumer safety.

Discretionary policies, on the other hand, confer benefits selectively on certain groups at the discretion of the policymakers, such as subsidies or tax breaks for specific regions or industries. Discretionary regulatory policies, meanwhile, are policies that call for an ad hoc decision each time an issue arises between the regulated and the regulators, instead of applying the same rules to each situation; the classic example is the "administrative guidance" so common in Japan. Here the bureaucracy wields tremendous discretion in deciding whether to apply the official rules, how strictly to apply them, or even whether to invent an ad hoc regulation for the situation at hand.

The second axis, socialized versus individual risk, gauges the degree to which society as a whole shares and lightens the individual's responsibility with respect to possible losses, injuries, disasters, and so forth. In the other direction, it gauges the degree to which the principles of individual responsibility and free competition prevail.

Market purists place the greatest emphasis on individual responsibility and thus individual risk, insisting that each person assume the risk of losing his or her job, going bankrupt, falling ill, and so forth. Policies associated with this orientation include tax cuts, deregulation, and other measures that call on each individual to take on the competition and accept responsibility for the outcome. In opposition to this thinking are those who insist that individuals may find themselves sick or unemployed through no fault of their own and that society as a whole should assume the risk and come to the aid of people who happen to meet such misfortune. They also believe that regulations governing the behavior of individuals and corporations are necessary to prevent environmental destruction and ensure consumer safety. With respect to the distribution of risk, policies associated with this orientation emphasize the use of tax revenues or social insurance premiums to pay for things like universal pensions and health care. Where regulation is concerned, policies reflecting this school of thought strive to minimize risk to the consumer through a regulatory regime, even if it means higher prices or fees than would result from free competition in a deregulated environment.

Using both axes, we can categorize policies according to the scheme shown in Figure 2. This process will aid us as we explore the reasons Japan's socioeconomic system has been termed socialistic or social democratic.

The first reason is that the Japanese system has functioned to socialize risk through public-works projects in the rural prefectures and through a regulated, uncompetitive environment, such as that embodied by the "convoy system" of the finance industry. As we have already seen, Japan's outlay for social programs is relatively low as a percentage of GDP, while its outlay for public capital

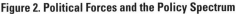

Figure 2. Political Forces and the Policy Spectrum

formation relative to GDP is three times that seen in the Western industrial nations. This reflects the government's generosity toward the rural prefectures through public works, which have helped create jobs in those regions. In addition, by curbing competition through its regulatory policies, the government has coddled such uncompetitive industries as agriculture and distribution and made them lucrative. The government has indirectly maintained a minimum living standard through public-works projects and regulations that allow companies to operate without regard for profitability or efficiency, and this has led some to describe the system as a social democracy.

The second basis for the label "social democracy" is the tremendous power wielded by the state bureaucracy by virtue of its discretion in the implementation of government policy. The majority of public-works projects are made possible by subsidies from the central government, and the division of the local-subsidy pie among the various prefectures is left to the discretion of the aforementioned bureaucrats. Another source of the mandarins' power lies in their administration of regulations, carried out not in keeping with clear and specific rules but through "administrative guidance"—in other words, ad hoc regulation adjusted to the situation at hand.

In short, the LDP has constructed a strong safety net beneath the weaker elements of the economy—be they individuals, companies, or prefectures—by socializing risk with subsidies and through such regulatory practices as the convoy system. At the same time, it has distributed profits at its own discretion through patronage and bid rigging.

The pitfalls of such a politico-economic system became painfully apparent in the 1990s, with the advance of globalization. One problem is the strain on government finances. Since the collapse of the bubble economy of the 1980s, stimulus measures centered on public works have helped prevent serious unemployment problems in the rural prefectures, but as a result Japan has accumulated a national debt of almost ¥700 trillion, the largest of any industrial nation. This is putting the entire economy at risk. The second problem is that competition-curbing regulation of industries has served to buoy up prices, creating a "high-cost society." The economic inefficiency resulting from this state of affairs can be regarded as the upshot of "Japanese-style socialism." The third problem is that the lack of transparency in this type of system breeds corruption, as many Japanese came to realize in the 1990s through a series of financial scandals involving bureaucrats as well as politicians. According to the neoliberal critics of "Japanese-style socialism," the problem was that the big corporations and wealthy individuals that drive the economy were forced to pay the price for the redistribution of assets in the form of high taxes, costs, and fees, and the bureaucrats and politicians used that money wastefully, resulting in inefficiency and corruption.

In the midst of all this, Koizumi made his entrance, calling for "structural reform." If we can take the prime minister's advisors at their word, the Koizumi administration's structural reform is aimed at instituting universal policies based on clear criteria, such as efficiency and profitability, and eliminating intervention by bureaucrats and politicians. This is the argument behind Koizumi's drive to privatize Japan's quasigovernmental organizations. The administration and its advisors also stress policies that will provide incentives for more individual and corporate risk-taking in a competitive environment. Koizumi also calls for more individual responsibility in such areas of risk as health care and pensions. The reform of the health-care system to shift more of the cost to patients and recent proposals for tax reform are all in line with the administration's emphasis on individual risk. The principle of individual responsibility is also being applied to the disposal of nonperforming assets; creditors are calling in their loans to small businesses, and bankruptcies are mounting.

The Japanese people are fed up with privileges that high-ranking bureaucrats have enjoyed. Therefore, it is quite natural that they support Koizumi's initiative for slashing inefficient and ineffective public sectors. However, the question now is whether this kind of structural reform, designed to root out the old "socialism," will put Japan in a position to solve its current economic woes, including continuing deflation, increasing unemployment, and financial jitters. Thus far, there is no indication that it will.

Whither the Koizumi Government?

Needless to say, Koizumi's structural-reform campaign is facing fierce resistance from the forces that have sustained the "socialist" policies of the past. Where the struggle within the LDP is concerned, the most likely outcome is a compromise rather than a clear victory for either side. In terms of the principles represented in Figure 2, the resulting setup is likely to emphasize individual risk on the one hand and discretionary policies on the other. The fact is that the LDP previously took steps to deregulate and open up markets back in the 1990s in response to economic globalization, but behind the scenes it practiced the same old politics of discretionary benefit distribution to cushion or console those vulnerable to competition; a typical example was the ¥6 trillion agriculture budget it pushed through the Diet to make up for its decision to open the rice market to imports. This time, however, relief will be forthcoming only in exceptional cases, as a special favor to the LDP's core supporters.

As for Koizumi's pet project, the privatization of Japan's postal services, the bill submitted to the Diet this year leaves most of the authority in the hands of the government, and private businesses are complaining that it effectively bars new entries into the market. As this example suggests, the current political dynamic seems to favor a combination of nominal reforms and continued administrative discretion as a way of maintaining the status quo.

It will be difficult for Koizumi to succeed as an agent of reform. The LDP represents such a hodgepodge of political inclinations that it can never reach a consensus on any clear-cut departure in policy, and this is the main reason its reformist leaders are hard-pressed to carry out their own policies. It is clear that the LDP has simply been taking advantage of Koizumi's anti-LDP, reformist image to hold on to its position as the ruling party, which it values above all else. And if that is the case, the only real chance for reform is a change of government. If a change of government occurs just once more, we can expect the LDP to splinter, setting in motion a more meaningful political realignment.

Searching for a Third Way in Japan

I would like to conclude by considering the kind of party needed to fill the present vacuum in Japanese party politics. What the country needs now is a political force that combines the ideals of universal policy and socialized risk. The goals of such a party would be to clean up the bureaucracy and put an end to political patronage, while at the same time laying the foundation for universal policies to protect and sustain the people—especially those buffeted by fortune—instead of leaving their fate to market forces. For example, instead of abandoning those displaced by shifts in the economic structure or devising ad hoc stopgaps one industry at a time, this party would seek to bolster unemployment insurance and strive for universal policies designed to get people back on their feet, such as government-subsidized education and training. The "welfare to work" policy of Britain's Labour government provides a good model.

If the tide of bankruptcies and unemployment continues to rise as the Koizumi administration pursues its blind quest for small government, it will be necessary above all to forge a policy to stabilize business and employment. This should be a strategic program centered on undertakings that simultaneously respond to other challenges facing Japan in the twenty-first century, such as the environment and an aging society—not the arbitrary doling out of funds or the anachronistic development and public-works projects carried out during the administrations of Obuchi Keizō and Mori Yoshirō.

At the same time, Japan desperately needs universal policies based on principles and rules. The rules for maintaining the economic system must be strict and unbending to ensure justice, while those aimed at assisting people in need should be fair and caring. As I mentioned earlier, the Koizumi administration seems to be pursuing a reform based solely on the principles of efficiency and profitability. Yet when it comes time to apply these rules to the actual economy, it reverts to the LDP's old discretionary approach. For example, regarding the disposal of nonperforming loans, the administration is not addressing the basic problem with a rational and consistent policy but merely applying band-aids here and there as the occasion demands—as in the bailout of supermarket chain Daiei. According to the rules, it should be calling for the full disclosure of bad loans, prompting the shoring up of write-off reserves, using public funds to make up the shortfall, and putting the failing banks under government control. The government needs to apply these rules strictly across the board in order to make a clean sweep of the moral hazard looming over Japan. Eliminating administrative discretion and political interference and applying the rules of capitalism consistently is a crucial prerequisite of true reform in Japan.

The other rules—the caring rules aimed at socializing risk—must also be fair and transparent. That means putting an end to the traditional LDP manner of socializing risk, as by keeping small businesses afloat and constituents employed with the special subsidies finagled through political clout. It means first seeing to it that unemployment compensation, pensions, and key social services like education and day care are reliably provided and then reforming the entire social welfare system to ensure that benefits are distributed equitably to those in need.

The policies I have just described are also those of the social democratic parties of Europe, where they are referred to as the "third way." The appellation suggests an alternative to both the welfare state built by the old social democrats (the "first way") and the cold-blooded capitalism of Thatcherism (the "second way")—that is, an economy in which market vitality coexists with a respect for humanity.

As a viable alternative to the LDP, the Japanese people need a party that can offer a third way tailored to the nation's realities. In Japan, we would have to call the first way LDP-style government for the vested interests, and the second way the American-inspired Koizumi reform. The next phase, then, should be a system that rests on the two pillars of a transparent, fair market and socialized risk to protect the health and welfare of the people—a Japanese third way.

Courtesy of the Japan Institute of International Affairs.

Originally published in the *Japan Review of International Affairs* 16, no. 3 (2002): 199–215.

III-(4) The Politics of Pension Retrenchment in Japan

Shinkawa Toshimitsu

Japanese Journal of Social Security Policy, 2003

Introduction

Pension reform is brought on the political agenda in Japan almost every five years in mandatory actuarial revaluation. Before 1985, pension reform meant the expansion of pension benefits with minimum increases in contributions. In the 1985 reform, however, the government reversed the trend by tightening the relationship between benefits and contributions. Most noteworthy is cost-containment by reducing the level of benefits, which was authorized for the first time in Japanese pension history. Benefit cuts and contribution hikes were repeated in the subsequent reforms of 1989, 1994, and 1999.[1] Pensionable ages in employees' pension schemes were raised in the 1994 and 1999 rounds. Thus, the keynote of pension reform in Japan has turned to retrenchment since the 1985 reform.

This paper aims to delineate the retrenchment process in Japan and analyze its major constraints and determinants. I argue that institution matters in the process of retrenchment in Japan as elsewhere but not in a conventional way. Institutional settings promote, rather than prevent, a change in Japan. Institutional fragmentation embedded in the Japanese pension system had caused financial tightness in specific pension schemes in the early 1980s before serious population aging took place, which compelled the government to embark on the overhaul of the pension system. I also argue that the retrenchment process in Japan can be traced considerably well with the idea of "blame avoidance."[2] Masterful skills of blame avoidance unfolded by policymakers successfully brought about the gradual and steady extension of retrenchment, but the politics of blame avoidance reached its limits in the face of accelerated population aging.

I first outline major features of the pension system in postwar Japan and clarify the influence of historical contingency and path dependency on its basic structure. Secondly, however, I argue that historically created, specific institutional settings brought about a crisis of the pension system, which in turn promoted its rearrangement. Thirdly, I introduce the idea of blame avoidance and show how it can neatly explain pension retrenchment in Japan. Finally, I address problems left unresolved, or exacerbated, by blame-avoidance politics.

1. Pension Development in Postwar Japan

Japan's pension system is based on the Bismarckian model. It is composed of occupationally fragmented social insurance schemes: Employees' Pension Insurance (EPI) for private-sector employees, various mutual-aid pension plans for governmental and paragovernmental employees, and National Pension Insurance (NPI) for those not covered by the above two types, including the self-employed and farmers. NPI provides flat-rate benefits, while employees' pension benefits are earnings-related. Employees' pension schemes used to have both flat-rate and earnings-related tiers, but the flat-rate tier was integrated with the NPI into the Basic Pension (BP) scheme in 1986.

All schemes are basically financed on a pay-as-you-go (PAYG) basis, but there is a clear difference between NPI and others. NPI is heavily subsidized by general revenue. A third of its expenditure is currently paid out of taxes, and the ratio of subsidization is scheduled to go up to half in the near future. The increase in arrears, combined with the shrinking workforce in agriculture and small independent businesses, exacerbated fiscal challenges for NPI. It is roughly estimated that a third of NPI members (those obliged to join the program) fail to pay their contributions. Since employees' schemes, on the other hand, have huge fund reserves for a PAYG scheme (for example, EPI keeps a reserve tantamount to its six-year expenditures), it is often referred to as partially funded schemes.

Occupational fragmentation, however, was not intentionally created. It was a by-product of another feature of Japan's pension system; that is, a mixture of private and public pension plans. During the turmoil following the end of World War II, the concern of public welfare was limited to the protection of the war victimized and extreme poor. Given the fact that public welfare could provide little for workers and their families, employers took the lead in responding to employees' demands. Together with company housing, lump-sum retirement payments came to be provided in major firms by the early 1950s and spread among smaller firms afterwards thanks to preferential tax treatment. The 1952 revision of the tax code made retirement payments nontaxable business expenses.

In the mid-1950s, the government embarked on the overhaul of public pension schemes as the economy got on the right track. Welfare bureaucrats hoped to reactivate EPI as an umbrella scheme covering all private-sector employees and providing major financial bases for their retirement life. Employers, however, were negative on the idea of expanding public pension schemes on the grounds that improved public pension benefits in addition to corporate retirement payments would cost too much. Employers' resistance successfully kept the level of EPI benefits low in the 1950s, reaching barely a third of its counterparts of mutual-aid schemes in 1960 (Tada 1991, 145). Such a low level of EPI benefits facilitated the proliferation of mutual-aid schemes. Employees in paragovernmental associations, such as teachers and clerks in private schools and employees of cooperatives in agriculture, forestry, and fisheries, left EPI to form their own mutual aid plans (Tada 1991, 147–53).

The level of EPI benefits was improved at last in the 1960s as a result of a compromise hammered out between welfare bureaucrats and employers. In the late 1950s, the Japan Employers' Association (JEA) demanded a change in the tax code to introduce the tax-qualified pension with the hope of leveling off annual expenses by shifting from lump-sum to pension payments. The Ministry of Health and Welfare (MHW) opposed the idea by arguing that the new corporate pension scheme would make the improvement of EPI more difficult than ever. A stalemate was broken by the JEA's proposal of Employees' Pension Funds (EPFs), which was publicized in November 1961 as a necessary condition for the improvement of employees' pensions. Accepting the proposal of the JEA, the MHW withdrew its opposition to the introduction of a new corporate pension scheme. Consequently, the tax code was revised in 1962 in such a way as to introduce the tax-qualified pension. The establishment of EPFs was allowed in 1966 in spite of labor's fierce resistance.[3]

To sum up, the historical contingency that corporate welfare provisions were developed first in postwar Japan defined the subsequent development of public pension schemes. Widespread retirement allowances made employers negative on the expansion of EPI. The resultant low level of EPI benefits in the 1950s in turn led to the proliferation of mutual-aid plans. Finally, the linkage between the introduction of the tax-qualified pension and the improvement of EPI benefits further complicated Japan's pension system.

2. Pension Retrenchment
2.1 Retrenchment in the 1980s
Population aging provides a quite powerful facilitator of pension retrenchment. Unless a pension scheme is completely funded, or as long as pension schemes are financed by the PAYG approach, population aging inevitably causes fiscal constraints, which in turn necessitate reform for cost containment. In this vein, Japan's retrenchment merits discussion. When Japan steered its pension policy toward retrenchment in the early 1980s, its population aging was not so serious as to cause a fiscal problem. Granted that the aged population in Japan gradually increased in the 1970s, Japan's aging ratio (the ratio of those aged over sixty-five to the whole population) was only 9.6 percent in

1982, which was much lower than its counter-parts in West European countries.[4] Social spending as a percentage of national income remained the smallest among the member countries of the Organization for Economic Cooperation and Development (OECD). Japan spent 10.1 percent of national income for social security in 1981, whereas France spent 26.6 percent, West Germany 22.5 percent, Sweden 20.7 percent, the UK 10.7 percent, and the US 10.2 percent (MHW 1984).

Nevertheless, "reconsideration of welfare" was a central theme of the political agenda in the early 1980s. That happened for specific reasons. One major reason was accumulated fiscal deficits in the 1970s, which was caused, first of all, by reduced tax revenues following the 1973 oil crisis, and, second, by expansionary fiscal policy to stimulate domestic demand (public works expenditures increased by an average of over 22 percent between 1976 and 1979). Social security expenditures also experienced a surge due to generous reforms in the early 1970s, though their ratio to national income was still low by comparison, as aforementioned. Consequently, public bond dependency reached 40 percent in the 1979 budget plan. Against this backdrop, the government started cutbacks, particularly in social security, to restore fiscal balance.

Social security systems had their own problems. Specific schemes suffered fiscal deficits in spite of relatively low spending for social security, due to institutional fragmentation. For example, NPI slipped into the red in the early 1980s, in spite of generous subsidies covering all administrative costs and a third of benefit payments. In addition to difficulties in collecting NPI contributions, a decrease in the number of farmers originally expected to be the core members of NPI exacerbated its finances. Agricultural employment fell from 8.42 million in 1970 to 5.02 million in 1982. The sector's percentage of the total workforce shrank from 16 percent to 9 percent.

To alleviate its fiscal constraints, NPI was integrated with flat-rate tiers of employees' pension schemes into the Basic Pension scheme in 1985. The new framework enabled NPI to receive financial support from other pension funds. Along with such "fiscal adjustment" across different schemes, generosity in benefits and entitlements were curtailed, not to mention increases in contribution. Consequently, the replacement rate of EPI was to be restrained below 70 percent. The minimum contribution period to obtain entitlements would also be extended gradually from twenty years to twenty-five years.[5]

To sum up, the pension reform of the 1980s was precipitated by deficits in overall public finance as well as fiscal constraints in specific schemes due to institutional fragmentation.

2.2 Retrenchment in the 1990s

After the 1985 reform introduced fiscal adjustment, raising pensionable ages became a major issue in subsequent reform rounds. It was considered necessary not only for cost containment but also for resolving a difference in the entitlement age between different types of insurants in the BP scheme. EPI members would obtain their entitlements at the age of sixty, while NPI members had to wait until sixty-five. A change in the pensionable age, however, was one of the most difficult items of reform because of its direct and clearly tangible loss imposed upon specific groups. Back in 1979, the MHW was forced to withdraw its proposal of raising the EPI entitlement age in the face of fierce resistance from various camps, including organized labor and pro-welfare groups. The MHW underwent a second setback in the 1989 reform.

A gap between the retirement age and pensionable age was a major cause of robust reactions. When major Japanese firms established the practice of lifelong employment, the ordinary retirement age of a male worker was fifty-five. Since the 1970s, the Ministry of Labour encouraged firms through various measures, including recommendations and subsidies, to extend employment up to the age of sixty, and retirement at the age of sixty finally prevailed by the end of the 1980s. A raise in the pensionable age would worsen the gap between the retirement age and pensionable age, which was disappearing at least among major firms. As the socialists and unions convincingly asserted, therefore, the extension of employment of those aged over sixty would be a precondition for the change.

Since the problem would not be solved in

the short run, a raise in the pensionable age was unlikely to be realized in the near future. Unexpectedly, however, the idea of raising the pensionable age was accepted with no serious challenge in the 1994 reform. The age of male employees' basic pension entitlement would be raised gradually up to the age of sixty-five during the transitional period between 2001 and 2013, and the same procedure would be applied to female employees between 2006 and 2018. A delay in the female case was due to the fact that the female pensionable age was in the process of rising from fifty-five to sixty by 1999.

To extend employment of those aged sixty and over and make a smooth connection between the retirement age and the pensionable age, various measures were introduced in the 1994 reform. First, actuarial deduction applied to working pensioners was modified lest it deprive them of work incentives. Under the former system, working pensioners were unable to increase their incomes much due to steeply progressive deduction from their pension benefits. Those who earned over ¥250,000 could receive no pension benefits. The revision allowed working pensioners aged between sixty and sixty-four to increase their total incomes in proportion to their earnings by modifying progressiveness in deduction. Those aged sixty-five and over were free from actuarial penalty.

Second, labor legislation, including the Worker Dispatching Law and the Elderly Employment Stabilization Law, was revised to expand the range of flexibility in the employment of older persons and thereby to encourage employers to hire more elderly workers. At the same time, the extension-of-employment allowance for those aged between sixty and sixty-four was introduced to compensate for wage cuts. When they continue to work and suffer substantial losses in their incomes (more than 15 percent of their previous salaries), elderly workers are provided with an allowance up to 25 percent of the salary (the total amount cannot be over ¥361,680) under the Employment Insurance Plan (EIP). On the other hand, the EIP was revised to prohibit receiving both unemployment and pension benefits, on the grounds that too much generosity would deprive the elderly of the work incentive.

Following the hike in the Basic Pension entitlement ages among employees in 1994, the 1999 reform raised the pensionable ages in earnings-related pensions. In addition, the indexation of benefits with wage raises was suspended, actuarial deduction in benefits was applied to those aged between sixty-five and sixty-nine, and earnings-related benefit standards of new beneficiaries were reduced by 5 percent.

Most noteworthy in the pension retrenchment of the 1990s was raising the pensionable ages. What brought about the 1994 breakthrough? What had changed between 1989 and 1994? Or what made a sharp contrast between the 1989 setback and the 1994 easy win. The measures that the 1994 reform introduced to create and extend employment for the elderly certainly distinguished it from the previous attempt, but their immediate effects were negligible in the economic downtrend. The newly introduced measures were unable to effectively increase elderly employment, at least in the short run.

Population aging certainly provided a condition in favor of further retrenchment, but it was not such a drastic change as to explain the sharp contrast between 1989 and 1994. Population aging is, after all, a continuous trend, not a sudden phenomenon, so it is not appropriate in explaining the specific timing of a new policy. Besides, the aging ratio of Japan was still the lowest among major advanced countries, except for that of the United States in 1993 (see Table 1). Table 1 also shows that Japan was quite successful in cost containment. According to Table 2, Japan spent only 7.8 percent of national income on pensions, while the figures of France and Sweden were more than double that of Japan.

A critical difference between 1989 and 1994 is found in political partisanship in government. Following the step-down of the LDP from power for the first time since 1955, all opposition parties except for the Japanese Communist Party (JCP) formed a coalition government in 1993. The Japan Socialist Party (JSP), which had played a central role in opposition, accepted a bill to raise the pensionable age in 1994. The JSP in the coalition government conceded in the reform to coalition partners for the maintenance of the non-LDP

Table 1. Social Security Expenditure as a Percentage of National Income and International Comparison of the Elderly Population

Country	Social security expenditure as a percentage of national income (FY 1993)	The aged as a percentage of the total population (1993)	Social security expenditure as a percentage of national income (FY 1997)	The aged as a percentage of the total population (1997)
Japan	15.2	13.6	17.8	15.7
US	18.7*	12.7	—	12.7
UK	27.2	15.8	—	15.8
Germany	33.3	15.1	—	15.4
France	37.7	14.5	—	15.7
Sweden	53.4	17.6	—	17.0

Note: US data for social security expenditure was not available.
*The figure for fiscal 1992 was used as a reference.

Table 2. International Comparison of Social Security Expenditure by Category as a Percentage of National Income

Country	Total Comparison with national income (%)	Category (%) Medical care	Pensions	Welfare & others	Total benefits (million units of national currency)	Benefits per capita
Japan FY 1997	17.8	6.5	9.3	2.0	69,418,725 yen	550,217 yen
FY 1993						
Japan	15.2	5.9	7.8	1.6	56,797,461 yen	455,239 yen
US (FY 1992)	18.7	6.8	8.4	3.5	906,195 dollars	3,494 dollars
UK	27.2	7.3	10.8	9.1	132,646 pounds	2,279 pounds
Germany	33.3	8.7	14.3	10.3	799,688 marks	9,901 marks
France	37.7	9.2	18.4	10.2	1,973,922 francs	34,313 francs
Sweden	53.4	10.0	20.1	23.3	557,135 kronor	63,708 kronor

Source: In Tables 1 and 2, figures for each country are based on the International Labour Organization (ILO) Social Security Survey, as estimated by the National Institute of Population and Social Security Research; there may thus be discrepancies with figures published by the ILO. Transcribed from www.ipss.go.jp.
Note: Benefits were calculated using the average annual exchange rates for the respective currencies; for comparison, benefits per capita were ¥442,461 for the US, ¥378,326 for the UK, ¥667,246 for Germany, ¥674,140 for France, and ¥910,585 for Sweden.

government. Its concession formed a watershed by bringing about an all-party consensus except for the JCP. The LDP in opposition had no reason to stand up against its originally formulated bill. Organized labor, which had opposed the idea most vehemently in the past, opted for "silence and compliance" this time, showing its support for the new government (Shinkawa 1999).

Compliance of organized labor is comprehensible using the logic of "Nixon goes to China" (Ross 2000). Nixon's decision to go to China was accepted among the conservatives in the US because they knew Nixon was anti-communist and had no intention of selling out. It can be said, by applying the same logic, that the pensionable age was successfully raised since the most vehement opponent in the past, the JSP, went for it. Organized labor yielded because of its affiliation with the JSP. The argument of "Nixon goes to China" can be placed in a broader context of "blame avoidance."

3. Politics of Blame Avoidance

R. Kent Weaver argues that "politicians are motivated primarily by the desire to avoid blame for unpopular actions rather than by seeking to claim credit for popular ones" (Weaver 1986, 371). Voters are more likely to notice relatively concentrated costs or benefits than those widely diffused. Besides, they tend to be more sensitive to real or potential costs than to gains (Weaver 1986, 373). Welfare retrenchment is an ideal case in which to examine how best the politics of blame avoidance works in reality, because it forces its tangible costs upon a limited number of people, while its benefits, such as fiscal balance and fairness, are not tangible rewards one can easily and immediately appreciate.

Taking into account arguments developed by Weaver and Paul Pierson (1996), this paper classifies five different strategies of blame avoidance. First, policymakers try not to be involved in retrenchment by limiting the agenda or keeping a blame-generating issue off the agenda (Strategy One). When they have to make a decision, they will redefine the issue, or prevent blame-generating by developing new policy options which diffuse or obfuscate losses (Strategy Two). Strategy Three is lowering visibility. Decision-makers can lower their visibility by passing the buck or delaying the effect of a policy upon specific groups until some point in the future. By so doing, it would be more difficult for affected groups and individuals to realize the impact of a decision as well as to trace responsibility for its effect back to particular decision-makers. Strategy Four is deflecting blame by finding scapegoats or by playing off one group against the other. Strategy Five is forming a consensus. A consensus formed across political partisanship on a blame-generating decision prevents political opponents from taking advantage of the issue, thus minimizing the risk of making a blame-generating decision (Weaver 1986, 384–90; Pierson 1996, 147).

Tracing the retrenchment back in the 1970s, we can detect the predominance of Strategy One. The LDP leadership kept the retrenchment issue off the government agenda in the late 1970s, in spite of reinforced calls for "reconsideration of welfare" within the government, especially among financial bureaucrats. The LDP, which barely maintained a majority in the upper house of the Diet at that time, cautiously avoided making a blame-generating decision. Gaining a stable majority in the 1980 election, the Liberal Democratic government decided to embark on welfare retrenchment but redefined the issue. Administrative reform, or fiscal reconstruction without tax increases, was the officially set goal. By mobilizing popular support with that slogan, the government legitimized welfare retrenchment as necessary for fiscal reconstruction. Welfare retrenchment was redefined as an attempt to avoid a trap of the stagnant welfare state and build a welfare society with (economic) viability.

Strategy Three was coupled with Strategy Two. To make an administrative reform plan, the government established the second Provisional Council for Administrative Reform (Daini Rinchō) and delegated decisions to it. Daini Rinchō not only lowered the visibility of politicians but also unexpectedly obtained zealous support among broad classes of people thanks to the charismatic chair, Dokō Toshio. Bureaucratic initiatives witnessed in the 1985 pension retrenchment are also understood in terms of Strategy Three. In contrast with political credit-claiming in pension reforms of the 1950s and 1960s, which ignored policy rationality and fiscal balance in administration, welfare bureaucrats took an initiative in retrenchment (cf. Nakano 1992; Shinkawa 1993). In short, Daini Rinchō set the course of pension reform and welfare bureaucrats took the lead in actual policymaking. The visibility of politicians, thus, was kept quite low in the 1985 reform. Deferred effects of cost containment also make sense in the context of Strategy Three.

A good example of Strategy Four, or finding a scapegoat, is witnessed in the idea of "Japanese-style welfare society" (JSWS), or welfare society with economic viability, which is a Japanese version of the neoconservative attack on the welfare state. Based on the perception that the welfare state caused the English/European disease of obese public finance, economic stagnancy, and work disincentive, the argument of JSWS stressed the necessity of welfare cutbacks in Japan to avoid the European disease and build a viable society with small government (Shinkawa 1993). Considering the fact that Japan's social security expenditures in the early 1980s occupied only a small portion of national income, Japan was free from the supposed European disease. Nevertheless, advocates of JSWS blamed social security provisions as a major cause of fiscal and moral deterioration in Japan.

Strategy Five explains strong political leadership exerted in the 1994 reform. The coalition government formed a special task force on pension reform in October 1993 to make a plan for pension reform in the following year. The final report of the task force was made in two months without delay. Such swift action was possible due to the turnabout of the Socialists, which contributed to consensus-forming within as well as without the government. The Nixon-goes-to-China logic was a key to the success of consensus-forming in this case, by which it was possible to diffuse blame. "No one has to stick their neck out: everyone provides political cover for everyone else, making it difficult for a future political opponent to raise the issue" (Weaver 1986, 389).

4. Concluding Remarks: Major Issues in the 2004 Reform

4.1 Playing-off strategy

Pension retrenchment conducted for the last two decades in Japan can be assessed as fairly successful in terms of blame avoidance. Masterfully combined various strategies of blame avoidance gradually but steadily transformed the pension system in Japan. A series of pension reform, however, fell short of realizing financial sustainability. Piecemeal or decremental changes through strategies of blame avoidance lack a grand design, which provides a vision and direction of reform necessary to integrate occupationally fragmented schemes and absorb the impact of accelerated population aging.

Based on the population projection released in 1992 that Japan would enter the stage of "super-aged society," or that a quarter of the Japanese population would be those aged sixty-five and over in 2025, the 1994 reform set a schedule to raise the EPI contribution rate up to the upper limit of 29.8 percent in 2025 (that of the NPI contribution was set at ¥21,700 in 2015). That scenario was blown away by the 1997 population projection, according to which Japan would become a "super-aged society" in 2015.

Accelerated population aging would push the EPI contribution rate up to 34.3 percent in 2025 and the NPI contribution to ¥24,300 in 2015 without further measures taken for cost containment.

The 1999 reform based on the 1997 population projection needs to be renewed now, according to the 2002 population projection. The latest projection is more pessimistic about the recovery of the fertility rate. The 1997 projection assumed that the fertility rate would recover to the level of 1.61 in 2025, but the unexpectedly robust downward tendency in the fertility rate impelled the 2002 projection to assume that the fertility rate in 2025 would remain at the level of 1.38.[6] Consequently, the latest medium-variant projection expects the peak of population aging to come with the figure of 35.7 percent in 2050, while the last one expected the figure of 32.3 percent in 2050.

As a result of continual reforms for cost containment with no grand design provided, intergenerational equity has been severely damaged. A widely circulated argument since the late 1990s is that future generations will receive less than the total amount of their payments whereas the balance is quite favorable to current beneficiaries. According to an intergenerational calculation, a model couple of 1940 (a couple composed of a male breadwinner, who was born in 1940, working between the ages of twenty and sixty, and living the average span of life, and a two-year younger spouse) gains 2.68 times the amount of payments, while a couple of 1960 gains 1.05 times, and a couple of 1980, 0.73 (Nishizawa 2003, 33–34).

The argument of intensified intergenerational unfairness pits retired generations against working generations, or older generations against younger generations. So far, the playing-off strategy has worked well to canalize discussions for the 2004 reform into a specific course of retrenchment. The government recently made a small, yet noteworthy step toward intergenerational equity. It decided to cut 0.9 percent of current benefit levels in fiscal 2003 by indexing them with a fall in prices, which had never been conducted before.

Another playing-off case is witnessed in the attempt to abolish the privilege of third-type insurants in the Basic Pension. Employees' spouses with income of no more than ¥1,300,000 are categorized as third-type insurants and require no contributions. "Free-riding" of third-type insurants is criticized as unfair to workingwomen who also take care of their families. Workingwomen are, thus, played off against housewives. The cancellation of the third type is asserted as necessary not only in terms of equity between workingwomen and housewives but also for the encouragement of female labor force participation.

The playing-off strategy is effective but is accompanied by a serious side effect. It surely provides a strong motivation toward reform on one hand but damages solidarity and unity in society on the other. The successful playing-off strategy created distrust for the pension system and consequently increased the number of NPI insurants in arrears, particularly among younger generations, as seen in Table 3.

Increased distrust for the pension system may discourage people to pay contributions. Research conducted by the Social Insurance Office in 1999 shows that the number of NPI insurants in arrears increased by 920,000 for the previous three years, from 11 percent to 16 percent of insurants except for noncontributory third insurants. If we add the number of those who are legally required but fail to join the NPI to that of first-type insurants and take the combined figure as the denominator, the percentage of those in arrears goes up to 36 percent. Although those explicitly showing distrust for NPI reaches only 12.2 percent among those in arrears, the percentage goes up to over 17 percent among those aged between twenty and thirty-five; 62.4 percent of those in arrears answered that insurance fees were too high for them, but their words cannot be taken literally, taking into account that more than half of those in arrears join private life insurance plans and 12.7 percent even hold individual annuities (SIA 1999).[7]

As for the status of third-type insurants, its simple cancellation would cause a serious problem; a considerable number of housewives would fail to pay their contributions and lose their own pension entitlements. It should be kept in mind that the third type was created in the 1985 reform to secure pension entitlements for housewives.

Moreover, given the fact that workingwomen's fertility rate is much lower than that of housewives, the government need expand public support for childcare, lest increased female labor force participation lead to a further decline of the fertility rate.

4.2 Overhaul of the system

It is widely perceived that Japan can no longer afford to have a fragmented pension system. Together with the establishment of the Basic Pension, the government intended to rearrange earnings-related pension schemes. The cabinet acknowledged in 1984 a time schedule indicating the integration of earnings-related pension schemes by 1994, which was never implemented. Certainly, mutual-aid pension schemes in public corporations were absorbed into EPI after they were privatized in 1987, and those in agricultural and fishery cooperatives dissolved and integrated into EPI in 2002. Their absorption, however, increased, rather than alleviated, burdens on EPI because those schemes decided to join EPI due to fiscal deterioration. Financially sound mutual-aid schemes for public employees are robustly opposed to the integration of their own programs with EPI.

To avoid an intergenerational war over pensions and regain the credibility of the public pension system, alternatives to the current PAYG approach have been presented by welfare economists. Considering difficulties in collecting contributions from first-type insurants in NPI, a number of experts insist on tax-financing the Basic Pension. Tax-financing the BP resolves not only a difficulty in collecting insurance fees but also ends the controversy over the free-riding

Table 3. Trust in Public Welfare

		(%)
Age	Trust	No Trust
20+	32	67
30+	27	72
40+	46	54
50+	58	41
60+	68	30
70+	71	22
Average	51	47

Source: *Asahi Shimbun*, June 21, 2003.

status of third-type insurants. As for earnings-related schemes, some argue for a shift to an integrated funded system, while others propose a PAYG system with no subsidies (current schemes receive subsidies covering administrative costs from general revenue).

Welfare bureaucrats are, however, negative on any major changes in the PAYG approach on the grounds that it blurs the relationship between benefit and payment, or entitlement and obligation. Besides, they insist, considering the fact that government subsidies currently cover a third of BP payments in addition to entire administrative costs and are scheduled to grow to half by 2004, further increases in subsidies from tax revenues are infeasible, implying that tax increases necessary to cover entire BP expenditures are politically impossible under the current stagnant economy (an interview with the chief of the Pension Bureau of the Ministry of Health, Labour and Welfare [MHLW], *Nihon Keizai Shimbun*, February 28, 2001). Another important reason for their opposition to tax-financing is that welfare bureaucrats are determined to keep pension fund reserves under their control.

The MHLW publicized in December 2002 a discussion paper for the 2004 reform. Noteworthy in the paper is a proposal to shift from a defined-benefit to defined-contribution format in the future. The current contribution rate of EPI set at 13.58 percent of total annual wages is to be raised gradually up to 20 percent by 2025 and kept at that level afterwards. The benefit level from that year onward will vary not politically but according to changes in demographic and economic factors, including life expectancy, the fertility rate, interest rates, prices, and so on. With this scheme, the MHLW insists that widespread anxiety about financial sustainability of public pensions in the future will be cleared away.

The MHLW projects that the replacement rate in the early 2030s would go down to 52 percent. The figure is 7 percent lower than the current replacement rate but still considered by critics to be difficult to attain. The MHLW's calculation is based on optimistic assumptions (the medium-variant projection for population, 2 percent annual wage raises, 1 percent annual

price increases, and a 3.25 percent nominal interest rate). A change in a single variable brings an enormous impact on the future replacement rate. If we use the low-variant—instead of medium-variant—projection for population, the replacement rate will be 45 percent. No one knows if other conditions would be met. It is impossible to predict precisely future replacement rates in a defined-contribution scheme, but widely believed is that they are likely to be lower than what the MHLW expects. Uncertainty as regards levels of benefits would reinforce anxiety over postretirement life and in turn erode the credibility of the public pension system and social solidarity.

Courtesy of the National Institute of Population and Social Security Research (IPSS).

Originally published in the *Japanese Journal of Social Security Policy* 2, no. 2 (December 2003): 25–33.

Notes

1. The 1999 round ended with the reform bill passed in the Diet in the spring of 2000.

2. The idea was originally created and developed by Weaver (1986). Though the idea is extensively employed by Pierson (1996) in the context of the "new politics of the welfare state," the politics of blame avoidance is witnessed also in old partisan politics. By employing the concept of blame avoidance, therefore, I have no intention of standing for the perspective of new politics against that of old politics, though class politics insights are missing in this article. I have discussed the role of class politics in the welfare state development of Japan in previous works (Shinkawa 1993; 1999; 2000).

3. Labor's opposition was based on the argument that an adjustment between public and private pensions was not legitimate, suggesting labor's loss.

4. The aging ratios in selected countries are as follows: 16.6 percent in Sweden, 15.3 percent in the UK and West Germany (1981), 13.5 percent in France, and 11.6 percent in the US (MHW 1984).

5. Those born between April 2, 1952, and April 1, 1953, are required to make a twenty-one-year contribution to obtain their pension entitlements. Everyone born after April 2, 1956, is required to make a twenty-five-year contribution.

6. When the fertility rate fell to 1.57 in 1989, it was called the "1.57 shock." Retrospectively, the figure of 1.57 was only a mid-point of the fall. The

fertility rate reached 1.33 in 2001. Comparing fertility rates as of 2000, Japan's figure of 1.36 is the same as that of Germany, but much lower than those of Sweden (1.55), France (1.89), and the United States (2.13) (*Asahi Shimbun*, September 10 and 11, 2002).

7. EPI has no difficulty in collecting contributions since they are automatically deducted from paychecks. Its finances, however, are not sound and stable. The coverage of EPI is shrinking; 20 percent of employees are not covered with EPI as of 2000. More employers in small businesses fail to pay to the public pension scheme due to deficits in business. Another reason for the decreased number of EPI participants is a change in employment, that is, the increased number of nonregular employees, who are excluded from EPI. EPI requires working more than thirty hours per week for membership. To prevent a further decrease in the EPI membership, the Ministry of Health, Labour and Welfare (created in January 2001 through the merger of the Ministry of Labour and the Ministry of Health and Welfare) recently proposed to allow the temporarily unemployed to stay in EPI and encourage part-time workers to join the plan by reducing required working hours from thirty hours to twenty hours per week.

References

In Japanese

Hatta Tsutomu and Oguchi Noriyoshi. 1999. *Nenkin kaikaku ron: Tsumitate hōshiki e ikō seyo!* [Theory of Pension Reform: Switch to the Reserve Method!]. Tokyo: Nihon Keizai Shimbunsha.

Kenkō Hoken Kumiai Rengōkai. 1985. *Shakai hoshō nenkan* [Social Security Yearbook]. Tokyo: Tōyō Keizai Shinpōsha.

MHW (Ministry of Health and Welfare). 1984. *Kōsei hakusho* [White Paper on Welfare].

Nishizawa Kazuhiko. 2003. *Nenkin daikaikaku: "Sakiokuri" wa mō yurusarenai* [Grand-Scale Pension Reform: "Postponement" Is No Longer Acceptable]. Tokyo: Nihon Keizai Shimbunsha.

Shinkawa Toshimitsu. 1993. *Nihon-gata fukushi no seiji keizaigaku* [The Political Economy of Japanese-Style Welfare]. Tokyo: San-Ichi Shobō.

———. 1999. *Sengo Nihon seiji to shakai minshushugi: Shakaitō, sōshyō burokku no kōbō* [Social Democracy in Postwar Japan: The Rise and Fall of the Socialist Party and the General Council of Trade Unions Bloc]. Kyoto: Hōritsu Bunkasha.

SIA (Social Insurance Agency). 1999. *99-nendo kokumin nenkin hihokensha jittai chōsa* [The 1999 Survey on NPI Insurants].

Tada Hidenori. 1991. "Bunritsu-gata kai-nenkin taisei no kakuritsu" [The Establishment of the Fragmented Pension System]. In *Nihon shakai hoshō no rekishi* [The History of Social Security in Japan], edited by Yokoyama Kazuhiko and Tada Hidenori, 140–62. Tokyo: Gakubunsha.

In English

Garrett, Geoffrey. 1998. *Partisan Politics in the Global Economy*. Cambridge: Cambridge University Press.

Pierson, Paul. 1996. "The New Politics of the Welfare State." *World Politics* 48 (January): 143–79.

———, ed. 2001. *The New Politics of the Welfare State*. Oxford: Oxford University Press.

Ross, Fiona. 2000. "'Beyond Left and Right': The New Partisan Politics of Welfare." *Governance* 13 (2): 155–83.

Shinkawa Toshimitsu. 2000. "Failed Reform and Policy Changes of the SDPJ." In *Power Shuffles and Policy Processes: Coalition Government in Japan in the 1990s*, edited by Ōtake Hideo, 152–82. Tokyo: Japan Center for International Exchange.

Shinkawa Toshimitsu and T. J. Pempel. 1996. "Occupational Welfare and the Japanese Experience." In *The Privatization of Social Policy?: Occupational Welfare and the Welfare State in America, Scandinavia and Japan*, edited by Michael Shalev, 280–326. London: Palgrave Macmillan.

Swank, Duane. 2002. *Global Capital, Political Institutions, and Policy Change in Developed Welfare States*. Cambridge: Cambridge University Press.

Weaver, R. Kent. 1986. "The Politics of Blame Avoidance." *Journal of Public Policy* 6 (4): 371–98.

III-(5) Lessons from the LDP Landslide

Kabashima Ikuo and Sugawara Taku
Japan Echo, 2005

The forty-fourth general election for Japan's House of Representatives took place on September 11 this year. The most striking result of this contest was the overwhelming victory of the ruling Liberal Democratic Party (LDP), which expanded its number of seats to 296, considerably more than the 241 required for a majority in the 480-seat body. (Table 1 breaks down the results of the last three general elections by party.) Along with the 31 seats won by the New Kōmeitō, the other party in the ruling coalition, the LDP has a comfortable two-thirds majority in the lower house of the National Diet, enough to override the rejection of legislation by the House of Councillors and force its bills through. Meanwhile, the Democratic Party of Japan (DPJ)—ostensibly the second option in the two-party political system many hope to see develop in Japan—suffered a severe blow in the contest, seeing its seats drop from a pre-election 177 to just 113.

One particularly noteworthy development in the September election was the surprisingly strong performance of the LDP in urban prefectures like Tokyo, Kanagawa, and Osaka, where it had historically been less popular. This election saw strong voter interest, with turnout climbing from 59.9 percent in the previous contest to 67.5 percent, and Prime Minister Koizumi Junichirō made the most of this attention, remaining in control of the public discourse the whole way. Following the rejection of a package of postal privatization bills in the House of Councillors, the prime minister directed a skillful production of what came to be called "the Koizumi theater," dissolving the lower house, withdrawing party backing for the LDP members who had opposed the reform bills,

and sending in high-profile "assassin" candidates to unseat them. Now, thanks to his party's convincing victory, Koizumi is set to stay in the prime minister's seat until his term as president of the LDP ends about a year from now.

This paper will first explore the significance of Koizumi's emergence within the Liberal Democratic Party. It will then examine the results of the September 11 election from four perspectives: (1) a comparison of voting patterns in urban and rural areas, (2) the relationship between rising voter turnout and the climb in votes garnered by the LDP, (3) the election results in districts where the LDP rebels ran, and (4) the impact of Kōmeitō and the Japanese Communist Party (JCP) on the contest. Building on all of these aspects, the paper will then take a look at just what the September 11 election results mean for Japanese politics.

The LDP System and Koizumi's Reforms

Since becoming prime minister in April 2001, Koizumi has delivered a consistent message on reform, stating that he will see through his structural reform policies even if it means "destroying" the LDP in the process. His insistence on this point is an important development in Japan's political history. The Liberal Democratic Party was formed in 1955 and immediately became a mammoth ruling party. Over the decades that followed it gradually built up what might be called "the LDP system," a political structure designed to perpetuate its hold on power. This system advanced policies aimed at boosting economic growth and sought to channel the benefits of that growth to groups in society that would not enjoy them otherwise. This politically motivated redistribution of wealth, with its goal of "equal growth," made the system quite socialist in nature.

This pursuit of "equal growth" was never formally a part of the LDP platform, but was rather a natural result of the support base the party enjoyed in the rural, largely agricultural regions of the country. Solid support from farming communities cemented the LDP's long-term rule, and in exchange for this support the party kept up a massive flow of funds to rural areas, including agricultural subsidies and public works projects. These policies prevented serious gaps in income from opening up between Japan's rural and urban regions, making Japan highly unusual as a nation that was able to maintain equal growth even as a democracy espousing a free economy.

Eventually, however, this LDP system began to show cracks. The nation underwent rapid urbanization and shifts in its industrial structure, causing rural populations to plunge. Urban residents came to make up the majority of the population, and a rise in the numbers of second- and third-generation city dwellers lessened the social and psychological ties between city and country. All these developments chipped away at the LDP system, but it was the end of the period of rapid economic growth in the early 1970s that seemed to threaten its complete collapse. This collapse did not occur, though: the LDP system, and the economic redistribution at its core, continued to thrive, and even grow to encompass new beneficiaries. Behind this continued existence of the system were the efforts of the Liberal Democrats themselves.

From the perspective of urban residents, who enjoy none of the benefits of the LDP system, this setup long represented a massive waste of their tax money. The transfer of wealth from the cities to rural areas through public works and the excessive protection given to various vested interests acted as impediments to open competition and causes of environmental degradation, and the network of ties between LDP politicians and those benefiting from their system appeared shady to city voters. In the 1990s these voters finally became a force capable of pushing back hard enough against the LDP to threaten the party's grip on power. Faced with these crises, the LDP formed a series of alliances with other parties and thereby managed to hold on to control of the government, but its losses in urban districts grew more pronounced with every new general election.

When Koizumi won the race for the LDP presidency in 2001 it was thanks to a revolution of sorts within the party. He saw the LDP system as the cause of the party's dwindling popularity and swore he would destroy this system once and for all. This began the process of the LDP's recovery of support from urban voters.

A look at the way Koizumi came into leadership of the party and the history of the LDP as a whole makes this year's introduction of the postal privatization bills and dissolution of the lower house seem like an entirely natural direction for these political developments to have taken. Koizumi's fierce attacks on the LDP rebels who voted against the postal legislation provided him with an effective way to reach the people who had found themselves outside the umbrella of the LDP system in the past.

Prior to the election it struck the authors as unlikely that the entire contest could revolve around an issue like postal privatization. For an issue to have a real impact on an election it must be one in which the electorate is deeply interested; it must have the support of a considerable number of people, and candidates must stake out clear positions on the matter. The postal reform question satisfied none of these requirements, though, and we expected the September election to be a referendum on Koizumi's reform record during the more than four years he had been in office. While the prime minister has managed to cultivate an image as a reformer, the problems in Japan's pension system have been put off, with needed reforms still unaccomplished. Koizumi has also made insufficient headway on spinning off powers from the central to local governments. Although the nation's fiscal deficits have continued to grow, we have seen no fundamental rethinking of public works spending: *shinkansen* bullet-train lines and expressways continue to spread across the land and dams continue to go up. If this election had been a judgment on Koizumi's actual reform record, his party would likely have gone down to defeat.

Table 1. Lower House Election Results

	Single-seat districts			Proportional-representation segment						Total		
				2000		2003		2005				
	2000	2003	2005	Seats won	Vote share (%)	Seats won	Vote share (%)	Seats won	Vote share (%)	2000	2003	2005
Liberal Democratic Party	177	168	219	56	28.3	69	35.0	77	38.2	233	237	296
New Kōmeitō	7	9	8	24	13.0	25	14.8	23	13.3	31	34	31
Democratic Party of Japan	80	105	52	47	25.2	72	37.4	61	31.0	127	177	113
Japanese Communist Party	0	0	0	20	11.2	9	7.8	9	7.3	20	9	9
Social Democratic Party	4	1	1	15	9.4	5	5.1	6	5.5	19	6	7
People's New Party	—	—	2	—	—	—	—	2	1.7	—	—	4
New Party Nippon	—	—	0	—	—	—	—	1	2.4	—	—	1
New Party Daichi	—	—	0	—	—	—	—	1	0.6	—	—	1
Independent	—	—	13	—	—	—	—	—	—	—	—	13
Liberal Party	4	—	—	18	11.0	—	—	—	—	22	—	—
Conservative Party	7	4	—	0	0.4	—	—	—	—	7	4	—
Other	21	13	5	0	1.5	—	—	—	—	21	13	5
Total	300	300	300	180	100	180	100	180	100	480	480	480

Koizumi managed to completely prevent the contest from being framed as such, though. He successfully narrowed the issues at stake down to the single topic of postal reform, thus heightening public interest in that one issue and increasing support for privatization. By sending in the "assassin" candidates, he made it crystal clear who was for and against the reforms on the table. This strategy also allowed the LDP to focus national attention on a handful of electoral districts—just a tenth or so of the 300 across the country—thereby successfully smothering the idea that this election was a broad clash between two major political parties. This strategy of raising the banner of postal privatization recast the election as a forward-looking contest, just as the July 2001 House of Councillors election had been, and presented voters with the image of a Koizumi LDP that would break away from the system of the past and move boldly ahead with structural reform efforts.

Making Gains among City Voters

The Liberal Democrats cannot remain a political force over the long term without boosting their support among urban voters. The introduction of single-seat districts and the subsequent adjustment of the number of seats in the House of Representatives shifted a large number of seats from rural to urban districts, giving city dwellers a bigger voice in national politics. A considerable percentage of these urbanites have no party affiliation, and wresting their votes away from the DPJ was a high-priority task for the LDP. Nobody understood this better than Koizumi. In response to a 2000 survey of ours that indicated anti-LDP voting trends among city populations, it was Koizumi who said:

The main problem with the LDP is the party's lack of independent initiative. In terms of policy, we can't be thorough about reforming the nation's administration and finances, so we resort to spending packages that target anything and everything. This sort of spending doesn't do much for the economy, and what is more, it is losing its effectiveness as a means of boosting support for the party when we direct it at the organizations that can get out the vote. Since the LDP hasn't been able to gain a simple majority of its own it's been forced to hold hands with groups like the Socialists and Kōmeitō, which is another factor dragging down our attractiveness to voters. . . . These survey results bear out all of this. It all comes down to the voter turnout. If elections start capturing the popular interest, and nonaligned voters begin heading to the polls in greater numbers, then the rising turnout numbers could give the DPJ a shot at taking power from us. (*Ronza*, March–April 2000)

In the 2005 election, however, Koizumi turned his own prediction on its ear: The election did capture the public's attention, and election turnout climbed, with unaligned voters flocking to the polls; but it was his own party, not the DPJ, that reaped the benefits.

Figure 1 shows this development clearly. The information is taken from all 300 of the lower house's single-seat districts. We have ranked these districts in order of urbanization (share of people living in densely inhabited districts) and have broken them down into three groups of 100 each, which we have labeled "urban," "intermediate," and "rural." The graph shows the results of the proportional-representation votes cast in three general elections: 2000, 2003, and 2005. By comparison with the 2000 election, which took place while the LDP was headed by Prime Minister Mori Yoshirō, the party made gains among urban voters in both 2003 and 2005, with its urban vote actually drawing level with the rural vote in 2005.

The LDP's urban gains have been just as clear in the voting for single-seat representatives. Table 2 presents the numbers of candidates fielded by the LDP and DPJ in the last two general elections, along with the numbers elected and the corresponding vote shares, again broken down according to urbanization level. In the space of just two years the Liberal Democrats more than doubled the number of their seats in urban areas, from 31 to 74, and gained an additional 13 seats in intermediate districts. The DPJ, meanwhile, saw its haul of seats in urban districts plunge from 60 to just 16. A look at Table 1 shows that while the DPJ did also lose seats in the proportional-representation voting, this drop was less pronounced, falling from 72 to 61. This accentuates the drubbing taken by the party in the urban single-seat districts. Of the 64 seats that the DPJ lost in all this year, 44, or some 70 percent, were in urban districts. This figure is all the more surprising

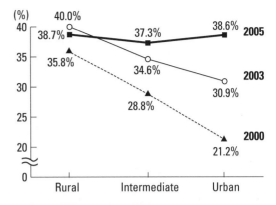

Figure 1. LDP Proportional-Representation Vote Shares by Type of District

when one considers that the 100 seats representing urban districts comprise just over 20 percent of the 480 seats in the entire lower house.

The rise of the LDP in the cities and the corresponding fall of the DPJ have both been major developments. We should note, though, that the Liberal Democrats made these gains thanks to a rise of just 7.5 percentage points in its share of the urban vote. How could such a small gain—and one enjoyed in districts accounting for only around a fifth of the total number of seats—lead to such huge jumps in the party's representation in the lower house? The answer lies in the single-seat districts, where even tiny leads in the voting at the district level can bring about lopsided victories in terms of Diet representation.

Growing Voter Turnout

Let us next look at the issue of voter turnout rates. Observers of the 2005 election have noted that "sleeper" unaffiliated voters went to the polls in greater numbers than ever before, giving their votes—and victory—to the Liberal Democrats. But is this interpretation borne out by the facts?

Figure 2 takes voter turnout figures for 300 single-seat districts, plotting the difference in turnout between the 2003 and 2005 elections (the horizontal axis) against the difference over the same two elections in the percentages of voters choosing the LDP in proportional-representation balloting (the vertical axis). According to this graph, the overall rise in voter turnout does seem

Table 2. LDP and DPJ Performance by Type of District

Liberal Democratic Party

	Candidates		Victors		Vote share (%)	
	2003	2005	2003	2005	2003	2005
Urban	89	91	31	74	41.6	49.1
Intermediate	93	100	58	71	47.2	49.4
Rural	95	99	79	74	55.1	49.7
Total	277	290	168	219	48.1	49.4

Democratic Party of Japan

	Candidates		Victors		Vote share (%)	
	2003	2005	2003	2005	2003	2005
Urban	99	99	60	16	42.8	37.4
Intermediate	92	98	35	26	42.5	40.4
Rural	76	92	10	10	35.0	34.6
Total	267	289	105	52	40.5	37.5

Note: The vote shares are averages of the percentages of votes won in all districts where the party fielded candidates.

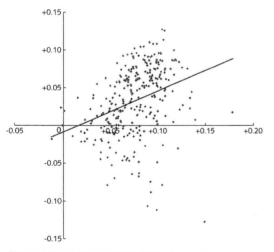

Figure 2. Voter Turnout and LDP Gains by Local District, 2005 versus 2003

Notes: The horizontal axis shows the change in voter turnout from the 2003 to the 2005 election. The vertical axis shows the change in the LDP proportional-representation vote share from 2003 to 2005. The data points are for single-seat districts.

to bring about a corresponding rise in votes for the ruling party. There are also, however, many districts where the party has seen its percentage of votes gained fall. There is not, in other words, a consistent connection between higher voter turnout and higher LDP popularity across the nation.

Ibaraki Prefecture's seventh district, the site of a fierce contest between the LDP-endorsed candidate and a rival conservative candidate, saw the largest leap in voter turnout, with the figure climbing by 17.8 points from the 2003 election. The proportional vote for the LDP in this district went up by just 1.7 points, though. The second-highest climb in turnout, 14.9 points, came in Toyama Prefecture's third district. Here, however, the LDP actually saw its share of the vote ratio drop by 12.8 points, due in large part to the votes siphoned off by incumbent legislator Watanuki Tamisuke, who opposed postal privatization and, having lost the LDP's endorsement, ran as head of the newly established People's New Party (Kokumin Shintō). The next four districts in order of the growth in voter turnout saw similar gaps between those percentages and the ratios of the proportional vote going to the Liberal Democrats: Saitama's eleventh district (13.9 points versus 0.7 points) and Gifu's first district (13.6 points versus 4.5 points) are two districts where the LDP rebels put up energetic fights against the party-backed candidates, and the next two, Wakayama's first district (13.4 points versus 2.3 points) and Kagawa's first district (13.4 points versus 3.6 points), saw strong performances by DPJ candidates.

All of the districts listed above fall into the rural and intermediate categories, not the urban one. There were many other areas where the rebels who had split from the LDP line on postal privatization or the Democrats enjoyed deep support, making for close contests with the LDP contenders. Many popular candidates succeeded in calling out the anti-Koizumi vote, thereby boosting voter turnout without sending many of those increased numbers of votes to the LDP.

A more detailed picture of these figures can be gained through regression analysis of the LDP's gains and losses in individual districts measured against three variables for each district: the degree of urbanization, the voter turnout rate, and whether the area was the site of a contest involving one of the LDP rebels. This analysis shows that the impact of shifts in turnout rates on changes in percentages of the total vote cast for the LDP was actually quite small.

In short, the simplistic and straightforward hypothesis that high voter turnout equals large gains for the Liberal Democrats does not hold water. The success the LDP enjoyed in this election can be attributed to the support it gained among the urban electorate. In Japan's cities greater turnout meant larger numbers of people going to the polls to vote for LDP candidates; in rural regions, meanwhile, greater turnout was generally the result of the anti-Koizumi forces getting out the vote. In terms of simple numbers the higher turnout rates look the same across the board, but the meaning of those rates differs widely depending on whether we are talking about rural or urban districts.

The Rebels in the Countryside

What do the results have to say about the LDP rebels? These candidates lost the backing of the party after opposing the government's legislation for postal service privatization. The 2005 election drew much attention to the contests between these rebels and the "assassins," the high-profile candidates chosen by the party to go up against them. Table 3 displays various election data relating to these contests.

There were 37 LDP members in the House of Representatives who voted against the postal bills. Of these, 24, or almost two-thirds, represented rural districts. This points to a key factor in Koizumi's strategy for this election: his positioning of "the Koizumi LDP" against the forces of "the traditional LDP" as represented by the rebellious legislators from rural districts.

Three of these rebels ended up stepping down, and one of them ran not in a single-seat district but only in the proportional-representation contest under the banner of a different party. Of the 33 candidates that remained in the running for single seats, 15 won reelection in their districts and 2 came back from defeat to win seats in the proportional vote. Of these 17 victorious candidates, more than half of the rebels who remained in the race, fully 15 came from rural districts. The remaining two hailed from districts classified as intermediate in our divisions: former minister of posts and telecommunications Noda Seiko (Gifu's first district) and Taki Makoto (Nara's second district; he lost locally but won a seat in the proportional ballot).

Table 3. Election Results for the LDP Rebels, 2005 versus 2003

2003 general election

	Rural	Intermediate	Urban	Total
Won single seats (as LDP candidates)	13*	4	3	20
Won single seats as independents, joined LDP later	5			5
Failed to win single seats, won proportional seats	3	3		6
Withdrew from local races at party's request, won proportional seats	3		2	5
Won proportional seats	—	—	—	1
Total	24*	7	5	37

*Includes one member who won a by-election in April 2004.

2005 general election

	Rural	Intermediate	Urban	Total
Single-seat candidates	23	5	5	33
Single-seat winners	14	1	0	15
Lost in local districts but won proportional seats	1	1	0	2

There were no successful rebels in urban electoral districts. This is far from a surprising result if we consider how this election took shape. In the countryside, though, these opponents of postal privatization enjoyed solid support. The 37 rebels actually included only 20 politicians who had been formally endorsed as LDP candidates in single-seat districts in the previous election; the remaining 17 had been elected either as independents or for proportional-representation seats. Five of the independents had even defeated LDP-backed candidates in rural districts to win their seats in 2003—a clear sign that an environment conducive to a split of the conservative camp was firmly in place in many of these rural areas. During the period leading up to the election, many predicted that the DPJ would win handily thanks to the divisions in the Liberal Democrats' ranks, but the results showed the overwhelming strength of the LDP, which left no openings for the Democrats to exploit even though the conservative camp was not putting up a united front in the campaign.

The DPJ may have suffered an additional blow from the fact that the rebel legislators ran for office in rural areas where the LDP traditionally held a strong position. Under Koizumi's lead the ruling party sent its team of assassins to do battle with the recalcitrant members, and the media concentrated its coverage on these 33 districts. The public interest was firmly focused on the "Koizumi versus rebels" story; what is more, this story played out in districts where the DPJ had no effective candidates in place to begin with. The Koizumi theater robbed the Democrats of their chance to play the part of one of two major parties on the Japanese political scene. The LDP, meanwhile, made skillful use of these 33 high-profile races where the DPJ stood little chance of winning to raise its image in the cities, where it went on to win numerous Diet seats.

Kōmeitō and the Communists

The sheer scale of the Koizumi victory in this election dealt a blow not just to the opposition DPJ but also to the Kōmeitō, the LDP's partner in the ruling coalition. Kōmeitō successfully defended its seat in Tokyo's twelfth district, but lost the first district in Okinawa Prefecture, as well as two proportional-representation seats, in the contest. During the campaign period the LDP candidates repeatedly urged voters to cast their proportional votes for Kōmeitō. While these calls did lead to a higher vote count for the party in the proportional balloting, the higher voter turnout across the board cancelled this out, and the coalition partner did not see a corresponding jump in its number of Diet seats.

In past elections the DPJ's urban popularity had made LDP candidates in the cities increasingly dependent on votes from Kōmeitō supporters. This time around, though, the Liberal Democrats managed to break away from the DPJ candidates on their own. Accurate data on proportional voting is available for 215 of the 219 single-seat electoral districts where LDP candidates won. In these districts, we first compared two figures: (1) the margin of victory—that

is, the difference between the number of votes cast for the winner and the number going to the second-place finisher—and (2) the total number of proportional votes cast for Kōmeitō—that is, the number of votes that the victor may be considered to have received from Kōmeitō supporters, on the assumption that 100 percent of them cast their votes for the LDP candidate. The former was lower than the latter in 95 cases, an increase from the 85 such districts in the 2003 election. But when we modify the assumption, we find a different picture. For example, if we assume that 80 percent of the Kōmeitō supporters voted for the LDP candidate, we find that the number of victors whose margin was smaller than their assumed Kōmeitō support fell from 77 in 2003 to 67 this year. And if we lower the assumption to 60 percent, we find that figure dropped from 53 to 50. In other words, unless we make the extreme assumption that 100 percent of those who backed the Kōmeitō in the proportional-representation voting cast their ballots for the victorious LDP candidate in their local constituency, it appears that the LDP was significantly less dependent on Kōmeitō support this year than it was previously. The sheer number of victorious LDP candidates in this fall's election means that the party needed to rely on Kōmeitō support much less than in previous years.

Many of the candidates who gained seats thanks to the Koizumi tailwind this year did so without a strong support base in the districts where they won. So long as this tailwind continues to blow for the LDP, the party will see its need to cooperate with the Kōmeitō dwindle. Many see the massive popularity of the Liberal Democrats in the September election as a one-time event, though. When it comes time for this election's winners to defend their seats, the first-time Diet members without solid support bases in their constituencies will probably need to rely on the powerful Kōmeitō machine for votes. The LDP's overwhelming victory is unlikely to weaken the party's ties with its coalition partner for the time being.

One new development in the September election was the Japanese Communist Party's decision not to field candidates in all 300 of the single seat districts. What sort of impact did this move have on the DPJ's performance? To gauge this we must examine the 25 districts where no JCP candidate took part in the race. Just 4 of these districts are classified as intermediate; the remaining 21 are all in rural areas. Only one of these (Shizuoka's fourth district) falls among the top half of the 300 districts as ordered by urbanization level. In the 2003 election the JCP had low rates of support in these areas, with Shizuoka's fourth district giving the party 7.9 percent of its proportional votes and the remaining 24 districts falling well below the Communists' nationwide average haul of 7.8 percent. In single-seat terms the party fared even worse, gaining only 7.4 percent of the votes in the best case and far less than that in most of these diffusely populated areas. These numbers point to the JCP's dismal support rates; in many of the local districts the percentages dipped so low that the party risked forfeiting the deposit it put up to register its candidate.

The Democrats also fared poorly in these 25 districts. In 2003 the DPJ fielded candidates in 19 of the areas, winning only Fukushima's third district, where Genba Kōichirō took a single seat. Six DPJ candidates who ran unsuccessfully in these districts got Diet seats from the proportional voting. In the 2005 election these same 19 districts provided similar results for the Democrats, with one candidate winning a single seat and seven losing locally but winning proportional-representation slots.

A quick look at the numbers gives the impression that the Communists did not have any serious impact on the Democrats by sitting out the 2005 election in these districts. But the DPJ candidates made solid gains in many of these races, both in terms of raw vote numbers and percentages, and many of the contests were close losses. The party acquitted itself quite well in these districts, considering the nationwide trend of overwhelming victory for the Liberal Democrats and the general decline of the DPJ. Some of these district contests may have been closer due to the presence of especially compelling DPJ candidates or because of the rift in the LDP, but on the whole it appears that the absence of the Communists in these districts was to the benefit of the Democrats.

Table 4 compares the average numbers of votes received by DPJ candidates in districts where JCP candidates ware also running and districts without JCP participation. The Democratic candidates extended their vote hauls over the last two elections in both of these types of districts, but the data clearly shows that the growth was larger in areas where there were no candidates with Communist backing. The gap is nearly 5,000 votes in rural districts and more than 9,000 votes in intermediate districts.

There are of course considerable differences between the conditions candidates faced in 2003 and the election situation in 2005, and there may be some other elements that contributed to the improved DPJ performance in rural districts. Not all of these gaps in vote numbers can be ascribed to the presence or absence of JCP candidates in those areas. Moreover, even if we can pin down this JCP effect, it still pales in comparison to the 20,000 to 30,000 votes that Kōmeitō and the Sōka Gakkai religious organization behind it can provide in many districts. The LDP still has an advantage here through its cooperation with Kōmeitō.

Just the same, these districts where the JCP fielded no candidates are mainly in rural areas

Table 4. DPJ Vote Tallies by District Type, with and without JCP Candidates

| | Races including JCP candidates | | | | Races without JCP candidates | | | |
| | No. of districts | Average votes per candidate | | | No. of districts | Average votes per candidate | | |
		2003	2005	Difference		2003	2005	Difference
Urban	98	90,162	92,318	+2,156				
Intermediate	89	85,788	94,020	+8,232	3	73,228	90,858	+17,630
Rural	56	69,590	75,267	+5,677	16	62,322	72,773	+10,451
Total	243	83,819	89,012	+5,193	19	64,044	75,629	+11,585

where both the Communists and Democrats are historically weak, and there was no deliberate cooperation between the two parties; the JCP did not offer its official backing to DPJ participants in these races. In this light the numbers we see take on greater significance, pointing to the potential for future moves involving both of these parties. If the Communists remove their candidates from a larger number of races in areas they cannot hope to win, and throw their support behind Democrats, the DPJ vote counts could continue to grow.

An important point to note, though, is that the JCP is not taking its candidates out of the running in order to work together with another party. The decision to withdraw from the 25 districts in question for the 2005 contest was nothing more than a move to lower costs for the organization. The way things are going now, it seems unlikely that the DPJ will be able to count on the Communists for any more cooperation along these lines—unless the Democrats are able to provide some sort of incentives in exchange for that help.

The Tasks Ahead

In preparing this paper we examined a considerable volume of data related to the past few elections. The results of this analysis, and the conclusions we reached, can be summed up as follows:

(1) Under Koizumi the LDP has been able to overcome the DPJ's traditional strength in the cities, winning a similar share of the proportional vote in both rural and urban districts.

(2) Even minor shifts in the votes received in single-seat districts can lead to major changes in the number of Diet seats held. The urban electoral districts were key to the massive increase in LDP power in the Diet this year, but this increase came about with a relatively small 7.5-point increase in the percentage of votes won by the Liberal Democrats.

(3) Higher voter turnout rates were not directly tied to the LDP's convincing victory in the 2005 election. This victory was rather brought about by the rising support among city voters, who cast their ballots for the party in greater numbers than ever before. In some rural districts, meanwhile, higher turnout rates were sparked by dissatisfaction with the LDP. The factors bringing people to the polls differed greatly between city and countryside.

(4) The LDP tactic of sending in its "assassins" to take on the rebel legislators was expected to benefit the DPJ, but in the end the Democrats were unable to exploit this fracture. The overwhelmingly conservative forces embodied by those rebellious party members provided the perfect back drop against which Koizumi could burnish his image as the enemy of vested interests and the old-fashioned LDP system.

(5) In this paper we pointed out the contributing role played by the Kōmeitō vote in furthering the LDP cause and the potential power of the JCP's support base. While the recent election appears to have attenuated both the LDP's need for Kōmeitō support and the chance for the Communists to play a larger role in helping the DPJ in the future, this is not necessarily the case. A wave of new LDP legislators representing constituencies where they do not have a strong support foundation in place could very well rely heavily on Kōmeitō support in future elections, and JCP decisions on where to field candidates will probably continue to affect the fortunes of the Democrats.

By focusing relentlessly on the issue of postal privatization in the September 2005 contest, Prime Minister Koizumi bolstered his image as a reformer and won the hearts of many unaffiliated voters in urban districts. The scale of his party's victory has caused some observers to view this election as a major shift in the nation's political structure, one that represents the emergence of a reinvigorated LDP at the top of a "2005 setup." But the Koizumi effect made itself felt in this dramatic fashion mainly because of the arrangement of the electoral system, with its single-seat districts, and it is likely to be only temporary. There is almost no guarantee that the city voters who flocked to Koizumi's banner this time around will remain faithful to the LDP in future elections.

Koizumi worked hard to keep this contest from being a referendum on his record over the last four years, but the next prime minister will not be able to do the same. The next general election will see great attention focused on what has actually been accomplished. With its sweeping majority in the Diet the LDP has great power to move forward with its policies, but it has also been saddled with heavy expectations. How the party uses the political capital gained through its crushing victory to tackle the issues facing Japan today will determine whether it is rewarded or punished the next time around.

The Democratic Party of Japan must be deeply frustrated with the results of the recent election. The party goal going into the contest was to wrest a majority away from the LDP and take control of the nation's government, but this proved a difficult task in the face of the ruling coalition's popularity. Today's DPJ has little ability to garner votes or to press ahead with its agenda, leaving it to drift aimlessly as a minor force on the political stage. The previous two general elections, in 2001 and 2003, made it clear that the LDP and Kōmeitō are able to gain a parliamentary majority solely through their strength in the single-seat balloting. An exit poll carried out by the daily *Yomiuri Shimbun* showed that a remarkable 80 percent of Kōmeitō supporters cast their votes for LDP candidates in the single-seat districts in this year's election; the parties are growing more tightly connected with time. The opposition parties, meanwhile, show no sign of wanting to work together at election time. They seem to be moving in the other direction, in fact, as can be seen from the Democrats' refusal to back any Social Democratic Party (SDP) candidates this year. The opposition parties will have to begin working together and joining forces if they want to stand against the ruling coalition with any chance at replacing it in Japan's driver's seat.

These overtures are not something for the Democrats alone to work on. The Social Democrats and Communists will also need to open themselves up to this sort of cooperation. The SDP and JCP are minor parties in the Diet now, and it makes no sense for them to both field large numbers of candidates in local constituencies. By splitting the opposition vote, this hands the contest to the LDP and Kōmeitō, and it is hardly a good way for these parties to serve their supporters.

In the September election, voters seemed to make a clear choice in favor of implementing postal privatization. If this is a fair reading of the results, it suggests that it no longer makes much sense for a political party to campaign on a platform of policies with no prospect of being implemented. Only if it actually takes power can a party turn its policies into reality and thereby show its own value. The JCP, which has no prospect of winning power for itself, has taken to proclaiming itself "the only reliable opposition party," but by splitting the ranks of opposition voters it is indirectly supporting the present ruling coalition. Surely this is not what its supporters really want.

Japanese voters learned something of the fearsome power of their votes in this House of Representatives election. Politicians and the parties they belong to also gained a fresh understanding of the decisive power that the election process wields in a democracy. In the end, the most noteworthy result of the September 2005 contest may have been a heightened tension in the relationship among voters, parties, and politicians in Japan.

Courtesy of Japan Echo.

English version originally published in *Japan Echo* 32, no. 6 (2005):10–17. Translated from "Chihō no shikaku ga yonda 'toshi no hōki,'" *Chūō Kōron* (November 2005): 108–18 (courtesy of Chūōkōron Shinsha).

III-(6) Koizumi Ushers in the "2005 Setup"

Tanaka Naoki
Japan Echo, 2005

A period of frustration with the decision-making process in the Japanese political system began early in the 1990s. Dark clouds had settled in over the nation, and although the government made a number of policy choices to relieve the sense of unending stagnation, none led to a brighter outlook. The electoral system was reformed in 1994 with a view to making politics more dynamic, but none of the three subsequent general elections, which were held in 1996, 2000, and 2003, was successful in shaking off the national lethargy. The new electoral system replaced the multiseat districts of the House of Representatives with a combination of single-member constituencies and proportional-representation seats. The hope was that the single-member districts would help the electorate express its preferences among the available policy choices, but the reality was that sufficient attention was not given to what voters were expecting, and victorious parties paid scant heed to what they had been entrusted with accomplishing.

The recent election of September 11 has engendered a fresh breeze that, we may hope, will blow the clouds away. To be sure, the circumstances of Japanese society are hardly simple, regardless of the need for new ways of reaching political decisions. I would nonetheless declare that as far as the public sees it, Prime Minister Koizumi Junichirō has unmistakably provided a new technique for making political choices. He has engineered a realignment of political forces along the lines of support for or opposition to his own policies and political posture. He has in effect created political space presenting the people with a new opening for making choices. I believe that he has given new life to politics aimed at serious reform and thereby rung the death bell for the "1955 setup," in which the conservatives monopolized power and protected vested interests.

With the establishment of this new political space, we can expect to see its continuing use as a place for presenting voters with reform themes and political alternatives. As a struggle goes forward among all who wish to fill this space, we can expect to see a realignment of forces into what will provide the framework for a "2005 setup."

Demise of the 1955 Setup

As a result of the advent of the new setup, what specifically within the 1955 setup, which defined the contours of Japanese politics over the period following World War II, will come to an end? In a word, it is the pork-barrel politics by which politicians, while granting licenses and permissions as they squeeze money out of companies, channel the distribution of social resources into vested interests.

The 1955 setup started out as a political division between the forces for and against amending the new Constitution adopted under the Allied occupation after World War II, including its war-renouncing provision, but it soon evolved into an overall framework for protecting vested interests in battles over political spoils. On the surface, the conservative Liberal Democratic Party (LDP) and the Socialist-led opposition had a relationship of confrontation and rivalry, but over the course of the policymaking process, they constructed a complementary relationship that became a mechanism providing social stability.

The upshot was that the 1955 setup came to be plagued by susceptibility to money-driven corruption. When politicians are in a position to act as go-betweens in the distribution of resources, individual political decisions can become buttons that trigger huge fund flows, and unless politicians are almost obsessively concerned with cleanliness, they will have a hard time avoiding the taint of money.

Within the LDP, a major political reform drive took place from the late 1980s into the early 1990s. It was motivated by a desire to sever the vicious circle in which faction leaders would spread money around to claw their way to the top, only to be forced to resign shortly thereafter on account of their involvement in money scandals. At the time, the introduction of single-seat districts to the House of Representatives was billed as a change that would promote policy-based political choices, but in reality it was also needed to rescue the LDP from faction-maintenance costs that had grown too heavy to support. The burden of these expenses made a shift to public subsidies for electoral campaigns a necessary component of the political reform.

In pursuing this reform in the 1990s, the political leaders did not have any intention of dismantling the 1955 setup's arrangements for political meddling in government appropriations. The starting point of their arguments was the circumstances of the political circles on the supply side, and thus the reform did not encapsulate the fervent wishes of the voters on the demand side. Precisely because of the reform's poor coordination with demand-side needs, little progress was made toward narrowing the policy options even after three rounds of elections with single-seat districts. Before political space for reform could be opened up, clearing the way for the advent of the 2005 setup, an opportunity had to be awaited, and it eventually came along in the form of Prime Minister Koizumi and his pet scheme for privatizing the postal services.

One Step at a Time

If Koizumi had the objective of creating political space for reform and shaking up the system of pork barreling from the start, why did he not come out in favor of full privatization of the postal services as soon as he took office in 2001? To answer this question, we need to evaluate the nature of his commitment to the continuity of rule by the LDP.

In 1997 the cabinet of Prime Minister Hashimoto Ryūtarō, acting on a proposal advanced by the Administrative Reform Council, an advisory body, began work on a major reorganization of the central bureaucracy. After considerable debate, it was decided to leave the government in charge of the three branches of the postal system—mail, postal savings, and postal life insurance. The services were to be reestablished as three operations of a public corporation, and all the postal workers were to retain their status as civil servants. Koizumi, who was then the minister of health and welfare, had long been arguing that privatization was imperative, and he made his position very clear in 1998 when the basic law for overhauling the bureaucracy was being drafted. By threatening to resign unless his demands were met, he secured an agreement on a reform in the way funds were funneled from postal savings into the government's fiscal investment and loan program, along with a promise that attention would be given to allowing private operators to enter the mail business. But the law that was eventually passed had a stipulation slipped in stating that "no review shall be conducted for privatization or other purposes."

At the start of 2001 the overhaul of the government's ministries and agencies was put into effect, and in April an election was held for president of the LDP. In his campaign for the post, which would also make him prime minister, Koizumi affirmed his basic stance on reform in these words: "Let us entrust to the private sector anything it can handle and delegate to the regions anything they can handle. I have not changed my basic thinking on privatization of postal operations, but for the time being let us go ahead and place the three postal services under a public corporation and achieve private entry into the postal services, after which we can proceed with further reforms."

Having won the presidential election and taken office as prime minister in April 2001, Koizumi started the process of setting up the state corporation that became known as Japan Post, and in June he set up a discussion group to give further thought to the postal services. These moves made clear his political intention to keep the flame of reform burning. In his thinking, the advent of the state corporation was to be but a steppingstone on the way to privatization. Japan Post was officially founded in April 2003, and shortly thereafter, during the campaign for the November 2003 general election, Koizumi made his first formal pledge to pursue full privatization of the postal services.

It was back at the time of the 1979 general election that the leaders of the political world first took serious note of Koizumi's potential, recognizing that he might someday become prime minister. That was his third successful bid for a seat in the House of Representatives. The main issue in the election was the controversial call Prime Minister Ōhira Masayoshi had made for the introduction of a general consumption tax. Other young and middle-ranking legislators shied away from endorsing this unpopular measure, fearful that voters would desert them. But Koizumi gave it his unequivocal support, declaring that the government should not be allowed to go on running up deficits, and he won reelection.

Around this time Koizumi began to assert that allowing the private sector to handle anything it was capable of handling was a principle that should be applied to the postal services. In the course of the private campaign he then embarked on, he was made aware of the structure of the forces lined up against his position. Among the politicians standing in his way were many of the ilk of the legendary former prime minister Tanaka Kakuei (1972–74).

Post Offices for Collecting Funds

It is fair to say that Tanaka put the finishing touches on the structure of intervention by politicians in government appropriations. One of the key components of the structure is a kind of special post office that does not operate mail delivery routes but does provide postal savings and life insurance services in addition to selling stamps and the like. Tanaka was a promoter of the policy to expand the numbers of these small post offices in the environs of big cities.

At the time of the establishment of the 1955 setup, Japan had 8,420 of these special post offices. By the second half of the 1960s Japan was well into the high-growth period, and during the six years of the Izanagi boom (1965–70) alone, the nation's production capacity, which was centered on heavy industry, approximately doubled. Public works, which required huge infusions of capital, were going forward full swing, and this provided the justification for the arrangements by which money was collected at post offices in the form of deposits and life insurance premiums and funneled into the public and semipublic "special corporations" that were carrying out public works. The authorities were hard put to supply infrastructure as fast as the need for it expanded, and they also had to make a response to worsening problems of environmental destruction. In this setting, people took it for granted that the government should be deeply involved in economic affairs.

Within this business model, the establishment of additional special post offices helped secure a greater flow of funds for infrastructure projects. These post offices were set up at the rate of 300 a year during the 1964–67 period. The pace slowed later, but from 1955, when the LDP took power, to 1993, when it was briefly booted out, as many as 6,334 of these special post offices were newly created.

The aim behind this manipulation of the postal services was the creation of a network of concessions capable of gathering money and votes at the same time. The funds made available by postal savings and life insurance were channeled into public works and other projects through the institutions handling the government's fiscal investments and loans, and they also became a source of the political funds flowing into the coffers of politicians from companies engaged in activities like road construction. The members of the LDP banded together into *zoku*, or "tribes" of legislators working closely with bureaucrats and the industries under their jurisdiction, and five of these groups came to assume a central place in the structure for parceling out economic benefits. These were the *zoku* legislators specializing in road construction, postal services, agriculture, education, and health and welfare. At the same time, the members of these five *zoku* developed an affinity for each other, and many of them gathered together in the Tanaka faction. In fact, this faction held so many influential *zoku* specialists working to protect industrial clients and remedy their complaints that people called it a "general hospital." Within this faction it was easy to see the benefits of the interconnections among *zoku* legislators.

The habit of the five *zoku* to act in concert developed into something of a secret ritual within the LDP. Thus when Koizumi embarked virtually unaccompanied on his quest to privatize the postal services, he was bound to run into a wall of resistance erected by all five *zoku* working together. When in his 2001 campaign for LDP president he raised a call for "destroying the LDP," what he meant was that the vested interests of the united *zoku* legislators should be smashed. He was not mouthing this war cry just to pander to voters. He was in fact declaring the start of a political battle.

When Koizumi formed his first cabinet after his victory, he refused to accept the names the LDP factions handed him for appointment to cabinet positions. This was not a sign that he opposed the existence of the factions, however. He had his sights set on consolidating the reform camp within the LDP, and he wanted to make it quite clear to each of his ministers that he had picked them personally. If we recognize that even at that point he could foresee the possibility of a showdown in which the cabinet would pass a resolution dissolving the lower house, thereby forcing an election with the potential to destroy the LDP as happened this year, we can appreciate that he wanted to be sure that his cabinet would follow his lead.

The Post–Cold War Global Economy

After the Soviet Union unraveled in 1991, Japan ceased to be bothered by external forces seeking to destroy democracy and the market mechanism. This development had direct meaning for the future of Japan's political system. It unfastened the tight bonds of the Cold War years, when the constraints of the East-West conflict required that there be no crack in the nation's armor. If there is no act that can be construed as serving the interest of the enemy, then no external framework can be imposed on the political system to limit reform, and no reason exists for exercising restraint when lashing out at the corruption of money politics.

At the same time, in the days of the Cold War Japan's involvement in the international community could only go so far, and Japan was also able to use these limits craftily to secure a degree of freedom in its relations with the United States. Now, however, the removal of these Cold War restraints from all countries has put Japan in a position where it cannot refrain from total involvement in international affairs on the basis of decisions it arrives at independently.

The maintenance of the 1955 setup had required that attention be devoted only to ways of distributing wealth domestically, but cries of distress came to be heard from parties asserting that this is not enough. Japan has found that it does not have sufficient human talent for dealing with international affairs, and it also needs to come up with principles for domestic economic management that are consistent with all-out international involvement. In this age of the global economy, Japan must move ahead with a market-opening program that satisfies the need for coherency in its international involvement even in such fields as government procurement and agricultural policy. In this light, we can appreciate that the 1955 setup was a framework for the power structure designed for the days when Japan needed only to be partially involved in the international community.

We need also to bear in mind that the rapid evolution of the global economy has made it imperative for the Japanese to grapple in earnest with the creation of value in the domestic economy. What was important in the 1955 setup was dividing up the economic pie in ways that could hold domestic fissures to a small size. Acting under the slogan of balanced development nationwide, practically all of the country's 3,000 local government bodies drew up community development plans premised on population growth. In Hokkaido, for instance, the great majority of municipal governments unveiled plans even in the 1990s based on the expectation that development would cause the local population to expand. After all, if they did not project an increase in residents, they would be unable to secure money from the central government for making new investments in port and harbor infrastructure and road construction. The mandarins in Tokyo, meanwhile, were happy to accept this overall design, for it meant that their job was only to make adjustments in fund allocations. In this way the 1955 setup spread a protective umbrella over a structure that increasingly became a fabrication.

The general line politicians took under the 1955 setup involved coming up with ways to reduce the differentials of a dual economy, in which both efficient and inefficient businesses were present, and to mend the fissures within society. For a short time, this led to the emergence of a society in which everyone claimed membership in the middle class. But the advent of the global economy began to undermine the society's sustainability, and government policies needed to be reoriented, with less emphasis placed on distribution of resources and more on value creation. Despite this momentous shift in the premises on which the setup rested, though, many politicians were slow to bring their thinking into line with the new realities. And at just that juncture Japan's bubble economy collapsed, setting the stage for the slump of the 1990s.

Infrastructure for an Investment Society

One more factor to bear in mind when considering the demise of the 1955 setup is Japan's aging population. The 1955 setup came to be supplied with a full set of social security policies. In 1961 the construction of systems providing universal coverage for pensions and health insurance was completed, and in 2000 a system of nursing care for the elderly was launched. These were the outcome of the spread of the thinking that society as a whole should manage the risks that individuals will someday confront. In the current phase of huge deficits in public finance, however, much of the funding of these insurance schemes has been shifted to subsidies funneled into the government's insurance accounts, and these public expenditures fall on the shoulders of taxpayers.

If there were a match in each period between the size of contributions and the size of the benefits, it would be possible to attain sound management of the social security safety net. In practice, however, Japan's public pension and insurance schemes were designed from the start to rely to some extent on infusions of subsidies

from the treasury. At present there is such a huge shortfall in the receipts of the social security system that government bonds cover close to half of the expenditures. In principle each generation should pool sufficient funds to meet the risks its members face, but in fact the current generation has blithely moved a large portion of its own charges onto the credit cards of its children and grandchildren. This is nothing but duping investors by shifting losses between accounts, and it bodes ill for the prospects of sustaining Japanese society in the future.

Overseas scholars of demographics say that the remarkable decline in Japan's birthrate signifies nothing less than a revolution in the consciousness of Japanese women. The 1955 setup was supposed to bring a gentle society into being, but what it in fact gave birth to can be summed up as a generation that hardly pauses to think before passing on to future generations the bills for its own lavish treatment. If this generation is serious about pooling money to meet its own risks, it needs to use a mix of three reforms to attain financial health in social security finances. These are to increase the size of contributions, lower the level of benefits, and streamline the operations of the bodies administering the various schemes to make them more efficient.

Japan's pensions need to be shifted from the current pay-as-you-go financing to a fully funded basis. If we fail to come up with the resolve to make this change, the generations to come will sense a growing burden on their shoulders. As things stand, the policy system of Japan's postwar democracy lies open to the charge that it is bereft of the concept of self-support. When in this way the 1955 setup is exposed to the harsh light of a historical reassessment from the bottom up, it cannot help but begin to crumble. It was under the setup that the structure of extravagance in the social security system took shape, creating what is essentially a vested interest of the current generation. At least until very recently, nobody showed much interest in making a political issue out of this structure of extravagance, and this failure to act in itself reveals a flaw in the setup's design.

Another flaw in the design can be seen in the shortage of infrastructure for building a society supported by portfolio investments. The immaturity of this infrastructure could even deal a fatal injury to Japan's old-aged society. This is because such a society moves through two phases, one in which savings are accumulated and the other in which they are drawn down. To the wage earner pressed by the circumstances of everyday life and intent only on making ends meet from month to month, infrastructure for an investment society may sound like a needless luxury, but even those whose family budgets are in the red month after month are regularly paying pension premiums, since the money for this comes out of their wages before they receive them. In this light, every single Japanese wage earner is also an investor. And what would happen if pension funds failed to swell smoothly with the passage of time? For pensioners in the old-aged society, life could become quite bleak.

Investments are a means by which economic resources are apportioned at some point in the future. It goes without saying that training for making wise investments should not be neglected. The investment society cannot flower unless it is provided with the requisite investment infrastructure, including that for investor training.

Executing a Deep Cut

One-fourth of the Japanese people's financial assets have accumulated in the savings and life insurance accounts of Japan Post. Money flows naturally into accounts of this type, since they have a government guarantee. Seen from the vantage point of consolidating infrastructure for an investment society, however, such fund flows are retrogressive. In addition, the government guarantee inevitably has an effect on the structure of the assets managed by Japan Post. This is because of the iron rule that government-backed assets must be managed so as to assure full repayment.

Because the removal of government guarantees from financial assets constitutes the first step toward the rounding out of the investment society, privatization of the postal services cannot be avoided. But when the package of postal-privatization bills was placed before the National Diet this year, it went down to defeat at the hands of legislators still operating under the assumptions of the 1955 setup. It was at that point that

the lower house was dissolved to hold a general election, and voters made it quite clear that they were in favor of privatization. Having been kept informed by the media, the public was well aware of the whereabouts of the problems.

Japan is at a point where a whole series of reforms must be carried out in order to maintain the health of society over the years to come. The seriousness of the crises we confront can be observed from the steep decline in the number of children and the very low level of the voting rate of young adults. It was essential that the political world perceive this situation and present voters with concrete remedies for the various ills, but awareness of this need was slow to spread. If political space for reform was to be created, accordingly, some way had to be found to promote the withdrawal of those Diet members who had become unable to extricate themselves from the web of vested interests. A scheme for enticing these legislators to cut their own throats had to be found, even if it was in the nature of a confidence trick.

Koizumi moved into power with the valuable experience of once having received high marks from the LDP top brass when, daring to part ways from the defenders of vested interests, he ran for reelection without abandoning his conviction that the public would suffer from the debts the government was building up. Because of this, he chose not to leave the LDP even after he began to champion thoroughgoing reform. This was a party, he was convinced, that was capable of reform from within even in the face of internal resistance so deeply embedded that it had to be surgically removed. Thanks to his belief, a foundation is now being laid for the construction of the 2005 setup.

It perhaps is only proper that the postal services have provided the starting point for the new reform drive. With a host of new special post offices coming into being, especially in the 1960s, postal administration provided the turf where the defenders of vested interests in the LDP erected their core defense installations. And given the affinity of all the *zoku* legislators for each other, Koizumi and his fellow crusaders undoubtedly presumed that the postal services could best expose to light the network of vested interests that had crystallized around the core.

The Democratic Party of Japan (DPJ) also waves the banner of reform. Expecting it to take the lead, the LDP groups opposed to reform were slow to take note of all the preparations that were going forward on groundwork for the 2005 setup. As a result, the LDP ended up having to execute a deep cut to excise the resistance within it. If we see the ultimate objective as nothing less than the formation of a "new LDP" and a new regime, we can appreciate that postal reform merely marks the start of a whole series of changes. In that event, all the forces interested in ensuring the sustainability of Japanese society will need to take part in reviewing and reforming the ties of collusion between interest groups and Diet members.

Ending Cozy Relationships

In the agricultural sector, for instance, the interest groups with connections to the farming, forestry, and fishing industries need to be examined. Between 1990 and 2004 there was a 46 percent decline in the number of full-time farming households, which fell from 710,000 to 386,000. Despite this, there was no appreciable decline either in the some 10,000 members of local agriculture commissions or in the roughly equal number of employees of land improvement districts, who work out of agricultural extension centers. There are also about 10,000 staff members of agricultural mutual-aid associations, as well as 250,000 employees of agricultural cooperatives. These are not people directly engaged in production, and we need to ask if they are continuing to be employed in such large numbers only because their wages can be taken out of budget appropriations for the support of the agricultural sector.

In the fields of medical care and nursing care, meanwhile, the functioning of the administering bodies, whose operations may not be up to par in terms of sustainability and efficiency, needs to be thoroughly investigated. Under the 1955 setup, the LDP had a cozy relationship with medical societies and related organizations, but the new LDP is likely to develop relations with them that are tenser than could ever have been imagined until now.

It is common knowledge that the *zoku* legislators who have gathered around MEXT, the Ministry of Education, Culture, Sports, Science, and Technology, are opposed to cuts in the treasury subsidies for compulsory education. The crisis in the schools is so critical that parents are convinced that the only remedy is to give free rein to the ingenuity and originality of the educators on the front lines, but the MEXT *zoku* legislators are desperately defending the state's direct involvement in education. They are apparently using the name of the state's responsibility for compulsory education to conceal the realities of the protection they extend to vested interests. The establishment of the 2005 setup will require the new LDP and the DPJ to raise the flag of reform jointly and set off on a quest to formulate specific reform guidelines. The result should be further progress in the demolition of the five *zoku*'s alliance.

There seems to be some confusion about why moves toward a change of setup have begun at this point. Perhaps what is needed is a framework for interpreting the state of Japanese society in the period since World War II. I would say that under the 1955 setup, this society was one in which a number of "equilibrium solutions" existed simultaneously. Each quarter of society worked out a solution providing it with a reasonable degree of stability, and each put forward its own representatives to champion its interests.

A plain illustration of the coexistence of multiple solutions is provided by the arrest of the vice-president of Japan Highway Public Corporation for breach of trust. The case involves a bid-rigging scheme that parceled out bridge-building work among companies, and because the scheme drove up the project costs paid by the corporation, it was possible to lodge the charge of breach of trust. Much of the pork barreling by politicians involves just such scattering of money about for government-funded work. The administrative systems of the central government's ministries and agencies came to be entangled in the ties of collusion, and the procedures the mandarins typically relied on to parcel out work tended to artificially elevate costs and thus had the potential to violate the trust of the taxpayers. In this light, the 2005 setup will also thoroughly shake up the culture of the mandarins. In fact, the star of the mandarins will fall with the collapse of the 1955 setup, which they have been busily propping up.

In summary, we can see that in the context of transformations in the external environment and accumulating changes on the domestic front, a broad wave of reform has been set in motion by the approach of a situation that will threaten the very existence of Japanese society if steps are not taken to reshape it. Although a variety of fortuitous circumstances were involved, a display of powerful leadership aimed at creating political space for reform just happened to come along at this time. But this was also a logical development. All those in favor of bringing the 2005 setup into being will no doubt redouble their efforts. Now that the political arena has been broadened, we can expect young lawmakers to set up more platforms from which to broadcast their positions. What is certain is that whoever is to follow Koizumi will have to undergo rigorous training in this arena.

Courtesy of Japan Echo.

English version originally published in *Japan Echo* 32, no. 6 (2005):18–23. Translated from "'05 nen taisei' no tanjō to shōgeki," *Chūō Kōron* (October 2005): 59–69; abridged by about one-fourth (courtesy of Chūōkōron Shinsha).

What's Gone Wrong with the Abe Administration?

Nonaka Naoto
Japan Echo, 2007

Last September, Abe Shinzō swept to victory in the Liberal Democratic Party (LDP)'s presidential election, winning about two-thirds of the votes in the race to succeed Koizumi Junichirō as leader of the ruling party and, by extension, prime minister. Following up on this impressive entrance, which was made possible by his nationwide popularity, Abe visited China and South Korea soon after his inauguration as prime minister and succeeded in improving Japan's relations with these two neighbors. He continued his positive start by taking a strong stand against North Korea's nuclear test, spearheading international criticism of Pyongyang. It was not long, though, before the new administration's fortunes took a turn for the worse. "Team Abe," as the prime minister's inner circle has been dubbed, began to malfunction. The administration was buffeted by a series of gaffes by senior LDP figures, friction between Abe's inner circle and LDP members of the House of Councillors over this summer's upper house election, and flip-flopping over the return to the LDP fold of lawmakers who opposed postal privatization and over the handling of tax revenue set aside for road construction. There was also no letup in a stream of political funding scandals involving cabinet ministers.

Why has the administration failed to function in the manner that Prime Minister Abe would have wished? One oft-cited cause is that in choosing cabinet ministers and party executives, Abe unashamedly rewarded those who had helped to make him prime minister, with the result that many top positions are held by people not well suited to their jobs. There has been a steady stream of complaints that Chief Cabinet Secretary Shiozaki Yasuhisa, LDP secretary-general Nakagawa Hidenao, LDP Policy Research Council chairman Nakagawa Shōichi, Deputy Chief Cabinet Secretary Matoba Junzō, and Executive Secretary to the Prime Minister Inoue Yoshiyuki are not fulfilling the roles expected of them in terms of keeping the administration on an even keel.

Another problem is the lack of clarity in the delineation of the roles and powers of the many panels established to advise the prime minister directly, such as the Education Rebuilding Council, and of his five special advisors. This vagueness has led to confusion and stagnation in the policymaking process. The increasing willingness of LDP lawmakers in the House of Councillors to take an independent line has added to the sense of disarray. What is more, Abe's style of politics, which he himself has compared to Chinese herbal medicine—producing results in a steady, unspectacular manner—has failed to capture the imagination in the way that Koizumi did with his prescriptions of potent potions for reform.

What is certain is that as people have begun to make unfavorable comparisons between Abe and his predecessor, and as errors in apportioning key government jobs and indecision over the return of the postal privatization rebels to the LDP have come to light, Abe's reputation for strong leadership, which was forged through his handling of the abductions of Japanese nationals by North Korea, has quickly dissipated. And with disappointment spreading among the public, the Abe cabinet's approval ratings—the prime minister's biggest weapon—have been on the slide.

Falling approval ratings are not the only thing sapping the administration's strength, however. It also faces a more serious, structural problem, and without understanding this it is impossible to gain an overall picture of the problems Abe faces.

It has long been a criticism of LDP administrations that a dualistic government-party structure and collusion between bureaucrats and "tribes" of lawmakers representing special interests lead to government guided by vested interests, not principles, and to a lack of leadership. These are, of course, important issues. Comparisons with the structures and histories of governments in other industrialized democracies reveal a slightly different picture, however. I would like to analyze the workings of the Abe administration using the concept of the "core executive."

Core executive theory is a means of examining all of the influential individuals and groups that are involved in a government's central decision-making structure. It considers the respective roles and mutual relationships of the prime minister, other cabinet ministers, ruling party executives, and senior central government bureaucrats, and it also takes a look at the national legislature and, in some cases, the opposition parties. By analyzing all those involved, the theory clarifies the leadership attributes of the prime minister and his office. It also illuminates any constraints on this leadership, on how the policymaking process is coordinated overall, on the relationships and division of roles between politicians and bureaucrats, and on other aspects of policymaking. In short, through comparisons with other countries this concept sheds light on the characteristics of how decisions are actually made at the heart of the Japanese government based on the nation's constitutional and legal framework.

Two Pillars That Support the Core Executive

How are political leadership and high-level policy coordination exercised in Britain and France, for example? The textbook answer is that in these and other countries with a parliamentary cabinet system, a mechanism has evolved over the years for centralizing power in a government led by a prime minister. (France also has a president, but its government essentially operates on the basis of the confidence placed in it by the National Assembly.) Under such systems, the people choose a parliament (in particular, a lower house) through direct elections, and the government is headed by a prime minister selected on the basis of support by a majority in the lower house. The government both requires the confidence of and is answerable to the lower house. This results in a system of close collaboration between the parliament and the government and enables the prime minister, who has the effective power to dissolve parliament, to exercise strong leadership. This is the typical understanding of how such systems function.

While these countries may share the same basic parliamentary cabinet system, however, it goes without saying that the actual mechanisms of government vary greatly according to each nation's institutions and historical experiences. Deducing from British and French history and political reality, it is possible to identify two major preconditions for the exercise of strong political leadership.

One is that the main political parties must have a centralized structure in which executives exercise clear leadership. The other is the rationalization of the parliamentary process—meaning, for example, that one house must enjoy clear primacy in a bicameral system and that the government must possess the authority to manage parliamentary affairs.

Britain and France differ greatly in terms of their historical experiences and the political roles played today by their administrative elites, but broadly speaking both countries fulfill the two conditions described above. This results in clarity regarding such fundamental issues as where political power and authority lie and what actions political leaders can take. With authority, of course, comes responsibility; these cannot be separated. They are founded on interparty competition based on election manifestoes and on intraparty democracy based on rigorous debate among party members, adoption of resolutions at party conferences, and elections for the party leadership.

In Britain the centralized structure of major parties originated as a means of countering royal authority within Parliament and was reinforced from the nineteenth century onward as parties modernized to cope with expanded suffrage. In France, meanwhile, centralized party structures quickly took hold after the constitution of the Fifth Republic was adopted in 1958, heralding the introduction of single-seat electoral districts for elections to the National Assembly (lower house).

The rationalization of the parliamentary process, which I cited as the second condition above, consists of two specific elements: rationalization of the bicameral system and the reinforcement of government control over parliamentary affairs. As for the former, both the British House of Commons and the French National Assembly have clearly established primacy as the lower houses in their respective countries' parliaments. In Britain, the power of the House of Lords to veto legislation from the House of Commons has been gradually reduced since the beginning of the twentieth century, and now the most that the upper house can do is to delay the enactment of legislation by a short time. There is also a well-established convention that the House of Lords will not oppose major items of legislation that the governing party promised in its general election manifesto. In France, meanwhile, although the constitution of the Fifth Republic allows for legislation to be passed back and forth between the two houses, it also makes clear that the ultimate power to pass a law lies with the National Assembly.

It was also in Britain that government control over parliamentary affairs first became an established practice. The original parliamentary mechanism, in which the sovereign controlled the convening and dissolution of Parliament, became a mere skeleton as the government's authority to decide parliamentary schedules and procedures gradually became institutionalized. During France's history of repeated revolutions and revolts, the country lurched between two extremes: authoritarian regimes that completely incapacitated the parliament and regimes in which sovereignty rested with the parliament. The establishment of the Fifth Republic and the introduction of the principle of *parlementarisme rationalisé*, however, gave the government sweeping powers to control and intervene in a broad range of parliamentary affairs, such as the schedule of parliamentary business, the handling of debates and amendments, and methods for passing legislation. In other words, both Britain and France are governed through a rationalized parliamentary process, with the lower house having manifest primacy over the upper house and the government possessing robust powers to intervene in parliamentary affairs.

The Traditional Structure of LDP Administrations

A centralized party structure and a rationalized parliamentary process form the bedrock on which the core executive is built. How does the traditional setup in an LDP administration measure up to these requirements? The answer, in short, is that past LDP administrations have not met these conditions.

The LDP has always been a conspicuously decentralized, unintegrated party. Internal decision-making was essentially a bottom-up, consensus-based process, factions competed for influence, and the party's headquarters had little control over the LDP prefectural federations serving as the party's regional organizations. Under the system of multiseat districts for elections in the lower house (House of Representatives), which was in effect through the early 1990s, the success or failure of a candidate depended not on the party organization but on the supporters' associations of individual lawmakers and candidates. Under these circumstances, there was no prospect of establishing a centralized party setup.

Of course, centralizing party power carries the risk of creating an internal dictatorship. Yet a quasi-democratic internal party setup whose sole purpose is to ensure that LDP legislators get convenient opportunities to speak their minds (with potential veto power) also presents serious problems, because it signifies a lack of accountability to voters. Under these circumstances, a certain degree of centralization is unavoidable if we are to build a highly transparent intraparty democracy and a system in which parties fulfill their responsibility to voters through manifestoes.

No progress whatsoever has been made, meanwhile, on the task of rationalizing the parliamentary process in Japan. The prime minister's authority to dissolve the legislature applies only to the House of Representatives and does not extend to the House of Councillors, effectively giving this, the upper house in Japan's bicameral system, tremendous power. The turmoil caused when the House of Councillors rejected Prime Minister Koizumi Junichirō's postal privatization plan in 2005 illustrates the severity of this problem, and it is also notable that the need to secure a majority in the upper house has been the motivating factor behind the formation of a series of coalition governments since the 1990s. What is more, while defeat for the ruling party in an upper house election does not signify a change of government, it is generally regarded as sufficient to bring about a change of prime minister. The fact that the House of Councillors has so much sway effectively doubles the frequency of national elections in which the government's survival is at stake, making it extremely difficult run an administration in a normal way.

The fact that the government has almost no direct means of controlling parliamentary affairs is one of the singular features of the Japanese constitution. This, along with the sheer duration of LDP rule, is what gave rise to the practice by which *zoku*, "tribes" of lawmakers linked to particular special interests, screen government bills in the LDP's Policy Research Council before they are presented to the Diet. In countries like Britain and France, there is no need for governments to gain party approval in advance of submitting bills to the legislature. Demands from the ruling party are handled as part of the parliamentary process (usually at the committee stages), with the government taking the lead. The Japanese government, however, has no means to control the Diet and so has no option but to rely heavily on the ruling party. It is the nature of Japan's parliamentary process, including the flaws of the nation's bicameral system, that is at the root of the peculiar relationship between the government and the Diet and the role of the ruling party as an intermediary between them.

Centrifugal Force at the Heart of Power

Based on the above, let us now examine how the core executive actually functions in Japan. The main features of the core executive in LDP administrations are powerful centrifugal tendencies, the central role of the bureaucratic chain of

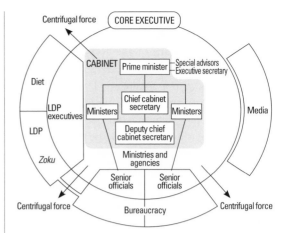

Figure. The Structure of the Core Executive in Japan

command, and the limits on the prime minister's room for maneuver.

The attached figure is a schematic representation of this setup. The centrifugal tendency has two main sources. The first is the system in which each ministry has responsibility for its own area of policy. The ministers who are charged with overseeing each field of administration do not have the resources to match their authority, making them heavily dependent on the organizational resources of their ministries' respective bureaucratic machines. Ministers effectively become administrative representatives working according to bureaucratic logic and interests, with each bringing the thinking of the administrative organ he or she heads to the cabinet and the core executive, resulting in a compartmentalized government that is pulled in all directions.

The second source of centrifugal force is the decentralized nature of the ruling LDP and its bottom-up policymaking process. As noted earlier, the government's inability to control the Diet has resulted in the institutionalization of a system by which the ruling party is allowed to screen government bills before they are presented to the Diet. What is more, the divisions and departments of each ministry and the *zoku* groupings of lawmakers have built up a structure of close collaboration that also involves special-interest groups. This "iron triangle" spearheaded by the *zoku* members is located on the margins of the formal structure, pulling the decision-making process ever further away from the center.

The second feature of the core executive in an LDP administration is the central role of the bureaucratic chain of command. The core of the government structure is quite plainly a bureaucratic mechanism. The overall coordination of major policies is undertaken by the chain of officials leading from the chief cabinet secretary via the deputy and assistant chief cabinet secretaries down through the Cabinet Secretariat, and bureaucratic thinking dominates this mechanism almost right to the top. The deputy chief cabinet secretaries play a major administrative role in this process. The chief cabinet secretary, who is a politician, plays a vital role, but functions more as a coordinator than as a decision-maker. To be sure, the top LDP executives have significant influence, but this is exercised mainly within the party itself and in Diet affairs. In other words, overall policy coordination even high up the core executive is conducted largely through bureaucratic functioning.

The biggest feature of the core executive, though, is the impotence of the mechanisms that are supposed to assist the prime minister directly in exercising political leadership and the number of constraints on the prime minister's actions. The easiest way to understand this is to compare the mechanisms in Japan with those in Britain. The British prime minister traditionally possesses a wide range of powers to make personnel decisions, covering everything from the recommendation of people for honors to the appointment and dismissal of cabinet ministers. The prime minister also has the power to set up and select the members of cabinet committees, which serve as alternatives to full cabinet meetings and enable ministerial-level decisions to be reached more swiftly and flexibly. Furthermore, the prime minister is empowered to adapt major planks of the administrative machinery as he or she sees fit, including the so-called ministerial code, the prime ministerial support apparatus, and the configuration of offices in each ministry. What is more, there is no need to pass a law each time such a change is made. The right to sum up discussions in cabinet meetings is another powerful tool at the prime minister's disposal.

In Japan, by sharp contrast, administrative authority lies not with the prime minister but with the cabinet, a collegial body. There are a variety of constraints on how the authority is used, such as the laborious procedures for submitting a policy to the cabinet, consensus-based cabinet decision-making, and the established principle that each minister is responsible for managing his or her own area of policy. This situation may be a reflection of the traditional Japanese view of power, which holds that it should be separated from authority. Whatever the reason, the conditions that would enable the prime minister to be directly involved in policy as a political leader are simply not in place. This is very different from the situation in countries like Britain and France, where the prime minister and his or her support apparatus play a decisive role in a wide range of policy fields.

Koizumi's Success, Abe's Challenge

The nature of the core executive in LDP administrations has slowly begun to change since the implementation of institutional reforms, such as the introduction of a combination of single-seat constituencies and proportional representation for the lower house, which was first implemented in the 1996 general election, and the overhaul of central government organs crafted under Prime Minister Hashimoto Ryūtarō (1996–98), which was implemented in 2001. Even so, the core executive continues basically to lack cohesive power and remains strongly influenced by bureaucratic dynamics and characterized above all by constraints on the exercise of leadership. Why was Prime Minister Koizumi, who took office in 2001, able to achieve a certain degree of success under this setup? And how has his successor, Abe Shinzō, fared so far?

Two principal factors explain Koizumi's success. The first is that he gained popularity by adopting the position of an un-LDP-like reformist "maverick," attacking his powerful opponents within the party as being in the grip of vested interests. This was an adept, populist way of controlling public opinion; it created a struggle within the LDP in which Koizumi held the upper hand, and it reduced the opposition parties to irrelevance. The other factor behind Koizumi's success was his strategic use of the Council on Economic and Fiscal Policy (CEFP). The CEFP was created as part of the administrative overhaul implemented shortly before Koizumi became prime minister, and he gave it a central role throughout his premiership. He brought in Takenaka Heizō, a private-sector economist, as a member of his cabinet, and he put him in charge of a team that operated the council strategically and adopted various tactics to maximize its effectiveness, such as making use of papers produced by the council's private-sector members.

The important point in terms of the core executive is that Koizumi made the CEFP function not as an ordinary policy-coordination body under the chief cabinet secretary but as a separate, strategic policymaking organ charged with addressing key political issues. What is more, Koizumi succeeded in retaining a firm grip on the tiller of his government by refusing to allow the LDP to be involved in setting the basic direction of the council, thus deliberately engineering a confrontation with his own party and taking full advantage of his most important resource, his popularity with the public. This, combined with his adept use of prime ministerial powers over personnel matters, was the setup that enabled him to be so successful. To put it another way, by harnessing the unique resource of his personal popularity, Koizumi was able to strengthen and maintain the cohesive force of his administration, thus transcending the flaws of a core executive characterized by powerful centrifugal forces and leadership constraints. He made strategic use of the CEFP as a policymaking instrument under his own control, separate from the bureaucratic chain of command in the Cabinet Secretariat.

How about the current prime minister, Abe Shinzō? Bearing in mind the features of the core executive in Japan, the situation under the Abe administration can be summarized as follows. First, the channel between the chief cabinet secretary and the prime minister's executive secretary, which should be a pillar of the administration, is not functioning well. Chief Cabinet Secretary Shiozaki Yasuhisa has tried to intervene in each and every issue as a decision-maker, rather than a coordinator, and Executive Secretary Inoue Yoshiyuki's failure to control politicians' and bureaucrats' access to the prime minister effectively has made matters worse. While Abe's attempt to bolster his authority by increasing the number of prime ministerial special advisors had a certain logic to it, there is a considerable risk that competition among them over loyalty and access to the prime minister may destabilize the core executive, as reports of a feud between Shiozaki and Sekō Hiroshige, the special advisor for public relations, show. To be sure, the prime minister's direct support apparatus is extremely weak. This is because the Cabinet Secretariat, which is at the heart of the core executive, is controlled by the chief cabinet secretary. An ill-considered expansion of this apparatus, however, is liable to cause even more instability by muddying the workings of the core executive as a whole.

Like the prime minister's special advisors, the panels established directly under the prime minister also pose a problem in terms of their status and role. This could even conflict with the principle of each ministry being responsible for administering its particular area of policy and with the principle that ministers are accountable to the Diet, which is close to the heart of the parliamentary cabinet system. The panels may answer directly to the prime minister, but their real significance is that they lie outside the Cabinet Secretariat chain of command headed by the chief cabinet secretary. The basic problem is that the discussions in these bodies—with the special advisors at the core—cannot on their own produce final decisions regarding government policy.

The appointment of these special advisors is said to be in imitation of the American system of presidential advisors, and it has also been proposed to establish a national security council on the US model. But in the American system of government, featuring a clear separation of powers among three branches, executive authority is strongly concentrated in the hands of the president. Since Japan's administrative setup and core executive are strongly centrifugal, it is questionable whether arrangements based on direct imitation of US models will function effectively here.

Another problem with the Abe administration

is its sense of distance—or lack thereof—from the ruling party. As I have already stated, the LDP is a highly decentralized party, and parliamentary process in the Diet has not yet been rationalized. This is why the ruling party and the upper house have so much autonomy, as demonstrated by the jostling over fiscal resources earmarked for road construction. Keeping a proper sense of distance means having a clear understanding of which government policy proposals are likely to provoke fierce opposition from within the ruling party and acting accordingly to develop strategies for implementation of the reform agenda. Political acumen and strategy are essential if the administration is to overcome opposition within the ruling party and implement genuine reforms. The Abe administration does not appear to be equipped with such a strategic approach, including effective ways of utilizing the CEFP.

This spring, as his approval ratings continued to fall, Prime Minister Abe appeared to throw caution to the wind and began pursuing controversial policies rooted in his own convictions. But the initiatives he has taken—the bill on referendums for approving constitutional amendments, educational reforms, and restrictions on *amakudari* (the practice of bureaucrats' retiring to take jobs in sectors they formerly regulated)—give the impression of a scattershot approach. Taking this kind of approach is one of the political options open to a prime minister, but in this case it seems to be an indication of extreme frustration on Abe's part. Unable to find a strategy for breaking free of the constraints on the core executive, the prime minister appears to be displaying an almost desperate sort of defiance, using the approach of the House of Councillors election as an excuse to do as he likes.

At this point everything depends on the verdict of the voters in the upcoming election. Whatever the result of the voting, though, the basic setup of a core executive lacking in cohesive power will remain. Even if it comes through the upper house election unscathed, the Abe administration will need to fundamentally rethink how the core executive functions if it is truly to stamp its authority on the political process.

Courtesy of Japan Echo.

English version originally published in *Japan Echo* 34, no. 4 (2007): 35–39. Translated from "Abe seiken no shissei chūsū wa, naze kinō shinai no ka," *Ronza* (June 2007): 92–99 (courtesy of the Asahi Shimbun).

The DPJ at the Helm

After three ineffective Liberal Democratic Party (LDP) cabinets in as many years, the party went down to a disastrous defeat in the 2009 general election. The Democratic Party of Japan (DPJ) won a majority in the House of Representatives and seized the reins of government. In this section's leading essay, "Who Ended the LDP's Reign?" Taniguchi Masaki, Uenohara Hideaki, and Sakaiya Shirō trace the events leading up to that reversal and analyze the voter behavior that yielded such a dramatic outcome.

After decades of almost uninterrupted rule by the LDP, there was intense interest in the new regime's prospects and progress. Writing shortly after DPJ leader Hatoyama Yukio formed his cabinet, Iio Jun surveys the challenges facing the fledgling government in "What Will the Change of Government Bring to Japanese Politics?"

In the end, the DPJ proved unequal to those challenges, and its stumbles provided endless food for commentary in the three-odd years before it was voted from power—criticism that doubtless accelerated the party's fall from public favor. This section includes two articles that look back on the DPJ regime and analyze its collapse. In "The Manifesto," Nakakita Kōji focuses on the DPJ's inability to deliver on the promises of its much-vaunted manifesto and considers the factors behind that failure, including the internal process by which the platform was drafted and adopted. Kamikawa Ryūnoshin, by contrast, adopts a historical-institutional perspective in "The Failure of the Democratic Party of Japan." While acknowledging problems within the DPJ, he puts greater emphasis on systemic obstacles raised by the persistence of mechanisms and processes that took hold during the long period of single-party dominance.

Who Ended the LDP's Reign?

Taniguchi Masaki, Uenohara Hideaki, and Sakaiya Shirō
Japan Echo, 2010

In May 1989 the ruling Liberal Democratic Party (LDP) adopted a document titled "Outline for Political Reform," which included the following passage: "The strengths of the ruling and opposition parties have become fixed over a period of many years, and it is hard to see the possibility of a change of government. . . . Fundamental reform of the existing system of [multiple-seat] electoral districts [for the House of Representatives] will involve pain for our party, which has maintained a majority for many years under this system. However, in order to achieve a 'people-oriented,' 'policy-oriented' system of party politics, we will undertake a fundamental reform of the electoral system based on introduction of small [single-seat] electoral districts." In this way, the long-dominant LDP itself raised the issue of a change of government. Twenty years later this has finally come to pass as a result of the victory of the Democratic Party of Japan (DPJ) in the August 2009 House of Representatives election.

On the occasion of this lower house election, our group of researchers at the University of Tokyo and the newspaper publisher Asahi Shimbun conducted a survey of candidates in the race and of 3,000 voters around the country. This survey directed many of the same questions to both candidates and voters, making it possible to directly compare the views of the candidates and those of the public on various issues. Another feature is that we have implemented the same sort of survey at the time of earlier elections, making it possible to track the changes in candidates' and voters' views over time. Table 1 compares the voting intentions reported by those surveyed with the results of the election for the proportional-representation seats in the lower house.

The findings of any survey are bound to differ somewhat from the actual outcome of the voting, but we can see that the distribution of voting behavior (party selections) among those surveyed corresponded fairly closely to actual results.

Many commentators have noted that a major cause of the DPJ's landslide victory over the LDP was that quite a few of the latter's supporters deserted it this time. We would like to start by offering our analysis of why the LDP is in even more serious straits than commonly recognized.

When one asks, "What percent of the LDP's supporters voted for it?" the answer depends on how one defines "LDP supporters." Most commonly these are taken to be the people who name the LDP when asked what party they currently or ordinarily support. But the concept of "supporting" a party actually covers a range of meanings, including (1) intending to vote for it, (2) having a long-term sense of affiliation with it, and (3) doing more than just voting for it—for example, contributing to it, taking part in rallies and the like, and perhaps becoming a party member. If the definition of supporters is based on item (1), then the question becomes almost tautological: "What percent of those who intended to vote for the LDP voted for the LDP?" So, for the purposes of our survey, we have used item (2), asking people which party they were inclined to support over the long term. By this measure, we found that the percentage of LDP supporters who voted for the party in the election last August was only 59 percent (Table 2). In other words, over 40 percent of the LDP's supporters deserted it this time, even though they knew it was in danger of losing the reins of power to the DPJ. In what follows we will consider the process that led to this development.

Results since 2009

We at the University of Tokyo have conducted surveys in tandem with the Asahi Shimbun in advance of each national election since 2003, and the survey questionnaire addressed to candidates has gauged their policy orientation with a set of questions that have been kept the same in each survey. For our presentation in this article, we have used the statistical technique of factor analysis in order to present an intuitively easy-to-grasp view of the diachronic changes in the average positions of the candidates of each of the major parties, summing up their views on a variety of issues by plotting them against two axes, as presented in Figure 1.[1]

This diagram shows the average positions of the candidates of each of the major parties at the time of the three most recent general elections for the lower house: in 2003, 2005, and 2009. The horizontal axis represents the range of opinions on a variety of foreign policy, national security, and social issues, such as the strengthening of Japan's defense capabilities, the legitimacy of preemptive attacks, and the appropriateness of allowing permanent foreign residents to vote in local elections. The scale goes from "liberal" on the left to "conservative" on the right. The vertical axis represents opinions on issues relating to economic policy, including the appropriateness of public works spending and fiscal stimulus. Here the scale goes from "reform-oriented" on the bottom to "traditional" on the top. The latter refers, for example, to support for the use of public works spending to create jobs and of fiscal stimulus to counter economic downturns. "Reform-oriented," by contrast, refers to support for macroeconomic policy that does not rely on Keynesian measures of this sort.

Koizumi Junichirō, who became prime minister in April 2001, adopted the slogan "No growth without reform," and he declared that he was going to "destroy" the LDP, his own party. This sort of outspoken sloganeering helped him win an unprecedented level of support for his administration, and in the House of Councillors election held that July, the LDP made great gains. Koizumi came under criticism in connection with some subsequent developments, notably his

sacking of Minister for Foreign Affairs Tanaka Makiko, but he managed to hold on to high level of support, helped by the success of his dramatic trip to North Korea in September 2002 and his cabinet reshuffle and appointment of Abe Shinzō as secretary-general of the LDP a year later.[2]

In the general election held in 2003, there were no prominent policy issues, and so the focus was largely on whether Koizumi's popularity would continue. The party leadership under Koizumi was clearly reform-oriented, but the LDP's members in the lower house included many belonging to the "forces of resistance," as the prime minister called them, favoring the traditional approach to economic policy. The average position of the LDP candidates in this election (marked LDP 03 in the diagram) thus ended up in the middle of the vertical range—"moderate," if one wishes to describe it favorably, though one could also call it "wishy-washy." The position of the DPJ candidates (DPJ 03), meanwhile, was clearly on the reform-oriented side.

The LDP came out of the 2003 election with fewer seats than before, but the ruling coalition, including the New Kōmeitō and the New Conservative Party, secured an absolute stable majority in the lower house.[3] The DPJ fared better: Before the election it merged with the Liberal Party to form the new DPJ, which performed well in the election, winning more than 100 seats in the single-member districts for the first time. It thereby solidified its position as a major opposition force aiming to take control of the government.

The July 2004 election for the upper house was fought on pension reform and the situation in Iraq, issues that worked against the Koizumi administration. In addition, Koizumi himself disappointed many when he casually brushed off irregularities in his own participation in the public pension system during one period of his career. The DPJ managed to win one more seat than the LDP.

After this election, Koizumi reshuffled his cabinet and started working in earnest on the centerpiece of his reform agenda, privatization of the postal services. But opposition to this move ran deep within the LDP, and Koizumi found himself battling the "forces of resistance" led by Kamei

Table 1. Proportional-Representation Vote Shares, 2009

(%)

	Surveyed voters	Election results
Democratic Party of Japan	47	42
Liberal Democratic Party	29	27
New Kōmeitō	8	11
Japanese Communist Party	6	7
Social Democratic Party	3	4
Your Party	4	4
People's New Party	2	2
Other	2	2

Table 2. Supporter Retention Rates, 2009

(%)

	Voted for								
Party affiliation	DPJ	LDP	Kōmei	JCP	SDP	YP	PNP	Other	None
DPJ	**85**	5	2	2	2	2	1	1	0
LDP	27	**59**	6	2	1	2	2	0	0
Kōmeitō	15	4	**79**	1	0	0	0	0	0
JCP	16	2	3	**72**	2	0	2	0	3
SDP	16	3	5	8	**65**	0	3	0	0
Your Party	33	8	4	4	0	**42**	0	8	0
PNP	43	14	0	0	0	0	**43**	0	0
Other	71	0	0	0	0	0	0	**29**	0
None	52	15	7	7	4	7	3	2	**3**

Note: Party affiliation refers to support for a party based on a long-term sense of affiliation with it, as reported by surveyed voters.

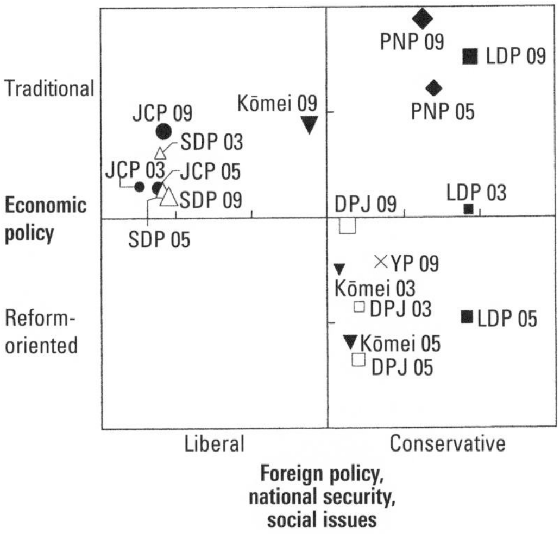

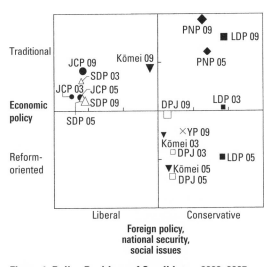

Figure 1. Policy Positions of Candidates, 2003, 2005, and 2009

Shizuka over passage of the government's privatization package. The legislation was approved by the lower house in July 2005 despite the negative votes of Kamei and other LDP legislators in the anti-privatization camp, but it was voted down by the upper house the following month. Koizumi responded by dissolving the lower house and calling a general election. He had the party withhold its nomination from Kamei and others who had voted against the privatization bill; instead the LDP nominated new candidates, popularly referred to as "assassins," to challenge these incumbents, some of whom joined to form the People's New Party (PNP), while others ran as independents.

The position of the People's New Party in the diagram (PNP 05) clearly reflects that it was made up of legislators who favored traditional economic policies. Meanwhile, the position of the LDP (LDP 05) moved significantly toward a reform-oriented stance by comparison with 2003, reflecting the addition of the "Koizumi children"—the contingent of new candidates, many relatively young, who were nominated to run under Koizumi's banner of postal privatization.

The average position of the DPJ's candidates going into this election (DPJ 05) was still more reform-oriented than that of the LDP's candidates. But the DPJ found itself eclipsed by the overwhelming presence that Koizumi projected as he battled for his privatization agenda. The LDP scored a landslide victory, capturing 296 of the 480 seats in the lower house.

In September 2006 Koizumi stepped down voluntarily, and he was succeeded by Abe Shinzō. The new prime minister, while proclaiming his commitment to continuation of the Koizumi reform drive, came out with calls for revision of the Basic Act on Education and for upgrading the Defense Agency to the status of a ministry. These were part of his drive to make "a clean break with the postwar regime"—meaning the reversal of some of the reforms implemented in the wake of Japan's defeat in World War II.

Abe's administration enjoyed a high level of support at its launch, but before long its ratings plunged as the result of a series of developments, such as the readmission to the LDP of legislators who had voted against Koizumi's postal privatization legislation, political funding irregularities by State Minister for Administrative Reform Sata Genichirō, and verbal gaffes by Defense Minister Kyūma Fumio. On top of this, the problem of missing pension records came to the surface in May of the following year, causing people to lose trust in the LDP-led government.[4]

The House of Councillors election held in July 2007 thus resulted in a big win for the DPJ, which emerged as the largest party in the chamber, and the ruling coalition found itself in the minority in the upper house. Abe initially declared his intention of staying on as prime minister even after this major setback, but in September he was forced to step down because of bad health. The administration of his successor, Fukuda Yasuo, was dogged by the difficulty of getting bills enacted through the opposition-controlled upper house. Fukuda tried at one point to form a grand coalition with the DPJ, but that attempt fell through, and in September 2008, just after he reshuffled his cabinet, he announced his resignation. Like Abe, he was prime minister for only one year. This rapid turnover further eroded public confidence in the LDP.

When Asō Tarō took office as Fukuda's successor, there was less than one year remaining in the term of the members of the House of Representatives. And Asō himself originally intended to call a lower house election promptly in order to seek a popular mandate for his administration. But just then the world started feeling the effects of the global financial crisis. Asō decided to put off calling an election and instead to focus on measures to shore up the economy. But the approval ratings of his administration fell to very low levels as the result of the prime minister's repeated verbal missteps and the resignation of Finance Minister Nakagawa Shōichi, who showed signs of inebriation—including slurred speech—at a press conference following a February 2009 meeting of the Group of Seven in Rome. Asō was unable to take advantage of the emergence of alleged irregularities in the fundraising activities of DPJ president Ozawa Ichirō around this time as an opportunity to call an election and campaign on terms favorable to the LDP. In the July election for the Tokyo Metropolitan Assembly, the LDP lost its position as the top

party, and some within the party started pushing for Asō to be replaced as LDP president. It was under these highly unfavorable circumstances for the LDP that Asō finally dissolved the House of Representatives and called a general election in August 2009, less than a month before the September deadline.

The LDP Changes Course

The policy stances of the candidates of all the parties going into the 2009 lower house election strongly reflected the impact of the worsened economic conditions Japan was experiencing. According to Figure 1, they responded to this situation by shifting their positions substantially, moving away from favoring structural reform toward support for traditional economic policies. The shift was particularly extreme in the case of the LDP, as seen in the movement from LDP 05 to LDP 09 in Figure 1.

To examine this point more closely, we have calculated the shares of the LDP and DPJ candidates who expressed support for public works spending and, separately, those who expressed support for fiscal stimulus. In both cases, we used the total of those who expressed outright support and those whose support was more muted. The results are shown in Figure 2. They clearly show the increase in support for traditional economic policy measures among LDP candidates in 2009 by comparison with 2005. In the case of fiscal stimulus, the share in favor actually grew by a whopping 73 percentage points. The direction of movement was the same in the DPJ, but the scale of the change was far bigger in the LDP.

How did voters evaluate this shift? To gauge this we created a diagram showing the policy stances of the voters we surveyed in 2009 according to the same factor analysis we used in our survey of the candidates. In Figure 3 we present the results—both for all surveyed voters and for voters broken down by party affiliation—along with the 2009 results for the candidates of each of the parties. (For easier viewing, we doubled the scale of the vertical axis relative to the horizontal axis.)

As this diagram indicates, the average position of the LDP candidates was quite distant from that of the electorate as a whole, particularly along the vertical axis of economic policy. We should note that the candidates' position was distant not just from that of the entire electorate but also from that of voters who identified themselves as LDP supporters. The LDP politicians shifted course in response to criticisms of the strains resulting from the Koizumi reform program and to the deterioration of the economy in the wake of the Lehman shock, but they seemed to have pushed the rudder too far.

The average position of the DPJ's candidates was much closer to that of voters. Even the position of LDP supporters was roughly halfway between that of the LDP's candidates and that of the DPJ's. Meanwhile, the average position of those with no party affiliation was, like that of DPJ supporters, quite close to that of the DPJ candidates. If we assume that people vote for the party whose policy stance is the closest to their own, it seems reasonable to surmise that the DPJ was able to attract votes not just from its own supporters and independents but also from the more reform-minded group of voters among those supporting the LDP.

Another factor contributing to the LDP's defeat may have been the unpopularity of its leader, Prime Minister Asō. In our survey of voters, we measured their "emotional temperature" toward the various parties, their respective leaders, and their local candidates in the voter's own district. Emotional temperature is an indicator ranging from 0 to 100 degrees, where 50 degrees represents a neutral feeling, 100 degrees is the highest possible level of favorable feeling, and 0 degrees represents the strongest possible aversion. In Figure 4 we show the results for the LDP and DPJ and their respective leaders, broken down by the voters' party affiliations. As is only natural, voters tended to feel "warmer" toward the party they supported and the leader of that party. But what stands out in the results is the low temperatures of voters' feelings for Asō. The reading was below 50 degrees not just among DPJ supporters as expected, but even among LDP supporters, indicating that many of them felt aversion toward the prime minister. Meanwhile, though the temperature of their feelings toward DPJ leader Hatoyama Yukio was also below 50 degrees, it

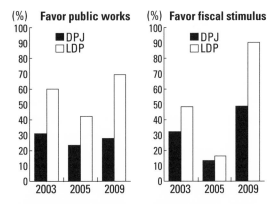

Figure 2. Shares of DPJ and LDP Candidates Favoring Public Works and Fiscal Stimulus Policies

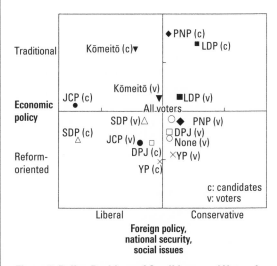

Figure 3. Policy Positions of Candidates and Voters by Party Affiliation, 2009

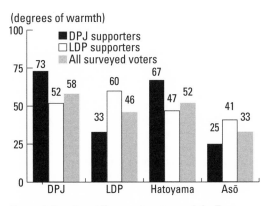

Figure 4. Emotional Temperature toward the Top Parties and Their Leaders

was higher than that of their feelings toward Asō. This suggests that many of them were ready to accept the idea of Hatoyama becoming the country's top political leader. And it relates to the fact that, as we noted at the beginning of this article, only 59 percent of the LDP's supporters actually voted for it in the August 2009 election.

Who Switched, and Why?

Next let us examine which of the voters who cast their ballots for the LDP in 2005 swung to the DPJ in 2009. For the purposes of our analysis, we limited ourselves to looking at the voters in three groups: those who voted for the LDP in both 2005 and 2009 (group A), those who voted for the DPJ in both 2005 and 2009 (group B), and those who voted for the LDP in 2005 but for the DPJ in 2009 (group C). We based our reading of voting behavior in both elections on the ballots cast in the proportional-representation voting. The three groups together accounted for a bit over 60 percent of those surveyed who voted in both elections; as a share of this larger class, group A accounted for 24 percent, group B for 20 percent, and group C for 18 percent. Below we will focus mainly on the characteristics of group C—those who shifted to the DPJ this time.

Figure 5 presents the averages of the responses from the members of these three groups on twenty policy issues. As is readily apparent from the diagram, the average positions of the group C voters were somewhere in the interval between those of the group A voters and the group B voters on almost all of the policy issues. And if we compare the voters of group C with those of group A, we find that the former showed a more liberal tendency than the latter on issues of foreign policy, national security, and social values, and they were more inclined to favor reform-oriented economic policies. This is congruent to our earlier hypothesis that the more reform-oriented group of voters among the LDP's supporters probably swung to the DPJ in the most recent election.

The group C voters also place between those of group A and group B with respect to their emotional temperatures toward the various parties and their leaders (Figure 6). In other words, among those who voted for the LDP in 2005, the ones who swung to the DPJ in 2009 were a group with relatively cool feelings toward the LDP and Asō.

Next let us consider the characteristics of these group C voters, who switched their votes to the DPJ in 2009, in terms of gender, age, and occupation. By gender, while women accounted for 46

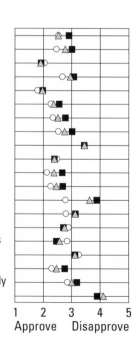

Revision of the Constitution
Strengthening defensive power
Maintaining the three nonnuclear principles
Preemptive attacks
Permanent seat on UN Security Council
Pressure on North Korea rather than talks
Collective self-defense
Overseas missions for Self-Defense Forces
Small government
Permanent employment
Public works to provide jobs
Fiscal stimulus to support the economy
Maintaining budget for roads
Hiking the consumption tax
Funding the basic pension with taxes
Voting rights for foreigners in local elections
Use of foreign workers
Limits on individual rights for public safety
Education stressing tradition over individually
Abolition of the death penalty

1   2   3   4   5
Approve   Disapprove

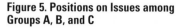

○ Group A: Voted for LDP in 2005 and 2009

■ Group B: Voted for DPJ in 2005 and 2009

△ Group C: Voted for LDP in 2005 but for DPJ in 2009

Figure 5. Positions on Issues among Groups A, B, and C

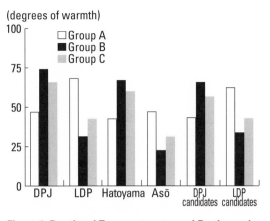

(degrees of warmth)

Figure 6. Emotional Temperature toward Parties and Leaders by Group

percent of group B (those who voted for the DPJ in both elections), they accounted for 52 percent, or slightly over half, of group C. Their switch from the LDP to the DPJ resulted in an increase in the female share of the total vote for the DPJ this time. The DPJ has up to now been said to be relatively weak among women voters, but this tendency seems to have been somewhat alleviated. By age group, those in their forties were the largest cohort in group C, followed by those in their thirties, twenties, and sixties. In these four age groups only about half of those who voted for the LDP in 2005 voted for it again in 2009. By contrast, the LDP has maintained its popularity among those in their seventies or above (Figure 7).

The voters in their thirties and forties, of whom a relatively large percentage switched from the LDP, include many who stand to benefit from the introduction of the child allowances that the DPJ called for in its campaign manifesto. Did this pledge draw them to cast their votes for the DPJ in 2009? To investigate this, we asked the respondents to our survey this time whether they had children aged fifteen or under. Those who said they did accounted for 44 percent of the voters in all three groups. Figure 8 shows the shares of the three groups among those with children and those without. The distribution does not differ that greatly between the two categories, so at least as far as the results of our survey are concerned, we cannot establish a link between the promise of this benefit and the additional votes that the DPJ won.

Finally, let us look at the breakdown of the three groups by occupation. Traditionally the DPJ has been considered to be strong among salaried workers and the LDP to be popular with those in the agricultural sector, such as farmers and fishers. Our survey indicates that the LDP continues to have a support base among this portion of the population, but that the DPJ has managed to eat into this base to a certain extent. Figure 9 presents the occupational breakdown by group. The composition of group C, those who switched to the DPJ this time, is closer to the overall composition (the sum of the three groups) than that of either group A or group B is. So as a result of these people's switch, the composition of the DPJ's voters in 2009 (group B plus group C) in terms of occupations also became closer to the overall composition. This suggests that the DPJ is turning into a "catch-all" party capable of drawing votes from a broad range of groups within the population. Meanwhile, among those in nonregular employment (temporary workers, part-timers, and the like), group C accounts for the largest share. This would seem to indicate that the negative impact on the employment situation from the economic downturn, which affected these workers directly, pushed a fair number of them to switch their votes from the LDP to the DPJ.

The DPJ's Win: Deviation or Realignment?

The results of an election are commonly classified according to three categories: "maintaining," "deviating," and "realigning." "Maintaining" election refers to cases in which the results correspond to the previously existing distribution of party affiliations among voters. "Deviating" refers to cases in which a party with a relatively low rate of support is able to come out ahead because of special circumstances. And "realigning" refers to cases in which the election is accompanied by a major change in the distribution of party affiliations.

Do the results of the 2009 election represent a deviation or a realignment? The outcome was certainly dismal for the LDP, which won a mere

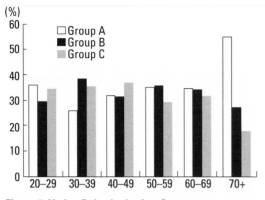

Figure 7. Voting Behavior by Age Group

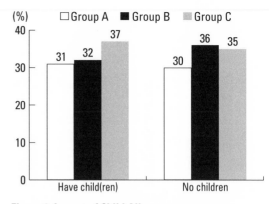

Figure 8. Impact of Child Allowances

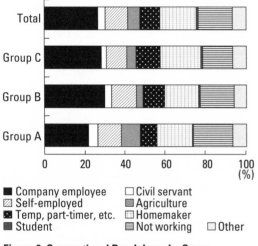

Figure 9. Occupational Breakdown by Group

The DPJ has probably established itself as a party that is capable of replacing the LDP at the helm of the government. But will it be able to get through its initial test period as the ruling party successfully and engineer a realignment under which it gains a higher level of long-term support? Or will the LDP continue to be the default leader in terms of the distribution of party affiliations, while the DPJ manages from time to time to win power—in other words, will we see a pattern in which elections that maintain the predominance of the LDP are mixed with deviations that allow the DPJ to take the helm temporarily? The true historical significance of the 2009 election will be determined, we believe, by the way the DPJ governs and the LDP conducts itself as an opposition party in the period to come.

Courtesy of Japan Echo.

English version originally published in *Japan Echo* 37, no. 1 (2010): 19–25. Translated from "2009 nen sōsenkyo: Dare ga Jimintō seiken o owaraseta no ka?" *Sekai* (December 2009): 74–82 (courtesy of Iwanami Shoten).

Notes

1. For our factor analysis we used the results of surveys of candidates' positions at the time of three lower house elections (2003, 2005, and 2009), analyzing their answers concerning nine issues that were included in the same form all three times, namely, whether they approved or disapproved of (1) strengthening of (Japan's) defense capabilities, (2) preemptive attacks, (3) a permanent seat (for Japan) on the United Nations Security Council,

119 seats, while the DPJ garnered a record-high 308. But it would be premature to label this a realignment. It is possible for voters to cast their ballots for a different party only temporarily. When we asked the voters in our survey which party they were inclined to favor over the long term, 41 percent named the LDP and just 25 percent the DPJ. By this measure the LDP still enjoys a big lead.

That is not to say that voters have given the LDP a slap and are now satisfied. When asked which party they would vote for if an election were held tomorrow, 45 percent picked the DPJ and just 29 percent the LDP. Even though the LDP has been thrown out of power, many voters evidently have not yet forgiven it.

(4) small government, (5) permanent employment, (6) public works, (7) fiscal stimulus, (8) voting rights (in local elections) for foreign residents, and (9) an emphasis on public safety (crime fighting). Items (6) and (7) relate strongly to the vertical axis ("economic policy") in Figure 1; the other items relate strongly to the horizontal axis ("foreign policy, national security, social affairs").

2. Abe, who was serving as deputy chief cabinet secretary, had won wide recognition and favorable appraisals for his hard-nosed approach to dealing with North Korea in getting that country to return abducted Japanese citizens.

3. An "absolute stable majority" is a majority with enough members to retain a majority on all of the lower house's standing committees even after the designation of committee chairs.

4. In the spring of 2007 the government admitted that, because of sloppy management of payment records by the Social Insurance Agency, there were as many as 50 million pension contributions whose payers could not be determined.

IV-(2) What Will the Change of Government Bring to Japanese Politics?

Iio Jun
Social Science Japan Journal, 2010

In the lower house general election held on August 30, 2009, the Democratic Party of Japan (DPJ) won 308 of 480 seats and secured a significant majority. With this victory, the Liberal Democratic Party (LDP)-Kōmeitō coalition government crumbled, and the DPJ-led Hatoyama Yukio cabinet was inaugurated on September 16. The LDP yielded its long-held reins of power to its opponents.

The significance of the DPJ's victory lies in the fact that it was essentially the first time in the history of Japanese party politics that a "true change in government" was achieved through an election. Under the current Japanese Constitution, the Katayama Tetsu cabinet of 1947 and the Hosokawa Morihiro cabinet of 1993 were also formed as the result of seat changes after general elections. So, in this sense, the Hatoyama cabinet is not the first change in government resulting from a general election; but both the Katayama and Hosokawa cabinets were formed by negotiating coalitions after general elections, and those administration changes may not have taken place if the coalitions' negotiations had played out differently. In contrast, the recent change in government occurred due to a fierce two-party competition for power that resulted in a dramatic shift in the majority in the lower house, and from this point of view it can be considered a "true change in government."

If we examine this further, we can see that the DPJ did not accidentally come into power but that conditions paved the way for a change in government. Signs of changes to come were indicated by the fact that in many opinion polls, the approval ratings of the DPJ had outstripped those of the LDP for quite some time—which was

an unprecedented phenomenon—and since the election followed on the heels of this trend, most voters, including supporters of the ousted LDP, accepted the outcome. What is more, the DPJ had captured the highest number of seats in the 2004 and 2007 upper house elections, so this is not the first time they emerged as the leading party in a national election.

In other words, the DPJ not only had a secure foundation to work from in the lower house, which serves as the constitutional backbone for the cabinet, but since it was only a few seats shy of a single-party majority in the upper house, it cooperated with the Social Democratic Party and the People's New Party—with which it formed a coalition—to secure a majority in the upper house and maintain a solid basis for passing legislation. In the light of these earlier achievements, the foundation for the DPJ government is firm, and there is sufficient potential for the party to retain power as long as the lower house is not dissolved midway through its four-year term.

Furthermore, in the general election of 2009 the lower house electoral system, which combines single-seat districts and proportional-seat representation, provided important clues indicating the potential for changes in government due to massive seat fluctuations. In the previous lower house general election held in 2005, the LDP secured a major victory with 296 seats, and its coalition partner Kōmeitō won 31 seats, while the DPJ suffered a major loss by only winning 113 seats. In 2009, the election results shifted 180 degrees with the LDP and Kōmeitō only holding on to 119 and 21 seats, respectively, and the DPJ sweeping to victory with 308 seats. The sudden reversal was possible because a mere handful of Japan's 300 electoral districts are "safe districts" that reliably vote for a particular party. This means that large-scale seat turnovers such as what we have just witnessed will remain possible in the future. Looking at the two most recent general elections, one can safely say that party politics in which change in government is possible is starting to take root in Japan.

While the DPJ was able to effect a change in government, the predominant view is that the election was less a victory for the DPJ than a loss for the LDP, which is the correct assessment. However, one must take care not to infer that a change in government simply means that the ruling party has fallen out of favor. In Japan, where changes in government through elections have not been the norm, the LDP was not simply the leading political party; it had secured a symbolic presence as the ruling elite that also held the reins of government. In this sense, the fact that the LDP lost means that Japan's conventional political systems and ruling bloc have been rejected by the voters. Additionally, the DPJ is carrying a banner for "ending dependence on bureaucrats" and emphasizing the "elimination of government waste" precisely because of these kinds of voter trends. Seen in this light, the 2009 change in government has the potential to alter government structures and transform the social order. Given this potential, what effects will the establishment of a DPJ-led cabinet via a change in government have?

First, the DPJ seeks to change how decisions are made within the government and has been steadily achieving reforms since coming to power. The DPJ has presented a clear policy of politician-led government and has begun to develop systems in which ministers and other high-ranking officials make their own decisions rather than rely on the bureaucrats under them as they used to. The ministers together with the already installed senior vice-ministers and parliamentary secretaries constitute the top three official posts, and the administration has established that these top officials will make decisions in their respective ministries and agencies. In the past some matters used to only be reported to ministers and agency heads without requests for decisions, but with the top three officials now working in unison, the

number of cases being decided by the ministers and agency heads is rising. Cabinet-level decision-making, too, has been reformed. Cabinet meetings in which bureaucrats used to coordinate and fix issues in advance are giving way to a system of several cabinet committees in which cabinet ministers coordinate policy together, and this system is gradually starting to kick into gear. These reforms have served to remedy the disparity between nominal power and actual power so that those individuals who possess official authority will now make substantive decisions.

In this context, the standard practice in Japan of keeping the government and the governing party separate and not having Diet members serve in government positions has been overhauled such that members of the ruling party now play major roles in government decision-making; the rule of "a uniform cabinet stance on policy" has been put into effect. These reforms will likely serve to gradually streamline the decision-making process of the Japanese government.

However, since the government is in a transition phase and coordination among ministers remains inadequate, disparate remarks by ministers on foreign policy and other issues are starting to make the administration's stance appear shaky, but as the ministers and other top officials familiarize themselves with the ins and outs of running a government, these problems will most likely sort themselves out.

Second, a major transformation in the relationship between politicians and bureaucrats is imminent. As I have already mentioned, the DPJ-led cabinet has reformed government decision-making systems to phase out the old practice of behind-closed-doors fixing by bureaucrats, and because of this, the roles of bureaucrats are undergoing drastic changes. At present, politicians tend to object to consulting with bureaucrats on policy in order preserve their autonomy.

As a result, the overall capacity for governance has declined somewhat. In any case, the administration is moving from the old system in which politicians and bureaucrats teamed up to make decisions to a new division of roles for each camp based on the assumption that politicians' and bureaucrats' areas of responsibility should be separated from each other. However, a climate in which changes of government are possible means that the opposing LDP could once again regain its grip on power, so the DPJ has decided that it must switch to a separate functional relationship between politicians and bureaucrats, instead of maintaining the heretofore unchallenged symbiotic relationship.

Third, these kinds of changes mean that altering Diet management will be unavoidable. Until now maneuvering surrounding the agenda-setting of the ruling and opposing parties was the primary work undertaken by Japan's Diet. This practice was based on the assumption that the relationship between the two parties was unchanging; however, with role-switching now possible, this tendency towards inefficiency and disregard for real debate is increasingly becoming a target for reform. For example, one tactic that was often used to set agendas was to request the minister of foreign affairs or another minister to attend the Diet, forcing him or her to cancel overseas business trips even if the opposition parties have no intention of asking the minister questions, but criticism of this kind of senseless behavior will probably increase.

Fourth, shifts in party structures will progress. In addition to the single-seat electoral system, discipline by party officials is starting to take effect on the structure of Japan's political parties. This trend is especially strong in the DPJ, which is promoting the unification of the government and the ruling party. For this reason, political parties are expected to evolve from groups of lawmakers to more organized entities.

Fifth, relationships between the state and interest groups will have to change. For instance, as the roles of politicians and bureaucrats are separated, the government and ruling party unify, and political parties become more organized, the number of access points to the government and ruling party, which used to be countless, may be confined into routes of expressed social interest. Against this backdrop, the heretofore amalgamated state-society relationship will most likely move slowly towards a relative decoupling.

Sixth, one can expect a shift in public awareness stemming from a sense of release. The change

in ruling systems by way of the change in government is giving people who were not involved in politics in the past a sense of new possibilities. This may raise people's interest in politics, or it may provide an escape from an administrative straitjacket. Increased activity in a heretofore weak area will boost social mobility, and that in and of itself could hold a certain measure of political meaning.

At this point in time, many of these predictions remain mere possibilities, but we must focus attention on the prospect that the impact of the change in government could be greater than expected.

Originally published in *Social Science Japan Journal*, no. 42 (March 2010): 3–5.

The Manifesto
Why Was the DPJ Unable to Keep Its Campaign Promises?

Nakakita Kōji
The Democratic Party of Japan in Power, 2016

The Democratic Party of Japan (DPJ) came to power in the general election of August 30, 2009, by capturing 308 of the lower house's 480 seats. However, in the general election of December 16, 2012, voters handed the DPJ a severe reprimand: the number of DPJ-controlled seats dropped to just 57 in a massive defeat for the party. The DPJ was an opposition party once more.

Yet one cannot deny that DPJ government policies had met with considerable success. In terms of domestic policy alone, doctor shortages in hospitals were alleviated by the first revision to medical fees in a decade, while the public high school waiver program reduced the number of high school dropouts. The DPJ also created new safety nets by establishing a support system for job seekers, extending unemployment insurance to nonregular workers, and reviving a supplementary assistance scheme for single-parent households receiving social welfare. These can all be described as successful DPJ policies. More generally, the fact that the DPJ, with its slogan of "from concrete to people," reduced public works spending and increased government support for social welfare and education was far from insignificant. Above all, the DPJ government should be commended for a series of "children first" policies that supported child-rearing from pregnancy and childbirth through university graduation.

Given this track record, it is all the more surprising that DPJ government policies have been evaluated so poorly. The DPJ's failure to implement the policies promoted in the 2009 campaign manifesto was likely a primary reason for this poor assessment. During the Kan Naoto and Noda Yoshihiko administrations, a proposed increase in the consumption tax, aimed at restoring the state of public finances, came to dominate the policy agenda. What drew such censure was the fact that the DPJ's 2009 campaign manifesto had made no mention of a consumption tax hike. The DPJ manifesto was ultimately referred to as "a pack of lies."

Where did the DPJ go wrong with its much-vaunted manifesto? This chapter seeks to answer this question through an objective analysis of DPJ policies.

The DPJ's Failure to Secure Adequate Funding

Policy successes and failures

Let us begin by reviewing the extent to which the DPJ government followed through on its 2009 manifesto pledges. The DPJ issued a report assessing the government's progress toward implementing manifesto policies on November 20, 2012 (DPJ 2012b). The report categorized 149 of the 166 manifesto articles as either "achieved," "partially achieved," "started," or "not yet started" (foreign policy items were excluded from the count). According to this report, only 51 manifesto articles had been fully "achieved," 63 were listed as "partially achieved," 26 as "started," and 9 as "not yet started." While avoiding the more common conclusion of "total defeat," the DPJ acknowledged it had only managed to achieve one-third of its manifesto goals.

Next, let us examine in detail several of the party's priority policies, known as the "Five Pledges." Of these, the DPJ was most successful at implementing the high school tuition waiver program, and it also introduced an annual subsidy of ¥118,800 for students attending private high schools. Furthermore, the DPJ implemented an income support scheme for commercial farming households, which compensated farmers for the difference between the production costs and market prices of their products. A full 98 percent of large-scale rice farmers (farming more than five hectares) joined this program.

On the other hand, more than a few policies ended in failure. Just months after assuming power, the Hatoyama Yukio administration abandoned the manifesto proposal to eliminate the temporary tax rate for gasoline and other products. And while the elimination of highway tolls was given a limited trial on 20 percent of the nation's highways in 2010, this trial was suspended following the Great East Japan Earthquake and Fukushima Daiichi nuclear disaster.

The DPJ's greatest stumbling block was the new child allowance (*kodomo teate*)—a uniform, monthly payment of ¥26,000 per child for all children under the age of fifteen. Initial payouts of half this amount (¥13,000) began as scheduled in 2010. Due to a shortfall in finances, however, full payouts did not begin as planned in the following year. In 2012, following the Great East Japan Earthquake and the Liberal Democratic Party (LDP)'s recapture of the upper house, the DPJ was forced to impose an income cap on allowance recipients. The name of the allowance also reverted back to that of the LDP-era "childcare allowance" (*jidō teate*). To be sure, the scope and value of the revised allowance remained greater than that of the previous childcare allowance. As the new, universal child allowance (*kodomo teate*) scheme originally proposed by the DPJ, however, the policy can only be described as a failure.

The DPJ's promise to suspend the construction of the Yanba Dam, a symbolic example of wasteful public works spending, also ended in disappointment. Maehara Seiji confirmed his intention of honoring the manifesto pledge to suspend construction during his very first visit to the Ministry of Land, Infrastructure, Transport, and Tourism as minister. But this met with growing criticism from local residents, local governments, the Tokyo Metropolitan Government, and the five prefectures jointly involved in the project. Each successive minister retreated further from the DPJ's original position. In late 2011, Maeda Takeshi,

the Noda cabinet's minister of land, infrastructure, transport, and tourism, finally announced that construction of the dam would resume.

An acute shortfall in financial resources

There are many reasons why the DPJ government was unable to implement manifesto policies. However, the DPJ's failure to abolish the temporary tax rate and highway tolls, or implement the child allowance as planned, was primarily the result of a shortfall in financial resources.

The 2009 manifesto included a chart depicting the financial resources required to fund important policies in a future DPJ government (shown in Table 1.1). For what would be the DPJ's fourth year in power, the projected savings through the "elimination of wasteful spending" were estimated to be ¥9.1 trillion, while tapping "buried treasure" (surplus and reserve funds within special government accounts) would yield ¥5 trillion. A further ¥2.7 trillion would be generated through tax reform, including a review of special tax measures. In total, the DPJ predicted that an additional ¥16.8 trillion could be raised in government funds. According to the manifesto, these funds would be used to implement new policies, such as the child allowance and high school tuition waivers. Based on these assumptions, the manifesto "roadmap" (reproduced in Table 1.2) depicts a small initial output that increases with each year of DPJ government: ¥7.1 trillion in year one, ¥12.6 trillion in year two, ¥13.2 trillion in year three, and ¥16.8 trillion in year four.

The progress report released by the DPJ on November 8, 2012, shows the government fell far short of these projections (Figure 1.1). To be sure, the fiscal 2010 budget, compiled in the first year of DPJ government, succeeded in securing an additional ¥9.8 trillion—exceeding initial projections by ¥2.7 trillion. But a breakdown of the fiscal 2010 budget reveals that the one-time use of "buried treasure" amounted to ¥6.4 trillion of this total, while cuts to "wasteful spending" yielded ¥2.3 trillion and tax reform just ¥1.1 trillion. Due to the subsequent decrease in "buried treasure," the DPJ government's second budget, for fiscal 2011, produced ¥6.9 trillion in new funds. The DPJ's third budget, for 2012,

Table 1.1. The Manifesto's List of New Financial Resources under DPJ Government

1. "We will make the state's ¥207 trillion budget vastly more efficient, eliminating wasteful spending and non-essential, non-urgent programs."

(¥ trillion)

Category	Budget allocation (FY 2009)	Explanation of DPJ policies	Cost savings
Public works	7.9	*Cancel the Kawabe River and Yanba dams. Completely review anachronistic large-scale projects under direct state control. *Build only essential roads after strict cost-benefit analysis.	1.3
Personnel costs	5.3	*Cut personnel costs by various methods including: transfer most administrative functions to local governments as part of decentralization; review personnel numbers and benefit levels (e.g., allowances and retirement pay) for national civil servants; and (after civil service reform) revise pay scales through labor management negotiations.	1.1
Government-related institution costs	4.5	*Cut policy implementation and procurement costs by reviewing the payments (approx. ¥12 trillion annually) to independent administrative institutions, special corporations, and public service corporations (all providers of *amakudari* jobs), and by reviewing government contracts (worth ¥8 trillion annually, about half this amount in discretionary contracts).	6.1
Contracting costs	0.8		
Government facility costs	0.8		
Subsidies	49.0	*Cut subsidy-related administrative and procurement costs through reforms. Enable low-cost, high-quality government services by allowing standards adapted to local conditions and not imposing national standards excessively. *Thoroughly review the work of independent administrative institutions, special corporations, and public service corporations, and abolish entities and tasks that exist to provide *amakudari* jobs, thus reducing subsidies.	
Debt repayment and associated costs	79.6	*Costs are almost entirely to fund maturing national debt.	—
Pensions and social insurance payouts	46.1	*Cost of paying pensions, medical and employment insurance.	—
Transfer, loan, and investment funds	9.9		—
Others	2.5	*Fewer Diet seats will mean lower cost of member's salaries. *Stricter budget assessment.	0.6
	206.5		Subtotal: 9.1

2. "Tax money presently sitting in 'buried treasure' funds or idle assets will be put to work for the people."

Target of reform	Explanation	Amount to become available
Effective use of "buried treasure"	To implement policies, put to work part of the numerous ill-defined "funds" set up in the FY 2009 supplementary budget, and also part of the Fiscal Investment and Loan Special Account and the Foreign Exchange Fund Special Account (estimated combined profits in FY 2008: ¥5 trillion).	4.3
Planned sale of government assets	Sell state-owned assets (such as unused land, employee housing, office buildings, and shares in privatized companies) on a planned basis.	0.7
		Subtotal: 5.0

3. "We will review special taxation measures, among other tax policies."

Target of reform	Explanation	Amount to become available
Create a fair and transparent taxation system	Review all special taxation measures, which lack transparency, and abolish any that are not clearly effective or that have outlived their purpose. Switch from tax exemptions to allowances by abolishing the spouse and dependent income tax deductions and creating a "child allowance."	2.7

*The special tax deduction for dependents, tax deductions for the elderly, and tax deductions for disabled persons will be continued. With regard to taxation of pensions, deductions of public pensions and other pensions will be increased and tax deductions for the elderly will be revived. This will mean that while the tax deductions for spouses will be abolished, the tax burdens of pensioners will be decreased.

New fiscal resources to be realized in FY 2013	16.8

Source: Adapted from the DPJ's 2009 manifesto, official English translation.

Table 1.2. The DPJ Manifesto "Roadmap" for Policy Implementation

Item	FY 2010	FY 2011	FY 2012	FY 2013
Child allowance, childbirth benefit Child allowance of ¥312,000 p.a.; lump-sum childbirth benefit	50 percent of p.a. child allowance implemented in the first year ¥2.7 trillion	¥5.5 trillion		
Effectively free public high school tuition With equivalent subsidies to private high school students	¥0.5 trillion			
Pension reform Addressing pension record problems; creating a new pension system	Concentrated efforts on record problems (¥0.2 trillion) (National consensus on pension system)		System design	Drafting and enacting legislation
Renewal of medical care and long-term care Resolving the doctor shortage; emergent influenza countermeasures and related programs; upgrading pay of long-term care workers	Phased measures to relieve the doctor shortage, etc. ¥1.2 trillion		¥1.6 trillion	
Individual (household) income support for agriculture Income support for commercial farm households	Studies; model projects; system design	¥1.0 trillion		
Abolition of provisional tax rates Abolishing or reducing provisional tax rates on gasoline, etc.	¥2.5 trillion			
Elimination of highway tolls Eliminating highway tolls in principle	Stepwise implementation		¥1.3 trillion	
Employment measures Expanding employment insurance to nonregular workers; job-seeker assistance and related measures	¥0.3 trillion	¥0.8 trillion		
Estimated costs	¥7.1 trillion	¥12.6 trillion	¥13.2 trillion	¥13.2 trillion
Measures not listed above (Abolition of the health insurance scheme for people aged 75 and over; expansion of university scholarships; raising minimum wage levels; assistance to SMEs, etc.)	To be implemented step by step, while securing financial resources		¥3.6 trillion	

Source: Adapted from the DPJ's 2009 manifesto, official English translation.
Note: Projected costs in FY 2013 came to ¥16.8 trillion.

produced ¥4.4 trillion. In a complete reversal of the DPJ's projections, there was an annual *decrease* in the total amount of new funds the administration was able to generate for policy implementation (DPJ 2012a).

And this was not all. The financial shortfall was actually even more acute, as revealed by another DPJ document. The DPJ's mid-term assessment of manifesto implementation, dated August 26, 2011, discusses the 2010 budget as follows: "From the existing budget we secured ¥9.9 trillion with which to meet the projected ¥7.1 trillion required to implement manifesto policies, but much of this was allocated to address an unexpected shortfall in tax revenue and a natural increase in social security spending, leaving ¥3.1 trillion for manifesto policy implementation" (DPJ 2011). In the first year of DPJ government, the funds raised for new manifesto policies amounted to just ¥3.1 trillion, not ¥9.8 trillion or ¥9.9 trillion.[1] The fact that additional funds would be required to cover the natural increase of over ¥1 trillion per year in social security spending, among other issues,

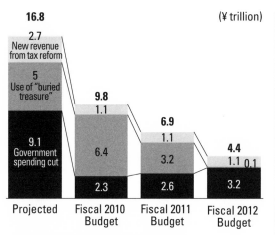

Figure 1.1. The DPJ's Fiscal Shortfall
Source: Adapted from a 2012 DPJ progress report on the manifesto.

went completely unheeded in the DPJ manifesto. In order to implement manifesto policies without damaging the government's overall finances, far more than the projected ¥16.8 trillion for year four would be required. Nor had the manifesto made any provisions for a potential economic downturn or natural disaster.

Two perspectives

The reasons why the government proved unable to secure adequate funding for manifesto policies are still being debated within the DPJ today, to no satisfactory conclusion. Indeed, this dispute contributed to the eventual split within the party.

According to one influential perspective, the DPJ's failure to secure adequate financial resources can be blamed upon the unrealistic manifesto produced by Ozawa Ichirō, who became the party's president in 2006. Sengoku Yoshito claims that it was in the 2009 manifesto that Ozawa, who focused exclusively on elections and the political climate, made "promises that were completely infeasible from a financial perspective." The 2009 manifesto was based upon the party's "Basic Policies for Government" (also referred to as the DPJ's "policy Magna Carta"), the prototype for the 2007 upper house manifesto. Sengoku says he protested at the time that "creating policies that can't be backed up financially was a major problem, which could cost us

the public's trust." According to Sengoku, his protests went unheeded.

Having led the party to victory in the 2007 upper house election, Ozawa began to throw his weight around, demanding obedience to the party leadership and suppressing internal debate. This state of affairs remained unchanged through the September 2009 alternation in power, despite Ozawa's May 2009 resignation due to a campaign finance scandal, and his replacement by Hatoyama Yukio. According to Sengoku, it was precisely this situation that led to the failure of the manifesto.

Azuma Shōzō, a former leader of the Ozawa group, disagrees strongly with Sengoku's assessment. Azuma believes it should have been possible for the DPJ to implement manifesto policies, including the monthly child allowance of ¥26,000. According to Azuma, the DPJ should have cut low priority items from the existing budget to fund the higher priority manifesto policies. Why, then, did the DPJ government fail to do so? According to Azuma, the DPJ's leaders shirked from making politically difficult decisions and came to rely on the bureaucracy: "In a politician-led system, you have to promise to take responsibility for the cuts you make." Azuma also believes the manifesto could have been implemented successfully had Ozawa, with his experience and leadership skills, remained at the center of the DPJ administration.

Was Ozawa to blame? Or could manifesto policies have been implemented more successfully with Ozawa at the helm? The failure of the DPJ manifesto cannot be discussed without addressing these questions. Let us begin by examining the claim that Ozawa created an unrealistic manifesto.

Did Ozawa Create an Unworkable Manifesto?

Okada's secret proposal for revision

Ozawa's critics are convinced that the DPJ government could have succeeded had the party stuck to the manifesto prepared for the 2005 general election, which was drafted largely by Sengoku (then the party's policy chief) under the leadership of DPJ president Okada Katsuya. In their view, this manifesto was ruined by Ozawa, who took over the party leadership in 2006.

According to Fukuyama Tetsurō, who helped draft successive party manifestos, "The 2005 manifesto was the best." And, reasoning that the 2009 general election signified an LDP defeat rather than a DPJ victory, Okada claims, "Even something along the lines of the 2005 manifesto would have brought us to power in 2009."

We should thus take note of Okada's proposed amendments to the 2009 manifesto, entitled "New Policies and the Problem of Financial Resources."[2] On May 11, 2009, DPJ president Ozawa announced his resignation due to the Nishimatsu Construction campaign finance scandal. With Ozawa's support, Secretary-General Hatoyama Yukio narrowly defeated Okada in the subsequent party leadership contest. Okada took over the post of secretary-general instead and began raising his objections to the 2009 manifesto. On June 3, Okada submitted a two-page proposal to revise the manifesto. Okada recalls that the manifesto originally "claimed we could generate about ¥19.8 trillion in new funds. I proposed lowering this estimate to at least ¥10 trillion."

Okada's proposal to amend the manifesto was premised on the idea that a future DPJ government's "cuts to wasteful spending" would yield less than predicted. Okada thus divided manifesto policies into two categories: "category X" policies, to be implemented unconditionally, and "category Y" policies, to be implemented once progress had been made in reducing annual government expenditures and the economic outlook became clearer. Okada then sought to contain his estimate of the additional financing needed to implement category X policies within the total of ¥10 trillion. One manifesto policy to receive a clear downgrade was the proposed elimination of the temporary tax rates on gasoline and other products. Okada made this a category Y policy, in part because lowering gasoline prices contradicted the party's proposed countermeasures against global warming. Okada also tried to rein in expenditures by phasing in or reducing the scope of certain policies, such as the new child allowance, the elimination of highway tolls, and the income compensation scheme for farming households.

The DPJ's 2005 election manifesto, prepared under Okada's leadership, had called for a ¥17 trillion reduction in government spending. Of this, ¥7 trillion would be diverted to new manifesto policies, while ¥10 trillion would be used to return Japan to fiscal health. Okada explains that the Koizumi Junichirō administration's Trinity Reforms, introduced shortly after the 2005 election, depleted the government's resources by ¥6.2 trillion through the transfer of tax revenue sources to local governments. Subtracting this amount from ¥17 trillion yields—more or less—the ¥10 trillion total proposed by Okada in 2009. Changes to Japan's economic and fiscal situation make a straightforward comparison of the two documents difficult, but the same ideas clearly inform the 2005 manifesto and Okada's proposal to revise the 2009 manifesto.

Okada's proposal did yield one concrete result: the DPJ lowered its projections of the new funds required by the manifesto to ¥16.8 trillion. In fact, the projected total could have been reduced even further. According to Okada, "With Hatoyama's consent, we tabled such policies as the elimination of temporary tax rates, thereby reducing the overall scope to ¥14.3 trillion. But in the end, Ozawa and Hatoyama overturned these changes." When DPJ president Hatoyama, deputy leaders Ozawa, Kan Naoto, and Koshiishi Azuma, and Secretary-General Okada finalized the 2009 election manifesto, the policy of eliminating temporary tax rates was again discussed. With votes of support from Ozawa and Hatoyama, the policy was ultimately included in the manifesto.

Had the DPJ government entered a fourth year, however, it could not have generated even the ¥10 trillion proposed by Okada—much less the ¥16.8 trillion specified for new policy implementation in the 2009 manifesto.

A surplus of new policies

The circumstances surrounding Okada's proposal for revision comprise one basis for the claim that Ozawa created an unworkable manifesto. There is another perspective, however. As the deputy policy chief, Hosono Gōshi, was involved in the drafting of the 2009 election manifesto. Like Okada, Hosono had long been troubled by the total funds required to implement manifesto

Election Year	Elimination of highway tolls	"Minimum guarantee" pension	The new child allowance (*kodomo teate*)	Income support for commercial-farming households	High school tuition waivers	Abolition of the provisional tax rate on gasoline and other products
2003 general election		("national basic pension")				
2004 upper house election			No specified value	(direct payment system)		
2005 general election			¥16,000 per month			
2007 upper house election			¥26,000 per month			
2009 general election						

Figure 1.2. The Accumulation of "Priority Policies"
Note: Dotted lines indicate policies originally introduced in different form.

policies and pushed unsuccessfully for a reorganization of the manifesto's finances. Since 2003, the party members responsible for drafting the manifesto had more or less remained the same, and they disliked the idea of changing policies accumulated over the years. Hosono says, "We needed a justification for changing policies we had previously promoted, but as an opposition party it was difficult to come up with a basis for making changes." Okada acknowledges this, to a certain degree: "This is true. In terms of the child allowance, Ozawa abruptly increased the monthly total from ¥16,000 to ¥26,000 and this became the norm, so there was resistance to reverting to the earlier value. I was surrounded and told off by a number of female Diet members for trying to curtail our spending on the child allowance." Thus, while Ozawa is clearly to blame for blocking Okada's proposed revisions to the 2009 manifesto, there is obviously more to the story.

An analysis of the changes to the manifesto's key policies is also enlightening. One clear trend revealed by such an analysis is the DPJ's addition of new signature policies with each election (see Figure 1.2). According to Fukuyama Tetsurō, "Once Ozawa took over, the funds necessitated by our manifesto grew and grew." On the other hand, Fukuyama argues, "The 2009 manifesto wasn't just an attempt to 'spend and win' (*baramaki*). The number of policies we wanted to implement grew with our time in the opposition."

This accumulation of new policies was the result of several interconnected factors. With each election, the party leadership, centered upon the party president, sought to highlight new policies to grab the attention of voters. Matsumoto Takeaki served as policy chief from the party presidency of Maehara Seiji to that of Ozawa and acknowledges, "It was acceptable for the party leader to introduce new policies without any prior discussion within the party. Ozawa announced the increased child allowance at the Diet without any advance notice to the party. Kan added the policy of eliminating highway tolls while we were drafting the manifesto."

It is difficult to revoke or reduce the scope of new policies introduced in this way. Rejecting the policies of the former leadership generates friction. Moreover, policy proposals are supported not only by the various subcommittees of the party's Policy Research Council but also by voters and interest groups. This means that any modification to these proposals must be explained to the public and mass media. The priority policies included in the manifesto have a "downward rigidity," so to speak.

This is confirmed by an examination of the projected expenditures for new policies included in each successive party manifesto. The first DPJ manifesto, compiled in 2003 under Kan Naoto, projected a total of ¥2.5 trillion in new policy expenditures. This total had grown to ¥7 trillion by the 2005 general election, ¥9 trillion by the 2007 upper house election, and ¥16.8 trillion by the 2009 general election. Projected expenditures nearly doubled in value with each election.

It is thus clear that even if Ozawa can be held responsible for creating a financially infeasible manifesto, the DPJ's campaign methods and organizational structure were also to blame.

Returning Japan to fiscal health and the consumption tax hike

Having reviewed the additional financial resources necessitated by new manifesto policies, there are now two more points for us to consider with regard to the claim that Ozawa created an unworkable manifesto.

The first is the fact that the DPJ had effectively abandoned its goal of restoring Japan to fiscal health. The DPJ had originally been far more zealous on this issue than the LDP. The 2003 manifesto, drafted under Kan's leadership, touted plans for fiscal consolidation but did not include specific numbers. Under Okada, the issue was brought further to the forefront of the DPJ platform. In the 2005 general election manifesto, the DPJ declared it would not only produce ¥7 trillion for the implementation of new policies but also restore Japan to fiscal health by cutting ¥10 trillion from annual expenditures over three years, thereby containing the issuance of new government bonds below ¥30 trillion and halving the government's primary budget deficit.

Under Ozawa's leadership, the DPJ retreated from this plan. While the 2007 upper house election manifesto promised to restore the primary balance to surplus within four years, measures for achieving this goal were not displayed numerically. The 2009 manifesto, meanwhile, made no mention whatsoever of Japan's fiscal health. Okada's proposal for revising the 2009 manifesto had emphasized the need to specify "new fiscal consolidation targets," but his recommendation was not adopted.

Second, members of the DPJ had lost their enthusiasm for a consumption tax hike. Specifically, from the time of Kan's presidency the DPJ manifesto had called for the establishment of a basic "minimum guarantee pension," entirely funded by tax revenue. Under Okada, the 2004 upper house election manifesto specified the introduction of a consumption tax hike to fund the pension system, assuming a 3-percent increase in the tax rate. But the 2007 upper house election manifesto, drafted under Ozawa's leadership, made no mention of raising the consumption tax to fund the pension system. Instead, the 2007 manifesto explained how the existing consumption tax rate of 5 percent could be allocated entirely to the minimum guarantee pension system if annual expenditures were reduced by ¥6.3 trillion.

While the 2009 manifesto called for the "establishment of a minimum guarantee pension funded by the consumption tax," the implementation of such a system was put off until after the next election. At a press briefing to announce the 2009 manifesto, DPJ president Hatoyama declared, "No tax hike will be necessary for the next four years" (*Asahi Shimbun*, July 28, 2009). In response, Okada wrote in his proposal for revision, "We should state that we will not raise the consumption tax for four years," but added, "we should take the stance that it is essential to discuss a consumption tax hike to support the pension system and other social security measures."

Here it is important to note that even under Okada's leadership, the DPJ manifesto had always cited cuts to existing expenditures as the means of restoring Japan to fiscal health and identified a consumption tax hike as the potential source of funding for the minimum guarantee pension scheme. In other words, up until the 2009 change of government, the DPJ had never identified the consumption tax hike as a strategy for fiscal consolidation. Yet those estranged from Ozawa were acutely aware of the need to raise the consumption tax for precisely this purpose. According to Kan, "Social security spending increases by ¥1 trillion every year, so we already knew that the consumption tax would have to be raised." Sengoku makes the same assertion. Moreover, in a panel discussion with Yosano Kaoru, published in the July 2008 issue of *Chūō Kōron*, Maehara Seiji stated, "We will not flinch from persuading the public if a tax hike exceeding the 3 percent designated for the pension system becomes necessary to pay for medical and nursing costs" (Yosano et al. 2008, 41).

Yet in the end, the DPJ did not take steps to raise the consumption tax in order to restore Japan's fiscal health. Why not? According to Naoshima Masayuki, who as policy chief authored the 2009 manifesto, "It was difficult to ask voters to accept a consumption tax hike in order to pay off a fiscal deficit." And as Sengoku recalls, "Even proposing a consumption tax hike to pay for pensions drew heavy criticism. Proposing a tax hike to pay off the deficit would have made it impossible to win elections."

Could Ozawa Have Implemented the Manifesto?

The drafting of the 2010 budget and the party's top demands

Let us now return to the claim that manifesto policies could have been implemented successfully under the strong leadership of Ozawa. To evaluate this assertion, the first issue to consider is the eighteen-point list of party demands regarding the 2010 budget. This list was presented to the government when DPJ secretary-general Ozawa, accompanied by many top party leaders, attended a meeting at the Prime Minister's Office in late 2009. Let us first review the events leading up to this meeting.

The fiscal 2010 budgetary requests submitted on October 16, 2009, including those funding new manifesto policies, amounted to a record-breaking ¥95 trillion. At a November 2 meeting of the lower house Budget Committee, Prime Minister Hatoyama announced his intention of curtailing these initial budgetary requests and curbing new government bond issuance through the budget screening process and other measures designed to eliminate wasteful spending. Hatoyama promised to do his best not to exceed the total bond issuance of ¥44 trillion set by the Asō Tarō administration's fiscal 2009 budget and supplementary budget. At the same time, Hatoyama declared, "Manifesto policies will be steadily implemented one by one, as they represent our contract with the nation."

According to Sengoku, who then served as the government revitalization minister, the move to keep the total of new government bonds under ¥44 trillion was led by Minister of Finance Fujii Hirohisa and Sengoku himself, both of whom valued fiscal discipline. Sengoku suggested to Fujii that they abandon the elimination of temporary tax rates, but Hatoyama insisted upon honoring manifesto promises. This left the government caught in a trap of its own design.

What is more, the Japanese economy deteriorated significantly amid the global financial crisis. In mid-November 2009, estimated tax revenue for the 2009 budget dropped from ¥46 trillion to ¥37 trillion. On November 11, the Government Revitalization Unit began a review of government spending with the aim of exposing any waste within the 2010 budgetary requests. This resulted in cuts of approximately ¥700 billion—far less than the ¥3 trillion the DPJ had predicted. While the issuance of new government bonds was thus limited to "approximately ¥44 trillion," the budget process remained fraught with difficulty.

It was Ozawa who took action. Hosono, then the DPJ's executive deputy secretary-general, quotes Ozawa as saying at the time, "If we exceed the quota we exceed it—we simply have to assign priorities." There was deep dissatisfaction within the party regarding the reduced scope of ¥44 trillion, but Ozawa accepted the limit set by the government. The list of party demands submitted to the government by Ozawa on December 16 proposed amending the manifesto by continuing the temporary tax rate for gasoline and other products and placing an income cap on recipients of the new child allowance. In Hosono's words, Ozawa's list "threw a lifeline" to a government brought to a standstill by financial woes. Prime Minister Hatoyama rejected the idea of income caps for the child allowance but accepted a continuation of the temporary tax rate for gasoline. On December 15, the 2010 budget proposal was approved by the cabinet.

Significantly, it was Ozawa who first amended the manifesto in order to address the problem of the DPJ government's financial shortfall. Noda Yoshihiko is thus accurate in his assessment, "While it was Ozawa who gave up on the idea of eliminating the temporary tax rate, the entire party shares responsibility for failing to implement the manifesto." We should not forget that while Sengoku and Fujii both pushed to continue with temporary tax rates from within the government, it was the strong leadership of Ozawa that finally achieved this by breaking the government's adherence to the manifesto.

With an eye to the upcoming upper house election, Ozawa also included in his list of demands the halving of budgets for bullet train and highway development and agricultural land improvement. The reduction by half of the budget for agricultural land improvement drew attention because it represented the effective defeat of Nonaka Hiromu, chairman of the National Federation of Agricultural Land Improvement Contractors (Zendōren), an important LDP support group. Here Ozawa flexed his muscles and demonstrated his readiness to increase or slash budgets as necessary to win votes or rip away at the LDP's support base. According to Matsui Kōji, "The list of party demands may have destroyed the unity of the administration and ruling party, but it also saved the administration. Ozawa picked up the support of the trucking association by promising to leave some subsidies uncut but halted the elimination of the temporary tax rates. This secured tax revenue two digits greater than that of the trucking subsidy. Politically, this was a success."

Taking all of this into account, the following testimony from Hosono is probably evenhanded: "Ozawa might have been able to implement a higher percentage of manifesto policies, but given how quickly he abandoned the policy of eliminating the temporary tax rate, I think even Ozawa realized it was impossible to accomplish everything." Ozawa accepted revisions to the manifesto in part because he could not deny the need to restore Japan to fiscal health and resigned himself to the ceiling of ¥44 trillion for new government bond issuance. This fact will prove equally important in our subsequent consideration of the DPJ's decision to pursue a consumption tax hike.

The "phantom" Hatoyama manifesto for the upper house election

As we have seen, the 2009 manifesto made no mention of raising the consumption tax as a measure for improving Japan's fiscal health. Prime Minister Noda apologized for this omission following the passage of legislation for the comprehensive reform of social security and tax on August 10, 2012. Disagreements within the DPJ over the consumption tax hike culminated in the defection of the Ozawa camp. But was Ozawa really so thoroughly opposed to raising the consumption tax, which was aimed at improving public finances, out of loyalty to the manifesto? Here let us examine a few points.

While abandoning the proposed elimination of the temporary tax rate, the 2010 budget proposal adhered to the manifesto by including plans to initiate payouts of half the total sum of the new child allowance, provide income compensation for farming households, and issue high school tuition waivers, thereby necessitating a record-breaking ¥44.3 trillion in new government bonds. This marked the first time in the postwar period that the national debt exceeded tax revenue in the initial budget. It was at this point that the proposal for a consumption tax hike to address the state of Japan's public finances first surfaced.

Sengoku was the first to raise the issue. During an appearance on a December 27, 2009, NHK discussion program, the government revitalization minister warned that public finances would give out if nothing was done to initiate debate on a consumption tax hike and seek the approval of the public in the next general election. Sengoku reflects, "Since our time in the opposition I knew that cutting wasteful spending would only produce limited financial reserves, and we would need to raise the consumption tax. But I only truly understood this after taking part in the budget screening process." Sengoku's message was taken up by Kan Naoto as he left the post of national strategy minister to head the Ministry of Finance. Kan had always been positive on the subject of a consumption tax hike, but his sense of urgency deepened when, in the wake of the worldwide financial crisis, he attended the February 5, 2010, meeting of the G7 (Group of Seven) in Canada. There, Kan was told repeatedly of the general unease with Japan's finances. Kan turned to the consumption tax as a means of pursuing Japan's fiscal recovery.

Meanwhile, work had begun on the DPJ's manifesto for the 2010 upper house election. A first draft was produced during the Hatoyama administration. A detailed examination of this "phantom" Hatoyama manifesto reveals an entry at the very end on "restoring Japan's fiscal health," with the goal of halving the fiscal 2010 deficit (against potential GDP) by fiscal 2015 and eliminating the deficit entirely by fiscal 2020.[3] To that end, the manifesto called for the rapid implementation of fundamental reforms to the tax system—including the consumption tax—after the next general election. This was the first time that the DPJ had proposed a consumption tax hike specifically to address Japan's fiscal crisis. The Hatoyama draft made further revisions to the 2009 manifesto. With regard to the child allowance, for example, "The amount will be raised from the ¥13,000 currently distributed once financial resources are secured." And, "Taking into account regional circumstances, the amount of increase may be exchanged for in-kind services." In effect, this revoked the original plan to increase the new child allowance to the full amount of ¥26,000 from 2011.

The fact that this initial "Hatoyama manifesto" was drafted with Ozawa's approval is extremely important. From the government side, the manifesto was prepared by State Minister for National Strategy Sengoku and Senior Vice Minister Furukawa Motohisa of the Cabinet Office. From the party, they were joined by Chief Deputy Secretary-General Takashima Yoshimitsu and Executive Deputy Secretary-General Hosono. According to Hosono, "Ozawa emphasized repeatedly how difficult the election would be if we mentioned the consumption tax hike, but in the end we persuaded him to give his consent." Ozawa may have been reluctant, but he accepted the proposal of a consumption tax hike in order to improve Japan's fiscal health. This is of enormous significance in our search for the reasons behind the DPJ's downfall. Setting aside the question of whether or not the DPJ could have won the upper house election on the strength of the Hatoyama manifesto, Ozawa's acceptance of a proposed consumption tax hike suggests the growing conflict over this issue within the party could actually have been prevented. The DPJ's split was not inevitable, after all.

Defeat in the upper house election and internal conflict

Hatoyama announced his resignation on June 2, 2010. Cabinet approval ratings had plummeted due to the campaign finance scandals involving both Hatoyama and Ozawa, Hatoyama's wavering on the issue of the Futenma base relocation, and the Social Democratic Party (SDP)'s withdrawal from the coalition government. Remarking that Ozawa "should keep quiet for a while," Finance Minister Kan won the subsequent party leadership contest (*Asahi Shimbun*, June 4, 2010). Cabinet approval ratings shot up after Kan became prime minister on June 8.

Looking ahead to the upper house election in July, Kan began to revise the Hatoyama manifesto. Specifically, Kan moved the topic of "robust public finances" to the beginning of the manifesto, and identified "beginning multiparty discussion of the fundamental reform of the tax system, including the consumption tax, with the aim of reaching a conclusion in the short term" as a measure "to be undertaken immediately" (DPJ 2010). Hosono worked over three consecutive nights to rewrite the manifesto and emphasizes these revisions demonstrated "Kan's strong determination." Hosono reminds us that Kan made revisions to what had been a last-minute compromise with Ozawa on the consumption tax issue. According to Hosono, these revisions—and Kan's decision to bring the consumption tax hike to the forefront of the manifesto—deepened the divide between Kan and Ozawa.

Kan went even further. During a June 17 press conference to introduce the new manifesto, Kan announced he would consider increasing the consumption tax rate to 10 percent, as had been proposed by the LDP. Kan acknowledges this declaration was a "strategic mistake." Azumi Jun, then director of the DPJ's general election strategy committee, offers the following explanation: "Public opinion polls gave us 60 seats—a remarkably good prediction. If the numbers had been worse, Kan would probably not have attempted something so risky."

Once Kan realized the DPJ faced a much tougher election fight as a result of his reference to a 10 percent consumption tax, he began discussing measures aimed at low-wage earners, but his message lost coherence and only elicited further criticism. The DPJ captured 44 seats in the July 11 upper house election, for a 10-seat reduction overall. With a combined total of just 109 seats in the chamber, the DPJ and its coalition partner, the People's New Party, had lost their majority. As the SDP had already left the ruling coalition, the DPJ also lacked the two-thirds seat share in the lower house required to overturn a negative vote in the upper house.

The divided government or "twisted Diet" (*nejire Kokkai*) brought about by the DPJ's upper house election defeat dealt a severe blow to the DPJ government. According to Azumi, "The upper house election defeat was our Battle of Midway. After that, we lost even our ability to act independently." The DPJ government's ability to secure the passage of legislation to raise financial resources and other important bills was severely curtailed, making it all the more difficult to implement manifesto policies.

This was not all. The manifesto lost legitimacy following the DPJ's upper house election defeat. The 2009 manifesto was supposed to have been replaced by the 2010 manifesto, which proposed a consumption tax hike in order to restore Japan's fiscal health. The DPJ's failure to win voters' support for this change plunged the party into a needless confrontation between the Ozawa group, who urged compliance with the 2009 manifesto, and the anti-Ozawa group favoring revision. This led to the direct confrontation between Kan and Ozawa in the September 14, 2010, party leadership contest. While Kan emerged victorious, antagonism within the party grew all the more intense.

The Great East Japan Earthquake of March 11, 2011, made it decisively difficult for the government to secure resources. Like the child allowance and the elimination of highway tolls, other 2009 manifesto policies were pushed back time and again. Meanwhile, the Kan and Noda administrations continued to pursue a consumption tax hike to address the nation's fiscal woes—driving Ozawa from the party in the process. Ozawa announced his decision to leave the DPJ on July 2, 2012. At his press conference, Ozawa

spoke as if he had played no part whatsoever in amending the 2009 manifesto, declaring, "It is a clear reversal of the natural order of things when those trying to keep their promise to the people are purged by those willing to set aside their promises" (*Asahi Shimbun*, July 3, 2012).

Did Ozawa create an unworkable manifesto? Or could the manifesto have been implemented under Ozawa's leadership? Both claims are persuasive up to a point yet remain oversimplified stances emerging from the final deadlock over the manifesto. Blaming one person for the failures of the manifesto obscures more essential problems. We should keep our sights trained upon problems intrinsic to the manifesto itself.

Explaining the Manifesto's Failure
The manifesto's list of financial resources and roadmap

In the words of Fukuyama Tetsurō, "When we tried to make revisions [to the manifesto] to address declining tax revenue due to the global financial crisis and the natural increase of ¥1.3 trillion per year in social security spending, we were told we were violating the manifesto. But when we adhered to the manifesto, we were criticized for over-prioritizing campaign pledges. For three-and-a-half years we were criticized, regardless of the direction we took." Why were such fierce and inconsistent criticisms leveled at the manifesto? To begin with, what is a manifesto?

In its July 7, 2003, "urgent proposal regarding policy pledges (manifestos) for administration," the 21-Seiki Rinchō (People's Conference to Create a New Japan) defines a manifesto as "a contract between the public and the government" and a "package of policies that the party will promote in government, clearly specified for the operation of government, including specific goals that can later be examined or assessed (through the use of numerical targets, a clear timeline for completion, or an explanation of policy financing), a framework and mechanisms for execution and a schedule (or 'roadmap') for policy implementation" (21-Seiki Rinchō 2003).

Campaign pledges had previously been party wish lists, enumerating a wide range of abstract goals. Many pledges could not be implemented or evaluated easily. As a result, people could not cast their votes—in other words, choose a government—based on policy. Political parties were thus told to unify their campaign pledges with their policies in office, fight elections based on manifestos that included numerical targets, timelines for completion, details on financing and a "roadmap," and once in office, to exercise political leadership to implement this "contract with the people."

At the same time, when the manifesto was first introduced to Japan from the United Kingdom, it was precisely this definition of the manifesto as a "contract with the people," complete with the clear numerical specification of financial resources, which led to the type of contradictory criticisms of the DPJ discussed above. Unifying campaign pledges with policies in office leaves no flexibility to respond to changed circumstances. Moreover, given the reality that not everything goes as planned, making numerical pledges for future evaluation inevitably invites the criticism of "broken promises."

Following the recommendations of the 21-Seiki Rinchō, the DPJ took the initiative in adopting a manifesto for the 2003 general election. At first, the party's manifesto was considerably vague on the subject of funding new policies. The 2007 upper house election manifesto raised the bar dramatically in this regard by outlining the costs of implementing priority policies, and identifying potential sources of funding. The first section of the 2009 manifesto, dedicated to the DPJ's priority policies, also included a "roadmap" depicting how policies would be implemented in the first four years of a DPJ government. Significantly, the very definition of a "manifesto" necessitated the inclusion of the roadmap and a list of financial resources. Fukuyama explains, "the very definition of a manifesto is the clear specification of policy financing, targets, and deadlines, and this is what we tried to enhance." The manifesto was also intended to challenge the LDP by demonstrating the DPJ's ability to govern. According to Fukuyama, "In political debates, the LDP's primary source of ammunition was the demand that the DPJ come up with counterproposals or explain how policies would be funded. We had to respond to these demands."

According to Matsumoto Takeaki, the DPJ's policy chief during the 2007 upper house election, the DPJ took the manifesto even further in an effort to go on the offensive after its enormous defeat in the 2005 general election. Furthermore, "After talking for so long about the sources of funding for policies and deadlines, we had no choice but to produce them." As one of the party members to announce the 2009 manifesto roadmap, Matsumoto says, "We came up with the roadmap as a way to phase in policies and push their implementation back past our first four years in government. This way we could limit the amount we needed to raise." In other words, the introduction of the roadmap was intended to make funding policies more feasible.

After the 2009 election, the manifesto became the DPJ's "contract with the people," complete with a roadmap, list of potential resources, and detailed numbers. The new administration thus found itself trapped. Any amendment to the manifesto in response to changed circumstances, no matter how slight, drew fierce criticism. On the other hand, if the DPJ tried to avoid criticism by adhering to the manifesto at all costs, it lost flexibility. Ultimately, members of the administration revised the manifesto in order to fulfill their duty to manage the government—and earned the title of "liars" in the process.

Explaining the manifesto's inflated numbers

Of course, the DPJ could have avoided such criticism had the manifesto included more realistic numbers. If it was so difficult to calculate clearly the feasibility of funding policies, why did the DPJ not limit its use of specific numbers? Put more bluntly, could not the DPJ have prevented the manifesto from becoming a numerical version of a campaign "wish list?"

As we have seen, Ozawa bears considerable responsibility for failing to back up the numbers presented in the 2009 manifesto. According to Naoshima, the DPJ's former party policy chief, when questioned about funding policies Ozawa repeatedly asserted, "It will work out—there is always more money" (Naoshima 2012, 82). This is corroborated by Ozawa's aide, Suzuki Katsumasa: "Ozawa honestly believes there is no need to worry about money—the Ministry of Finance will always provide more." Several others recall that Fujii Hirohisa, who went on to head the Ministry of Finance during the Hatoyama administration, made remarks similar to Ozawa's before the DPJ assumed power. Significantly, Ozawa and Fujii's seniority prevented more skeptical DPJ lawmakers from challenging their assertions. Added to this was the shared concern for winning elections. New "priority policies" began to accumulate as a result.

Given this, one could hardly have expected an accurate estimate of the financial resources required for implementing new policies, much less reliable estimates of future revenue. Recessions and natural disasters cannot be predicted accurately. Yet the 2009 manifesto included a four-year roadmap to the next election that somehow failed to incorporate even the natural increase of ¥1 trillion per year in social security spending. Hosono has an explanation for this: "There was a discussion about whether we should run a simulation of economic growth to predict changes in tax revenue when planning the budget, but it was given up because we couldn't make an accurate prediction. It was clear that tax revenue would decrease after the financial crisis, and we also knew about the natural increase in social security spending. But if we factored this in, we would also have to include forecasts for tax revenue over the next four years to maintain consistency. In the end, we kept all such factors abstract." Fukuyama mentions another reason: "Had we produced a 'discounted' manifesto that predicted declining tax revenues, the media would probably have criticized us for getting cold feet when faced with the prospect of governing. To be honest, we wanted to avoid this criticism in order to take power."

The DPJ could not predict with any accuracy how circumstances would change in the future and wanted to exclude any factors likely to have a negative impact on the election. The DPJ's failure to implement the manifesto on schedule was thus somewhat inevitable. While the government exceeded earlier estimates by securing between ¥9.8 trillion and ¥9.9 trillion in funds for the 2010 budget, only ¥3.1 trillion could be allocated to new manifesto policies because of the decline in tax revenue following the global financial crisis and the natural increase in social security spending. Out of concern for its impact on the election, the DPJ also excluded from the manifesto a proposal to raise the consumption tax in order to improve the nation's fiscal health.

The insider's manifesto

Conflict within the DPJ over whether or not to amend the manifesto, which ultimately led to the split within the party, was exacerbated by the process through which the 2009 manifesto was produced. This process began with the submission of between five and ten policy items by each subcommittee of the party's Policy Research Council, led by a minister of the DPJ's "Next Cabinet." The policy chief then led a working group in aggregating and refining these proposals. At this early stage, just four or five people joined the policy chief to draft the manifesto in total secrecy. Later, the team expanded to include ten people, and the party president became involved at the end to ensure his opinions were reflected. Finally, the manifesto was approved by the party executives at a meeting of the top three party leaders (Naoshima 2012, 67–70).

As Naoshima's account makes clear, the most important phase of the drafting process, during which decisions were made regarding which policies to adopt, their organization, and the nuances of their presentation, occurred behind closed doors and involved just a few DPJ Diet members and the party's top leadership. This approach was adopted out of concern for the effects of publicizing the manifesto too early in the election campaign. Fukuyama disputes this, saying, "The content of the manifesto didn't appear out of nowhere, it was the accumulation of discussions ongoing since the party's formation." He adds, however, that "we worried the manifesto's content would become fodder for negative campaigning if it was shared too soon and that we would be criticized for the infeasibility of particular policies or for what we had left out."

DPJ Diet members who had been left in the dark until just before the election complained, "The manifesto was completed before we knew it," and "the decision-making process was unclear."

Agricultural associations and DPJ lawmakers with close ties to the issue objected to the manifesto policy of concluding a free trade agreement (FTA) with the United States. In order to avoid a negative impact on the election, the revised manifesto promised only to "promote negotiations" on the subject of the FTA. That the manifesto was insufficiently shared not only with party members and support groups but even among the DPJ's own Diet members was a clear vulnerability.

By contrast, Fukuyama testifies that in the first manifesto election of 2003, the party used an inclusive process, soliciting and reflecting the input of the regional organizations within their support base, as well as the Japanese Trade Union Federation (Rengō). This practice was adopted from the British Labour Party, the originator of the campaign manifesto. At the final stage, however, priority policies with voter appeal were incorporated from the top-down. These included the elimination of highway tolls pushed by DPJ president Kan and a review of the five-day school week system. Before long this inclusive manifesto drafting process fell by the wayside, along with concerns for openness and consensus-building.

Since 2003, the DPJ has required all candidates to sign a written pledge confirming their commitment to the manifesto as a condition for party endorsement. This regulation is rendered meaningless, however, once the manifesto is amended by the very party leaders with authority over such candidates. The fact that the manifesto had not been adequately shared even among DPJ Diet members was exposed once amendments were made for the operation of government. Amid harsh circumstances, the party failed to unite behind the manifesto.

One former minister who joined the administration following Kan's September 17 cabinet reshuffle recalls that "among cabinet ministers, there was little sense that the manifesto had to be implemented at all costs. There was a widespread feeling that the manifesto was Ozawa's creation and didn't have anything to do with us." In order to demonstrate his own legitimacy, meanwhile, Ozawa fought to protect the manifesto, which the DPJ's election victory had transformed into the government's "contract with the people."

Should they honor or amend the manifesto? Disagreement over these two alternatives led to the DPJ's split.

Overcoming the failures of the manifesto

As we have seen, significant problems were intrinsic to the manifesto. With insufficient information on raising funds—much less regarding future developments—campaign strategy dictated inflated numbers. Similarly, concerns for the election led to a secret drafting process that kept the DPJ's own Diet members in the dark. These issues came back to haunt the administration: together with the difficult conditions created by the "twisted Diet," they necessitated revisions to the manifesto that drew the criticism of "broken promises" and led to the party's split.

The DPJ's 2012 general election manifesto represented a significant departure from its predecessors. The party substantially reduced the number of numerical targets and cut both the list of financial resources and the roadmap from the manifesto. Instead, the manifesto began by introducing the "Principles of the Democratic Party of Japan." Meetings to report progress on manifesto policies were held throughout Japan. Within the party, including the regional chapters, opinion exchanges were conducted before drafting began. While the title "manifesto" remained, the contents marked a significant retreat from those of the manifesto as previously defined.

Opinion will be divided as to whether this development should be evaluated positively or negatively. The results of our survey of DPJ lower house members show that respondents were split on the question of whether or not the party should continue to specify numerical targets, deadlines, and sources of funding in the manifesto. A slight majority favored continuing with this model. In many cases, however, even those in favor added comments such as "We must also ensure that we can respond flexibly to changed circumstances" (Okada Katsuya) and "Demonstrating our principles and a simple course of action is sufficient" (Noda Yoshihiko).

The same held true in our interviews. On one hand, Fukuyama Tetsurō maintains, "It was because of the manifesto that the DPJ administration could implement so many policies." And according to Ōsaka Seiji, "While it led to our defeat, you cannot deny the fact that we did not make vague campaign pledges but rather produced a manifesto that could be held up for evaluation." In response, Azumi Jun argued, "It was nonsense to seek detailed numbers for four years into the future." And according to Sengoku Yoshito, "Politically, it was naïve to think that setting specific numerical targets would ensure that everything went smoothly."

Hosono Gōshi, who oversaw the drafting of the 2012 election manifesto, says, "We fully realized that to have something as unforeseen as the Great East Japan Earthquake occur before our eyes and still attempt to conduct politics according to the roadmap we promised voters would have been exceedingly unrealistic and a total abdication of our responsibility as politicians. There is nothing wrong with presenting the public with certain clearly specifiable policies—but apart from that, shouldn't politicians expound principles for voters to decide upon, and then make responsible decisions in accordance with the current situation?" After the fall of the DPJ government, Hosono became the party's secretary-general and immediately began to clarify the party's platform, which was adopted at the February 24, 2013, party convention.

The DPJ's renewal—and more broadly, the renewal of the DPJ's capacity to take over the reins of government from the LDP—depends entirely upon whether or not the party can face up to and overcome the failings of the manifesto during the DPJ's three years and three months in power. This task has only just begun.

Reprinted by permission of Taylor & Francis Ltd.

Originally published as chapter 1 of *The Democratic Party of Japan in Power: Challenges and Failures*, edited by Funabashi Yōichi and Nakano Kōichi, translated by Kate Dunlop (London: Routledge, 2016): 7–29.

Notes

1. Various DPJ documents refer to the total amount of funds secured as both ¥9.8 trillion and ¥9.9 trillion.

2. This document is an internal memorandum shared with the author by Okada Katsuya.

3. This is a private document shared with the author by Hatoyama Yukio.

References

DPJ. 2009. "Manifesto 2009: The Democratic Party of Japan's Platform for Government." August 18. Accessed November 30, 2015. http://archive.dpj.or.jp/english/manifesto/manifesto2009.pdf.

———. 2010. "Manifesto 2010: The Democratic Party of Japan's Policy Platform for Government." June 17. Accessed December 1, 2015. http://archive.dpj.or.jp/english/manifesto/manifesto2010.pdf.

———. 2011. "Manifesuto no chūkan kenshō" [Midterm Assessment of the Manifesto]. August 26. Accessed November 30, 2015. www.dpj.or.jp/download/4571.pdf.

———. 2012a. "Manifesuto wa doko made susunda ka" [Progress Report on the Manifesto]. November 8. Accessed December 4, 2015. https://www.dpj.or.jp/article/101565.

———. 2012b. "2009 sōsenkyo manifesuto: Jisseki kenshō ni tsuite" [The Track Record for the 2009 General Election Manifesto]. November 20. Accessed December 1, 2015. https://www.dpj.or.jp/article/101657.

Naoshima Masayuki. 2012. *Tsugi no, Nihon: Jidai no seichō senryaku e; Nagare wa kawaru* [The Next, Japan: Toward the Next Generation Growth Strategy; The Trend Will Change]. Tokyo: Jiji Tsūshinsha.

Yosano Kaoru, Maehara Seiji, and Tahara Sōichirō. 2008. "Jimin to Minshu wa hontō ni chigau no ka?" [Are the LDP and the DPJ Really Different?]. *Chūō Kōron* 123 (7): 34–43.

21-Seiki Rinchō. 2013. "Seiken kōyaku (manifesuto) ni kansuru kinkyū teigen" [An Urgent Proposal regarding Policy Statements or Manifestos]. Accessed November 26, 2015. http://www.secj.jp/pdf/20030707-1.pdf.

The Failure of the Democratic Party of Japan
The Negative Effects of the Predominant Party System

Kamikawa Ryūnoshin
Social Science Japan Journal, 2016

1. Introduction

Nothing set politics in Japan more apart from other democracies than the continuity of Liberal Democratic Party (LDP) rule from the party's founding in 1955;[1] with the exception of a brief period in 1993–94, there was no change of government. Among non-Western nations, Japan was an early adopter of democracy, but some critics argued that democracy had not been fully achieved because Japan had so little experience with transfers of power. However, on August 30, 2009, the LDP and Kōmeitō suffered a crushing loss in the lower house general election, and in September, the Democratic Party of Japan (DPJ) and its coalition partners took power, and a true change of government was achieved.

Unfortunately, the DPJ government fell far short of voters' expectations. The DPJ's mistakes included not fulfilling most of the campaign promises in its policy manifesto, inept policy implementation due to the exclusion of career bureaucrats from the policymaking process, internal party divisions over increasing the consumption tax that led one politician after another to leave the DPJ, a series of gaffes by cabinet members, the worsening of Japan-US relations due to the Futenma base relocation issue, and mishandling of the collision between a Chinese fishing vessel and Japan Coast Guard patrol boats near the Senkaku Islands. Its mismanagement of domestic and foreign affairs caused the party to lose the public's trust and to lose badly in the December 2012 general election.[2]

The electorate's mistrust of the DPJ runs deep, as the outcome of the December 2014 general election demonstrates. Prime Minister Abe Shinzō's policy proposals were not all that popular among voters, but nevertheless the LDP and Kōmeitō won another decisive victory, and it appears as if Japan will not have another change of government for some time to come.

As for why the DPJ failed, a common answer is that the party's Diet members lacked the ability and the experience to govern. Recently published academic research also points to the electoral system and rifts within the party that could not be bridged due to the DPJ's organizational structure. We can assume these interpretations are, for the most part, correct.

However, this is not to say that the reasons above fully explain the DPJ's misfortunes. This paper provides a structural perspective on the impacts of Japan's predominant party system, which has received little attention to date. I find that the DPJ's attempts to govern were greatly constrained by the legacy of decades of single party dominance. The following discussion uses the budget process and tax reform to demonstrate the obstacles the DPJ confronted in making policy after it assumed power.

Of course, there is some debate about whether or not Japan has had a predominant party system since the change of government in 1993–94. Although the LDP was only briefly out of power, it was argued that the possibility of losing again affected how the LDP and other parties acted. One could also conclude that Japan has had a two-party system since the 2003 merger of the DPJ and the Liberal Party. Despite these alternate interpretations, this paper regards the LDP as a predominant party that succeeded in keeping power for decades, except for a brief period, until 2009. As a result, the particular institutions and practices of one-party dominant government remained in place, as discussed below.[3]

The structure of this paper is as follows. First, prior research on the failures of the DPJ is summarized, and the differences between that research and the nature of the analysis in this paper are explained. Next, research on the effects of predominant party systems on the political process is presented and considered. Then, the specific issues involved in the budgetary process and tax reform efforts, the central concerns of the DPJ government, are outlined. Finally, the effects of the predominant party system on the DPJ's ability to govern are examined.

2. Literature Review

This section provides an overview of prior research on the DPJ government and what kept it from succeeding. It also explains how this paper differs in its approach to analyzing the sources of the DPJ's problems. Lipscy and Scheiner (2012) attribute the DPJ's inability to significantly change policy once it took power to the characteristics of Japan's electoral system. They begin their analysis with policy convergence. The elections for the House of Representatives use a mixed-member system with more representatives elected in single-member districts. As Downs (1957) argues, in two-party systems the policy positions of the main parties tend to converge, and that convergence generally precludes dramatic policy swings when the government changes hands. Moreover, policy changes that impose costs on the electorate are risky and difficult to enact.

Second, the policy platforms of the LDP and DPJ were similar, which meant voters had to find other criteria for evaluating candidates. Many opted for candidates who appeared most committed to reform. Parties that win based not on their ideas but on their image are presumably less inclined to undertake major reforms once they are in power. Third, swing voting has become prevalent in every national election. Therefore, politicians who push for reforms, especially candidates who are young or lack political experience, are less likely to remain in the Diet for long, making reform all the more difficult.

Fourth, the first-past-the-post election rule makes it very difficult for new parties to gain traction. This barrier to entry at the party level keeps politicians from leaving their party regardless of whether their own policy positions conform with the party platform. In addition, the barrier to exit at the individual level makes it more difficult for parties to maintain consistent policy positions and leads to chronic policy conflict among party members. Fifth, although the overrepresentation of rural voters in the Diet has been significantly reduced, rural politicians still possess a great deal of influence and impede reform. This influence is found not just in the LDP but in the DPJ as well. Many of the DPJ's Diet members were from rural districts, especially in the House of Councillors, which wields nearly as much power as the lower house. Winning a majority in the upper house requires winning single constituency seats in rural areas, ensuring that rural areas retain their political clout and fostering intra-party divisions over policy between representatives of rural and urban districts (Lipscy and Scheiner 2012; Scheiner 2013).

As I see this line of argument, the first three explanations Lipscy and Scheiner present account for why the DPJ was unable to develop policies that were markedly different from those of the LDP. And yet, the DPJ did propose new policies that the LDP had never promised. The DPJ's loss of power was due more to its inability to keep its manifesto promises to enact the reforms. This means that the first three factors listed above cannot sufficiently explain the failures of the DPJ government.

The fourth and fifth factors account for policy-based rifts within the DPJ. Lipscy and Scheiner link the DPJ's troubles in government to dissenting DPJ legislators and a party organization—itself a product of the electoral system—that could not bring its members into line. This analysis is persuasive, but, as the authors themselves note, all five factors and the electoral system from which they sprang should affect the LDP as much as the DPJ. Surely the first Abe Shinzō cabinet and the cabinets of Fukuda Yasuo and Asō Tarō were plagued by intense internal party strife that contributed to their inability to enact reforms during their brief tenures. These examples make it appear as if the failures of the LDP and the DPJ resulted from the same causes. However, this argument cannot explain how the same electoral system also produced the long-lived Koizumi Junichirō and second Abe administrations that demonstrated strong leadership.

Kushida and Lipscy (2013) add three more explanations for the DPJ's ineffectual reform efforts to the electoral-system-based characteristics in Lipscy and Scheiner (2012). First, the DPJ excluded the bureaucracy from policymaking but lacked the internal capacity to compensate for the loss of expertise in policy implementation. Second, an economic downturn reduced revenues while the fiscal burden of the aging population continued to grow, leaving too little in the government's coffers to offer new programs. Third, foreign policy occupied more of the political agenda as Japan's relationship with China abruptly worsened due to conflict over the Senkaku Islands. There was not enough expertise, money, or time for the DPJ to launch major policy initiatives. The sluggish economy and the spike in tensions with China were unfortunate events for the DPJ rather than products of missteps by the party. The DPJ's shortfall in policy implementation capacity, on the other hand, was a self-inflicted problem not seen in LDP governments. What led the DPJ to follow such an ill-advised course of action will be discussed further below.

The DPJ's failure can also be looked at as the successful outcome of the LDP's strategy while in the opposition. Using tactics learned from Ozawa Ichirō, leader of the DPJ from 2006 to 2009, the LDP effectively went on the offensive. One of Ozawa's tactics was to attack individual cabinet ministers. In the 2010 election, the DPJ lost control of the upper house. The LDP took advantage of this by passing a series of censure motions against DPJ cabinet ministers, some of whom were eventually forced to resign. The LDP also capitalized on its 2010 gains by thwarting the enactment of the DPJ's manifesto proposals. The LDP avoided appearing obstructionist by using its ability to derail legislation sparingly and by accepting amendments to important bills, such as those written in response to the 3.11 disaster. Finally, the LDP rejected the DPJ's offer to form a grand coalition and opted instead to continue calling for the dissolution of the Diet and a general election. With these tactics, the LDP weakened the DPJ without reforming its own party organization. In 2012, the LDP's strategy paid off, and it regained control of the government (Endo, Pekkanen, and Reed 2013).

The LDP's political maneuvers left the DPJ with no real alternative to dissolving the Diet. But why was the DPJ unable to quickly respond to the LDP's tactics when those tactics were taken from Ozawa Ichirō's opposition party playbook? The DPJ must have expected the LDP to fight to regain power, and yet it failed to adequately defend itself against opposition party stratagems. Although the LDP and Kōmeitō were adept in using parliamentary tactics, one could also argue that the DPJ's lack of experience as a governing party was evident in its mishandling of parliamentary procedures. In other words, the fall of the DPJ government is attributable more to the weakness of the DPJ than to the strength of its political opponents.

Prior studies on the fall of the DPJ offer many valid explanations, but a full comparison of how the LDP and the DPJ governed has been lacking. This paper makes this comparison and shows that the DPJ was at a significant disadvantage vis-à-vis the LDP for reasons beyond its lack of experience and electoral system constraints. As will be demonstrated below, the LDP's long tenure as the predominant political party gave it a structural advantage over the DPJ that remained in place after the DPJ assumed power.

3. Political Processes in a Predominant Party System

This section covers the existing literature on how single-party dominance affects a nation's political process. The most notable early study of predominant party systems is Arian and Barnes (1974; Murakami 1986). Arian and Barnes found that political processes in these systems have several distinguishing characteristics, three of which will be described here. First, predominant party systems demonstrate flexibility in response to social change. According to Maurice Duverger, predominant parties must adapt to avoid falling behind the societies they govern in order to remain in power (Pempel 1990b; Pempel,

Muramatsu, and Morimoto 1994). In other words, the more flexible a ruling party is, the longer it can rule. Predominant parties are also more likely to maintain their power if they become "inclusive parties" that seek the support of as much of the public as possible. In addition, predominant parties can continue to be predominant only when the public believe in their dominance and regard it as legitimate. Opposition party supporters that challenge this narrative should be consistently labeled as illegitimate or delegitimized. The LDP exhibits all three characteristics. It is manifestly flexible—if the public supports a certain policy, the LDP will enact it regardless of which party originally proposed it or whether it reverses prior LDP policies. Enacting popular policies wins the LDP popular support and has kept it in power. For example, in the late 1960s, candidates for local government office backed by reformist parties, such as the Japan Socialist Party (JSP) and the Japanese Communist Party (JCP), were elected based on their support for controlling pollution and expanding welfare. The LDP co-opted these issues by increasing environmental protection and welfare programs at the national level, thereby quelling public dissatisfaction with the LDP. In the 1980s, the LDP sought to win the support of urban, white-collar men by promoting administrative reform and privatizing three public corporations. The flexibility, or "creative conservatism," demonstrated by the LDP kept it in power (Pempel 1982; Krauss and Pierre 1990, 257–58; Pempel 1990b, 349–51; Pempel, Muramatsu, and Morimoto 1994, 23).

As for party inclusivity, it goes without saying that the LDP has epitomized inclusivity, which in turn leads to more flexibility. Interest groups seek good relationships with ruling parties, especially parties that govern for long periods. An interest group may have greater affinity with an opposition party, but when the group needs something, it must go to the ruling party to get it. The LDP successfully established regular lines of communication with groups such as social welfare organizations and labor unions in major firms. These relationships made the LDP's ideology harder to discern as the party transformed itself as needed in its pursuit of public support.[4]

The LDP has also worked to delegitimize other parties. As Pempel and others note, in speeches and publications in the 1950s and early 1960s, the LDP regularly denounced the JSP as "a class party, anti-parliamentarian, pro-Communist bloc." Then, in the 1963 House of Representatives general election, the LDP shifted from red-bashing to calling all opposition parties "irresponsible" (Pempel 1990b, 346–48; Pempel, Muramatsu, and Morimoto 1994, 19–20). Calling the opposition parties irresponsible was a way to convince the public they were unfit to govern. Delegitimizing their opponents was one more LDP tactic for remaining in power. The LDP's disparagement of opposition parties should not be dismissed as predominant party propaganda. A party that has resigned itself to being in the opposition for ages would lack the experience to be anything but amateurish if given the chance to rule, as the DPJ repeatedly demonstrated. An opposition party that has never led a cabinet may also be prone to drafting unrealistic policies, what I term the "unrealism of opposition parties."

Matoba (1986, 305) describes another way political process differs in predominant party systems: when a party is entrenched in power, it easily builds close-knit relationships with the bureaucracies of central ministries. Because civil servants expect the same party to be in power for the foreseeable future, they do not have to maintain a neutral stance to protect their own positions, making the bureaucracy more prone to politicization. This is not to say that the political neutrality of Japan's bureaucratic institutions in general has diminished (Yamaguchi 2009, 23–26). In fact, their neutrality might have increased since cracks began to appear in the predominant party system in the 1990s (Muramatsu 2010).[5] Nevertheless, there is no question that the LDP politicians had developed very close relationships with the bureaucracy during its nearly uninterrupted tenure as Japan's dominant party (Muramatsu 2010; Iio 2011, 381–83; Takada 2012, 62–63). At least from the opposition parties' perspective, the LDP and the bureaucracy appeared to be co-conspirators, as demonstrated by the frequently repeated accusations of "politician-bureaucrat collusion."

To summarize, in a predominant party system, the ruling party uses four tactics to shape the political process to its advantage: flexibility, inclusivity, delegitimizing opponents, and politicizing the bureaucracy. In addition, opposition parties became unrealistic. In the case of Japan, the use of these tactics by the LDP for decades created conditions that made governing much more difficult for the DPJ once it took power. The next section describes how the LDP's tactical legacy constrained the Hatoyama Yukio, Kan Naoto, and Noda Yoshihiko cabinets in their efforts to win approval for their budgets and tax reform.[6]

4. The Hatoyama Cabinet's Policy Operations

4.1 The 2009 manifesto

In 2009, the DPJ issued a manifesto for the general election campaign with the slogan "Putting people's lives first." The DPJ pledged to eliminate wasteful spending of tax revenues and redirect what had been wasted to improve the lives of the people. More specifically, the DPJ promised a new child allowance (*kodomo teate*), a childbirth support, the elimination of fees at public high schools, pension system reform, an overhaul of the health care and long-term care systems, income support paid to individual farm households, rescinding of provisional tax rates,[7] elimination of highway tolls, and employment support. The manifesto also included deadlines and cost estimates. The projected cost for the 2010 fiscal year was ¥7.1 trillion. In the 2013 fiscal year, the government would need to spend ¥16.8 trillion. To pay for these programs, the DPJ planned to use "buried treasure," funds that had been set aside under prior administrations, money raised through the judicious sale of publicly owned assets, and money saved by rationalizing government revenues and expenditures.

On the spending side, the DPJ planned to reorganize the entire general budget of ¥207 trillion, including special accounts, and end wasteful spending. Proposed cost-cutting measures included abolishing payments to support golden parachute *amakudari* jobs for former civil servants and instituting zero-based budgeting for special accounts, independent administrative institutions, and public service corporations. Collusion between government officials and private firms would no longer be permitted in the government contract bidding process, and opaque no-bid contracts would also be done away with. The Kawabe River and Yanba dam construction projects would be canceled, as would other unnecessary public works construction. Personnel costs would be cut 20 percent by transferring more administrative functions to local governments as part of decentralization, through civil service system reforms, and by cutting the cost of administering national subsidies to local governments. To carry out this agenda, a new office, the National Strategy Office (NSO, if the legislation had been enacted, it would have been renamed the National Strategy Bureau) was created and tasked with developing budgets. The Government Revitalization Unit (GRU) was also established to investigate all government policies and expenditures in order to identify and stop wasteful spending.

On the revenue side, the DPJ pledged to review all special tax exemptions to determine their effectiveness in achieving their intended goals. If their effectiveness could not be proven, or if they had already served their purpose, the exemptions would be eliminated. To reduce income inequality, the tax system would switch from using deductions, which are difficult for low-income earners to qualify for, to offering "allowances" or cash payments that would benefit more people. For example, deductions for spouses and dependents would be replaced with cash benefits for each child. To turn these proposals into reality, the DPJ disbanded its tax system research commission and replaced it with a government tax commission authorized to create new tax policy and also required to make its plenary sessions open to the public and the press.

Afterwards, however, the DPJ's commitment to centralizing policymaking within the cabinet began to weaken. During the cabinet of Kan Naoto, who took office in June 2010, a DPJ tax reform "project team" was formed. In September 2011, during the Noda Yoshihiko administration, the DPJ resurrected its tax system research committee. DPJ members disagreed over what reforms should be enacted, and they made their preferences quite clear to the government tax reform committee. The views of the DPJ were then reflected in the commission's tax reform recommendations (Kamikawa 2014).

4.2. The budget process in the first and second supplementary budgets of 2009

When Hatoyama Yukio became prime minister, his administration scrutinized the first 2009 supplementary budget (created under his predecessor, Asō Tarō), hoping to find ¥3 trillion that could be redirected toward achieving the manifesto's goals. Instead of imposing fixed cost-cutting targets on each ministry, Hatoyama required cabinet ministers to compete over funding by having them report on how much they were willing to cut and why they were unable to make deeper cuts. This approach did not produce the desired savings, leading the GRU and the Ministry of Finance (MOF) to impose additional cuts on each agency that totaled ¥2.93 trillion.

However, at that time the value of the yen spiked while the value of the stock market fell sharply, prompting the government to enact new stimulus measures in a second supplementary budget at a cost of ¥7.1 trillion. Kamei Shizuka of the People's New Party, appointed as minister of state for financial services and the postal system, demanded that supplemental spending be raised to ¥8 trillion. In the ensuing uproar, a scheduled extraordinary meeting of the cabinet had to be cancelled. Kan Naoto, then deputy prime minister and minister of state for national strategy (head of the NSO), and Kamei got into a heated debate over the issue, the result of which was an additional ¥100 billion in government-bond-financed public works construction that brought the total cost of the supplementary budget up to ¥7.2 trillion.

4.3. The 2010 budget process and tax system reform

The DPJ changed the 2010 budget compilation process by ending the practice of having the MOF issue "budget request guidelines" or spending ceilings to each ministry at the start of the budget process. Instead, each minister was entrusted

with independently developing a budget proposal for their department. The ministries' budget requests, delivered on October 15, totaled ¥95.04 trillion, nearly ¥3 trillion more than the budget enacted by the Asō cabinet before the change of government. Moreover, the final figure was expected to reach ¥97 trillion once unspecified "item requests" were included.

The next step was having the GRU conduct a "program review" to evaluate the necessity of each government program and identify duplication of effort. The GRU's goal was to identify ¥3 trillion in unnecessary spending. This target had to be reached to fulfill Prime Minister Hatoyama's pledge to limit government borrowing in 2010 to ¥44 trillion, the amount of government bonds issued for the 2009 general budget and the first 2009 supplementary budget. Unfortunately for Hatoyama, the GRU was able to find only ¥1.6 trillion in potential savings. In the actual budget, the savings shrank to ¥692 billion, far short of what was needed to fulfill the promises of the DPJ manifesto. Kan Naoto, head of the NSO, asked ministers to cut back on their manifesto-related budget requests. He asked for high school fees to be eliminated for lower income families instead of all families, for shifting some of the costs for the DPJ's child allowance away from the national government, and for a reduction in the direct payments made to farm households. The ministers were, however, less than forthcoming with budget concessions.

The deadlock was broken by Ozawa Ichirō, DPJ secretary-general. On December 16, Ozawa strode into the prime minister's official residence and handed Hatoyama the party's budget and tax reform demands. These demands included elimination of public high school fees and highway tolls, and income support for farm households as promised in the campaign. On the other hand, the party endorsed keeping provisional tax rates in place and limiting child allowance payments based on family income. Ozawa openly questioned whether the government had succeeded in taking control of policymaking out of the hands of the bureaucracy: "We're calling this government by politicians, but is that really true? I doubt it." Ozawa criticized the cabinet ministers for continuing to rely on bureaucratic expertise, saying, "When making budget decisions, top officials need to master the details of their departments' spending themselves and not just act as if they understand those details." Ozawa also took it upon himself to reconcile the budgets of each ministry, a task that should have been handled by the office of the prime minister (Asahi Shimbun Seiken Shuzai Sentā 2010, 249–51). Thanks to Ozawa's intervention, the final budget adjustments were made quickly and the budget was completed before the end of the year.

By the end of the budget compilation process, in the first year of the DPJ government, it was obvious that the party could not deliver on one manifesto promise after another. The LDP's child allowance (jidō teate) was provisionally revised in 2010 as a monthly payment of ¥13,000 under a cost-sharing arrangement with local governments and employers. As for rolling back provisional tax rates, the national automobile weight tax increase was cut by half, and that was all. The provisional tax increases on gasoline and the delivery of light fuels were rescinded in April 2010 but were replaced by special tax increases, of roughly equivalent value, that were to remain in place "for some time."[8] The tax deduction for dependents was amended to exclude children aged fifteen or younger, but deductions for dependents aged twenty-three to sixty-nine remained in place, as did the deduction for spouses. The proposed tax cut for small and medium enterprises was postponed.

Many of the manifesto's pledges could not be fulfilled due to budget shortfalls made far worse by the global recession. In response to the economic slowdown, the government had to increase spending as tax revenues fell dramatically. The ¥2.9 trillion that the DPJ had trimmed from the first supplementary budget of 2009 was meant to be spent in the 2010 budget on manifesto programs. Instead, the money went to the second supplementary budget of 2009 to stimulate the economy. In addition, to help make up for a steep drop in predicted 2009 tax revenue, from ¥46.1 trillion to ¥36.9 trillion, ¥9.3 trillion in additional government bonds were issued. Tax revenue for 2010 was expected to be ¥37.4 trillion. When Hatoyama first pledged to limit new

government bonds to ¥44 trillion, it seemed like a fairly easy target to hit, but the severity of the recession quashed that expectation.

From this perspective, it appears that the global financial crisis that began in 2008 was a major reason the DPJ was unable to live up to its manifesto, but the DPJ's overly rosy predictions should not be ignored. The party promised to slash government spending yet made little progress toward that goal. The DPJ also neglected to factor in the natural yearly increase in social security spending of approximately ¥1 trillion, or the additional ¥2.5 trillion cost of raising the government's share of basic pensions funding from 36.5 percent to 50 percent (Tanaka 2013, 97). Finally, the severity of the financial crisis was unmistakable from the autumn of 2008 and so too was the inevitability of lower tax receipts and higher government spending.

The manifesto also included a pledge to review special tax measures. The 2009 Dubai financial crisis raised fears of another economic downturn and a "special tax recession." These fears caused the DPJ to keep many of the tax breaks in place despite their effect on the budget deficit. Election campaign strategy also played a role. The party would not commit to eliminating the tax deductions for dependents and spouses ahead of the 2010 upper house election (Asahi Shimbun Seiken Shuzai Sentā 2010, 266–68).[9]

5. Policy Operations in the Kan Cabinet
5.1 Prime Minister Kan's inauguration and the consumption tax hike
Having failed to resolve the issue of relocating the Futenma military base, Hatoyama announced that he was stepping down on June 2. Kan Naoto was chosen as his replacement. Hatoyama's cabinet had a difficult relationship with some ministries due to its efforts to remove bureaucrats from the policymaking process. After becoming prime minister, Kan immediately set out to rebuild ties with the bureaucracy. At the first meeting of his cabinet, Kan announced that developing close relationships between his administration and the bureaucracy was his top priority. He declared that relationships between the three highest political appointees in each ministry and its civil servants

would be characterized by "open and reciprocal sharing of information, efforts to achieve mutual understanding, and a unified approach to solving problems" (*Asahi Shimbun* 2010).

Kan also initiated major policy shifts. His experience as head of the NSO and finance minister made him fully aware of how rising government debt was making budget planning ever more difficult. Kan also attended the Group of Seven meeting of finance ministers and central bank governors in Iqaluit, Canada, in February 2010, where he learned of the extent of the Greek debt crisis. Kan began to campaign for raising the consumption tax under the slogan "strong economy, strong public finances, strong social safety net."

In a June 17 press conference called to announce the DPJ's platform for the upper house election in July 2010, Kan signaled his interest in raising the consumption tax by referencing the LDP's proposal to raise the consumption tax to 10 percent. The House of Councillors election turned out badly for the DPJ and its coalition partner, the People's New Party, and they lost control of the chamber, thereby creating a "twisted Diet," or divided government. Kan's statements about raising taxes were blamed for the DPJ's loss, and he fell silent on the topic as criticism toward him escalated. This is not to say that Kan gave up on the idea; discussions about raising the consumption tax continued to move forward within the DPJ.

5.2. The 2011 budget compilation process

On June 22, the Kan cabinet adopted a "medium-term fiscal framework" for government revenues and expenditures in 2011–13 as part of a "fiscal management strategy." The strategy included a commitment to do everything possible to avoid issuing more than ¥44 trillion in new government bonds and to continue working to further reduce annual deficits. The Kan administration also pledged to cap 2011 government expenditures at ¥71 trillion, the same level as in 2010 (not including debt servicing costs). In drafting the 2011 budget, Kan included a special ¥1 trillion fund for a "revitalize Japan" scheme that would target seven areas as part of the cabinet's "new growth strategy" that

aimed to "modulate" the budget. To cover the cost of the scheme, all ministries were given new budget guidelines and instructed to reduce their 2011 budget requests by 10 percent, instructions that perhaps reflected the lessons the DPJ had learned from trying to overhaul the entire budget.

Genba Kōichirō, minister of state for national strategy (head of the NSO) and DPJ policy chief, was appointed as chair of an evaluation committee tasked with vetting proposals from ministries in a public "policy contest" that would determine how the ¥1 trillion special fund would be allocated. Having the contest and its results made public was touted as a way of bringing transparency to the budget process. Although the special fund was meant to stimulate the economy through innovative projects, the Ministry of Defense proposed using the money to cover the cost sharing ("sympathy budget") for US forces stationed in Japan. The Ministry of Education cut its financial contribution to the management of compulsory education by ¥216 billion under the new budget guidelines; its special fund proposal was to use ¥225 billion to reduce class sizes for first and second grade students to thirty-five. Instead of being inspired to innovate, ministry after ministry asked for special funds to pay for existing programs that were slated for cuts under the budget guidelines. These requests caused the proposed size of the special fund to swell to ¥2.1 trillion, of which only ¥900 billion would go toward "new growth strategies." The Kan government once again conducted a program review looking for ways to cut costs but identified only ¥300 billion in wasteful spending.

In short, the DPJ failed to live up to its manifesto again in its 2011 budget framework. Because tax exemptions for children were eliminated from national and local income taxes, the child allowance was increased by ¥7,000, limited to children under the age of three. The maximum allowance for older children was to remain at ¥13,000, and the DPJ relinquished its commitment to raise the allowance to ¥26,000. The DPJ's plan to end highway tolls stalled at a ¥120 billion appropriation for a pilot project in a limited area. The DPJ leadership could not hide the fact that their manifesto was in tatters and had no choice but to announce they were going back to the drawing board.[10]

The Kan government was also stymied by the opposition's control of the upper house. The Great East Japan Earthquake led to a temporary truce among the parties and a 2011 budget was adopted before the end of the fiscal year. According to public finance laws, the government cannot issue special deficit-financing bonds (*akaji kokusai*) without specific enabling legislation and therefore a "special deficit-financing bond act" must be passed every year. The LDP and Kōmeitō blocked passage of the bond act in the upper house until the DPJ made several concessions, including cutting the budget for its manifesto programs.

Consequently, the funds meant to cover the loss of revenue from ending highway tolls would not be included in the 2012 budget request. As for the child allowance, a stopgap measure passed in September 2011 to keep the monthly benefit at ¥13,000. From October 2011 to March 2012, a special measures law would raise the payments to ¥15,000 for children under age three, lower payments to ¥10,000 for children aged three to twelve (families with three or more children would receive ¥15,000) and middle school students. In April 2012, the DPJ's child allowance would be repealed and the LDP's *jidō teate* child allowance would be reinstated. Only households with annual pretax incomes below ¥9.6 million would be eligible for the benefit (Takenaka 2011, 51–55). After receiving these concessions, and a commitment from Kan that he would resign as prime minister, the LDP and Kōmeitō finally approved the special deficit-financing bond act on August 26.

5.3. The 2011 tax reforms

To support job creation and avoid layoffs, Kan had advocated for an across-the-board cut of corporate tax rates, and he included a 5 percent rate cut in the package of tax revisions for 2011. His revisions also included income redistribution measures targeting wealthy individuals, such as limiting earned income deductions for high-wage earners, cutting the standard deduction for inheritance tax, raising the tax rate on the highest income bracket, and reviewing the preferential tax treatment given to retirement allowances.

The proposed tax reforms included some steps toward fulfilling manifesto pledges. Although the DPJ was blocked from delivering on its pledge to repeal tax deductions for adult dependents, the tax reforms would place an income cap on those deductions. In place of the manifesto's promise to cut the corporate tax rate for small and medium enterprises from 18 percent to 11 percent, the tax package would cut the rate to 15 percent. The manifesto proposed an anti-global-warming tax, although the same effect could have been achieved by increasing taxes on fossil fuels beginning in October 2011. Also included was an expanded deduction for charitable donations, a change that Hatoyama had championed during his administration.

Once again, the tax proposals were blocked by the upper house, with some exceptions. Legislation creating tax incentives to support employment, encourage environment-related investment, and expand charitable giving was passed on June 22. A reduction in corporate tax rates, expansion of the tax base, and repeal of the 10 percent personal income tax deduction for retirement income finally passed on November 30, but were not implemented until 2012.[11] All other changes to the tax code were tabled until 2012 (Matsuura 2012, 1). During the 2011 budget compilation, as it became increasingly clear that the government would have to take on more debt, Kan renewed his calls to increase the consumption tax. In the January 2011 cabinet reshuffle, Kan appointed Yosano Kaoru, a former LDP member, as minister of state for economic and fiscal policy and minister of state for total reform of social security and tax.

When Yosano was appointed as minister of state for economic and fiscal policy in the Asō cabinet, the following statement was added to supplementary provision 104, paragraph 1, of the Act for Partial Revision of the Income Tax: "In order for the government to increase the state's contribution to basic pensions to 50 percent and fund health care, long term care and other social security programs, including those addressing the needs of an aging society, once the targeted economic stimulus policies have their desired effect, presumably by 2010, legislative measures to enable comprehensive reforms of the tax system, including the consumption tax, shall be drafted no later than the 2011 fiscal year." Yosano seized on this provision as justification for drafting a bill to raise the consumption tax in the 2011 fiscal year, an initiative supported by Kan. Yosano led the writing of a draft for comprehensive social security and tax reform. However, there was intense opposition to raising the consumption tax within the DPJ and so, at the June 30 cabinet meeting, the draft was accepted only as a "cabinet report" rather than being approved as a "cabinet decision."

5.4. Kan steps down

Following the 3.11 disaster, the ruling and opposition parties had a period of détente, but that spirit of cooperation ended as the opposition increasingly challenged the Kan administration's response to the crisis. Kan's rival, Ozawa Ichirō, teamed up with Mori Yoshirō of the LDP to introduce a no-confidence motion against Kan (Yomiuri Shimbun Seijibu 2011, 175–86). To keep DPJ members from voting against him, Kan announced at a DPJ meeting on June 2 that he would soon resign. Two supplementary budgets were passed on May 2 and July 25 in response to 3.11. These budgets covered only immediate emergency measures. Instead of new government bonds, the funding for these budgets was found through a spending review and accounting surpluses, and no new bonds were issued.

Kan set three conditions for his resignation: passage of the second supplementary budget, a special deficit-financing bond act, and a law to support renewable energy. The last of these were enacted in late August, and Kan stepped down immediately thereafter. The DPJ held an election for party president on August 29, and Noda, who was backed by supporters of the Kan administration, became prime minister.

6. Policy Operations Under the Noda Cabinet

6.1. Noda's installment as prime minister and the 3.11 recovery budget

After the change of government, Noda was appointed as vice minister and then minister of finance. Some called him an "internal candidate from the MOF" due to the closeness of his relationship

with the ministry. From the time he campaigned to become the president of the DPJ, Noda argued that disaster recovery required higher taxes. As for raising the consumption tax, Noda said, "A bill will be introduced in the ordinary session of the Diet next year. There's no arguing against it." In order to fulfill supplementary provision 104 of the Act for Partial Revision of the Income Tax, Noda felt it was necessary to introduce a bill to raise the consumption tax in the Diet in 2011.

The Finance Ministry did not hide its complete support of Noda. When Noda became prime minister, one of the MOF's "ace" officials, Budget Bureau deputy director Ōta Mitsuru, was sent in to serve as Noda's secretary. Noda also replaced Deputy Chief Cabinet Secretary Takino Kinya, who was from the Ministry of Internal Affairs and Communications and had opposed the MOF over local tax revenues, with Taketoshi Makoto, administrative vice minister of land and infrastructure, who had close ties with Katsu Eijirō, administrative vice minister of finance. Moving currently serving administrative vice ministers into key posts in the cabinet was all but unheard of and led critics to say the Noda cabinet was run by the MOF.

The bulk of the disaster recovery budget (¥9.2 trillion) was contained in the third supplementary budget, which was adopted by cabinet decision on October 21 and went into effect on November 21. A bill to secure resources for reconstruction was also approved by cabinet decision on October 28. This bill set a ten-year limit on how long the higher taxes for reconstruction funding could be in effect. Negotiations with the LDP and Kōmeitō led to the time limit being raised to twenty-five years. Thus amended, the bill was enacted on November 30.[12] Moreover, the fourth supplementary budget, which included funding to help disaster victims pay off the loans they had taken out for houses that no longer existed, was passed on February 8, 2012. The funding source for this budget was higher than expected tax revenue and previously issued government bonds.

6.2. Compiling the 2012 budget

In the 2012 budget, public works spending was cut by 8.1 percent (3.2 percent if lump sum grants are excluded), and support for small and medium enterprises was cut by 8.5 percent, making it seem as if substantial budget cuts had been achieved. In fact, adding the ¥3.8 trillion in the special funding for disaster recovery reveals that the public works budget grew by 6.6 percent (11.4 percent excluding lump sum grants), while the budget for small and medium businesses grew 70.5 percent.

The 2012 budget was also notable for resurrecting large-scale public works that had been attacked by the DPJ as wasteful, such as the Yanba dam, three new high-speed train routes, an outer ring road for Tokyo, and super levees. The backers of these projects argued that the 3.11 disaster demonstrated the importance of infrastructure and that the new construction would help prepare the country for future disasters by providing alternate transportation routes.

Maehara Seiji, DPJ policy chief and former minister of land and infrastructure in the Hatoyama cabinet, demanded cancellation of the Yanba dam construction, but his successor, Maeda Takeshi, formerly an official in the Ministry of Construction, refused to give in. Ultimately, Noda approved including the project in the budget proposal. After that decision, the DPJ was judged to have abandoned its commitment to change the government's focus "from concrete to the people."

6.3. Total reform of social security and taxes

Unfazed by adamant opposition within his own party, Noda continued to press forward on raising the consumption tax. His cabinet accepted a framework for social security and tax reforms, and a bill to raise the consumption tax was expected to be submitted to the Diet before the end of the 2011 fiscal year (March 31, 2012). When Noda became prime minister, he committed to gaining the party's approval prior to introducing major legislation, and therefore his tax bill had to be vetted by DPJ committees. On March 28, 2012, with no consensus in sight, DPJ policy chief Maehara declared an end to the party's internal review of the tax plan and announced, over the shouts of protesting DPJ members, that the plan had, in fact, been approved by the party. Later that day, a majority of the executive committee

of the DPJ's Policy Research Council approved the bill. Noda met with Ozawa and asked him to support raising the consumption tax, but to no avail. Noda then changed tack and reached out to the LDP and Kōmeitō. Negotiations with these parties lasted until June 15, at which point the government had reached agreement with the LDP and Kōmeitō over the Noda administration's consumption tax bill and the LDP's proposed amendments to the Basic Law for Social Security System Reform.

During the negotiations, the DPJ had to make several concessions on social security policy to the LDP, including the following items: (a) no increases in income tax or inheritance tax until the 2013 tax system amendments; (b) postponement of the introduction of a guaranteed minimum old-age pension benefit; (c) replacement of pension contribution subsidies for low-income earners with cash benefits; (d) postponement of a reduction in national pension benefits for people with high incomes; (e) delayed expansion of eligibility for pension benefits to nonregular workers and reduction in the types of workers who will be eligible; (f) postponement of the cancellation of the medical care system for people seventy-five and older, and (g) withdrawal of the DPJ plan to develop "comprehensive early childhood centers" (sōgō kodomoen) in favor of expansion of the existing "accredited early childhood centers" (nintei kodomoen). Noda's willingness to concede almost the entire slate of DPJ social security proposals showed that raising the consumption tax was his highest priority.

On June 19, at a joint meeting of DPJ members from both chambers of the Diet, Maehara again declared an end to internal debate, this time over the compromise social security and tax bills that emerged from the three-party talks. The legislation was passed in the House of Representatives on June 26. Fifty-seven DPJ members voted against the bills and sixteen more either abstained or were absent. Ozawa and forty-eight other DPJ members left the party and formed the "People's Life First" party. Before these bills could be voted on in the upper house, six of the smaller opposition parties began organizing to force a vote of no-confidence in the lower house. In an effort to pressure Noda to declare when the lower house would be dissolved, the LDP also threatened to introduce a motion of no-confidence against the cabinet in the lower house and censure motions against Noda in the upper house. Noda eventually promised to "verify the people's trust in the near future." This commitment was enough for the LDP to abstain from the no-confidence vote and on August 10 the social security and tax increase package was approved by the upper house.

6.4. Disaster reconstruction funding controversy and the dissolution of the lower house

In October, problems in how disaster recovery funds were being used came to the surface. First, much of the funds were being spent beyond the affected areas on projects such as retrofitting public buildings for earthquake resistance and road construction. Only 6 percent of the money allotted to a subsidy for private businesses in affected locations was spent in the disaster zone. More controversy arose when it was discovered that funds earmarked for recovery were being spent on things that had little or no relationship to local revitalization, including increasing security for whale hunting ships against animal rights activists. The DPJ government was attacked by the press and the public for mishandling the disaster recovery. Despite the outcry, when the recovery budget was being written, considered by panels of experts, and then approved by the Diet, it was always clear that some of the funds would be spent in unaffected areas to make them less vulnerable to natural disasters.

This intention to help the "entire nation" recover and prepare is clearly set forth in Article 2, paragraph 1, of the Basic Act on Reconstruction in Response to the Great East Japan Earthquake:

The cessation of economic activity in the disaster zone has negatively affected businesses and citizens around the country, making it a national problem. Therefore, recovery efforts should not be limited to physically restoring the regions that were directly affected. Instead, with the understanding and support of the public, and with an eye toward making Japan a vibrant nation once more, we propose

dramatic policy shifts to enable each and every person to move past the current difficulties and lead a rich life. We must take this opportunity to implement policies to create new communities that fulfill the vision of what Japan should be in the mid-twenty-first century.

This law was passed with the support of the LDP and Kōmeitō as well as the DPJ, which is to say that the LDP and Kōmeitō were in no position to criticize the DPJ over diversion of recovery funds. The DPJ also complained about criticism from the press, which had covered the process and knew this history well.

Being able to share the blame did not save the DPJ from facing a major crisis over the spending of recovery funds on completely unrelated projects. The DPJ was especially vulnerable to attack because of its insistence on putting politicians instead of bureaucrats in charge of budget compilation. Having ministers and vice ministers poring over accounts and punching numbers into calculators was seen as no substitute for the work of experienced civil servants, but the real problem was the lack of a system for elected officials to effectively oversee how the agencies were using their budgets. In other words, although the DPJ tried to take control from the bureaucracy to the point of getting involved in matters they should have stayed out of, they had no choice but to delegate a considerable degree of responsibility to bureaucrats, much as the LDP had done when in power. The DPJ either ignored or failed to catch bureaucratic misconduct.

Former prime minister Abe Shinzō, who was reelected to the post of LDP president in September, called Noda a "liar" for not having yet delivered on his commitment to dissolve the House of Representatives and pressed for dissolution before the year ended. A group of DPJ members started a "dump Noda" campaign and threatened to force Noda to step down if he moved to dissolve the lower house. In a party leaders' debate at the Diet on November 14, Noda abruptly, and unilaterally, announced that he would dissolve the parliament in two days if the LDP and Kōmeitō would vote for the annual special deficit-financing bond act and for electoral system reform legislation that would reduce disparities in voter representation in the Diet and reduce the number of seats in the lower house. In spite of the opposition within his own party, Noda committed to calling snap elections on December 16. As anyone could have predicted, the DPJ was thrashed at the polls, and the LDP returned to power.

7. Analysis

To summarize the events described above, the DPJ campaigned on a manifesto promising programs that required a great deal of money. The party claimed they could deliver on their pledges by eliminating waste and "reorganizing" the budget. Hatoyama also pledged not to raise the consumption tax for four years if elected. In reality, the necessary funds could not be squeezed out of the existing budget, and most of the promised benefits never materialized, but taxes were raised all the same. Over the vehement opposition of DPJ backbenchers, Prime Minister Noda partnered with the LDP and Kōmeitō to increase the consumption tax. Decrying Noda's tax hike and abandonment of the DPJ manifesto, Ozawa and his supporters defected from the party. The denouement was a massive defeat for the DPJ in the general election.

There are many, many possible explanations for why the DPJ government lost the support of the public: the Futenma military base relocation problem, the mishandling of foreign affairs—such as the furor sparked by the ramming of Japan Coast Guard patrol vessels by a Chinese fishing boat near the Senkaku Islands—the cabinets' amateur efforts to make policy and govern without relying on bureaucratic leadership, Hatoyama's and Ozawa's financial scandals, and the gaffe fests presented by a series of cabinet members. This paper credits the DPJ's fall to its inability to deliver on its unworkable manifesto and its willingness to ignore the public's opposition to raising the consumption tax. The DPJ was plagued with internecine conflict over enacting the manifesto and the consumption tax, conflict that resulted in the party breaking up.

Not everyone sees the breach of manifestos as a major cause of the DPJ's problems. In a public opinion poll conducted by the *Asahi Shimbun* after the DPJ's victory in the 2009 general election, 81 percent of respondents said the DPJ won because people wanted the LDP out of government. Only 38 percent credited the DPJ's victory to public support for their policies. Similarly, a *Yomiuri Shimbun* opinion poll conducted immediately before the DPJ's party president election in September 2010 found little public attachment to the 2009 manifesto; 79 percent of respondents agreed the manifesto should be revised given the changes in the political and economic environment since its creation, while only 15 percent disagreed (Pekkanen and Reed 2013, 9, 11).

Although the public might not have been wedded to the particulars of the 2009 manifesto, their confidence in the DPJ was seriously damaged when the party proved to be unable to live up to its commitments. The fights within the DPJ over enacting the manifesto further weakened the public's trust in the party's ability to govern. A *Nihon Keizai Shimbun* survey asked respondents why they did not support the Noda cabinet. The most popular responses were "poor handling of government and party affairs" and "lack of leadership." These articles commented that the respondents felt that the DPJ's poor management "reflected the deep policy divisions within the government" and "disapprove because the DPJ members fight with each other over every important policy" (*Nihon Keizai Shimbun* 2012a,b,c).[13]

Of course, one could say that much of the conflict within the DPJ was less about policy than Ozawa Ichirō's personal ambitions and political maneuvering against the mainstream faction of the DPJ. It would be wrong, however, to treat policies as just props in a power struggle. If the manifesto did not matter, its abandonment would not have been brandished as a casus belli by DPJ insurgents. The fate of the manifesto was a central issue in the DPJ's internal struggles. It is worth noting that during LDP governments, we have not seen opposition parties continually condemn the LDP for violating its campaign promises, nor has the LDP had endless bouts of infighting. This comparison with the LDP merits consideration when examining the failures of the DPJ government.

The questions remain as to why the DPJ filled its manifesto with promises it could not keep and why it then fought incessantly over those promises. Understanding the fall of the DPJ requires answering these questions. This section explains how the overpromising and the infighting can be traced back to the constraints created by the predominant party system.

7.1. Why the DPJ reached for the unreachable in its manifesto

7.1.1. A strategy of say anything to get elected?

It is not unreasonable to suspect that the DPJ was fully aware that it could not deliver on some of its manifesto promises, yet made them anyway in order to win the election. For example, its manifesto for the 2005 lower house election included a monthly child allowance of ¥16,000 that would be paid for by eliminating tax deductions for dependents and spouses.

However, this deficit-neutral plan was upended by Ozawa, who was elected as DPJ party president in 2006. Ozawa claimed, "In national election campaigns, women get very keyed up when talking about children or grandchildren, so the *kodomo teate* child allowance should be the flagship policy of the DPJ manifesto for the upper house election." This pronouncement raised the issue of how the allowance would be paid for. During Diet questioning in January 2007, Ozawa abruptly announced that the DPJ's child allowance would cost ¥6 trillion, enough to make the monthly payment ¥26,000 per child. Later the DPJ claimed this amount was appropriate because it would cover the average cost of raising and educating a child through elementary and middle school (*Sankei Shimbun* 2009; Yakushiji 2012, 179–80).

In fact, there were already doubts within the DPJ about whether the manifesto could be paid for without adding to the government's debt. In a dialogue with Yosano published in *Chūō Kōron* in July 2008, Maehara criticized the DPJ's manifesto for the 2007 upper house election stating, "Finding ¥18 trillion through administrative reform is utterly impossible." He added, "I think that unless the DPJ admits and corrects this mistake, it cannot govern responsibly" (Yakushiji 2012, 46).

Moreover, by the time Ozawa resigned as DPJ president in May 2009, the price tag for the manifesto had risen above ¥20 trillion. Okada Katsuya, the DPJ's new secretary-general, cut ¥3.2 trillion from the manifesto's goals and pledged that some policies whose cost would amount to ¥3.6 trillion would be "incrementally implemented while ensuring sources of revenue" (Yakushiji 2012, 21–24).

In fact, Okada was already planning to roll back provisional tax increases in the second year of the DPJ administration and wanted to cut spending accordingly. His concerns were not shared by Hatoyama, Ozawa's successor as party president, who was intent on quickly executing his own policy agenda. Okada's budget concerns were also dismissed by Ozawa who, as acting party president, claimed, "Funding will become available once we are running the government. This is the decision by the party president" (Mainichi Shimbun Seijibu 2009, 131–32).

7.1.2. The distant relationship between the DPJ and the ministries

Were Ozawa's critics right to accuse him of deciding unrealistic policies deliberately as an election ploy? Ozawa might have sincerely believed that the MOF could produce more funds if ordered to do so, and he was also dissatisfied with the Hatoyama cabinet's budget compilation process. On December 14, after Hatoyama announced a ¥44 trillion cap on new government bonds for the next fiscal year, Ozawa urged Kamei to question whether that would be enough money (Nihon Keizai Shimbunsha 2010, 213).

As noted earlier, on December 16, Ozawa handed the prime minister the party's budget and tax reform demands and accused the cabinet ministers of failing to exercise leadership over the bureaucracy. When Ozawa ran again for party president in 2010, he insisted that national subsidies to local governments should be switched to lump sum, no-strings-attached state subsidies and claimed that if politicians assumed more control, they would be able to cut all wasteful spending and thereby pay for new policies. Setting aside whether or not Ozawa was right, he was convinced the DPJ government was unable to live up to its manifesto because other DPJ leaders were under the thumb of the MOF. Judging by their subsequent defections, many DPJ members agreed with Ozawa's criticisms in 2009.

Why did so many DPJ members embrace Ozawa's version of events? One possible explanation is the chilly relationship that existed between the DPJ and the ministries while the DPJ was in the opposition. Long before the DPJ assumed power, it drew up various policy proposals, including those that made their way into the manifesto. But the DPJ did not consult with the relevant ministries to find out how much of their budgets could be redirected toward the party's policies, which is to say the DPJ never asked the bureaucrats if their plans were realistic (Kitamura Wataru, cited in Rengō Sōgō Seikatsu Kaihatsu Kenkyūjo 2012, 45–46).

In the UK, which has a two-party dominant system and fairly frequent transfers of power, members of Parliament not in the cabinet are forbidden to have contact with civil servants. The only exception to this rule is during a specified period prior to a general election when the prime minister may give leaders of opposition parties access to officials in government departments. Opposition parties then consult with those officials regarding the viability of their policy platforms and revise their proposals accordingly (Fujimori and Ōyama 2004, 47–49; Kitamura Wataru, cited in Rengō Sōgō Seikatsu Kaihatsu Kenkyūjo 2012, 45–46). Because the LDP was in power for decades, Japan lacked a similar system for preparing opposition parties to govern by giving them access to the bureaucracy. This missing link is part of the institutional legacy of Japan's predominant party system.

Despite the lack of an institutionalized precedent, there was presumably no obstacle keeping the DPJ from informally conferring with ministry officials as its chances of winning in 2009 grew favorable. In fact, there was some contact. But the ministries did not closely review the DPJ's proposals for the following reasons.

7.2. Why the DPJ did not consult with the ministries over the manifesto's viability

7.2.1. Politicization of the bureaucracy

The first reason for the distance between the DPJ and ministries is the unusual closeness between the ministries and the LDP, a relationship that deepened over the decades of LDP rule. Members of the DPJ viewed the bureaucracy and the LDP as two sides of the same coin or saw the bureaucracy as LDP collaborators. DPJ members who saw civil servants as their adversaries would scarcely consider seeking their advice prior to an election. The bureaucrats had their own worries. They feared the LDP would retaliate against them if the party discovered they were advising an opposition party on how to govern, and therefore no such overtures were made to the DPJ. In short, the politicization of the bureaucracy made it more difficult for the DPJ to consult with them on the feasibility of the manifesto.

The DPJ's antipathy toward the bureaucracy was not entirely unfounded. For example, at a June 2009 press conference, administrative vice minister of the Ministry of Agriculture, Forestry, and Fisheries Ide Michio criticized the DPJ's agricultural plans as "difficult to implement and unrealistic" (Nihon Keizai Shimbunsha 2010, 60–61). More seriously, documents released through the Wikileaks site revealed that officials in the Ministry of Foreign Affairs and the Ministry of Defense had advised US officials not to compromise with the DPJ administration (Yamaguchi 2012, 131–32). According to Nagatsuma Akira, minister of health, labour and welfare, ministry officials who opposed him leaked stories to the press about Nagatsuma behaving abnormally toward civil servants, actions of which he himself had no recollection (Nagatsuma 2011, 126–27).

After the first DPJ cabinet was formed, ministry officials complained the top political leaders (minister, vice minister, and parliamentary secretary) of the ministries were excluding them from policy deliberations and that high-ranking bureaucrats were getting too little information from the political leaders. Stories appeared in the press about politicians using calculators to review documents and trying to micromanage instead of letting the civil servants take care of the details.[14]

The DPJ's attempts to reserve all decision-making powers showed the extent of their distrust of the bureaucracy and revealed that many DPJ members saw civil servants as adversaries.

7.2.2. The flexibility of the LDP in its inclusive party strategy

In addition to having scant access to bureaucratic expertise, the DPJ's manifesto writing was also hampered by the LDP's willingness to claim any DPJ idea as its own and thereby scuttle the DPJ's campaign strategy. Edano Yukio (2006) helped write the 2003 general election manifesto while serving as chair of the DPJ Policy Research Council and described his experience with LDP policy poaching:

> Leading up to the 2001 Tokyo Metropolitan Assembly election, the DPJ campaigned by making promises based on abstract slogans, but as soon as Koizumi Junichirō became president of the LDP, they started campaigning on the same issues as those we emphasized. We lost an important way to show voters how we were different from the LDP. If we cannot promise the voters something that the LDP cannot offer, it will come back to bite us. An experienced Diet member who had been in the Japan Socialist Party said, "Whatever we proposed, within two to three years the LDP would take the teeth out of it and repackage it as their own idea." With the LDP's track record in mind, we made every effort to come up with ideas the LDP could not support. The LDP liked to campaign on abstract values, so we made our platform as concrete as possible (p. 115). . . . Our strategy was to unveil flagship policies all at once, just before the election. Otherwise we would lose the surprise effect and risk having the LDP upstage us by claiming our ideas. (p. 118)

Because the DPJ felt compelled to pursue policies the LDP would not support, and because the LDP was an inclusive party, the DPJ may have ended up with plans that were unlikely to be achieved. One example of an unrealistic policy, explained in more detail below, was a ban on *amakudari* sinecures for elite civil servants. Returning to the

DPJ's fears of being copied by the LDP, the Asō cabinet originally opposed the DPJ's proposals for eliminating highway tolls and creating a new child allowance program but later reduced highway tolls and increased the amount of the LDP's existing *jidō teate* child allowance. The DPJ not only postponed its manifesto announcement until immediately before the election, it may have also avoided a party-wide discussion and limited the number of DPJ members who knew of the manifesto's contents to keep information from being leaked to the LDP.

According to Naoshima Masayuki, chair of the DPJ Policy Research Council and person in charge of creating the 2009 manifesto:

> If we wanted some feedback about the manifesto and contacted an outside expert to ask for advice, usually it would be leaked to the press by the following day. That's why we became secretive. . . . We treated the manifesto like it was top secret because it was the flagship of our campaign. If word leaked out, our strategy would become known. That's why we made a practice of not showing our hand until right before the election. . . . Diet members did complain that manifestos were decided before they knew anything about them and that the process was not transparent. However, from a strategic viewpoint, we had little choice but to keep everything secret until just before an election. Openness and transparency were supposed to be part of the DPJ brand, but we imposed strict information controls. (Naoshima 2012, 68–71)

It follows that if the manifesto drafters were unwilling to share information with fellow party members, they would hardly be willing to seek input from the bureaucrats that worked hand in glove with the LDP. Writing the manifesto behind closed doors had other negative consequences. DPJ members did not share an understanding of the principles that underlay specific policies (Naoshima 2012, 49). For example, the party split over placing an income limit on the DPJ's *kodomo teate* child allowance that was intended as a universal welfare policy.[15]

As mentioned above, the LDP is not new to copying the policies of opposition parties. Also, when an interest group that holds policy positions close to an opposition party needs something from the government, it asks the LDP, the dominant party. The LDP uses the inclusive party strategy to maximize votes, and if changing policy for that interest group wins the LDP more public support, it will not hesitate to do so, whether or not that policy change was first proposed by an opposition party.[16] The fact that the LDP is completely open to adopting the policies of other parties is both cause and effect of the predominant party system. Confronted with the LDP's "inclusiveness" and opportunism, the DPJ was unable to reveal its policies until the last minute.

7.3. The causes of the series of manifesto failures

7.3.1. Clear goals make for clear failures

Because the DPJ could not achieve all of the objectives in its manifesto, it was repeatedly accused of dishonesty while in government, despite the fact that breaking campaign promises is not uncommon. There was no equivalent scrutiny of prior LDP manifestos at election time. The LDP's campaigns feature many vague or abstract ideals, the attainment of which cannot be easily measured. According to Bill Emmott, in the UK, where the use of manifestos dates back over a century, "Governments breaking campaign promises is an everyday occurrence" (Nihon Keizai Shimbunsha 2010, 183). Moreover, the primary function of UK manifestos is expressing the parties' fundamental principles; they are not action plans featuring numerical targets for budgeting and time required. (Fujimori and Ōyama 2004, 143–46; Yamaguchi 2009, 144–45; Nakakita 2012, 201–2)

In its manifesto the DPJ did not stop at presenting concrete policies that clearly set it apart from the LDP. It went on to include specific budget amounts and time frames for implementation. This clarity made it easy to identify when the DPJ fell short of its goals. In regard to the child allowance, for example, instead of being able to claim a victory for expanding eligibility and raising the allowance, the DPJ was attacked as "liars"

for not raising the benefit to ¥26,000. Beginning with the Kan cabinet, Ozawa and his supporters accused the DPJ leadership of not upholding the manifesto. This recurring internal conflict kept the manifesto issue alive and kept the DPJ's credibility under attack.

7.3.2. Delegitimization

What led the DPJ to include specifics in its manifesto is worth considering. Naoshima (2012) offers the following explanation:

> With each election, the DPJ grew stronger, eventually reaching the point where it seemed likely to win control of the government. As the odds of the DPJ's winning increased, so did pressure from the LDP, the mass media, and political commentators to go beyond criticizing the LDP and offer its own policies complete with price tags. Looking back, I can't say that we weren't baited into getting carried away, but at the time we believed that explaining our plans as rationally as possible would help people to better understand the DPJ. (pp. 48–49)

Naoshima also admitted that some DPJ members warned about the risks:

> Diet members who had been bureaucrats cautioned, "If you explain in too much detail, you'll regret it later." Ozawa, as president of the DPJ, said, "For that sort of thing, it's enough to lay out the logic of the policy," and ordered that there should be no need to go into great detail about costs and funding. Naoshima argued, "If we don't show where the funding will come from, the voters won't believe our policies are feasible." Then, Ozawa answered, "It will all work out. There's enough money to cover it." (pp. 75, 82)

However, these words of caution were not enough to quell demands to make the manifesto more specific. In the end, the manifesto drafters decided to add up the costs of implementing the manifesto and then find the necessary funds. In short, goaded by the LDP and eager to prove the viability of its policies to voters, the DPJ was boxed into including specific figures in its manifesto. This tactical misstep was closely connected to delegitimization. The LDP sought to delegitimize the DPJ by consistently portraying the party as too inexperienced to govern. In order to disprove this allegation, the DPJ had to demonstrate it was prepared to lead the nation.

Of course, it is extremely hard for a party to prove that it can govern while in opposition. When Maehara was party president (September 2005–April 2006), instead of opposing whatever the LDP cabinet proposed on whatever grounds, the DPJ set out to proactively present alternative policies to show that it had the capacity to govern and make policy. However—given that the LDP had no qualms about incorporating opposition policies into its own platform—if a DPJ bill became law, the LDP grabbed the lion's share of the credit. The DPJ was forced to use tactics that had little chance of succeeding, proving that the LDP's delegitimization strategy was highly effective.

Ozawa, who succeeded Maehara as party president, led the DPJ in a go-for-broke campaign against the LDP. The DPJ capitalized on the pension scandal and took control of the upper house in the 2007 election but was still vulnerable to LDP accusations that it was unfit to govern. Although Ozawa was unfazed by the criticism, the writers of the manifestos felt compelled to prove that the DPJ's policies could be implemented. The manifesto for the 2007 House of Councillors election explained what the policies would cost and where those funds would come from. In the 2009 manifesto, the DPJ went still further and included detailed timetables for implementation. These details would come back to haunt the DPJ after it unseated the LDP.

7.3.3. Why did the DPJ's infighting become chronic?

The next topic to consider is why the DPJ's internal conflicts over implementing the manifesto and the necessity of raising the consumption tax became severe enough to result in the party breaking up. Much of the conflict can be credited to nonideological power struggles among DPJ members. However, Kan Naoto, Okada Katsuya, Sengoku Yoshito, Noda Yoshihiko, Maehara Seiji, and Edano Yukio saw increasing the tax as a necessary evil from the start; Ozawa and his supporters strongly opposed the increase. At the time of the 2009 House of Representatives election, the Ozawa group was the mainstream faction, but partway through the term the other side got the upper hand.

In a campaign speech before the 2004 upper house election, DPJ president Okada proposed pension reforms that went beyond what the manifesto contained. Okada proposed changing the national pension (basic pension) into a fully tax-based system with a minimum guaranteed pension. Okada wanted to raise the consumption tax rate by 3 percentage points and earmark the increased revenues to pay for pension reforms (Okada 2008, 184–85). Although the 2005 general election manifesto did not provide details on raising taxes, it did feature a monthly minimum pension of ¥70,000, which Okada publicly stated should be paid for with the consumption tax hike (Yakushiji 2012, 16–17).[17] Ozawa, however, had other ideas as party president. In the DPJ platform written in 2006, dubbed the "policy Magna Carta," Ozawa stifled Okada and Maehara's protests and pledged to keep the consumption tax at 5 percent. This pledge was repeated for the 2009 general election when Hatoyama promised not to increase the consumption tax for the next four years (Minezaki 2010, 103).

The point here is the DPJ's persistence in pushing for a higher consumption tax, dating back to the Kan cabinet, can be seen as proof that Kan and Noda were co-opted by the Finance Ministry. While not denying that entirely, it is also true that the members of both Kan's and Noda's cabinets who formed the "mainstream" faction had been advocates for raising the consumption tax and therefore may have found the MOF's arguments more convincing.

The DPJ has often been criticized for having a random assortment of policies and ideology, but this lack of a common agenda is not surprising given the circumstances. When Japan replaced multi-member districts with single-seat constituencies, it simultaneously attempted to graft a two-party system onto an entrenched one-party predominant system. Given that the heretofore predominant party was still in existence, any claimant to the second party slot would find it difficult enough to recruit electable candidates without worrying about upholding party orthodoxy. Therefore, a lack of unity is the inevitable price, as this paper has made clear (Nakakita 2012; Yomiuri Shimbun Seijibu 2012, 289–90).[18] There can be no doubt that the inclusion of members with varying policy positions kept the DPJ from developing an organizational structure that could put an end to party infighting.

7.4. "Opposition parties are fantasists"

The DPJ had no experience in government prior to 2009, and it showed. The manifesto demonstrated that the party was incorrigibly naive. Three examples are discussed here. First, the manifesto's budget figures were optimistic in the extreme. Fukuyama Tetsurō, who came up with the funding estimates, said he assumed there would be a savings of 20 percent if national subsidies to local governments were switched to lump sum, no-strings-attached state subsidies. This assumption overlooked the fact that local governments were not in a position to accept a 20 percent cut.

> The existing national subsidies imposed a lot of restrictions on local governments, and it was argued that they could spend a lump sum payment more efficiently and get by with 20 percent less. Unit costs are higher when the national government is the buyer, so we assumed having local governments make their own purchases would cut costs. But the local governments and the Ministry of Internal Affairs and Communications (MIC) were dead set against even a nominal budget cut. (Yakushiji 2012, 187)

First, the DPJ should have foreseen that the agencies in charge of programs relating to national subsidies would be deeply averse to switching to a lump sum system, and therefore the party should not have assumed that all national subsidies would be simultaneously converted to block grants. The majority of national subsidies go

toward social security and education, programs that are difficult to significantly cut and are prized by the party (Minezaki 2010, 105). It was also overly optimistic for the party to presume that local governments and the MIC would simply go along with transforming national subsidies. It seems reasonable to conclude that the DPJ's failure to anticipate how the MIC and local governments would respond was a consequence of the tenuous relationship the DPJ had with these groups due to the predominant party system.

The second example of the DPJ's excessive confidence was its pledge to prohibit *amakudari* postretirement job postings for elite civil servants and to abolish the public interest corporations that were *amakudari* fronts. This practice proved much more difficult to uproot than the DPJ anticipated. Maehara reported:

> It wasn't until after the change of government, when I became a cabinet minister, that I first realized ending *amakudari* would be a time-consuming problem. I recognized *amakudari* fronts could not be shut down overnight. . . . The catch was the public interest corporations didn't employ only retired bureaucrats, they also had proper, white collar employees who would have to find new jobs if we closed the *amakudari* organizations. I didn't think about that when we were in the opposition. . . . We also thought that if we combined the internal reserves of these organizations, it would add up to a large sum that could be spent on other programs. Only after I took office did I learn that much of those reserves would be eaten up if we had to provide early retirement benefits to non-*amakudari* employees. . . . If someone were to ask me how I could have not understood that from the beginning, all I can do is apologize. (Yakushiji 2012, 65–66)

It seems that a ruling party would have understood this all along, but for the DPJ, a party that had spent its entire existence lobbing criticisms at the government and the LDP, that was not the case.

The third example was the DPJ's commitment to take decision-making powers away from elite bureaucrats and exert direct control. The party announced, "Once we are in power, we will tell administrative vice ministers and all officials at the bureau chief rank or higher to submit their resignations. Only those who adhere to our policy direction will receive political appointments." Yet again, after the DPJ formed a government, the party walked back this pronouncement, in this instance because of "civil service protections" (*Asahi Shimbun* 2012).

According to the deputy chief cabinet secretary in the Hatoyama cabinet, Matsui Kōji, "Making all bureau chief posts in every ministry political appointments would require firing all of the current bureau chiefs simultaneously. That would in fact violate the current National Public Service Act and we could not do such a thing" (Yakushiji 2012, 234). If civil service protections are in fact why the DPJ watered down its commitment to establish political control over the bureaucracy, the party should have known about such laws while still in the opposition. It has to be said that the DPJ was called irresponsible for its ineptitude. Opposition parties with ambitions to rule but no experience are the most liable to blithely promise the unachievable. The DPJ's naive overconfidence can, one could argue, also be blamed on the predominant party system.

8. Conclusion

This paper has examined how the DPJ was greatly constrained by the formal and informal institutions and networks that had evolved during the decades of single party dominance; it has also shown how these constraints contributed to the mistakes the DPJ made after assuming power. The DPJ set itself up for failure with its unrealistic manifesto that led to a spiral of problems. The party's internal conflict over violating the manifesto's promises led to a schism, it did not develop a good working relationship with the bureaucracy, and the government went off the rails. At that point, the party turned to the MOF, with its long experience in administering the government. The DPJ grew more dependent on the ministry and entrusted it with more areas of responsibility. The party that had feared its policies would be copied by the LDP ultimately followed in the LDP's policy footsteps by reviving large-scale public works and increasing the consumption tax. This paper does not go so far as to claim that similar constraints will be faced by opposition parties in other predominant party systems, as that will require further study. To assess how generalizable my findings are, two cases worth comparing are Italy in the mid- to late 1990s and France in the early 1980s. In short, this paper is more of a preliminary sketch than anything else, and further study is needed.

Originally published in *Social Science Japan Journal* 19, no. 1 (2016): 33–58. https://doi.org/10.1093/ssjj/jyv030.

Notes

1. For more on the reasons behind the LDP's enduring political power, see Scheiner (2006).

2. Pekkanen and Reed (2013) provide a chronology of the DPJ government from start to finish.

3. In recent years, the predominant party system concept introduced by Sartori (1976) has rarely been applied in political party system research. There have been almost no comparative empirical studies using this concept since Pempel (1990a). Nwokora and Pelizzo (2014) amend the definition of predominance and argue that the concept remains useful in empirical research.

4. Hamamoto (2012) presents a detailed description of the relationships between interest groups and the LDP.

5. Mabuchi (1997) reports that after the change of government in 1993, the relationship between the LDP and the Ministry of Finance grew less close and changed from being best described as "partners" to being "neighbors." As reported in Tatebayashi (2005), a study in 1977 found a positive relationship between the rank of ministerial officials and the closeness of their policy preferences to those of the LDP. A similar study in 2002 found no such indication of stronger support for LDP policies among elite bureaucrats.

6. The DPJ proposals listed below were widely covered in newspapers when the manifesto was released. No specific articles are cited here for the sake of simplicity. The DPJ's 2009 manifesto is available online at http://www.dpj.or.jp/policies/manifesto2009.

7. "Provisional tax rates" refers to a temporary increase in the rates of gasoline taxes, local road

taxes, automobile acquisition tax, automobile weight tax, and light oil delivery tax, which are collected for road construction.

8. If the price of crude oil continued to soar, the government was prepared to suspend the provisional tax increase on fuel as the original fuel taxes would generate sufficient revenue.

9. The DPJ appeared to deliver on its "from concrete to people" promise to shift spending from public works to meeting citizens' needs when it cut the projected 2010 budget for public works by 18.3 percent (¥1.3 trillion) compared to the 2009 budget. By October 2010, however, the strong yen and worries over deflation prompted the cabinet to enact emergency stimulus measures that included over ¥800 billion for public works projects that had been slated for the following fiscal year. More than 60 percent of the DPJ's cuts to public works spending were thus restored to the construction industry. At this point, the DPJ was constrained by the opposition parties that controlled the upper house. Nevertheless, the DPJ's commitment to its "from concrete to people" principle appeared to be wavering.

10. In response to DPJ members' demands to execute the manifesto, Genba replied, "We told that we would find ¥16.8 trillion to reallocate, but the first year we found ¥3.3 trillion, and in the second only ¥600 billion. That's where we are. As a ruling party we must reassess all of our priorities" (*Asahi Shimbun* 2011).

11. A 10 percent surtax was added to corporate taxes to pay for 3.11 reconstruction. The surtax was to be levied for the 2012–14 fiscal years.

12. The government's projected budget for reconstruction was ¥23 trillion to be spent over ten years, of which ¥19 trillion would be spent in the first five years. However, ¥4 trillion for reconstruction was included in the first supplementary budget and ¥2 trillion more was appropriated in the second supplementary budget. In total, ¥15.2 trillion was budgeted for the first year of reconstruction.

13. In a public opinion poll conducted by the *Nihon Keizai Shimbun*, the most common reasons given for not supporting the Hatoyama and Kan cabinets were "lack of leadership," "poor handling of government and party affairs," and "no sense of stability." Immediately after the incident involving the collision with the Chinese fishing boat around the Senkaku Islands, "lack of international awareness" became the top reason for not supporting the Kan government.

14. Relations between Nagatsuma and Ministry of Health, Labour and Welfare (MHLW) bureaucrats were especially antagonistic. According to newspaper reports, Nagatsuma issued "over one thousand" directives to high-ranking MHLW officials and repeatedly castigated them for not providing enough documentation. Nagatsuma was also described as a slow learner who needed to have the same material presented over and over and was said to have insisted on reviewing settlements of accounts one by one. The minister's methods created an administrative bottleneck that frustrated the civil servants (*Asahi Shimbun* 2010; Nihon Keizai Shimbunsha 2010, 146). For a refutation of these allegations, see Nagatsuma (2011, 104–6).

15. Uekami and Tsutsumi (2011) argue that, within the predominant party system, the DPJ had trouble accessing private and public resources and therefore criticized the LDP's clientelistic use of its discretion and called for universalist policy measures.

16. Tsutsumi and Uekami (2011) compared the manifestos of the DPJ and LDP and found that the LDP's copying of major DPJ proposals increased over time.

17. It was extremely optimistic to conclude that raising the sales tax by 3 percentage points would bring in enough revenue. In a budget estimate released by the DPJ in 2012, introducing a minimum guaranteed pension would require raising the consumption tax by 12 percentage points.

18. The defections the DPJ ultimately suffered in 2012, and the emergence of some small parties in the 2012 general election, also stem in part from the incentive to join a new party offered to individual candidates by the proportional representation part of the election ballot (Machidori 2012).

References

Arian, Alan, and Samuel H. Barnes. 1974. "The Dominant Party System: A Neglected Model of Democratic Stability." *The Journal of Politics* 36 (3): 592–614.

Asahi Shimbun. 2010. "'Kan-kan' itten yūwa e" [Prime Minister Kan and Bureaucrats Turn to Reconciliation]. June 10, 2010, morning edition.

———. 2011. "Minshu zaigen-an gohasan" [DPJ's Budget Funding Plan Has Gone Bankrupt]. January 13, 2011, morning edition.

———. 2012. "Minshutō seiken shippai no honshitsu 1: Yosan mo jinji mo kekkyoku, Zaimushō" [Essence of the DPJ Government's Failure 1: DPJ Government Ultimately Depends on the Ministry of Finance for Budget Compilation and Personnel Affairs]. April 5, 2012, morning edition.

Asahi Shimbun Seiken Shuzai Sentā [Asahi Shimbun Center for Government News Coverage]. 2010. *Minshutō seiken 100-nichi no shinsō* [The Real Story of the DPJ's First 100 Days]. Tokyo: Asahi Shimbun Shuppan.

Downs, Anthony. 1957. *An Economic Theory of Democracy*. New York: Harper and Row.

Edano Yukio. 2006. "2003 Shūgiin sōsenkyo to Minshutō manifesuto" [The 2003 General Election and the DPJ Manifesto]. In *Manifesuto ni yoru seiji gabanansu no kakuritsu: Ōmoji no manifesuto o kake* [Establishing Government by Manifesto: Write an All-Caps Manifesto], edited by Nihon Keizai Chōsa Kyōgikai [Japan Economic Research Institute], 114–25. Tokyo: Nihon Keizai Chōsa Kyōgikai. Available at http://www.nik-keicho.or.jp/wp/wp-content/uploads/nomura_all.pdf (accessed December 27, 2014).

Endō Masahisa, Robert Pekkanen, and Steven R. Reed. 2013. "The LDP's Path Back to Power." In *Japan Decides 2012: The Japanese General Election*, edited by Robert Pekkanen, Steven R. Reed, and Ethan Scheiner, 49–64. New York: Palgrave Macmillan.

Fujimori Katsuhiko and Ōyama Reiko. 2004. *Manifesuto de seiji o sodateru* [Developing Politics With Manifestos]. Tokyo: Garyūsha.

Hamamoto Shinsuke. 2012. "Seiken kōtai no dantai-seitō kankei e no eikyō: Futatsu no hikaku ni yoru kenshō" [Interest Groups and Political Parties in Japan: Comparative Study of the Two]. In *Nenpō seijigaku 2012(2): Gendai Nihon no dantai seiji* [The Annals of the Japanese Political Science Association 2012(2): Interest Groups in Japan Today], edited by Nihon Seiji Gakkai, 65–87. Tokyo: Bokutakusha.

Iio Jun. 2011. "Naikaku-kanryō-sei: Tōchi nōryoku no kōjō towareru" [Cabinet and Bureaucracy: Questioning the Rise of Cabinet-Bureaucracy Governing Capacity]. In *Zemināru gendai Nihon seiji* [Seminar: Japanese Politics Today], edited by Sasaki Takeshi and Shimizu Masato, 373–419. Tokyo: Nihon Keizai Shimbun Shuppansha.

Kamikawa Ryūnoshin. 2014. "Minshutō seiken ni okeru yosan hensei, zeisei kaisei: Minshutō no 'yotō-ka' to 'Jimintō-ka'" [Budget Compilation and Tax Reform under DPJ Government: The DPJ's Evolution toward Being a Ruling Party and LDP-ization]. In *Minshutō seiken no chōsen to zasetsu: Sono keiken kara nani o manabu ka* [The Endeavors and Failures of the DPJ Government: What Their Experience Teaches Us], edited by Itō Mitsutoshi and Miyamoto Tarō, 119–69. Tokyo: Nihon Keizai Hyōronsha.

Krauss, Ellis S., and Jon Pierre. 1990. "The Decline of Dominant Parties: Parliamentary Politics in Sweden and Japan in the 1970s." In *Uncommon Democracies: The One-Party Dominant Regimes*, edited by T. J. Pempel, 226–59. Ithaca: Cornell University Press.

Kushida, Kenji E., and Phillip Y. Lipscy. 2013. "The Rise and Fall of the Democratic Party of Japan." In *Japan Under the DPJ: The Politics of Transition and Governance*, edited by Kenji E. Kushida and Phillip Y. Lipscy, 3–42. Stanford: The Walter H. Shorenstein Asia-Pacific Research Center.

Lipscy, Phillip Y., and Ethan Scheiner. 2012. "Japan Under the DPJ: The Paradox of Political Change without Policy Change." *Journal of East Asian Studies* 12 (3): 311–22.

Mabuchi Masaru. 1997. *Ōkurashō wa naze oitsume-rareta no ka: Seikan kankei no henbō* [Why Was the Ministry of Finance Cornered?: The Transformation of the Relationship between Politicians and Bureaucrats]. Tokyo: Chūōkōronsha.

Machidori Satoshi. 2012. "Keizai kyōshitsu: Shin seiken towareru jikkō-ryoku (3)" [Economics Classroom: The Questionable Abilities of the New Government]. *Nihon Keizai Shimbun*, December 24, 2012, morning edition.

Mainichi Shimbun Seijibu [Mainichi Shimbun Political Department]. 2009. *Kanzen dokyumento Minshutō seiken* [Fully Documenting the DPJ Government]. Tokyo: Mainichi Shimbunsha.

Matoba Toshihiro. 1986. "Ittō yūi seitō-sei ron no tenbō" [Debating the Future of the Predominant Party System]. *Hōgaku Ronsō* [Kyoto University Law Review] 118 (4–6): 286–327.

Matsuura Shigeru. 2012. "Heisei 24 nendo zeisei kaisei-an no gaiyō" [Summary of the 2012 Tax System Reform Bill]. *Chōsa to Jōhō* [National Diet Library Issue Brief], no. 734.

Minezaki Naoki. 2010. "Minshutō seiken wa naze zaigen mondai ni kurushimu yō ni natta no ka" [Why Did the DPJ Government Come to Suffer from Budget Problems?]. *Ekonomisuto* [Economist], October 11, 2010, 102–5.

Murakami Shinichirō. 1986. "Ittō yūi seitō shisutemu" [Predominant Party Systems]. In *Hikaku seiji no bunseki wakugumi* [Analytical Frameworks for Comparative Politics], edited by Nishikawa Tomokazu, 197–218. Kyoto: Minerva Shobō.

Muramatsu Michio. 2010. *Seikan sukuramu-gata rīdāshippu no hōkai* [The Demise of Scrum-style Leadership among Politicians and Bureaucrats]. Tokyo: Tōyō Keizai Shinpōsha.

Nagatsuma Akira. 2011. *Manekarezaru daijin: Sei to kan no shin rūru* [The Uninvited Minister: The New Rules for Politicians and Bureaucrats]. Tokyo: Asahi Shimbun Shuppan.

Nakakita Kōji. 2012. *Gendai Nihon no seitō demokurashī* [Political Party Democracy in Modern Japan]. Tokyo: Iwanami Shoten.

Naoshima Masayuki. 2012. *Tsugi no, Nihon. Jidai no seichō senryaku e. Nagare wa kawaru* [The Next Japan. Growth Strategy for a New Era. The Tide Is Changing]. Tokyo: Jiji Tsūshin Shuppankyoku.

Nihon Keizai Shimbun. 2012a. "Shōhi zōzei meguru 'nejire': Seifu no setsumei busoku nado haikei ni"

[The "Twist" over the Consumption Tax Increase: A Look at the Lack of Government Explanation and Other Factors]. February 20, 2012, morning edition.

———. 2012b. "Ugokanu seiji, fuman kakudai: Honsha yoron chōsa." [Static Politics, Growing Dissatisfaction: A Company Survey]. March 26, 2012, morning edition.

———. 2012c. "Shushō, genpatsu sai-kadō, shōhi zōzei de shōnenba" [Prime Minister at a Critical Juncture in Nuclear Power Plant Restart and Consumption Tax Hike]. April 23, morning edition.

Nihon Keizai Shimbunsha, ed. 2010. *Seiken* [Political Power]. Tokyo: Nihon Keizai Shimbun Shuppansha.

Nwokora, Zim, and Riccardo Pelizzo. 2014. "Sartori Reconsidered: Toward a New Predominant Party System." *Political Studies* 62 (4): 824–42.

Okada Katsuya. 2008. *Seiken kōtai: Kono kuni o kaeru* [Change of Government: Change This Country]. Tokyo: Kōdansha.

Pekkanen, Robert, and Steven R. Reed. 2013. "Japanese Politics between the 2009 and 2012 Elections." In *Japan Decides 2012: The Japanese General Election*, eds. Robert Pekkanen, Steven R. Reed, and Ethan Scheiner, 8–19. New York: Palgrave Macmillan.

Pempel, T. J. 1982. *Policy and Politics in Japan: Creative Conservatism*. Philadelphia: Temple University Press.

———, ed. 1990a. *Uncommon Democracies: The One-Party Dominant Regimes*. Ithaca: Cornell University Press.

———. 1990b. "One-Party Dominance and the Creation of Regimes." In *Uncommon Democracies: The One-Party Dominant Regimes*, edited by T. J. Pempel, 333–60. Ithaca: Cornell University Press.

Pempel, T. J., Muramatsu Michio, and Morimoto Tetsurō. 1994. "Ittō yūi-sei no keisei to hōkai" [The Rise and Fall of Predominant Party System]. *Revaiasan* [Leviathan], Special Supplemental Issue (Winter): 11–35.

Rengō Sōgō Seikatsu Kaihatsu Kenkyūjo [Research Institute for the Advancement of Living Standards]. 2012. *Rengō Sōken bukkuretto No. 8, seisaku kettei purosesu o kenshō suru: Seiken kōtai kara sannen: Wākushoppu kiroku-shū* [Research Institute for the Advancement of Living Standards Booklet No. 8, Policymaking Process Under Review: Proceedings of the Workshop on the First Three Years of the DPJ Government]. Tokyo: Rengō Sōgō Seikatsu Kaihatsu Kenkyūjo.

Sankei Shimbun. 2009. "Kodomo teate wa ko o umu ka: Kuru kuru kawaru seisaku ito." [Does the *kodomo teate* Childcare Allowance Produce Children?: Continually Changing Policy Intentions]. October 28, 2009, morning edition.

Sartori, Giovanni. 1976. *Parties and Party Systems: A Framework for Analysis*. New York: Cambridge University Press.

Scheiner, Ethan. 2005. *Democracy without Competition in Japan: Opposition Failure in a One-Party Dominant State*. New York: Cambridge University Press.

———. 2013. "The Electoral System and Japan's Partial Transformation: Party System Consolidation without Policy Realignment." In *Japan under the DPJ: The Politics of Transition and Governance*, edited by Kenji E. Kushida and Phillip Y. Lipscy, 73–101. Stanford: The Walter H. Shorenstein Asia-Pacific Research Center.

Takada Hideki. 2012. "Kokka Senryaku-shitsu no chōsen: Seiken kōtai no seika to kadai" [The National Strategy Office's Challenge: The Outcomes and Problems of the Change of Government]. Available at http://www.geocities.jp/weathercock8926/nationalpolicyunit.html (accessed December 27, 2014).

Takenaka Harukata. 2011. "2010 nen San'in senkyo-go no seiji katei: Sangiin no eikyō-ryoku wa yosan ni mo oyobu no ka" [Political Process after the 2010 House of Councillors Election: Does the Upper House's Influence Extend to the Budget?]. *Senkyo Kenkyū* [Elections Research] 27 (2): 45–59.

Tanaka Hideaki. 2013. "Keizai to zaisei: Henkaku e no chōsen to zasetsu" [The Economy and Public Finance: Reform Efforts and Setbacks]. In *Minshutō seiken shippai no kenshō* [Examination of the DPJ's Failures], edited by Nihon Saiken Inishiatibu [Rebuild Japan Initiative], 87–124. Tokyo: Chūōkōron Shinsha.

Tatebayashi Masahiko. 2005. "Kanryō no seiji-teki kontorōru ni kansuru sūryō bunseki no kokoromi" [Attempts to Quantitatively Analyze the Political Control of the Bureaucracy]. In *Nenpō seijigaku 2005(1): Shimin shakai ni okeru sanka to daihyō* [The Annals of the Japanese Political Science Association 2005(1): Participation and Representation in Civil Society], edited by Nihon Seiji Gakkai, 201–27. Tokyo: Bokutakusha.

Tsutsumi Hidenori and Uekami Takayoshi. 2011. "Minshutō no seisaku: Keizoku-sei to henka" [DPJ Policy: Continuity and Change]. In *Minshutō no soshiki to seisaku: Kettō kara seiken kōtai made* [Organization and Policies of the DPJ: From Party Founding to Party in Power], edited by Uekami Takayoshi and Tsutsumi Hidenori, 225–53. Tokyo: Tōyō Keizai Shinpōsha.

Uekami Takayoshi and Tsutsumi Hidenori. 2011. "Minshutō no keisei katei, soshiki to seisaku" [The Formation of the DPJ, Its Organization and Policies]. In *Minshutō no soshiki to seisaku: Kettō kara seiken kōtai made* [Organization and Policies of the DPJ: From Party Founding to Party in

Power], edited by Uekami Takayoshi and Tsutsumi Hidenori, 1–28. Tokyo: Tōyō Keizai Shinpōsha.

Yakushiji Katsuyuki. 2012. *Shōgen Minshutō seiken* [Testimony: Inner Politics of the Democratic Party of Japan]. Tokyo: Kōdansha.

Yamaguchi Jirō. 2009. *Seiken kōtai-ron* [An Argument over Change of Government]. Tokyo: Iwanami Shoten.

———. 2012. *Seiken kōtai to wa nan datta no ka* [What Did the Change of Government Amount To?]. Tokyo: Iwanami Shoten.

Yomiuri Shimbun Seijibu [Yomiuri Shimbun Political Department]. 2011. *Bōkoku no saishō: Kantei kinō teishi no 180-nichi* [The Ruinous Premier of a Ruined Nation: 180 Days of Paralysis in the Office of the Prime Minister]. Tokyo: Shinchōsha.

———. 2012. *Minshu gakai: Seikai daikonmei e no 300-nichi* [The Collapse of the Democratic Party of Japan: 300 Days of Heading toward Political Turmoil]. Tokyo: Shinchōsha.

Part
V

"Kantei Leadership" and
the Twilight of Heisei

The Liberal Democratic Party (LDP), led once again by Abe Shinzō, swept the Democratic Party of Japan (DPJ) from power in late 2012 and entered into a coalition with its partner, Kōmeitō. Under Prime Minister Abe, the coalition achieved a string of electoral triumphs. Initially, these successes were attributed to voters' disillusionment with the failed DPJ regime, but the focus later shifted to Abe's consummate strategic management of government and the opposition's ongoing disarray and fragmentation. From this period on, we begin to see a large volume of analysis focusing on the Abe cabinet's method of governing, quite apart from the merits of its policies.

From this current of commentary comes the term "Kantei leadership," which uses the name of the prime minister's office and official residence as a metonym for the administrative and policymaking apparatus surrounding the prime minister. The emphasis here is not so much on Abe's personal leadership skills as on the efficient division of labor among the aides and cabinet officials underneath him. "The Role of the Kantei in Policymaking," by Makihara Izuru, uses a comparative approach to trace the evolving role of the Kantei, culminating in the forceful top-down Kantei leadership of the Abe era. In "Institutional Foundation for the Abe Government's Political Power," Takenaka Harukata focuses more closely on the internal organization and governing mechanisms of the second Abe administration. (The analysis of the Abe cabinet has continued to progress in recent years, but the latest studies lie outside the scope of this volume.)

Under ordinary circumstances, the Heisei era would have ended only with the death of the emperor, since Japanese law makes no provision for abdication. But after Emperor Akihito indicated that he wanted to step down, the government passed special legislation to accommodate his wishes. The emperor's announcement stirred some politically charged debate, as did the government's decision to permit him to abdicate. Mikuriya Takashi, a member of the advisory council formed to deliberate the abdication issue, gives a frank and revealing account of that body's deliberations in "An Inside View from the Advisory Council." As Mikuriya's essay makes clear, there is an urgent need to debate issues confronting the imperial household, including succession, that the government has hitherto failed to address.

Emperor Akihito stepped down on April 30, 2019. The following day, Crown Prince Naruhito was enthroned as the new emperor, and the curtain fell on the Heisei era.

The Role of the Kantei in Policymaking

Makihara Izuru
Nippon.com, 2013

In recent years the role of the prime minister's office in policymaking has been an enduring theme in media coverage of Japanese politics. This focus on forceful leadership from the Kantei, as the prime minister's official residence and office are known, was particularly intense during the administration of Prime Minister Koizumi Junichirō (April 2001–September 2006), who electrified the nation by appointing cabinet members in defiance of his own party's powerful faction leaders and pushing through controversial reforms over the objections of key government agencies and ministries.

Of course, no prime minister can make policy single-handedly. At the Kantei, a large permanent staff lays the groundwork for decision-making through information gathering, policy analysis, and clerical and administrative support of every type. Technically referred to as the Cabinet Secretariat, this organization currently numbers more than 800 regular employees, many of them assigned to various policymaking "headquarters" within the cabinet (including the Headquarters for Japan's Economic Revitalization, established by the new administration of Prime Minister Abe Shinzō in December 2012). The Kantei today is empowered to formulate a response to any and all of the key political issues facing the prime minister and the cabinet.

It has not always been thus. As part of the massive constitutional and administrative overhaul imposed by the Allied occupation after World War II, the Cabinet Secretariat was established as a tiny unit consisting merely of the chief cabinet secretary and the prime minister's secretaries. The rest of the prime minister's support typically came from units ("offices") set up under the Sōrifu (Prime Minister's Office), the portfolio then assigned to the prime minister as "first among equals" in the cabinet. But the powers and capabilities of the Cabinet Secretariat grew over the years. Then in 2001, as part of a major reorganization of central government, the secretariat was accorded general planning authority, opening the way for its emergence as a vast organization empowered and equipped to draft concrete policies.

This growth process mirrors the evolution of the prime minister's leadership role over the postwar era. Pressure for change began to build during the second half of the twentieth century, as international summit diplomacy facilitated comparison with other heads of government and highlighted the weakness of the Japanese prime minister—particularly in comparison with the president of the United States, Japan's ally. By the beginning of the twenty-first century the government was under intense pressure to follow the lead of Japan's global corporations in replacing the cumbersome, bottom-up, consensus-building model of management of old with a more agile top-down decision-making process adapted to a rapidly changing world. In this sense, the emergence of a stronger prime minister and better-equipped Kantei might be seen as a product of the always-tense give-and-take between the nation's political and economic leaders.

In the following, I examine this historical process in greater detail with a view to shedding light on the meaning of "Kantei leadership" under the second cabinet of Abe Shinzō.

The Era of One-Party Dominance

When the Allied occupation of Japan came to an end in September 1951, the postwar Japanese government faced the challenge of managing affairs of state under a brand-new Constitution without the benefit of instructions from occupation headquarters. Without the support of the occupation forces, the cabinet of Prime Minister Yoshida Shigeru faltered. Politicians previously purged from public life because of their prewar or wartime role had staged an electoral comeback in both houses of the Diet. New laws gave more power to the Diet, allowing members to submit bills. The bureaucrats wielded their technical expertise in an effort to squelch the politicians' initiative, while the politicians threatened to decimate the bureaucratic ranks with sweeping administrative reforms. This institutional power struggle defined Japanese politics and government in the 1950s.

In 1955, the two feuding branches of the Japan Socialist Party (JSP) reunited, and Japan's conservative forces merged to form the Liberal Democratic Party (LDP). Although the conservative merger was in large part a reaction to developments on the left, it was also intended to settle the aforementioned institutional power struggles once and for all. The result was the so-called 1955 system, under which the LDP progressively consolidated power, while the JSP settled into the role of perennial opposition. Under the 1955 system, LDP rule continued uninterrupted for thirty-eight years, until the rise of an anti-LDP coalition cabinet in 1993.

It was during this period of uninterrupted LDP rule, as the bureaucracy took an increasingly active role in policymaking, that the need for a "stronger cabinet" emerged as a recurring theme of administrative reform. The third cabinet of Prime Minister Hatoyama Ichirō (November 1955–December 1956) made the first moves in that direction at the initiative of Kōno Ichirō, minister of the (now defunct) Administrative Management Agency. Kōno's stated goal was to enhance the leadership role of the nation's "top management," by which he meant the prime minister and his cabinet ministers. In regard to the former, Kōno elevated the prime minister's support apparatus, the Cabinet Secretariat, to the position of undisputed "control tower" in charge of policy coordination and mediation among the cabinet ministries, superseding the Prime Minister's Office. To strengthen the leadership of the other ministers, he proposed augmenting the number of high-level ministry officials answerable to them. Kōno's original plan would have given each ministry additional parliamentary vice-ministers—Diet politicians appointed as aides to a cabinet minister—plus a new civil-service post directly under the administrative vice-minister. In its final form, the plan allotted additional parliamentary vice-ministers only to the Ministries of Finance, International Trade and Industry, and Agriculture, Forestry, and Fisheries and installed a "director of the minister's secretariat" (a post already in existence, though only at few select agencies) at every ministry as the second-ranking civil servant under the administrative vice-minister.

This move to expand the support apparatuses directly under the prime minister and his cabinet ministers continued off and on under the 1955 system, peaking with the administration of Nakasone Yasuhiro (November 1982–November 1987). As the leader of a minor LDP faction, Nakasone had been obliged to forge an alliance with the dominant Tanaka Kakuei faction in order to assume leadership of the party. Resolved to exercise strong executive leadership nonetheless, he used his own advisory panels, private councils, and think tanks to build support for his own policies outside the Diet, circumventing the party apparatus. In addition, he sought to bolster executive leadership by strengthening the Kantei. Adopting the recommendations of the second Provisional Council for Administrative Reform, which he himself directed as minister of the Administrative Management Agency under the previous administration of Suzuki Zenkō (July 1980–November 1982), Nakasone expanded the Cabinet Secretariat by adding two "cabinet councilors' offices," one for internal affairs and another for external affairs. To head the newly beefed-up Cabinet Secretariat as chief cabinet secretary, he chose bureaucrat-turned-politician Gotōda Masaharu, a former head of the National Police Agency known for his crisis-management and intelligence-gathering prowess. With Gotōda's help, he asserted the authority of the Cabinet Secretariat and its chief—and by extension, that of the prime minister—over the other cabinet ministries and agencies. With the help of private consultants, Nakasone also used the mass media to maximum effect. In this way, he leveraged both the official staff of the Cabinet Secretariat and an unofficial team of private advisors to strengthen the Kantei's hand in the decision-making process.

Such developments notwithstanding, ministry bureaucrats remained at the center of the policymaking process during most of this period. The LDP's factions and policymaking apparatus weighed and conveyed the competing demands of their key constituencies, while the party's top three officials under the president (secretary-general, chair of the Policy Research Council, and chair of the General Council) ironed out conflicts between ministries. This approach functioned adequately thanks to the expanding economy, which had resumed its heady growth once it had weathered the energy crises of the 1970s. It was easy to satisfy or mollify various interest groups by drawing from an ever-expanding pool of resources. Free from the necessity of tough allocation decisions, the government had little need to exert strong top-down leadership. As a result, it continued to place priority on the policymaking capabilities of each ministry rather than those of the Kantei.

The Years of Coalition Government

In 1993, a split within the LDP paved the way for the first non-LDP administration in thirty-eight years. In August that year the House of Representatives passed a no-confidence resolution against the cabinet of Prime Minister Miyazawa Kiichi (November 1991–August 1993). In the general election that followed, the LDP failed to secure a majority of lower house seats, opening the way for a coalition of eight parties and parliamentary groupings under Prime Minister Hosokawa Morihiro (August 1993–April 1994). Thus began a period of changing multiparty coalitions and alliances. In the absence of a secure Diet majority, the prime minister was obliged to set policy in consultation with the heads of his coalition partners. Meanwhile, with the end of the Cold War and the rise of a global economy, Japan faced an urgent need for agile,

top-down policymaking to respond to a changing international environment. A major expansion and upgrade of the Kantei organization was inevitable.

The first administration to address this need was that of Prime Minister Hashimoto Ryūtarō (January 1996–July 1998), who personally presided over the Administrative Reform Council.[1] Charged with the reorganization of central government, Hashimoto pushed for a more powerful Kantei and fewer cabinet agencies and ministries in order to speed resolution of turf battles within the bureaucracy. After agreeing on the need for extra-ministerial policymaking mechanisms, the council drew up a plan to significantly expand the powers of the Cabinet Secretariat, create top-level advisory organs (such as the Council on Economic and Fiscal Policy) in which cabinet ministers could consult with experts from the private sector, appoint special ministers of state to coordinate policy on key issues, and create a mechanism for active policy coordination between the Cabinet Secretariat, the special ministers, and the ministries. The reforms went into effect in January 2001.

The Koizumi Cabinet

LDP maverick Koizumi Junichirō took office in April 2001, shortly after the Hashimoto reforms came into effect, and he took full advantage of the new Kantei organization.

Under the reorganization, the Cabinet Secretariat was accorded new planning powers in addition to its existing role in coordinating policy. Prior to the 2001 reorganization, basic procedure assigned the job of drafting new policies to the individual ministries and agencies; on paper, at least, the Cabinet Secretariat's role was simply to work out a compromise in the event of conflicts with other ministries. Now, with its new planning authority, the secretariat was empowered to draft its own policies and even shut down objections from the ministries in the name of carrying out the basic policies of the prime minister and the cabinet.

For this purpose, a number of policymaking "headquarters" were set up within the cabinet under the general management of the Cabinet Secretariat and staffed with bureaucrats culled from various ministries and agencies. As a consequence, the staff of the Cabinet Secretariat mushroomed under the Koizumi cabinet, swelling from about 200 prior to the reorganization to more than 800. To oversee policy coordination between the Cabinet Secretariat, ministries, and councils in the area of economic and fiscal policy, Koizumi tapped one of his own trusted aides, a Finance Ministry official who had served for a long period as Koizumi's secretary in the prime minister's office. For internal affairs, a deputy chief cabinet secretary (also a bureaucrat) with over five years' experience in the post performed the role of general coordinator.

Second, the role of the cabinet ministers underwent important changes at this time. Koizumi departed decisively from established LDP practice by appointing his ministers on the strength of their abilities and qualifications, rather than assigning cabinet posts on the basis of factional strength and seniority. Having done so, he expected his ministers to make full use of their abilities. The biggest test of their skills was probably the Council on Economic and Fiscal Policy, newly established under the cabinet. Minister of State for Economic and Fiscal Policy Takenaka Heizō played the leading role on the council. Communicating closely with the Kantei to ascertain the wishes of the prime minister, he proceeded to control the council's agenda by submitting one issue paper after another with the help of the council's private-sector experts. The regular cabinet ministers present (the minister of finance, minister of economy, trade and industry, and minister of internal affairs and communications) had to join the debate with both their individual ministries' policies and the cabinet's basic goals in mind. Gone were the days when a cabinet minister could get by delivering statements and papers prepared for him by bureaucrats.

Kantei leadership also played a key role in foreign policy under the Koizumi cabinet. After a series of blunders by Foreign Minister Tanaka Makiko early on, Chief Cabinet Secretary Fukuda Yasuo formed a Kantei foreign policy team, which helped engineer the administration's prompt enlistment in the US government's war on terror following the terrorist attacks of September 11, 2001.

Finally, Koizumi's top-down leadership was supported by high public approval ratings, the result in large part of his skilled use of the media to project a uniquely appealing public persona. Koizumi's longtime aide Iijima Isao played a central role orchestrating this highly effective public relations strategy. The success of Koizumi's five-year tenure (a long run by recent standards) owed much to a talented and dedicated Kantei team, including unofficial advisors as well as the official staff of the Cabinet Secretariat.

Abe, Fukuda, and Asō

Unfortunately, succeeding LDP administrations veered from the trail Koizumi had blazed. Both Abe Shinzō in his first stab at leadership (September 2006–September 2007), Fukuda Yasuo (September 2007–September 2008), and Asō Tarō (September 2008–September 2009) stumbled in three key areas: the Cabinet Secretariat, cabinet appointments, and unofficial staff.

The Cabinet Secretariat had grown so large and complex under Koizumi that a newly installed prime minister was at a loss to navigate it. From the standpoint of executive leadership, the ideal would have been to disband all the cabinet headquarters and reconstitute them in keeping with the priorities of the new cabinet, building up the organization gradually. However, as long as the LDP continued in power, each administration was obliged to take on the agenda of the previous one. This became an insurmountable obstacle during the waning years of LDP rule, as each succeeding leader struggled to dispose of his predecessor's unfinished business even while pursuing his cabinet's own agenda.

Among the pending problems weighing down the government at this time were serious issues of internal inefficiency and corruption, including the pension scandal. Born of structural problems that had taken root during decades of uninterrupted LDP rule, these were issues that neither the Kantei nor the individual ministries could adequately resolve in a short time, and they continued to weigh on successive cabinets.

Abe created further problems for himself by making key Cabinet Secretariat appointments without regard for the secretariat's customary personnel practices. These appointments under-mined the Kantei's ability to coordinate and mediate among the government's high-ranking bureaucrats, and because a system of this sort is very difficult to reinstate once it has broken down, the succeeding Fukuda and Asō cabinets were unable to rebuild the Kantei's coordinating capabilities.

Koizumi's successors also erred in their selection of cabinet ministers. Unlike Koizumi, they allowed their cabinet appointments to be guided by intraparty politics instead of the candidates' individual ability and experience. A succession of scandals plagued the Abe cabinet in particular, but in all three administrations, the appointment of poorly qualified ministers resulted in blunders, setbacks, erosion of public support, and an increasingly dysfunctional cabinet.

Finally, neither Abe, Fukuda, nor Asō managed to assemble the kind of talented media-savvy staff that had helped create Koizumi's appealing public persona, and this—more even than any basic failure of leadership—is why they lost the public's support and confidence so quickly. Another contributing factor was the rapid spread of social media during the period in question. The new technology enabled almost anyone to capture candid video images of politicians and transmit them over the internet in minutes or even seconds. With such a small margin of error, few politicians could have created and maintained the kind of charismatic image on which Koizumi had built his popularity.

Amid these struggles, the LDP suffered a major defeat in the House of Councillors election in July 2007, which cost the ruling coalition its upper house majority. In the absence of strong leadership from the Kantei, the cabinet was in no position to tackle the new issues facing the nation with a divided Diet. So it was that the Democratic Party of Japan (DPJ) was able to seize control of the government in 2009.

The Kantei's Role Following a Change of Government

The LDP reclaimed a majority in the House of Representatives in December 2012 and ousted the DPJ, but a new era of long-term dominance by the LDP seems unlikely any time soon. Faced with the prospect of an imminent change in government, recent cabinets have organized the Kantei with a view to quick results. But strong Kantei leadership requires a massive, complex organization. Moreover, constant preoccupation with the next election tends to strengthen the hand of the party apparatus, which manages election strategy. Both the DPJ and the LDP have been engaged in a process of trial and error as they grope for a way to maintain centralized control over both the ministries and the party and carry out policymaking in a responsive and decisive manner. Let us review their efforts to date, beginning with the DPJ.

Leadership Under the DPJ

Having campaigned and won in 2009 on a pledge to overhaul the government decision-making process at the national level, the new DPJ government was eager to strengthen institutional support for centralized decision-making by the prime minister. To this end, the cabinet of Prime Minister Hatoyama Yukio (December 2009–June 2010) unveiled two new advisory bodies to coordinate policy: the National Policy Unit and the Government Revitalization Unit. However, the relationship of these new organs to the Cabinet Secretariat and other existing bodies remained unclear until the government of Noda Yoshihiko (September 2011–December 2012) defined the National Policy Unit as the successor to the Council on Economic and Fiscal Policy, the Government Revitalization Unit as the body in charge of administrative reform, and the Cabinet Secretariat as the basic advisory office directly under the prime minister. As is customary, the government also assigned Diet politicians to serve as "senior vice-ministers" and "parliamentary secretaries" under each minister. It then abolished the conference of administrative vice-ministers that had traditionally preceded each regular cabinet meeting. The task of coordinating and mediating among the ministries was assigned to a conference of senior vice-ministers, chaired by the parliamentary deputy chief cabinet secretary—also a Diet member.

For this body to function, the political

executives at each ministry—minister, senior vice-minister, and parliamentary secretary—had to be in control of the ministry's operations. This never happened, however, because once the bureaucrats found themselves excluded from active policymaking, communications broke down, and the political executives were unable to obtain the information necessary for sound policy decisions. As a consequence, members of the cabinet were continually causing confusion and embarrassment with premature or ill-considered policy announcements. A notable example was Prime Minister Hatoyama's own statement on the relocation of US Marine Corps Air Station Futenma outside of Okinawa Prefecture, an option that was quickly revealed to be unfeasible.

In Britain, where power is continually alternating between parties, each new administration understands the need to prioritize the pledges in its election manifesto according to what it can reasonably hope to accomplish. The DPJ failed utterly in prioritizing its agenda, and largely as a result, the only major campaign promise it was able to fulfill was individual household income support for farmers, a policy for which preparations had begun relatively early.

Finally, of the three DPJ prime ministers, only Noda (who kept the government on a fairly even keel and even managed to push through major tax legislation) showed even the most basic understanding of political leadership. Hatoyama and his successor, Kan Naoto, surrounded themselves with incompetent advisors and proved woefully ill equipped to handle the mass media. Party unity collapsed over the key issues of the Trans-Pacific Partnership and reform of the social security and tax systems. The prime minister had lost control of his own cabinet and his own party.

Abe and the Return of the LDP

Amidst this chaos, the LDP staged a decisive comeback in the 2012 general election, and Abe Shinzō returned to the prime minister's office. Based on his performance so far, we can surmise that Abe has learned valuable lessons from the DPJ's failures.

First, both Abe and his ministers have resisted the temptation to grandstand or overreach on policy at this stage. Although one may regret the LDP's failure to transform itself during its years in exile, at least the LDP's policymaking apparatus—unlike a new cabinet organization—was fairly easy to reactivate, and it has provided the support and discipline the new administration needs at this stage. Working with the Kantei, the Tax System Research Commission and other LDP policy organs seem to have restrained the government from embarking on policy initiatives with little or no hope of success.

Second, the new cabinet has encouraged the bureaucracy to return to an active role in policymaking, and the Finance Ministry is making its voice heard throughout the government, as one can gather from the budget process and the prime minister's choice to fill such positions as chairman of the Japan Fair Trade Commission and governor of the Bank of Japan.[2] (Former Ministry of Finance officials have filled both posts.) It now seems fairly clear that a change in government will proceed without a major mishap, operating within fiscal constraints.

With regard to the Kantei, the chief cabinet secretary has established control over the Cabinet Secretariat as a whole, and new advisory organs are being launched with a view to making good on Abe's general-election pledges once the LDP has cleared the hurdle of the July House of Councillors election. New policy proposals will doubtless emerge after the election, and the Kantei will have the task of fleshing those out. If the LDP secures a majority in the upper house, that will clear the way for an era of strong policy leadership from the Kantei.

Unfortunately, bureaucrats from the Ministry of Economy, Trade, and Industry currently occupy most of the key Kantei posts, but because most of today's ministries are descended from the old Home Ministry, officials from those agencies are really needed to coordinate policymaking throughout the Kantei. In respect to economic policy—currently the Abe cabinet's major focus—the division of labor between the Council on Economic and Fiscal Policy, which has begun to function again, and the Headquarters for Japan's Economic Revitalization, established under the current cabinet, remains uncertain.

Because of issues like these, a complete reorganization of the Kantei is probably unavoidable at some point.[3] Thus the Abe government faces the challenge of rebuilding the Cabinet Secretariat into an instrument of responsive top-down leadership, even while addressing its immediate policy priorities. Assuming nothing forces a dissolution of the House of Representatives before the current members' terms expire in 2016, it will have three years between the end of the July upper house poll and the next national election. The big question is whether, in that brief time, the Abe government can fashion a new model of Kantei leadership tailored to an era of shifting party dominance.

English version originally published by Nippon Communications Foundation online at Nippon.com, August 7, 2013. Originally published in Japanese on June 27, 2013.

Notes

1. https://japan.kantei.go.jp/971228finalreport.html

2. "Profile of Kuroda Haruhiko, Governor of the Bank of Japan," Nippon.com, April 11, 2013, https://www.nippon.com/en/features/h00025/. Originally published in Japanese on March 21, 2013.

3. After the original paper was published, the Cabinet Secretariat further expanded its size and authority with the establishment of the National Security Bureau and the Cabinet Personnel Bureau in 2014.

Institutional Foundation for the Abe Government's Political Power

V-(2)

The Development of Prime Ministerial Control and Responsibility for National Policy

Takenaka Harukata
Discuss Japan—Japan Foreign Policy Forum, 2018

The Five Years of the Second Abe Administration

"The German chancellor Konrad Adenauer, who put Germany on the path to recovery after it lost World War II, became chancellor when he was seventy-four, continued in the job until eighty-eight, and then passed away one year later. To avoid any misunderstanding, I have absolutely no intention of continuing on in this job for that long, but what I am trying to say is that if everyone around the world is able to make full use of their abilities, then the world will become a more fulfilling place, and everyone will be able to lead more fulfilling lives."[1]

Prime Minister Abe Shinzō made this comment when he convened the first meeting of the Council for Designing 100-Year Life Society on September 11, 2017.

Prime Minister Abe reshuffled his cabinet on August 3, 2017, to halt the drop in his approval rating due to the Kake Gakuen issue. The prime minister has identified the "revolution in human resources development" as the most pressing issue for the reshuffled cabinet and established the Council for Designing 100-Year Life Society to discuss specific measures.

Although his term is much shorter than the fourteen years Adenauer spent in office, Prime Minister Abe's present term is approaching the six-year mark, reaching a total of 2,101 days on September 25, 2017. This is the third-longest tenure of a prime minister in the postwar period.

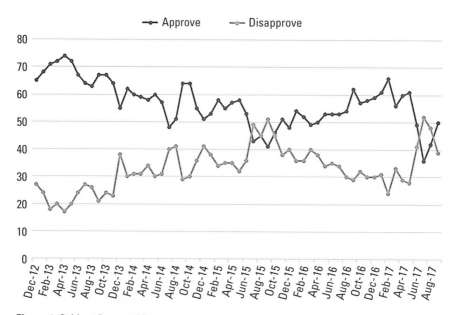

Figure 1. Cabinet Approval Rate

In December this year, the second Abe administration (here, this generic term refers to the second and third Abe cabinets) will mark its fifth anniversary in office. If Abe scores a win in the general election held this month, he will be eyeing the possibility of outlasting the term of Satō Eisaku, the longest-serving prime minister in the postwar period, notwithstanding his claim that he has "absolutely no intention of continuing on in this job for that long."

The second Abe administration has been characterized by its ability to secure a high approval rating from the public with the exception of the periods when he pushed through the Act on the Protection of Specially Designated Secrets and the new security legislation (Figure 1). Prime Minister Abe also has a certain number of achievements under his belt. In terms of diplomacy and security guarantees, he has exercised "diplomacy with a bird's-eye view of the globe," visiting a total of 127 countries and regions. He has worked with the Obama administration to deepen the alliance between Japan and the United States, and he has also built stable relations with the Trump administration. He has succeeded in having the negotiation of the Comprehensive and Progressive Agreement for Trans-Pacific Partnership (TPP 11) concluded in January 2018. He also has concluded an economic partnership agreement with the European Union in July 2018.

He has facilitated the exercise of the right to collective self-defense under certain conditions and established security legislation. On the economic side, he has realized a number of policies, including resolving the deflationary recession, reducing corporate taxes, dismantling the policy of reducing the acreage of rice cultivation (*gentan*), reforming corporate governance, and lifting the ban on private residences providing lodging services (*minpaku*).

Commenting on the stability of the Abe administration, the mass media now talks about Abe *ikkyō* (the Abe government's political predominance) or *Kantei shudō* (prime-minister-led initiatives). One of the factors behind the stability is that compared to his first administration, Prime Minister Abe himself is now more skilled at managing the administration.

But, more importantly, the power of the Japanese prime minister was systematically strengthened at the time of launching the second Abe cabinet. In Japan, two major reforms—political reform and restructuring of ministries and agencies—were implemented between the 1990s and the early 2000s, and prime ministerial power has been expanding ever since. The Abe government's political power overlaps with this buildup. We also need to pay attention to the fact that the prime minister's power base has grown even stronger under the second Abe administration.

But the growing power of the prime minister is also exposing cracks. This has been apparent in the past few months with fluctuating support for the cabinet and the lowest cabinet approval rating and the highest disapproval rate since the launch of the administration.

Since February 2017, the Abe cabinet has been criticized for selling state-owned land to Moritomo Gakuen, for approving an application by Kake Gakuen to open a veterinary school in a National Strategic Special Zone, and for concealing daily activity logs of the Self-Defense Forces posted to South Sudan on peacekeeping missions. The criticisms against the administration reappeared after it had become apparent in March this year that the Ministry of Finance had forged the official document used to approve the selling of state-owned land to Moritomo Gakuen after the approval.

The cabinet approval rating has been falling sharply since May when the spotlight was turned on the Kake Gakuen issue. Even a survey by the *Yomiuri Shimbun*, where one might generally expect a high approval rating for the Abe cabinet, recorded a decline in the approval rating from 61 percent in May to 49 percent in June, and 36 percent in July, while the disapproval rating rose from 28 percent in May to 52 percent in July (Figure 1). As a result, the Liberal Democratic Party (LDP) suffered an overwhelming defeat in the Tokyo Metropolitan Assembly elections in July, capturing a mere 23 seats in the 127-seat assembly.

The Abe cabinet was roundly criticized during the phases of deliberating the Specially Designated Secrets Act and the security legislation. But at this time, Prime Minister Abe himself is facing unprecedented and strong criticism over the Moritomo Gakuen and Kake Gakuen issues. In the *Yomiuri Shimbun* opinion poll, this is indicated point-blank by the sharp rise in the percentage of respondents who answered that they could not trust the prime minister—from 29 percent in May to 48 percent in June.

Why is the person of the prime minister criticized? To start with, the two issues have something in common. Firstly, there are the suspicions that a special relationship may exist between the prime minister and the operators of Moritomo Gakuen and Kake Gakuen. The prime minister has invited suspicions of the two educational organizations affording preferential treatment. Secondly, rather than the right or wrong of any decisions involving Moritomo Gakuen and Kake Gakuen, the important point about whether documents that clarify the relationship between the prime minister and public officials who were directly responsible for making a series of policy decisions related to Moritomo Gauen and Kake Gakuen exist or not has become a political issue.

So far, there is absolutely no evidence that the prime minister directly issued any instructions in the two affairs of Moritomo Gakuen and Kake Gakuen.

In the case of the Kake Gakuen issue, we have leaks of internal government documents. There are, however, misgivings concerning the testimony of the persons involved and suspicions that persons close to the prime minister may have exercised their influence.

There are only "suspicions" that persons close to the prime minister have exercised their influence in the policy decision process. There is no conclusive evidence of influence peddling in the documentation and testimony at the center of attention. The internal documents of the Ministry of Education, Culture, Sports, Science, and Technology that have been brought to light are no more than summaries of statements by Hagiuda Kōichi, deputy chief cabinet secretary, and the vice-minister for policy coordination of the Cabinet Office compiled by civil servants at the ministry. The prime minister has also denied any involvement during deliberations in the Diet, using the phrase "impression management" in his rebuttals (Committee on Audit and Oversight of Administration, June 5, 2017).

But the strengthening of prime ministerial powers over the past twenty years provides the context for the extent of the attention on the Moritomo Gakuen and Kake Gakuen affairs and for the criticism of the person of the prime minister.

It is symbolic that all the politicians and bureaucrats who are the focus of attention where Moritomo Gakuen and Kake Gakuen are concerned are persons whose jobs bring them into the periphery of the prime minister. For example, did Hagiuda Kōichi, the deputy chief cabinet secretary at the time, exert his influence on the process of selecting Kake Gakuen as a business operator in a special deregulation zone? Parliamentary officials noted for their competence, including Ozawa Ichirō in the Takeshita Noboru cabinet and Yosano Kaoru in the second Hashimoto Ryūtarō cabinet, have held the post of deputy chief cabinet secretary in the past. But, they were both experienced cabinet ministers, having clocked up seven election wins each. In contrast, Hagiuda, the previous deputy chief cabinet secretary, had won four elections and had no cabinet minister experience.

Reflecting on the series of issues in a television program broadcast on August 5, 2017, the prime minister said, "As the [Chinese] proverb says, 'Don't do up your shoe in a melon patch to avoid suspicions'; it is regretful that I always have to consider the possibility of misrepresentation."

In short, public opinion takes a stern view of the behavior of the prime minister because prime ministerial power has grown stronger, increasing the potential for strong criticism of any move that can be misrepresented. Although detailed testimony is an issue for the future, it has been pointed out that the broad coverage of the scandals involving lawmakers from the ruling parties in recent years has even influenced the cabinet approval rating (such as an article in the *Tokyo Shimbun*, July 19, 2017). The context here is, conceivably, the increasing power of the prime minister. In short, the prime minister now exerts more control within the administration, and as the head of the organization, he is perhaps held to account in a stricter manner than before.

In this article, I will keep the issues described above in mind while investigating the nature of prime ministerial power in the current political structure in Japan.

To start with, I would like to discuss how the power of the prime minister is understood. I would also like to reflect on the gradual expansion of the power of the prime minister since the 1990s. In addition, I would like to demonstrate in detail how the power of the prime minister has further expanded since the launch of the second Abe cabinet in 2012. Lastly, after addressing some anticipated objections to the arguments presented in this article, I would like to consider the political implication of the ongoing general election.

I would particularly like to focus the discussion on two matters. Firstly, the gradual expansion of prime ministerial power under previous administrations, which provides the context for the strong power exercised by the prime minister under the present Abe administration. Secondly, since the prime minister has obtained strong powers, he is in a position where he can introduce reforms to further expand his own powers.

Many publications have already focused on the recent expansion of prime ministerial power, including *Kantei gaikō* (Diplomacy Led by the Prime Minister) by Shinoda Tomohito, *Nihon no tōchi kōzō* (Political Structures in Japan) by Iio Jun, *Koizumi seiken* (The Koizumi Administration) by Uchiyama Yū, and *Shushō shihai: Nihon seiji no henbō* (Prime Ministerial Control: Transforming Politics in Japan) by Takenaka Harukata, among others. There has been a particularly strong focus on Prime Minister Koizumi Junichirō, but the current trend in the research is looking at the changes since the Koizumi administration. For example, *Abe ikkyō no nazo* (The Riddle of the Abe Government's Predominance) by Makihara Izuru, *Jimintō: Ikkyō no jitsuzō* (The LDP: Inside the Dominant Party) by Nakakita Kōji, and *Shushō seiji no seido bunseki* (An Institutional Analysis of Politics Led by the Prime Minister) by Machidori Satoshi. I would like to further develop the discussion based on this series of research.

Defining the Power of the Prime Minister

The power of the prime minister is supported by the following three elements. Firstly, there is the authority of the prime minister. Secondly, the resources, such as the politicians, staff, and organizations, which the prime minister can turn to in drafting policy. Thirdly, public opinion support.

The prime minister's authority can be further divided into two parts: his position as the head of the ruling party and his legal authority as prime minister.

In evaluating the power of the prime minister, we need to take into account the politicians, staff, and organizations assisting him, as he would find it difficult to show strong leadership in the process of drafting policy were he not given these resources.

In this article, I will focus on the civil servants and the organizations that are recognized in existing laws as resources available for the prime minister. Basically, I will treat the civil servants and organizations in the Cabinet Secretariat and the civil servants and organizations in the Cabinet Office as the prime minister's resources.

In addition, public support is important because of the current electoral system. Under the single-seat constituency system, the political parties fight elections with the party leader as the face of the election whose popularity influences the results for the party. The popularity of the prime minister is important for the ruling party. Whether or not the prime minister is able to freely exercise his power depends on whether or not he has secured sufficient support among the public. Due to space limitations, I will only point out how public opinion acts on the power of the prime minister.

The phrase *Kantei shudō*, which can be translated as "the prime minister's initiatives," is often used when the prime minister and the politicians, bureaucrats, and organizations around him put on a display of strength while drafting policy. Researchers and experts differ subtly on what constitutes Kantei.

Let us start from the authority of the prime minister. The power of endorsing candidacy and the right to allocate political funds are important sources of the prime minister as the leader of the ruling party. These two types of powers have become politically important because of the political reform introduced in 1994.

Under the political reform of 1994, the electoral system for the House of Representatives was reorganized from the single nontransferable voting system to a system combining the first-past-the-post voting system with the proportional representation system. For a candidate considering a run in an election under the single-seat constituency system, party endorsement is vitally important to win in elections. A candidate's ranking is also important when running under the proportional representation system. The controls over political funds have also been strengthened. As a result, it is no longer easy for individual politicians to acquire political funding. In the meantime, as public subsidies to the parties have been introduced.

The party leadership with the head of the party at the top controls party endorsement to candidates in the elections and has the power over how to distribute political funds within the party. Therefore, under the present system, the head of the party can project a strong influence on the party politicians.

The impact of the political reforms has gradually penetrated into Japanese politics. At the time of the general elections in 1996 and 2000, the electoral districts were adjusted among some of the ruling party candidates with the final decisions frequently taken by the party leadership. As a result of tighter restrictions on the collection of the political funds after the 1994 reform, there has also been a steady decline in the ability of factions to obtain funds. As a result, factions can no longer wield as much power as they did prior to the reforms.

The increasing power of the prime minister is vividly demonstrated in the way cabinet posts are filled. Traditionally, the prime minister would take account of the influence of the factions when allocating posts in his cabinet. He would also respect the recommendations of the factions when appointing the cabinet ministers. The prime minister had limited discretion to select cabinet ministers. However, when Prime Minister Obuchi Keizō assumed office in July 1998, he was able to appoint about half of the cabinet ministers at his discretion.

The reorganization of central government ministries and agencies in 2001 is important when considering the legal authority of the prime minister. Oddly enough, until that time, the prime minister of Japan had no clear formal authority to propose policy. In the cabinet, it was the ministers who had the prerogative to draft policy. Of course, the prime minister could take the initiative on substantial policy proposals. But in initiating policies, he had to rely on informal powers deriving from the position of the prime minister.

When the ministries and agencies were reorganized, amendments to the Cabinet Act assigned the prime minister the authority to propose policies. Specifically, Article 4-2 of the Cabinet Act was amended to affirm that the prime minister "may propose basic principles and related matters concerning important policies of the cabinet."

In addition, Article 12-2 of the Cabinet Act established that one of the tasks of the Cabinet Secretariat was the "planning, drafting, and overall coordination concerning the basic principles involving important policies of the cabinet." In short, providing assistance to the prime minister when he was formulating important policies was added to the tasks of the Cabinet Secretariat.

Prior to the reorganization of ministries and agencies, it was recognized that the Cabinet Secretariat retained the power to coordinate policy among the ministries and agencies, and it was possible to rely on this power to draft policy. For example, the Cabinet Secretariat formulated the bill on UN peacekeeping operations, which involved several ministries and agencies including the Ministry of Foreign Affairs and the Japan Defense Agency. However, this was an exception, and it was rare for the Cabinet Secretariat to take initiatives in formulating policy.

The Cabinet Office was established as a body to assist the prime minister with the formulation of policy in addition to the Cabinet Secretariat. The Council on Economic and Fiscal Policy for drafting economic and fiscal policies, and the Council for Science and Technology Policy for discussing science and technology policy (currently, the Council for Science, Technology, and Innovation) were set up under the Cabinet Office.

Prime Minister Koizumi took office in April 2001 amid the expansion of the authority of the prime minister and the enhancement of the supporting organizations.

Prime Minister Koizumi largely ignored the intentions of the faction in appointing ministers to his cabinet. He also implemented one policy after another that would have been unthinkable under a conventional LDP administration, including cuts in public construction expenditure, the privatization of the Japan Highway Public Corporation, and the privatization of the postal services.

Prime Minister Koizumi used the Cabinet Secretariat and the Cabinet Office when designing the policies that he wanted to focus on. In the process of formulating economic and fiscal policies, in particular, he made maximum use of the clout of the Council on Economic and Fiscal Policy, essentially using the council as the forum where he made decisions on key policies such as reducing public works expenditure, writing off non-performing loans, and privatizing the postal services. Takenaka Heizō, Prime Minister Koizumi's appointee to the post of minister of state for economic and fiscal policy, was put in charge of managing the council from April 2001 to October 2005.

Prime Minister Koizumi also made use of the Cabinet Secretariat with the formulation of important legislation. In terms of economic policies, for example, the Cabinet Secretariat prepared the bill related to the privatization of the postal services to implement the privatization, and the bill establishing the Promotion Committee for the Privatization of the Four Highway-Related Public Corporations to discuss the privatization of the Japan Highway Public Corporation. As security policies, the Cabinet Secretariat formulated the bill on anti-terrorism special measures to facilitate cooperation with the war on terror after 9/11, and the bill on special measures for humanitarian relief and reconstruction to dispatch the Self-Defense Forces to Iraq after the Iraq War.

After the Koizumi Cabinet

Prime ministerial powers have steadily expanded since the Koizumi cabinet. Nakakita Kōji, one of the authors listed above, has carried out a detailed verification of the expanding authority of recent prime ministers as leaders of the ruling party. Nakakita focuses on the percentage of politicians with no cabinet experience among those who have been elected to LDP seats in at least six lower house elections as an indicator of the prime minister's enhanced authority over personnel issues. Calculating the percentages immediately before general elections from the 1980s to the early 2010s, he points out that although the percentage used to be below 15 percent, it has leapt to the upper 20 percent level under the second Abe cabinet.

This indicator is significant because of substantial decline in the importance of factions in recent years. Conventionally, faction-related indicators were frequently used to scrutinize the strength of the prime minister's power in providing patronage, but it is now highly doubtful that these indicators have the ability to measure such strength.

The fading importance of factions is also indicated by the increase in Diet members who do not belong to a faction. At present, the number of LDP members of the House of Representatives who are not aligned with any faction has risen to sixty, which is on the same scale as the number of members in the largest faction, the Hosoda Hiroyuki faction.

The appointments to the posts of chief cabinet secretary and deputy chief cabinet secretary under the second Abe administration also symbolize the dwindling presence of the factions. Traditionally, with LDP administrations, the prime minister has appointed members of his own faction to the posts of chief cabinet secretary and deputy chief cabinet secretary. There are some precedents, including the appointment of Chief Cabinet Secretary Gotōda Masaharu (Tanaka Kakuei faction) under the Nakasone Yasuhiro cabinet, but, ultimately, these were exceptions. The second Abe cabinet appointed Suga Yoshihide as chief cabinet secretary, and Katō Katsunobu and Sekō Hiroshige as deputy chief cabinet secretaries, but Sekō is the only one who is a member of the prime minister's original faction (currently, Abe is not aligned with any faction).

Consequently, the percentage of LDP Diet members who have been elected at least six times without joining the cabinet is a significant indicator replacing the faction-related indicator. The customary practice in the LDP of focusing on the number of election wins is thought to have begun at the time of the Satō Eisaku cabinet. There is no doubt that the purpose was to guarantee the loyalty of LDP backbenchers to the prime minister and to restrain rebellions. If the power of the prime minister increases, it should be possible to step away from these practices and to appoint the right person to the right position as he wishes.

I have worked out the figures for each cabinet from the second Mori Yoshirō cabinet formed in July 2000 to the third reshuffle of the third Abe cabinet. My conclusions are essentially the same as those in Nakakita's study. The trend has remained unchanged since the 2014 general election, when the percentage of Diet members who had been elected at least six times without joining the cabinet leapt to 38 percent under the third Abe cabinet. The level after the third cabinet reshuffle was 26 percent, which is still high compared to the past (Figure 2).

Next, I will consider changes in the prime minister's authority and support system, both of which are aspects where prime ministerial power is expanding.

To start with, staff numbers at the Cabinet Secretariat, which is the core of the prime minister's support organization, are rising rapidly.

In fiscal 2000, prior to the reorganization of the ministries and agencies, there were no more than 377 regular staff at the Cabinet Secretariat, but by fiscal 2016 the number had risen to 1,119. With the number of persons holding concurrent posts also rising, the total number of regular staff and concurrent posts was 822 in fiscal 2000. By fiscal 2016, the number had more than tripled to 2,779 (Figure 3).

Within the Cabinet Secretariat, the number of divisions under the Cabinet Affairs Office and the assistant chief cabinet secretary, thought to participate closely in drafting policy, has also risen rapidly. In brief, under the reshuffled second Mori cabinet immediately after the reorganization of the ministries and agencies, there were only ten divisions. In contrast, the number increased to thirty-nine after the second reshuffle of the third Abe cabinet (Figure 4).

The Cabinet Office organization is also expanding. There were 2,210 regular staff at the time of the reorganization of the ministries and agencies in fiscal 2001, but the number had risen to 2,324 by fiscal 2016 (Figure 5). In addition, as outlined in the Act for the Establishment of the Cabinet Office, the Cabinet Office was

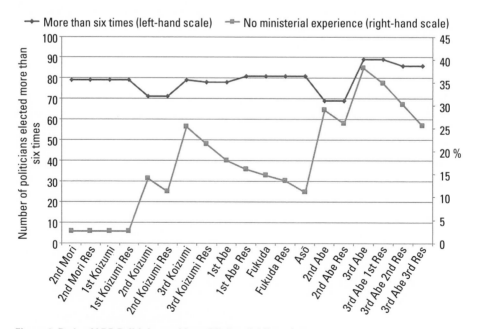

Figure 2. Ratio of LDP Politicians without Ministerial Experience
Source: Based on the *Kokkai binran.*

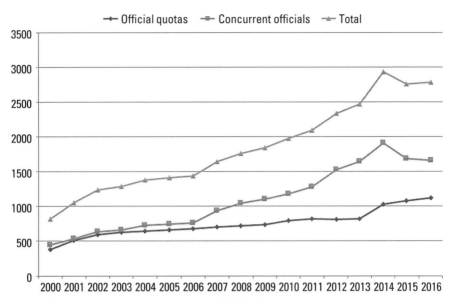

Figure 3. Number of Officers in the Cabinet Secretariat

Source: Based on the Cabinet Secretariat website and other sources.

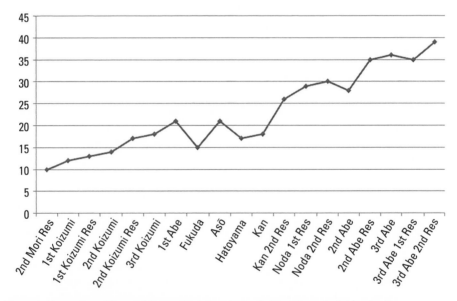

Figure 4. Expansion of Special Policy Divisions in the Cabinet Secretariat (under the Director General of Cabinet Affairs and Assistant Chief Cabinet Secretary)

Source: Based on the *Kokkai binran* and other sources.

responsible for 76 administrative tasks in 2001, but by the end of 2016, the number had reached 100. The number of councils under the Cabinet Office has also increased from twenty-four in 2001 to thirty-nine in 2016.

There are three trends in the expansion of the prime minister's support system.

Firstly, the Cabinet Secretariat, the Cabinet Office, and cabinet councils have been expanding continuously over the long term. This trend

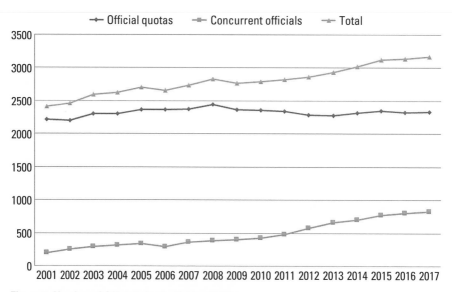

Figure 5. Number of Officials in the Cabinet Office
Source: Based on the Cabinet Secretariat website and other sources.

was no different under the administrations of the Democratic Party of Japan (DPJ), when policy-making was unstable.

Secondly, in terms of the structure of the Cabinet Secretariat, there was a period between 2009 and 2012 when the number of internal groups specifically created to take charge of policy decreased briefly due to changes in the majority parties controlling the government (Figure 4). This suggests that changes in majority parties managing the government are likely to lead to revisions of policies.

Thirdly, the Cabinet Secretariat structure and cabinet councils have expanded rapidly since the advent of the second Abe cabinet. At the end of 2012, shortly after the inauguration of the cabinet, the Cabinet Secretariat had 807 regular staff, but by the end of 2016, the number had risen to 1,119. When concurrent posts are included, the numbers have expanded from 2,331 to 2,779 posts (Figure 3). Directly after the inauguration of the second Abe cabinet, there were twenty-eight policy organizations, but by the third Abe cabinet, the number had risen to thirty-nine (Figure 4).

As a result, the prime minister, the Cabinet Secretariat, and the Cabinet Office are now directly responsible for an increasing number of policy domains. The current prime minister is, of course, in charge of foreign policy, security guarantees, and the economy, but his brief also ranges the whole gamut of policymaking from regional development to social security, and from the oceans to space.

The Second and Third Abe Cabinets
I would also like to take a close look at how prime ministerial powers have changed under the second and third Abe cabinets.

There are two distinct features. Firstly, institutional reforms have further broadened the legal authority of the prime minister. Secondly, as I have already described, the prime minister's supporting institutions have been expanded.

The second Abe cabinet has reformed the civil service based on the Basic Act for National Civil Service Reform enacted by the Fukuda Yasuo cabinet. In July 2013, an office for civil service reform was set up under the Headquarters for the Promotion of Administrative Reform at the Cabinet Secretariat to formulate a bill to deliver the reforms.

In November the same year, the bill related to the civil service reform was approved by cabinet decision, and the legislation was enacted in

April 2014. The legislation has two key dimensions. Firstly, to increase the prime minister's authority over the civil service and its executive leadership. The prime minister has taken charge of the civil service system, traditionally the responsibility of the Ministry of Internal Affairs and Communications (MIC). The prime minister has also acquired more political power in making the list which put the candidates for high-ranking officials at the grade of deputy director general and higher at each ministry and agency. In practice, the prime minister has entrusted the use of this authority to the chief cabinet secretary.

Those who have the authority to manage personnel affairs, including each minister, must choose among the candidates listed in this list when making appointments to high-ranking positions. They also have to consult with the prime minister and the chief cabinet secretary.

The Cabinet Bureau of Personnel Affairs was set up in May 2014 to help prepare the list of candidates for high-ranking positions and administer the civil service as a whole.

Prior to the reforms, the prime minister and the chief cabinet secretary exercised a certain degree of influence on the appointment of senior public officers at the ministries and agencies. In May 1997, the second Hashimoto cabinet agreed to set up an advisory panel on reviewing cabinet personnel affairs, which meant that all senior positions at the grade of director general and higher had to be reviewed in advance by the chief cabinet secretary and the deputy chief cabinet secretary. On such occasions, the opinion of the prime minister would, of course, be taken into consideration. But, it must be remembered that it was the relevant minister who had the right to appoint and dismiss bureaucrats and the authority to independently manage personnel affairs. The prime minister and the chief cabinet secretary may very well have rejected a proposed appointment, but it is difficult to find any examples where they would have endorsed a specific candidate for a post at a ministry or agency.

In this regard, Chief Cabinet Secretary Suga has made use of the new system to actively promote certain bureaucrats to senior positions in ministries and agencies. Specific examples include the vice-ministers at the Ministry of Agriculture, Forestry, and Fisheries, and at the Ministry of Defense, as well as the commandant of the Japan Coast Guard. In an interview with the *Asahi Shimbun*, the chief cabinet secretary has personally acknowledged that he has used his influence (*Asahi Shimbun*, online edition, February 27, 2017).

Another important institutional change was implemented at the same time as the civil service reforms in 2014. In brief, the prime minister gained the authority to set up new organizations and to make staffing decisions at the ministries and agencies (Cabinet Act Article 12-2, items 13 and 14). Seeing that the prime minister considers policy for the whole of Japan, it is only natural that he has the authority to make decisions about organization and staffing at each ministry. However, in the past, these tasks have been under the jurisdiction of the MIC. In this respect as well, the prime minister's influence over each ministry seems to be growing stronger.

Establishing the National Security Council

In December 2013, the Abe cabinet reorganized the Security Council, which designed such policies as principles of Japan's defense policy and National Defense Program Guidelines, into the National Security Council (NSC). In January 2014, the National Security Secretariat was established as the secretariat for the council.

The main purpose of the Security Council had been to discuss important matters related to the fundamental principles of defense policy as well as the National Defense Program Guidelines. In contrast, the NSC also discusses the principles for foreign and defense policies related Japanese security in addition to the policies discussed by the Security Council. Specifically, in principle, members of the four-minister meeting, which discusses foreign and defense policies, are limited to the prime minister, the chief cabinet secretary, the minister of foreign affairs, and the minister of defense. The establishment of this meeting was a major reform.

The Cabinet Secretariat prepared the bill to revise the law to create a NSC and the bill was enacted in November 2013. Since the establishment of the council and the National Security

Secretariat, the prime minister's ability to formulate security policies has increased significantly. The four-minister meeting is convened regularly. Since the assistant chief cabinet secretaries, respectively seconded from the Ministry of Foreign Affairs and the Ministry of Defense, serve as deputy secretaries-general of the National Security Secretariat, it has become possible to coordinate foreign and defense policies much more effectively on a constant basis.

Within the Cabinet Secretariat, there are three assistant chief cabinet secretaries who coordinate policies involving various ministries. The way they coordinate security policies have drastically changed since the establishment of the National Security Secretariat.

Their predecessor organizations are the Cabinet Office for Internal Affairs (COIA), the Cabinet Office for External Affairs (COEA), and the Cabinet Office for Security Affairs (COSA), which were set up by the Nakasone cabinet in July 1986. The posts have often been held by officials seconded from the Ministry of Finance, the Ministry of Foreign Affairs, and the Ministry of Defense. The COEA was responsible for coordinating matters related international relations, while the COSA coordinated policies related to national security. Prior to the revisions, Article 4 of the Order for the Organization of the Cabinet Secretariat clearly specified that matters under the jurisdiction of the COSA were "excluded" from the jurisdiction of the COEA. It is necessary to coordinate foreign policy and defense policy to design security policies, but since the COEA and COSA were separated, the Cabinet Secretariat could not effectively coordinate security policies. (In April 1998, the COSA also assumed responsibility for crisis management, and the name was changed to the Cabinet Office for Security Affairs and Crisis Management.)

The supporting institutions for the prime minister have expanded in an area which is not often noticed. In May 2013, the Abe cabinet amended the Cabinet Act to establish the post of deputy chief cabinet secretary for information technology policy with responsibility for coordinating issues involving information and communication technologies. The deputy chief cabinet secretary for information technology policy works on the integration of information systems at each ministry.

The Cabinet Secretariat and Economic Policy

In addition to the series of institutional reforms, the decision-making process within the Cabinet Secretariat has also changed since the launch of the second Abe cabinet. The prime minister, the chief cabinet secretary, the three assistant chief cabinet secretaries, and the secretary to the prime minister has come to meet regularly to facilitate communication among them. It is perhaps surprising that there were no regular meetings of the prime minister, the chief cabinet secretary, and the assistant chief cabinet secretaries under previous cabinets.

Under the second Abe administration, the Cabinet Secretariat has played a central role in numerous policy formulation processes. I would like to consider this from the perspective of economic policy.

As soon as Prime Minister Abe assumed office, he made it clear that he intended to press forward with the three arrows of Abenomics—bold monetary policy, flexible fiscal policy, and a growth strategy to stimulate private investment—as his fundamental economic policy. To formulate the growth strategy, the prime minister established the Headquarters for Japan's Economic Revitalization and created the post of minister in charge of economic revitalization. Under the auspices of the headquarters, he also set up the Industrial Competitiveness Council, which worked on the Japan Revitalization Strategy, an important cabinet policy, on an annual basis until 2016. (In September 2016, the Industrial Competitiveness Council was reorganized as the Council on Investments for the Future. In 2017, the council started coordinating the Investments for the Future Strategy in place of the Japan Revitalization Strategy.) To coordinate revitalization strategies, the General Secretariat for Japan's Economic Revitalization was set up as the secretariat for the Economic Revitalization Headquarters and for the Industrial Competitiveness Council.

Specifically, in 2013 and 2014, the revitalization strategies included, for example, corporate governance reform, the reform of the Government Pension Investment Fund (GPIF), reduction of corporate taxes, and establishment of National Strategic Special Zones. Each policy was delivered. Prime Minister Koizumi made maximum use of the Council on Economic and Fiscal Policy to formulate economic policy. In contrast, Prime Minister Abe has used the Cabinet Secretariat to formulate microeconomic policies.

After the general election in the fall of 2015, Prime Minister Abe launched "promoting the dynamic engagement of all citizens" as an important economic policy for the cabinet, adding "work-style reform" after reshuffling the cabinet in August 2016. He created the posts of minister in charge of promoting dynamic engagement of all citizens and minister in charge of work-style reform. He also established the National Council for Promoting the Dynamic Engagement of All Citizens and the Council for Promoting the Realization of Work Style Reform at the Cabinet Secretariat as the organizations with responsibility for each policy. By March 2017, the third Abe cabinet designed the policy for limiting overtime and levying penalties on firms found to be noncompliant.

Prime Minister Abe has also relied on the Cabinet Secretariat for the Trans-Pacific Partnership (TPP) negotiations. In March 2013, the prime minister announced that he would participate in the TPP negotiations and in April and set up the Governmental Headquarters for the TPP in the Cabinet Secretariat. He appointed Economy Minister Amari Akira the director of the headquarters. He also created the positions of chief domestic coordinator to make coordination within the government and chief negotiator to lead negotiations. The headquarters formulated basic policies for the TPP negotiations and handled domestic coordination. A general agreement was reached in October 2015. More than two and a half years passed since the Abe cabinet had announced that Japan would participate in the negotiations.

The Cabinet Secretariat and Security Policies

Next, I would like to take a look at security policies. As soon as Prime Minister Abe assumed

office, he indicated that he was considering a review of the right of collective self-defense. In February 2013, he also reconvened the Advisory Panel on Reconstruction of the Legal Basis for Security, which was established under the first Abe cabinet, to review the policies vital for the security of Japan including the exercise of the right of collective self-defense. The Cabinet Secretariat served as the secretariat for the panel. In May 2014, the advisory panel compiled a report recommending that the government be able to exercise the right of collective self-defense under certain conditions and that it should provide more flexibly rear support for other countries in times of international crisis, such as the Gulf War.

Subsequently, Prime Minister Abe had the cabinet make a cabinet decision to revise the constitutional interpretation of the right of collective self-defense and permit the government to exercise the right of collective self-defense under certain conditions. The Cabinet Secretariat did the groundwork for the cabinet decision. Based on the decision, Prime Minister Abe went ahead with preparations for a security-related bill. In May 2015, the Abe cabinet adopted the bill by cabinet decision, and the bill was enacted in September. The National Security Secretariat at the Cabinet Secretariat prepared and drafted the bill.

This is how Prime Minister Abe has developed, expanded, and made full use of his own supporting organizations to formulate important bills.

Reviewing the Support System

Prime Minister Abe has not only expanded his supporting organizations, but he has also carried out an institutional reform.

The reform was based on a recommendation by the LDP. The LDP considered that organizations of the Cabinet Secretariat and the Cabinet Office became excessive, and they asked for the reduction of the respective institutions. In January 2014, the LDP started to design plans for reductions and submitted a proposal to the government in November.

Based on the proposal, the Abe cabinet examined ways to slim down the Cabinet Secretariat and the Cabinet Office. The plan became official by a cabinet decision in in January 2015. In

September, the cabinet succeeded in having the Diet pass the bill to implement the plan.

The plan consisted of two pillars. First was to eliminate some organizations in the Cabinet Secretariat and to transfer some of them to the Cabinet Office, while moving some of the organizations from the Cabinet Office to other ministries and agencies. Many of the abolished or transferred organizations were introduced prior to the formation of the second Abe cabinet. It is possible to interpret that Prime Minister Abe has reorganized the two institutions in such a way that they truly serve his own policy goals.

The second pillar was to amend the National Government Organization Act and to set up a mechanism whereby the prime minister by a cabinet decision can assign each minister of state with the responsibilities of "comprehensive" coordination between ministries and agencies concerning important cabinet policies. Until this reform the Cabinet Secretariat and the Cabinet Office were the only organizations that had power to make comprehensive coordination among the ministries. Therefore, the prime minister basically had no choice but to rely on the Cabinet Secretariat or the Cabinet Office when formulating policies that involved multiple ministries and agencies. With the reform it has become possible for the prime minister to turn to each minister of state, as well as the organizations below the minister for comprehensive coordination. For example, in January 2016, Prime Minister Abe instructed Foreign Minister Kishida Fumio to be in charge of making comprehensive policy coordination within the government for the EU-Japan economic partnership agreement negotiations.

Evaluating the Political Developments between the First Abe Cabinet and the Noda Cabinet

So far, I have argued that the powers of Japan's prime minister have continued to expand both in terms of his authority as well as supporting institutions. Here, I anticipate that objections might be raised against the proposition of the continuous expansion of prime ministerial powers. The period between 2006 and 2012 was characterized by a series of short-lived governments. In fact,

the prime minister changed every year during this period. Even the longest-serving cabinet during this period, the Noda Yoshihiko cabinet, lasted only for one year and four months.

In brief, if the prime ministerial power is so strong, the objection would be to question why it was impossible for successive prime ministers to sustain their administrations for a long period of time.

Certainly, it would be difficult to claim that the prime ministers exercised strong power during the period between the first Abe cabinet and the Noda cabinet.

The first Abe cabinet and the Hatoyama Yukio cabinet were short-lived because the prime ministers poorly managed their administrations. A major reason for the short duration of the cabinets of Prime Ministers Fukuda Yasuo, Asō Tarō, Kan Naoto, and Noda is that the ruling parties were unable to secure a majority in the House of Councillors. The two chambers of the Diet were controlled by different parties, causing the policy process to stagnate.

However, even during this time, the prime ministers used their own support institutions to formulate many important policies. Basically, the function of formulating government policy was concentrated in the hands of the prime minister and those around him. The seeds for the expanding authority of the prime minister under the current Abe cabinet were sown in this period.

Under the three LDP cabinets after Koizumi, the number of councils where the prime minister was the principal minister increased, and the prime minister made use of the Cabinet Secretariat for formulating some important policies. For example, in 2006, Prime Minister Abe set up a council on strengthening the functions of the Kantei on national security, with its secretariat in the Cabinet Secretariat, to examine the possibility of establishing a National Security Council. This council recommended the establishment of the NSC. Prime Minister Abe then set up a task force at the Cabinet Secretariat to prepare for the establishment of the NSC, asking them to draft a legislation to amend the Act for the Establishment of the Security Council of Japan. (However, the amendments were not delivered at the time.) He also set up the Advisory Panel on Reconstruction of the Legal Basis for Security to examine the possible exercise of the right of collective self-defense and had the Cabinet Secretariat serve as the secretariat for the panel.

The Fukuda Yasuo cabinet asked the Cabinet Secretariat to prepare the bill for the Basic Act for National Civil Service Reform. A pillar of this bill was to set up a Cabinet Agency for Personnel Affairs to centralize the cabinet's management of personnel policy of the civil service. In the end, Prime Minister Fukuda did not set up the agency. Instead, he accepted a proposal from the Democratic Party of Japan to ask the chief cabinet secretary to prepare the register of candidates for senior-ranking officials for the ministries and agencies, and he decided to introduce a Cabinet Bureau of Personnel Affairs in the Cabinet Secretariat. The bill was enacted in June 2008.

When Prime Minister Asō set up the Council for the Realization of a Reassuring Society to reexamine the nature of social security in Japan, he also put the secretariat for the council in the Cabinet Secretariat. This council proposed the expansion of social security for the working generation of people in employment, which clearly marked a departure from the social security policies that have been pursued so far. Under the Asō cabinet, the Cabinet Secretariat also formulated the anti-piracy bill, which would allow the Maritime Self-Defense Force to guard private vessels from piracy off the coast of Somalia.

The DPJ administrations were unable to deliver on the plans for the centralization of policy formulation in the cabinet and the National Policy Bureau that was included in their manifesto for the 2009 general election, but even so, each prime minister used his supporting institutions to formulate several important policies.

Prime Minister Hatoyama established a National Policy Office instead of the National Policy Bureau. The National Policy Office formulated two important policies under the Hatoyama and Kan cabinets. Firstly, it set the targets for improving fiscal conditions in Japan that have been upheld in the second and third Abe cabinets. In July 2010, the office also compiled the New Growth Strategy as the key economic policy of the Kan cabinet. The strategy included

infrastructure exports, expansion of agricultural exports, construction of airport facilities, and the introduction of other concessions to social capital. These policies have continued under the second Abe administration.

The Kan cabinet was in power in March 2011 when the Great East Japan Earthquake and the Fukushima nuclear disaster occurred. The Kan cabinet has been criticized for its response, but it was the Cabinet Secretariat and the Cabinet Office that played the central role in designing policies in response to the earthquake and nuclear disaster.

The Kan and Noda cabinets also pushed for the comprehensive reform of the social security and tax systems with an increase in the consumption tax as an important pillar. Prime Minister Kan appointed Yosano Kaoru as minister for social security and tax reform, while Prime Minister Noda appointed Okada Katsuya as minister for social security and tax reform.

The Headquarters of the Government and Ruling Parties for Social Security Reform reviewed the reform proposals and the Office for Social Security Reform in the Cabinet Secretariat served as the secretariat for the headquarters.

Summary

As discussed at the outset, since the formation of the second Abe cabinet, the prime minister's strength has become apparent in the policy formulation process, a phenomenon often referred to as Abe *ikkyō*. Prime Minister Abe has, in actual fact, acquired more power than previous prime ministers. In addition to the expansion of the prime minister's legal authority, his supporting institutions centered on the Cabinet Secretariat and the Cabinet Office have also been strengthened.

The institutional strengthening of the prime ministerial powers has allowed Prime Minister Abe to manage the administration in a stable manner and to leave a record of steady policy performance through the first half of 2017. The prime minister used the Cabinet Secretariat as the forum for formulating security policies, including changes to the interpretation of the right of collective self-defense. He also used the Cabinet Secretariat to formulate a growth strategy, work-style reform, and other economic and social policies.

It should be noted that Prime Minister Abe has obtained stronger powers as a steady extension of the increase in prime ministerial powers since the 1994 political reforms. The prime minister's support system, in particular, has continuously expanded since the Koizumi cabinet.

When you look at the institution of the prime minister rather than the individuals in the post, it is interesting to note that the prime minister can use his supporting organizations to implement institutional reforms to secure even stronger powers. The establishment of the Cabinet Bureau of Personnel Affairs and the National Security Council are examples of the prime minister using the Cabinet Secretariat to expand his own powers even further. The beginnings of civil service reform, which introduced the Cabinet Bureau of Personnel Affairs, can be traced back to the first Abe cabinet, or from even a longer perspective, to the second Hashimoto cabinet (when the Final Report of the Administrative Reform Council was issued in 1997). Likewise, the discussions about the National Security Council started during the first Abe cabinet.

The political process under the second Abe cabinet also points to the risks of expanding his supporting institutions. The public has started to take a critical view of the prime minister as a result of the expansion of his powers. The problems involving Moritomo Gakuen and Kake Gakuen have shown that any action that can be interpreted as the prime minister's use of power to favor himself or those close to him is likely to shake the foundations of the administration. The emergence of documents suggesting the involvement of politicians and bureaucrats in the Cabinet Secretariat and the Cabinet Office in the Kake Gakuen issue also suggests problems with management at the continually expanding Cabinet Secretariat.

If the Cabinet Secretariat becomes bloated, it is likely that the prime minister and the chief cabinet secretary will be less scrupulous as regard to the management of the Cabinet Secretariat. If there is insufficient oversight, there is a growing risk that the politicians and bureaucrats in the Cabinet Secretariat will instruct the ministries of the alleged intentions of the prime minister in

the same way that Mito Kōmon (as Tokugawa Mitsukuni, 1628–1701, the second daimyo of the Mito Domain, was commonly known) brandishes his *inrō* seal in the television drama series.

The potential problems caused by a huge supporting structure for the prime minster were recognized when the Hashimoto cabinet reorganized the ministries and agencies. It had already been pointed out that if a single organization is given the responsibility for the supporting functions, the issue of how to manage such an organization emerges. Therefore, when the ministries and agencies were reorganized in 2001, the original idea was to divide the supporting functions for the prime minister among the Cabinet Secretariat and the Cabinet Office. The Cabinet Office would handle implementation and daily coordination, while the Cabinet Secretariat, as a small-scale organization, would only plan and formulate important policies.

Subsequent developments, however, suggest that the Cabinet Secretariat has become bloated. For example, the involvement of the Cabinet Secretariat in the process of deciding which university would be permitted to open new departments of veterinary medicine in the National Strategic Special Zones is now under suspicion. It is indeed doubtful that such matters can be considered important cabinet policies.

There is no doubt that the British system of government has been taken into account as a point of reference when implementing political system reform in Japan since the 1990s. If we compare the prime ministers of Japan and Britain, the powers of the Japanese prime minister fall far short of those of the British prime minister due to the authority of the Diet committees and the restrictions imposed by the bicameral system. There is still room for improvements in the Diet system. However, the concentration of powers into the hands of the prime minister with regard to formulation of policies and drafting of legislation has progressed to a significant degree. In terms of the appropriate scale of an organization managed by a small group of politicians comprising the prime minister, the chief cabinet secretary, and the deputy chief cabinet secretaries, it is doubtful that the Cabinet Secretariat will be able to continue to expand its personnel as it has done in the past.

Prime Minister Abe recovered his support rating when he reshuffled the cabinet on August 3, 2017. According to a *Yomiuri Shimbun* survey, support for the cabinet rose to 50 percent in September. The prime minister dissolved the House of Representatives on September 28, and general elections were held on November 22. There are undoubtedly two ulterior motives behind the sudden dissolution of the lower house. Firstly, there is the concern that the Diet will pursue the Kake Gakuen issue and that the support rating will once again fall if the matter is discussed at an extraordinary session of the Diet. Secondly, there is the ongoing excitement generated by the Democratic Party. It would be more advantageous to contrive a general election before it has a chance to join forces with the new party of Koike Yuriko, the governor of Tokyo, who is said to be making preparations for reentering the national political scene.

Although the prime minister's powers have been enhanced, it is up to the nation to decide whether the administration survives or not. The fact that the prime minister retains strong powers clearly indicates the seat of responsibility for national policy. Regardless of the prime minister's intentions, in this general election, there is a sense that a new wind is blowing with Governor Koike's new party (Party of Hope) and that it will "reset Japan." In this context, we are asked to make an overall assessment of whether or not to support an administration where the prime minister has accumulated certain achievements due to his enhanced power base, and where the management of the administration has started to unravel as a result of those enhanced powers.

English version originally published in *Discuss Japan—Japan Foreign Policy Forum*, no. 49, October 11, 2018. Translated from "'Abe ikkyō' no seidoteki kiban: 'Shushō-shihai' no hatten to kokusei e no sekinin," *Chūō Kōron* (November 2017): 98–115 (courtesy of Chūōkōron Shinsha).

Note

1. "Council for Designing 100-Year Life Society," The Prime Minister of Japan and His Cabinet, September 11, 2017, https://japan.kantei.go.jp/97_abe/actions/201709/11article5.html.

An Inside View from the Advisory Council
Looking Back at the Seven Months That Decided the Emperor's Future

Mikuriya Takashi

Discuss Japan—Japan Foreign Policy Forum, 2018

In April 2017, the Advisory Council on Easing the Burden of the Official Duties and Public Activities of His Majesty the Emperor (hereafter Advisory Council) put together its final report and concluded its work. In my role as acting chairman of the Advisory Council I was also its spokesman, so some readers may have seen me at post-meeting press conferences and other events.

There was absolutely no precedent for these discussions on imperial abdication, so it was inevitable that there would be some trial and error involved in the seven months of deliberation. Nevertheless, right now I feel that we produced the best report we could. But just what was this Advisory Council that captured the interest of the Japanese people? As our deliberations have now achieved their initial aim, I would like to explain as much as I can.

On April 21, 2017, the Advisory Council delivered its final report to Prime Minister Abe Shinzō. The report proposed permitting the emperor to abdicate and also establishing a special law on abdication instead of revising the Imperial House Law. The report also suggested that the emperor and empress be referred to as retired emperor and retired empress following abdication and that Prince Akishino be referred to as imperial heir.

In August 2016, the emperor himself used a video message to announce his strong wish to retire on account of his advanced age. Hearing his words, I was first struck by the thought that this is a "delicate" issue. I have spent my career studying politics, and it goes without saying that any political action by the emperor would be a violation of the Constitution. From my perspective as an academic, I certainly do not think it desirable for the emperor to influence Japanese politics by expressing his thoughts.

In his message, the emperor expressed his wish to abdicate and also negative feelings towards appointing a regent. On top of that, he said it was "impossible" for him to reduce his role as a symbol of the state. By saying so, I feel that he was pushing the limits of his status as a symbol. If one were to compare this to a sumo bout, his comments were akin to a wrestler's foot slipping slightly out of the sumo ring.

My Personal Connections to Imai Takashi and Sugita Kazuhiro

Basically, to date I have been critical of the Abe administration. So, I must admit that when I was approached about being a member of the Advisory Council that was due to start in October 2016, all sorts of worries cropped up. To begin with, the issue of abdication was unprecedented and difficult, so it was conceivable that the Advisory Council would become divided or dissolve without reaching a conclusion. I thought it would be bad if that happened.

Nevertheless, I accepted on account of how the emperor had entreated the people to deal with his own aging. I felt this issue of human compassion should be dealt with swiftly. I also had close personal connections to two other members of the Advisory Council: Imai Takashi and Sugita Kazuhiro, who was representing the Cabinet Office.

Eighty-six-year-old Imai Takashi is the manager of the venerable Nippon Steel Corporation. In order to understand the perspective of the emperor, it was important for the chairman to be older. Having someone of the same generation and with such gravitas helped give the Advisory Council authority.

Above all, I trusted Imai's steady character. Fifteen years ago, during the Koizumi Junichirō administration, I worked with Imai on the round table on establishing a memorial for mourning and prayers for peace. So, when I received the offer and heard that Imai would be the chair, I intuitively felt that it would go well.

My other personal connection was with the person who approached me, Deputy Chief Cabinet Secretary Sugita Kazuhiro. Sugita is about ten years older than me, went to the same university, and was a member of the same tea ceremony club. Although I did not know him when I was at university, we became friends through our alumni association and sometimes socialized together. At the time I was working on an oral history by Kasai Yoshiyuki of the Central Japan Railway Company (JR Tōkai), Sugita was an advisor to the same company and we often bumped into each other at meetings and other occasions. The present Cabinet Office is very strict about controlling information, and even the Advisory Council might not hear about some critical discussions. But I thought that if Sugita was a member, one way or another it would be OK.

On accepting the invitation to join the Advisory Council, as expected, the Cabinet Office's information control was thorough. When Cabinet Office staff turned up to give us an "explanation" before meetings, they took most of their materials back with them, leaving only a document titled "media warnings," which they said was OK to use. Nevertheless, apart from the official press conferences, having assigned me to the role of acting chair, which included media relations, the Cabinet Office gave me complete freedom.

The Advisory Council convened in the largest meeting room of the Kantei (prime minister's office). It was the same room that was used for meetings of the Reconstruction Design Council following the Great East Japan Earthquake in 2011. The Reconstruction Design Council included ten to twenty staff from the Ministry of Finance, the Ministry of Economy, Trade, and Industry, and other places, quickly becoming a big group of over fifty. This time the Advisory Council was led by the Cabinet Office and was a small group of around ten people from beginning

to end. The only staff from other departments were from the Imperial Household Agency, and we were not relying on force of numbers to get things done.

Also, the limited number of members was an important factor in the Advisory Council's smooth operation. The Reconstruction Design Council had over fifty members. With that kind of council, when there are more than ten people, the members start to feel less responsibility. Conversely, when they have too much zeal, a council can become divided.

This time, as well as myself and our chair Imai, the six-member Advisory Council included: Professor Obata Junko of Sophia University, President Seike Atsushi of Keio University, Professor Miyazaki Midori of the Chiba University of Commerce, and Professor Emeritus Yamauchi Masayuki of the University of Tokyo. Our meetings took two hours and involved much discussion. I lost count how many times, when the discussion became very heated, our chair Imai reminded members of the limited time available and the need to soon move on.

Another important point was that none of the six members was a specialist on the imperial house system. As a rule of thumb, specialists often get too attached to their own ideas, and the discussion does not move forward. When one person disagrees, others get dragged into the debate, and the meeting does not progress at all. It was wonderful how no one was late or absent to any of the fourteen meetings, and how we were able to hold frank discussions.

We Would Not Do Anything That Was Not Supported by the Public

When addressing the abdication issue, our most important consideration was the feelings of the emperor himself. Yet, if our discussions had directly reflected the opinions that the emperor had expressed, there would be a risk of unconstitutionality. Therefore, the premise behind the Advisory Council's creation was to go along with the feelings of the 90 percent of the Japanese people who heard the emperor's words and agreed with them.

At the first press conference I stressed, "You journalists are also participants. Please conduct polls and ascertain the direction of public opinion. We will reflect that." I believed that we could not discuss the issue while ignoring public opinion. The reporters seemed taken aback, but I wanted to explain that we would not do anything that was not supported by the public. Rather than being secretive, the idea was to disclose as much information as possible, thus giving the Advisory Council more viability and public support. In fact, when we look at the opinion polls that followed, the 90 percent public support for the emperor's feelings did not change. Although no member of the Advisory Council put this into words, I think we aimed for a result to suit a public mood that in itself reflected the emperor's feelings.

Although the Advisory Council was criticized by some as "directing the discussion according to instruction from the government," in actual fact we had no such instruction from the Cabinet Office.

One unexpected development occurred in early November when we began interviewing specialists. The Cabinet Office had started the interviews partly to avoid the media and public thinking we had decided on a particular direction for the discussions. But events took an unexpected turn for us.

The selection was made by Cabinet Office staff, and we members were only told of the result. When we looked at the final list, we found that it was not just researchers with expert knowledge of the imperial household but that the majority were journalists, commentators, and academics who had expressed opinions about the emperor's abdication, mainly in newspapers. Glancing at the list, we noticed that the number of commentators with what you might call right-wing views was relatively large, but no one expressed any objection to that.

There were sixteen interviews in total, with each person allocated twenty minutes. Beforehand, we gave the interviewees a list of ten questions, such as, "What are your thoughts on the role of the emperor within the Japanese Constitution?" We also said that they were welcome to submit a statement of their opinions or resume. Then, when we actually started the interviews, we found that opinions against abdication of the emperor were more numerous than we had expected, and more diverse.

For example, Hirakawa Sukehiro, a professor emeritus of the University of Tokyo, said that "the emperor is tired because he does unnecessary things" and that the emperor should perform rituals and the official duties specified in the Constitution. When we tried to question him, he was not an easygoing interviewee, replying, "I wonder if you can refute me?" Eventually, we ended getting a scolding, with Hirakawa saying, "there was no need for this Advisory Council in the first place."

Watanabe Shōichi, a critic who passed away recently, was another memorable interviewee, repeatedly saying, "It is OK to do nothing." As we were wondering how to handle the situation, he finally said, "As soon as I sat down here, I suddenly became deaf, and I haven't heard anything you said. If you will excuse me . . ." and then left.

Imai, who was sitting next to me, asked, "Was he ill?" and I had to laugh. I replied that it was "political deafness," a disease specific to Watanabe Shōichi. Yet, as soon as he left the meeting room he spoke to journalists, fluently laying out his thoughts on why the emperor should not abdicate, so I think he must have heard our questions very clearly.

In the statement of opinion she had submitted beforehand, critic Sakurai Yoshiko had written that she was in favor of abdication being limited to the current emperor. But on the day of her interview she had a sudden conversion and changed her statement. In her new statement, she wrote, "I would like to grant the wishes of the emperor and empress," adding that as a citizen of Japan she would like abdication to be made possible. Up to this point, the new statement matched the first, but following that she turned 180 degrees, writing, "Of course we must pay consideration to the advanced age of the emperor, but this is a different matter to thinking about the nature of the nation." She changed her mind right at the end of the statement, and I was quite struck by this deft shift in logic. I was also struck by how these right-wingers included "actors" who brought an array of "dramatic effects" to our interviews.

These opponents to abdication had an unexpectedly large impact; and the media seemed to assume that the Advisory Council might conclude not to accept abdication in accord with the emperor's expressed wishes. The newspapers wrote such things as "Eight in favor of abdication, six against, two expressing caution" and noted that if it came to a majority decision there would be deadlock.

Just as I started to worry about how the emperor must be reacting to these reports, one of his old school friends, Akashi Mototsugu, appeared in the media. He revealed that the emperor had expressed his feelings during a telephone call, saying, "I would like a system where abdication is possible, including in the future."

Akashi's remarks came exactly as the third specialist interview occurred, and around the time the trend was becoming clear. Given the timing, it is easy to imagine that the emperor felt a sense of crisis. As it happens, around that time Akashi approached me through an intermediary, saying he wanted to talk, but I politely declined, fearing that I might invite unwanted suspicions of a backroom deal. All the same, similar activities were going on behind the scenes.

These activities prompted a sense of crisis among both Advisory Council members and the Cabinet Office. The emperor's birthday was on December 23, and should he once again express his desire to abdicate, it would be impossible to deny that political intervention had occurred. Even more worryingly, some of the media had begun to speculate that the final report would simply set out both sides of the argument. If we sat on the fence, the Advisory Council would mean nothing. But luckily, right until the end all our members agreed on aiming for some kind of conclusion.

We Considered a "System of Mandatory Retirement"

In December, after all the interviews were finished, we reviewed the arguments. We started with the most important issue, permitting abdication or not permitting abdication, then examined one by one the issues and problems associated with those outcomes.

If abdication is not permitted, then the regency system stated in the law should be adopted. However, Article 16 of the Imperial House Law states that such a system would be adopted when the emperor cannot carry out official duties due to being "affected with a serious disease, mentally or physically, or there is a serious hindrance." At present the emperor is healthy, so this situation does not apply. In other words, the Imperial House Law would have to be revised to add a new condition.

On the other hand, if abdication was permitted what would the issues be? Article 4 of the Imperial House Law states, "Upon the demise of the Emperor, the Imperial Heir shall immediately accede to the Throne." It is written that imperial succession shall occur on the "demise" of the emperor and does not allow for the abdication of a living emperor. To make abdication part of the system, a new clause would have to be added here, too. In short, whether or not abdication is permitted, revision of the Imperial House Law would be necessary.

We also considered a system of mandatory retirement. But even though some emperors might express a wish to abdicate soon, other future emperors might want to keep going. It would be difficult to ask an energetic emperor to withdraw soon, and such a system would ignore each emperor's individual personality. What is more, if an administration of the time interpreted the clause according to the rules and encouraged abdication, that really would become an arbitrary intervention. Quite possibly, that could eventually destabilize the imperial throne.

Having thus reviewed the arguments, we stated our approval for a special exemption law, as laid out in the draft produced by the Advisory Council's secretariat. It read, "Although in principle, we should aim to revise the Imperial House Law, considering the current situation of the imperial throne, a debate on the issues of female houses and female succession would be unavoidable. Revision of the whole law would become necessary. If we are to avoid heading straight into a debate on amending the Imperial House Law and only make provisions to allow the current emperor to abdicate, we believe that a special exemption law is more appropriate."

Some in the public sphere have suggested that a one-off special exemption law is not the kind of solution the emperor desired, and the completely wrong course of action. But on this occasion, we faced a humanitarian issue, namely, helping the aging emperor, so it was imperative to implement a solution quickly. Precisely because it is a special exemption law, it is possible for the bill to detail the special situation of our current emperor and those reasons for his abdication of which most people in Japan are aware. Once it has become law, it will be followed as a precedent, and then after several occurrences will come to resemble something like a common law. In other words, I do not believe there is a conflict between a one-off special exemption law and making the change part of the system. And in the end, the course of action authorized by the Advisory Council was a one-off special exemption law.

It was December when the Advisory Council proposed abdication via a special exemption law, and around the same time new things started to happen in the Diet. Speaker of the House of Representatives Ōshima Tadamori and others stepped up to say that both houses should show independence and deal with the abdication issue.

We had been tasked by the government to discuss the issue based on a government proposal, so we thought it would be OK to continue our discussions, even in parallel with the Diet. But matters were not that simple.

I am the host of a current affairs program on TV called *Jiji Hōdan*, and all the politicians who appeared on the program around that time (either ruling party or opposition) made references to the Advisory Council. Most of them gave me a warning. "It is great that you are doing your best, but your members are not representatives of the people," they said. "It is we who have been chosen by the people, so don't get the wrong idea."

What is more, that December I gave a newspaper interview in which I said something along the lines of, "The special exemption law course of action is pretty much decided." In response, Speaker Ōshima said, "The Diet is not an organization that works for the Advisory Council." Probably, he believed that the Diet should not simply convert the Advisory Council proposal into a draft bill. Rather, it should independently decide on the content of the proposal itself. And I think that was a sound argument.

The Cabinet Office passed on our review of the issues to the Diet, and staff from the Advisory Council office also were summoned by the various factions to explain the situation. No further meetings of the Advisory Council were held until the bill was ready, and we entered a period of what you might call "hibernation."

We then waited for a summing up from speakers and deputy-speakers of the two houses before issuing the Advisory Council's final report on April 21. There was some criticism of the report as "having no depth" and "being too pragmatic," but I think this was partly due to not having put down the discussion process in writing. We feared that if we started to include the unused plans and the reasons why we did not use them, the debate would be reignited. That is how we made a deliberate and pragmatic decision to only put our conclusions in the report.

It Is Important to Expand the Imperial Family

One element of the final report that particularly captured the public's interest was that of titles: that post-abdication, the emperor and empress should be called retired emperor and retired empress, and Prince Akishino be called imperial heir. Prince Akishino has undertaken his official duties under his current title for almost thirty years and is still considerably attached to it, I have heard. So, it was difficult to simply suggest he abandon his Prince Akishino title and become the crown prince. Therefore, we came up with the suggestion of retaining the title Prince Akishino but also giving him the completely new title of imperial heir, which exists in the Imperial House Law but has no historic precedent. I believe we settled the issue in an appropriate manner.

As acting chair of the Advisory Council, I tried to address the abdication of the emperor not as an academic studying politics but as a Japanese citizen. If I were to view the issue as an academic, inevitably I would interpret it as an academic. A special exemption law is not an elegantly worded law, so I might have argued for amending the

Imperial House Law. Compromises of different kinds were made regarding various other aspects of the issue too. But if I had brought those up, the matter would never have ended. I made the pragmatic decision that, in order to resolve the issue, it would not be a good idea for me to get involved in situations that invited strong differences of opinion. Probably, the other members of the Advisory Council also acted according to their common sense and experience of the world. The final report of the Advisory Council contained decisions made by adults who had considered the issues as best they could, normally and with common sense.

As we were producing the final report, however, we all came to wonder whether it really was OK to let it end at this. Although this goes beyond our current remit, when we considered the imperial house so intensively we could not help but think about the imperial succession issue and more specifically whether the shrinking size of the imperial family was an acceptable situation.

When a new emperor is enthroned, that means there is one less heir. Just because we have Prince Akishino and Prince Hisahito, that does not mean we can rest easy. That is because Prince Hisahito is the only child from his generation in line to the throne. Increasing the size of the imperial family is one of the key issues relevant to removing this source of worry. During a dinner meeting that took place around the time we finished the first part of our work, the Advisory Council's chair Imai Takashi clearly conveyed this fact to Prime Minister Abe.

We felt that it was necessary to properly include these future issues in the final report, so we concluded the document with the following passage:

> In order for the imperial household to be able to continue its activities, we must quickly investigate measures to address the shrinking size of the imperial household. In the future, we hope that not only the government but also all sections and levels of society will discuss this issue in more detail.

Regarding the possibility of a reigning empress, there are many opponents to the idea, and it is not difficult to imagine a fierce debate. Advisory Council members were constantly mindful of the discussions about the shrinking size of the imperial family that will probably occur in the not too distant future.

We very much hope that Prime Minister Abe will proceed with revision for the Imperial House Law, including discussions such as these.

It is possible that it is easier for conservative politicians to bring reform to the imperial household issue than for liberal ones. I suspect that our conservative prime minister was not in favor of abdication from the first. Yet he considered both the support of the public and the feelings of the emperor and agreed with the current direction. A politician who can make that kind of decision should push the debate forward while he is still prime minister.

This issue is just as important as a constitutional revision. It has been reported that Princess Mako, the daughter of Prince Akishino, is planning to get married. There is no better time than now to consider how to deal with the female members of the imperial family. I hope that we will make use of this fortuitous opportunity to start a debate on the future nature of the imperial family.

English version originally published in *Discuss Japan—Japan Foreign Policy Forum*, no. 46, May 21, 2018. Translated from "'Tennō taii' yūshikisha kaigi no naijitsu: Kōshitsu no yukusue o kimeta nanakagetsu o furikaeru," *Bungei Shunjū* (July 2017): 172–80 (courtesy of Bungeishunjū Ltd.).

Chronology of the Heisei Era

Date	Event	Prime Minister
1989 Jan. 7	Death of Emperor Shōwa. Crown Prince Akihito enthroned. New era (beginning January 8) named Heisei.	Takeshita Noboru
Feb. 24	State funeral for Emperor Shōwa held.	
Apr. 25	Prime Minister Takeshita Noboru announces he will resign after enactment of fiscal budget to take responsibility for "political distrust" caused by Recruit scandal.	
May 12	Itō Masayoshi, chair of Liberal Democratic Party (LDP) General Council, declines the party's offer to become LDP president.	
May 30	Tokyo District Public Prosecutors Office announces close of Recruit scandal inquiry.	
Jun. 2	Takeshita cabinet resigns en masse. Uno Sōsuke appointed prime minister, forms cabinet.	Uno Sōsuke
Jun. 7	Foreign Ministry protests to Chinese ambassador over forcible suppression of Tiananmen Square demonstrations.	
Jul. 2	Japan Socialist Party (JSP) posts big gains in Tokyo Metropolitan Assembly election; LDP suffers major setback.	
Jul. 23	Ruling LDP loses upper house majority to opposition in 15th House of Councillors election.	
Aug. 10	Newly appointed prime minister Kaifu Toshiki forms cabinet.	Kaifu Toshiki
Sep. 10	JSP chairwoman Doi Takako releases "Doi vision" for a Socialist-led coalition government.	
Dec. 1	House of Councillors plenary session rejects settlement of accounts for FY 1987 and 1988 general account reserve funds (first time in 40 years).	
1990 Jan. 24	Prime Minister Kaifu dissolves House of Representatives, calls general election at start of session in break with precedent. Leaders of JSP and three other opposition parties agree to continue coalition talks.	
Feb. 18	LDP loses seats in 39th general election but retains secure majority in House of Representatives.	
Feb. 28	Prime Minister Kaifu forms second cabinet.	
Apr. 26	Government's Election System Council adopts report calling for parallel voting system for House of Representatives (roughly 500 seats, apportioned between single-seat districts and multi-member proportional-representation constituencies at a ratio of 6:4).	
Aug. 4	US president George H. W. Bush urges Prime Minister Kaifu to support sanctions against Iraq over invasion of Kuwait.	
Aug. 29	Prime Minister Kaifu announces package of cooperation and assistance to Middle East.	
Sep. 14	Cabinet approves second Middle East support package.	
Oct. 16	Kaifu cabinet submits UN Peace Cooperation Bill to Diet.	
Oct. 30	Government's Tax Commission adopts report recommending new land-holding tax.	

Date	Event	Prime Minister
Nov. 5	Kaifu cabinet withdraws UN Peace Cooperation Bill.	
Nov. 12	Enthronement ceremony for Emperor Akihito held.	
Dec. 29	Prime Minister Kaifu reshuffles second cabinet.	
1991 Jan. 17	Cabinet establishes Gulf crisis headquarters.	
Jan. 24	Government pledges additional $9 billion to support Gulf effort.	
Feb. 24	Government expresses full support for multinational force's ground assault into Iraqi-occupied Kuwait.	
Apr. 7	Suzuki Shunichi elected governor of Tokyo.	
Apr. 24	Government announces deployment of minesweepers to Persian Gulf.	
Jun. 22	Prime Minister Kaifu affirms "unwavering commitment" to political reform.	
Jul. 10	Cabinet approves three political reform bills.	
Sep. 30	Political reform bills die in committee by cross-partisan agreement after special committee chair Okonogi Hikosaburō calls for legislation to be scrapped.	
	Prime Minister Kaifu expresses deep disappointment with failure of political reform bills, speaks of "weighty decision."	
Oct. 4	Prime Minister Kaifu announces he will not seek reelection as LDP president.	
Oct. 27	Miyazawa Kiichi elected LDP president.	
Nov. 5	Newly appointed prime minister Miyazawa Kiichi forms cabinet.	Miyazawa Kiichi
1992 May 22	Japan New Party formed.	
Jun. 15	Act on Cooperation with United Nations Peacekeeping Operations and Other Operations (PKO Act) enacted.	
Jul. 26	LDP makes strong recovery in upper house in 16th House of Councillors election.	
Aug. 27	LDP vice president Kanemaru Shin announces resignation from post over receipt of ¥500 million in Sagawa Kyūbin scandal.	
Sep. 29	Kanemaru issued summary indictment and fined ¥200,000 by Tokyo Summary Court.	
Oct. 22	Obuchi Keizō chosen to replace Kanemaru as head of LDP's Takeshita faction. Splinter group led by Ozawa Ichirō and Hata Tsutomu announces formation of Reform Forum 21.	
Nov. 3	Sirius policy group formed centered on members of the Social Democratic Party of Japan (SDPJ, formerly JSP).	
Dec. 11	Prime Minister Miyazawa reshuffles cabinet.	

Date		Event	Prime Minister
1993	Mar. 31	LDP submits four political reform bills, including House of Representatives electoral reform (500 seats, all filled from single-seat districts).	
	Apr. 8	SDPJ and Kōmeitō jointly submit six political reform bills, including House of Representatives electoral reform (combination of single-seat districts and multi-member proportional-representation constituencies).	
	Apr. 17	Private-sector political reform council proposes House of Representatives electoral reform bill ("additional member" system of mixed voting: 300 seats filled from single-seat districts, 200 through proportional representation).	
	Jun. 9	Crown Prince Naruhito marries Owada Masako.	
	Jun. 13	Prime Minister Miyazawa loses no-confidence vote in House of Representatives, dissolves lower house.	
	Jun. 21	New Party Sakigake formed.	
	Jun. 23	Japan Renewal Party (Shinseitō) formed, setting in motion political realignment.	
	Jun. 27	Japan New Party scores big gains in Tokyo Metropolitan Assembly election.	
	Jul. 18	LDP loses absolute majority in 40th general election as three new parties post big gains in House of Representatives.	
	Jul. 22	Prime Minister Miyazawa announces resignation.	
	Jul. 23	Party leaders Hosokawa Morihiro (Japan New Party) and Takemura Masayoshi (New Party Sakigake) announce basic policy for coalition government dedicated to political reform.	
	Aug. 6	Doi Takako becomes first woman speaker of the House of Representatives. Hosokawa Morihiro selected prime minister by both houses of the Diet.	
	Aug. 9	Newly appointed prime minister Hosokawa Morihiro forms cabinet, presiding over eight-member coalition excluding LDP and Japanese Communist Party (JCP).	Hosokawa Morihiro
	Sep. 17	Cabinet approves four political reform bills featuring combination of single-seat districts and proportional representation in House of Representatives, a ban on corporate donations to individual politicians, and public funding for political parties.	
	Sep. 25	SDPJ holds party congress, affirms importance of anti-LDP coalition.	
	Nov. 18	Political reform legislation passes House of Representatives.	
	Dec. 16	Economic Reform Study Group (Hiraiwa Group) adopts final report.	
1994	Jan. 21	Political reform legislation voted down in House of Councillors plenary session.	
	Jan. 28	Prime Minister Hosokawa and LDP president Kōno Yōhei meet, reach compromise on political reform legislation.	
	Feb. 3	Prime Minister Hosokawa announces controversial plan for "national welfare tax" at early-morning press conference.	

Date	Event	Prime Minister
Mar. 4	Revised Political Reform Act enacted, combining single-seat districts and multi-member proportional-representation blocks in House of Representatives.	
Apr. 8	Prime Minister Hosokawa announces resignation.	
Apr. 26	SDPJ decides to leave coalition.	
Apr. 28	Newly appointed prime minister Hata Tsutomu forms minority cabinet.	Hata Tsutomu
Jun. 25	Hata cabinet resigns en masse.	
Jun. 29	SDPJ chair Murayama Tomiichi elected prime minister with support from LDP, SDPJ, and Sakigake, defeating Kaifu Toshiki (supported by Japan Renewal Party and Kōmeitō); many LDP and SDPJ politicians break ranks.	
Jun. 30	Newly appointed prime minister Murayama (SDPJ) forms coalition cabinet with LDP and Sakigake.	Murayama Tomiichi
Jul. 20	In Diet questioning, Prime Minister Murayama affirms constitutionality of Self-Defense Forces (SDF), pledges to maintain Japan-US security arrangements and to respect (then unofficial) Japanese flag and national anthem.	
Aug. 31	Prime Minister Murayama releases draft statement ahead of 50th anniversary of the end of World War II.	
Sep. 3	SDPJ reverses longstanding key policies.	
Sep. 6	Japan Renewal Party, Kōmeitō, Japan New Party, Democratic Socialist Party, and others enter into talks for merger into new party (excluding JCP).	
Sep. 20	Three ruling coalition parties agree on tax reform plan cutting income tax while raising consumption tax three years later, in 1997.	
Dec. 10	New Frontier Party formed.	
1995 Jan. 17	Great Hanshin-Awaji (Kobe) Earthquake strikes.	
Feb. 22	Basic Act on Reconstruction enacted.	
May 19	Decentralization Promotion Act promulgated.	
Jun. 9	House of Representatives adopts Diet resolution marking 50th anniversary of end of World War II.	
Jul. 23	LDP, SDPJ suffer major setbacks in 17th House of Councillors election; New Frontier Party doubles upper house strength.	
Aug. 15	Government releases "Murayama statement" on the 50th anniversary of the war's end.	
Sep. 22	Hashimoto Ryūtarō elected LDP president.	
Nov. 20	Japan-US Special Action Committee on Okinawa (SACO) meets for first time to discuss base issues.	
Dec. 19	Government, coalition parties approve infusion of public funds to dispose of nonperforming loans held by seven failing *jūsen* housing loan companies.	

Date	Event	Prime Minister
1996 Jan. 5	Prime Minister Murayama announces resignation, expressing intent to hand reins to LDP president Hashimoto.	
Jan. 11	Newly appointed prime minister Hashimoto forms cabinet.	Hashimoto Ryūtarō
Feb. 16	Minister of Health and Welfare Kan Naoto admits government culpability in infection of hemophilia patients with HIV through tainted blood products, apologizes to victims.	
Mar. 4	New Frontier Party, protesting *jūsen* appropriations, holds sit-in outside House of Representatives Budget Committee room to block action on budget bill.	
Jun. 18	Diet passes *jūsen* liquidation bill and five-bill package to shore up banking system.	
Jun. 25	Cabinet approves plan to raise consumption tax from 3 percent to 5 percent in April 1997.	
Sep. 11	Diet politicians from Sakigake, Social Democratic Party (SDP, established as a new party by former members of the SDPJ), etc., call for formation of Democratic Party of Japan.	
Sep. 18	SDP splits.	
Sep. 28	Democratic Party of Japan (DPJ) holds inaugural convention.	
Oct. 20	LDP makes gains in 41st general election, held under new House of Representatives electoral system; New Frontier Party loses seats, JCP nearly doubles strength.	
Nov. 7	Prime Minister Hashimoto forms second cabinet, all-LDP.	
Nov. 8	Prime Minister Hashimoto establishes administrative reform authority, pledging wholesale reorganization and consolidation of central government ministries and agencies by 2001.	
Dec. 2	SACO releases final report, calling for return of 11 US military installations or areas and construction of sea-based facility off east coast of Okinawa to replace heliport functions of Futenma air base.	
1997 Mar. 18	Prime Minister Hashimoto announces five principles of fiscal reform at Conference on Fiscal Structural Reform.	
Sep. 22	Satō Kōkō resigns as new director general of Management and Coordination Agency following sharp criticism of inaugural press conference; Prime Minister Hashimoto apologizes for appointment.	
Dec. 3	Administrative Reform Council adopts final report, calling for central government reorganization and reforms to strengthen policymaking and other powers of the prime minister.	
Dec. 27	New Frontier Party dissolves, splinters into several small parties.	
1998 Jan. 26	Finance Ministry officials arrested on suspicion of taking bribes, leading to resignation of finance minister two days later.	
Apr. 27	DPJ, Good Governance Party (Minseitō), New Fraternity Party (Shintō Yūai), and Minshu Kaikaku Rengō (Democratic Reform League) merge to form new Democratic Party of Japan (DPJ).	
Jun. 1	LDP, SDP, and Sakigake decide to terminate alliance.	

Date	Event	Prime Minister
Jun. 20	Group of 7 (G7) and Asian finance officials hold emergency meeting in response to falling yen, reaffirm international policy coordination.	
Jul. 12	LDP suffers massive defeat in 18th House of Councillors election; DPJ and JCP post big gains.	
Jul. 13	Prime Minister Hashimoto announces resignation.	
Jul. 30	Newly appointed prime minister Obuchi Keizō forms cabinet.	Obuchi Keizō
Sep. 28	Prime Minister Obuchi yields to opposition leaders in compromise on government's legislation to stabilize banking system.	
Oct. 16	Act on Emergency Measures for Early Strengthening of Financial Functions enacted following incorporation of opposition's revisions.	
Nov. 7	(New) Kōmeitō formed with merger of New Peace Party (lower house) and Kōmei (upper house).	
Nov. 19	Prime Minister Obuchi and Liberal Party head Ozawa Ichirō reach agreement on LDP-Liberal coalition ahead of ordinary Diet session.	
1999 Jan. 12	Headquarters for the Administrative Reform of the Central Government adopts draft guidelines for government reorganization beginning in 2001.	
Mar. 1	Top ruling and opposition parties agree to establishment of Diet commissions on the constitution.	
May 7	Information Disclosure Act enacted.	
Jul. 8	Diet passes package of bills for reorganization of central government and another for decentralization of administrative power.	
Jul. 26	Diet reform law enacted; party leaders' debate (*tōshu tōron*) and other reforms adopted.	
Aug. 9	Diet passes bills officially recognizing national flag (*hinomaru*) and national anthem ("Kimigayo").	
Oct. 5	Prime Minister Obuchi forms second cabinet; Kōmeitō joins LDP-Liberal coalition.	
Nov. 22	Okinawa prefectural government names Henoko district in Nago as site for replacement of Futenma air base facilities, seeks approval from city of Nago.	
Dec. 27	Mayor of Nago announces city will accept construction of Futenma replacement facilities provided use is limited to 15 years.	
2000 Mar. 16	Three coalition parties reach basic agreement on police reforms.	
Apr. 1	Liberal Party leaves coalition.	
Apr. 2	Prime Minister Obuchi hospitalized with massive stroke.	
Apr. 3	Liberal Party splits; group favoring coalition with LDP forms Conservative Party.	
Apr. 5	Newly appointed prime minister Mori Yoshirō forms coalition cabinet (LDP, Kōmeitō, Conservative Party).	Mori Yoshirō
Jun. 25	DPJ scores big gains in 42nd general election.	

Date	Event	Prime Minister
Jul. 21	26th Group of Eight (G8) summit (Kyushu-Okinawa Summit) kicks off.	
Oct. 26	Diet enacts House of Councillors electoral reform featuring proportional representation using open-list system, effective in 2001.	
Nov. 21	No-confidence motion against Mori cabinet by four opposition parties fails in House of Representatives after internal revolt led by Katō Kōichi ("Katō rebellion") aborts.	
Dec. 5	Prime Minister Mori forms second cabinet.	
2001 Jan. 6	Government reorganized into 12 ministries and Cabinet Office; posts of senior vice-minister and parliamentary secretary established.	
Apr. 24	Koizumi Junichirō elected LDP president.	
Apr. 26	Newly appointed prime minister Koizumi forms cabinet.	Koizumi Junichirō
Jun. 21	Council on Economic and Fiscal Policy (Cabinet Office) adopts basic policies for structural reform.	
Jul. 29	LDP and coalition partner Kōmeitō secure upper house majority in 19th House of Councillors election.	
Nov. 2	Anti-Terrorism Special Measures Act and associated legislation promulgated.	
Nov. 22	Coalition party leaders agree on plan to streamline and privatize Japan Highway Public Corporation and other highway and bridge authorities.	
Dec. 14	Revised PKO Act enacted.	
Dec. 22	Japan Coast Guard vessels engage in gun battle with suspicious ship.	
2002 Feb. 12	Foreign Ministry announces 10-point blueprint for internal reform.	
Apr. 21	Prime Minister Koizumi visits Yasukuni Shrine.	
May 28	Japan Federation of Economic Organizations (Keidanren) and Japan Federation of Employers' Associations (Nikkeiren) merge to form Japan Business Federation (today's Keidanren).	
Sep. 17	Prime Minister Koizumi visits North Korea, meets with General Secretary Kim Jong-il.	
Oct. 15	Five Japanese abductees living in North Korea temporarily reunited with families in Japan.	
Dec. 18	Act on Special Districts for Structural Reform promulgated.	
Dec. 24	Chief Cabinet Secretary Fukuda Yasuo, speaking at private gathering, calls for nonreligious national facility to honor Japan's war dead.	
2003 Mar. 20	Prime Minister Koizumi expresses support for US invasion of Iraq.	
Jun. 6	Diet enacts three security laws pertaining to emergency situations, including Armed Attack Situation Response Act.	
Jun. 18	Council on Economic and Fiscal Policy adopts basic policies for reform of local public finances (Trinity Reform).	
Aug. 1	Iraq Reconstruction Special Measures Act promulgated, opening way for dispatch of SDF to region.	

Date	Event	Prime Minister
Sep. 24	Liberal Party merges with DPJ.	
Nov. 9	DPJ gains seats in 43rd general election.	
Nov. 10	New Conservative Party merges with LDP.	
Nov. 13	Government commission on local administrative system issues recommendations for municipal mergers.	
Dec. 9	Cabinet approves basic plan for dispatch of SDF troops to Iraq.	
2004 Jan. 17	JCP congress adopts new, fundamentally revised platform.	
Jan. 31	Dispatch of SDF approved by House of Representatives (followed by House of Councillors on February 9).	
Mar. 30	House of Representatives Security Committee passes resolution on preservation of Japan's territorial integrity, including Senkaku Islands.	
May 22	Prime Minister Koizumi meets with North Korean leader Kim Jong-il in Pyongyang. Children of repatriated abductees reunited with parents in Japan.	
May 28	Saiban-in Act promulgated, establishing system for participation of "lay judges" (*saiban-in*) in criminal trials.	
Jun. 11	Pension reform law promulgated, establishing mechanisms for long-term balancing of burdens and benefits.	
Jun. 18	Seven emergency-related security laws promulgated (including Civil Protection Act).	
Jul. 11	DPJ gains seats in 20th House of Councillors election.	
Nov. 26	Government, ruling party agree on outlines of Trinity Reform of local public finance (reduction of subsidies, transfer of taxing authority to local governments).	
2005 Apr. 1	Personal Information Protection Act enters into force.	
Apr. 15	House of Representatives Commission on the Constitution adopts final report, including views on constitutional revision (followed by report of upper house commission on April 20).	
Aug. 1	LDP committee releases constitutional revision draft.	
Aug. 8	Postal privatization bill submitted by Koizumi cabinet voted down in House of Councillors, with LDP politicians breaking ranks. Prime Minister Koizumi dissolves House of Representatives, calls general election.	
Sep. 11	LDP scores landslide victory in 44th general election, winning commanding majority in House of Representatives.	
Oct. 14	Postal privatization law enacted.	
Dec. 27	National census results indicate first recorded decline in Japan's total population.	

Date		Event	Prime Minister
2006	Apr. 7	Government and city of Nago reach basic agreement on relocation of US Futenma air base facilities to Henoko.	
	Jun. 20	Government decides to withdraw Ground SDF troops from Iraq.	
		City of Yūbari in Hokkaido declares itself financially insolvent.	
	Sep. 26	Newly appointed prime minister Abe Shinzō forms cabinet.	Abe Shinzō
	Dec. 22	New Basic Act on Education promulgated.	
2007	Jan. 9	Ministry of Defense established.	
	Feb. 17	Social Insurance Agency's mishandling of public pension records comes to light.	
	May 18	Law on procedure for constitutional revision referendum promulgated.	
	Jul. 29	DPJ overtakes LDP as top party in upper house in 21st House of Councillors election.	
	Sep. 26	Newly appointed prime minister Fukuda Yasuo forms cabinet.	Fukuda Yasuo
	Oct. 1	Postal service privatized, Japan Post Group launched.	
2008	Jan. 16	New anti-terrorism law, required to continue Maritime SDF's refueling operations in Indian Ocean, promulgated after House of Representatives passes bill a second time, overriding House of Councillors.	
	Mar. 19	House of Councillors rejects government's nominee for Bank of Japan governor, leaving post vacant for first time since World War II.	
	Apr. 1	Health insurance scheme for persons 75 and older instituted.	
	Jul. 7	G8 Hokkaido Tōyako Summit kicks off.	
	Sep. 24	Newly appointed prime minister Asō Tarō forms cabinet.	Asō Tarō
2009	Feb. 16	Government announces that GDP for October–December 2008 contracted at an annual rate of more than 12 percent, largest decline since 1974 oil shock.	
	Jul. 1	Public Records and Archives Management Act promulgated.	
	Aug. 30	DPJ wins in landslide in 45th general election; LDP loses control of House of Representatives and government.	
	Sep. 16	Newly appointed prime minister Hatoyama Yukio (DPJ) forms coalition cabinet with SDP, People's New Party.	Hatoyama Yukio
	Nov. 27	DPJ government completes promised review of government programs, intended to cut wasteful spending from budget.	
2010	Apr. 1	DPJ government implements child allowance, free public schooling through high school.	
	May 30	SDP decides to leave coalition.	
	Jun. 8	Newly appointed prime minister Kan Naoto (DPJ) forms coalition cabinet with People's New Party.	Kan Naoto
	Jul. 11	DPJ suffers substantial losses in 22nd House of Councillors election.	
	Dec. 17	Cabinet approves new National Defense Program Guidelines.	

	Date	Event	Prime Minister
2011	Feb. 14	Government figures for 2010 show Japan fell behind China in nominal GDP, dropping to third in the world.	
	Mar. 11	Great East Japan Earthquake strikes; earthquake and tsunami trigger nuclear accident at Fukushima Daiichi Nuclear Power Plant; nuclear emergency declared.	
	Sep. 2	Newly appointed prime minister Noda Yoshihiko forms cabinet.	Noda Yoshihiko
	Dec. 2	Law on financing of reconstruction from Great East Japan Earthquake promulgated.	
2012	Feb. 10	Reconstruction Agency established.	
	Aug. 22	Law on social security and tax reform promulgated, mandating two-stage increase in consumption tax.	
	Sep. 11	Japanese government purchases three of the Senkaku Islands from private owner.	
	Dec. 16	LDP regains control of House of Representatives and government as DPJ suffers rout in 46th general election; Japan Restoration Party posts big gains.	
	Dec. 26	Newly appointed prime minister Abe Shinzō forms second cabinet.	Abe Shinzō
2013	Jan. 22	Government and Bank of Japan jointly set 2 percent inflation target, launch new monetary easing policy.	
	Mar. 15	Prime Minister Abe announces decision to enter negotiations for Trans-Pacific Partnership (TPP).	
	May 31	My Number Act promulgated, paving way for individual taxpayer ID numbers.	
	Jun. 14	Cabinet approves Japan Revitalization Strategy and Basic Policy on Economic and Fiscal Management and Reform, adopting new expansionary economic policy ("Abenomics").	
	Jul. 21	LDP-Kōmeitō coalition posts big gains in 23rd House of Councillors election, securing upper house majority; DPJ suffers massive losses.	
	Dec. 13	State Secrets Act promulgated.	
	Dec. 26	Prime Minister Abe visits Yasukuni Shrine; US government expresses "disappointment."	
2014	Jan. 7	National Security Secretariat established within Cabinet Secretariat to support new National Security Council.	
	Apr. 1	Consumption tax raised to 8 percent from 5 percent.	
	Jun. 20	Revised Act on the Organization and Operation of Local Educational Administration promulgated.	
	Jul. 1	Cabinet adopts resolution allowing Japan to engage in collective self-defense, previously seen as prohibited under the Constitution.	
	Nov. 18	Prime Minister Abe postpones until April 2017 planned increase in consumption tax rate from 8 percent to 10 percent (subsequently postpones it until 2019).	
	Dec. 14	Ruling coalition gains seats in 47th general election, maintains commanding majority in House of Representatives.	

Date		Event	Prime Minister
2015	Apr. 1	Government institutes new support system for children and child-rearing.	
	May 11	LDP and coalition partner Kōmeitō reach agreement on security legislation to expand scope of SDF's activities overseas.	
	Sep. 19	House of Councillors passes security bills (promulgated September 30).	
	Oct. 31	Ōsaka Ishin no Kai (Initiatives from Osaka), later renamed Nippon Ishin, holds inaugural convention.	
	Nov. 22	Candidates of reformist Osaka Restoration Association win election as mayor of Osaka and governor of Osaka.	
2016	Feb. 5	Cabinet approves bill to institute a reduced consumption tax rate for food and newspapers.	
	Mar. 27	Democratic Party (DP) formed through merger of DPJ and Japan Innovation Party (Ishin no Tō).	
	May 20	Diet enacts legislation to reduce number of seats in House of Representatives and address malapportionment.	
	May 26	G7 Ise-Shima Summit kicks off.	
	Jun. 1	Prime Minister Abe announces intent to postpone consumption tax hike two and a half years, to October 2019.	
	Jun. 19	Voting age lowered to 18 as revised Public Offices Election Act enters into force.	
	Jul. 10	LDP-Kōmeitō coalition gains 10 seats in 24th House of Councillors election to strengthen upper house majority.	
	Jul. 13	Emperor Akihito expresses wish to abdicate.	
	Oct. 26	LDP approves rule change extending party president's maximum tenure from six years to nine years (three consecutive three-year terms).	
	Dec. 9	Diet approves TPP, enacts related legislation.	
2017	Apr. 21	Government's advisory panel on easing emperor's official duties adopts final report.	
	May 31	Central government, Tokyo Metropolitan Government, and Olympic Organizing Committee reach basic agreement on cost sharing for Tokyo Olympic and Paralympic Games (scheduled for 2020).	
	Jun. 9	Diet enacts law allowing abdication of Emperor Akihito.	
	Jul. 2	Koike Yuriko's new Tomin First no Kai secures plurality in Tokyo Metropolitan Assembly election; LDP suffers rout.	
	Sep. 25	Tokyo governor Koike Yuriko forms national party Kibō no Tō (Party of Hope).	
	Sep. 28	Democratic Party (DP) leadership approves merger with Kibō no Tō.	
	Oct. 2	Constitutional Democratic Party (CDP) formed by left-leaning DP members.	
	Oct. 22	LDP maintains supermajority in House of Representatives in 48th general election.	

Date	Event	Prime Minister
2018 Mar. 9	Tax Agency chief Sagawa Nobuhisa resigns in connection with accusations of document tampering stemming from 2016 Moritomo Gakuen affair. Finance Ministry acknowledges documents were altered.	
May 7	Democratic Party for the People formed.	
Jun. 13	Age of majority lowered from 20 to 18 through revision of Civil Code.	
Jun. 29	Diet enacts legislation for work-style reform. Diet enacts legislation to ratify Comprehensive and Progressive Agreement for Trans-Pacific Partnership (TPP-11).	
Jul. 18	Revised Public Offices Election Act enacted, adding six seats to House of Councillors.	
Sep. 20	Prime Minister Abe elected LDP president for third consecutive term.	
Oct. 2	Prime Minister Abe reshuffles cabinet.	
Dec. 8	Diet enacts revised Immigration Control Act, opening way for influx of foreign workers.	
Dec. 30	TPP-11 trade agreement enters into force following ratification by sixth member.	
2019 Jan. 8	Ministry of Health, Labour and Welfare acknowledges irregularities in collection of wage data resulting in underpayment of benefits.	
Feb. 1	Japan-EU Economic Partnership Agreement enters into force.	
Mar. 27	Diet passes ¥101 trillion budget, first initial budget surpassing ¥100 trillion.	
Apr. 1	Government selects Reiwa as name of new era.	
Apr. 7	Osaka Restoration Association prevails in Osaka mayoral and gubernatorial elections.	
Apr. 30	Emperor Akihito abdicates.	
May 1	Crown Prince Naruhito enthroned, becoming 126th emperor in traditional order of succession. Era name changes from Heisei to Reiwa.	

About the Supervisor and Editor

Kitaoka Shinichi is professor emeritus of the University of Tokyo and Rikkyo University and special advisor to the president of the Japan International Cooperation Agency (JICA). He received his PhD in modern Japanese politics and diplomacy from the University of Tokyo and subsequently taught at Rikkyo University and his alma mater. He has held posts as Japan's ambassador extraordinary and plenipotentiary, and the deputy representative to the United Nations and president of the International University of Japan. He held the post of JICA president from 2015 to 2022. He has authored many English publications, including *The Political History of Modern Japan: Foreign Relations and Domestic Politics* (Routledge, 2018) and *From Party Politics to Militarism in Japan, 1924–1941* (Lynne Rienner, 2021), and was supervising editor for *A Western Pacific Union: Japan's New Geopolitical Strategy* (JPIC, 2023).

Iio Jun is professor at the National Graduate Institute for Policy Studies (GRIPS). He graduated from the Faculty of Law of the University of Tokyo, from where he also received his MA and PhD in political science. He has previously worked as associate professor at the Graduate School of Policy Science, Saitama University. He is the co-editor of *Policy Analysis in Japan* (Policy Press, 2015) together with Adachi Yukio and Hosono Sukehiro. His research interests include Japanese party politics, the role of the bureaucracy in the Japanese political system, and comparative public policy.

About the Authors

Inoguchi Takashi is former president of the University of Niigata Prefecture, professor emeritus at the University of Tokyo, eminent scholar-professor at J. F. Oberlin University (Tokyo), and senior fellow of research and development at Chuo University. He is former United Nations assistant secretary-general and has been a senior fellow at Chuo University's Comprehensive Research and Organization since April 2023. He received his BA and MA from the University of Tokyo and his PhD from the Massachusetts Institute of Technology (MIT). He is a member of the Science Council of Japan, founding editor of the *Japanese Journal of Political Science*, *International Relations of the Asia Pacific*, and *Asian Journal of the Comparative Politics*, director of the AsiaBarometer project, and chairman of the Asian Consortium for Political Research. He writes prolifically on education and politics in Japan, international affairs, and quality of life and typology of Asian societies. He received the Helen Dinerman Award in 2021 and is listed 1,226th globally and 1st in Japan in the 2023 Research. com ranking of best researchers in political science.

Kabashima Ikuo is governor of Kumamoto Prefecture (fourth term) and emeritus professor of the University of Tokyo. He received his BA in agriculture from the University of Nebraska, MPA from Harvard Kennedy School, and PhD in political science economy and economics from Harvard University. Before his career in public service, he was professor at the Graduate Schools for Law and Politics, University of Tokyo, and served as dean of the Graduate School of International Political Economy at the University of Tsukuba. He is the co-author of *Changing Politics in Japan* (Cornell University Press, 2009). His research interests include political parties, political participation, media, and elections.

Kamikawa Ryūnoshin is professor at the Graduate School of Law and Politics, Osaka University. He graduated from the Faculty of Law, Kyoto University, and received his MA and PhD from the Graduate School of Law at the same institution. Previously he was visiting associate professor at National Chengchi University in Taiwan and associate professor at Osaka University. He specializes in governmental process theory. His publications include *Nihon Ginkō to seiji* [Politics and the Bank of Japan] (Chūōkōron Shinsha, 2014), *Koizumi kaikaku no seijigaku* [A Political Analysis of Koizumi's Reforms] (Tōyō Keizai, 2010), and *Denryoku to seiji* [Electricity and Politics] (Keisō Shobō, 2018).

Machidori Satoshi is professor of political science at Kyoto University's Graduate School of Law. He graduated from Kyoto University's Faculty of Law and received his PhD from the same institution. He has previously worked as assistant professor at Osaka University and visiting researcher at the University of California, San Diego. He specializes in comparative politics. His publications include *Shushō seiji no seido bunseki* [The Japanese Premiership: An Institutional Analysis of Power Relations] (Chikura Shobō, 2012), which was awarded the Suntory Prize in Political Science and Economics in the same year, and *Political Reform Reconsidered: The Trajectory of a Transformed Japanese State* (Springer, 2023).

Makihara Izuru is professor at the Research Center for Advanced Science and Technology (RCAST), University of Tokyo. He graduated from the Faculty of Law at the University of Tokyo. His previous academic positions include professor at the School of Law, Tōhoku University and research scholar at the London School of Economics and Political Science (LSE). He specializes in public administration and political study, with a focus on postwar Japanese political history, judicial politics, and interdisciplinary public policy research.

Mikuriya Takashi is a fellow at the University of Tokyo's Research Center for Advanced Science and Technology (RCAST), professor emeritus of the University of Tokyo, and a member of the board of directors of Suntory Holdings Ltd. He graduated from the Faculty of Law, University of Tokyo, and received his DPhil from the same institution. He has previously been a visiting researcher at Harvard University and professor at the National Graduate Institute for Policy Studies (GRIPS), Tokyo Metropolitan University, and the Open University of Japan. He specializes in political history, oral history, and public policy.

Nakakita Kōji is professor at the Faculty of Law, Chuo University. He received his LLB from the University of Tokyo's Faculty of Law, and his LLM and LLD from the same university's Graduate School of Law. He has previously been visiting researcher at Harvard University and the Suntory and Toyota International Centres for Economics and Related Disciplines (STICERD) at the London School of Economics and Political Science (LSE), and taught as professor at Osaka City University, Rikkyo University, and Hitotsubashi University. He specializes in Japanese political history and contemporary Japanese politics.

Nakano Minoru (1943–2001) was a political scientist. He graduated from Waseda University's School of

Political Science and Economics and completed his doctoral studies at the same university. After teaching as an assistant at the University of Tokyo's Faculty of Law and as professor at the Faculty of Humanities, Ibaraki University, he taught as professor at Faculty of Law, Meiji Gakuin University. Among his publications available in English are *New Japanese Political Economy and Political Reform* (editor; European Press Academic Publishing, 2002) and *The Policy-Making Process in Contemporary Japan* (Palgrave Macmillan, 1997). He specialized in political process theory and Japanese politics.

Nonaka Naoto is professor at Gakushūin University's Faculty of Law. He graduated from the University of Tokyo's Faculty of Letters and received his DPhil in international relations from the Graduate School of Arts and Sciences at the same university. He has worked as a researcher and senior fellow at the Asia Pacific Institute of Research, assistant at the School of International Relations, University of Shizuoka, and was an overseas researcher at the Nissan Institute of Japanese Studies, Oxford University. His publications include *Saraba Garapagosu seiji: Kimerareru Nihon ni tsukurinaosu* [Farewell to Galapagos Government: Building a Japan that Can Decide] (Nihon Keizai Shimbun Shuppansha, 2013). He specializes in comparative political science.

Sakaiya Shirō is professor of Japanese politics in the Graduate Schools for Law and Politics, University of Tokyo. He graduated from the Faculty of Law, University of Tokyo, and received his MA and PhD in law from the same university. He also holds an MA in political science from the University of California. He has previously taught as an associate professor and professor at Tokyo Metropolitan University. His publications include *Kenpō to yoron* [The Constitution and Public Opinion] (Chikuma Shobō, 2017). His areas of interest include elections, political participation, public opinion, and ideology.

Sasaki Takeshi is professor emeritus of the University of Tokyo, president of the Japan Academy, and recipient of the Order of Culture. He has also been awarded the Grand Cordon of the Order of the Sacred Treasure and designated as a Person of Cultural Merit. He received his bachelor and doctor of law from the University of Tokyo. He has previously been professor and dean at the University of Tokyo Graduate Schools for Law and Politics, professor at the Gakushūin University Faculty of Law, and served as president of the University of Tokyo and also of the Japan Association of National Universities (JANU).

Sassa Atsuyuki (1930–2018) was the first director general of the Cabinet Security Affairs Office (1986–89). He graduated from the Faculty of Law, University of Tokyo, and joined the National Rural Police (now National Police Agency, or NPA). While at the NPA, he was responsible for handling the Yasuda Hall incident and the Asama-Sansō incident. He also worked for the Defense Agency and headed the Defense Facilities Administration Agency. After retirement, he was a frequent commentator on Japanese politics.

Shinkawa Toshimitsu is professor of politics at Hosei University, emeritus professor at Kyoto University, and the former president of the Japan Association for Comparative Politics (JACP). He received his PhD in political science from the University of Toronto. He has previously taught as associate professor and professor at Niigata University's Faculty of Law, and professor at the Hokkaido University School of Law and Graduate School of Law. He is the co-editor of *Ageing and Pension Reform Around the World* (Edward Elgar, 2005). His research interests include the welfare state and political economy.

Shinoda Tomohito is professor at the Graduate School of International Relations at the International University of Japan (IUJ) in Niigata, Japan. He received his BA in American studies from Osaka University of Foreign Studies, MA in international relations from IUJ, and his PhD in international relations from the Paul H. Nitze School of Advanced International Studies (SAIS), Johns Hopkins University. Before taking up his current role, he taught as assistant professor and as associate professor at IUJ. He also served as an advisor to the defense minister. His research interests include the history of international relations and foreign policy making. His publications include *Contemporary Japanese Politics: Institutional Changes and Power Shifts* (Columbia University Press, 2013).

Shinohara Hajime (1925–2015) was a political scientist and longtime professor at the University of Tokyo's Faculty of Law. Later he taught as professor at Seikei University's Faculty of Humanities. He specialized in European political history with a focus on Germany.

Sugawara Taku is an independent political scientist. After graduating from the Faculty of Law at the University of Tokyo, he completed his doctorate at the Graduate Schools for Law and Politics at the same institution. He taught as an associate professor at the Research Center for Advanced Science and Technology (RCAST). He currently lectures at universities, leads several political media surveys as a data scientist, and is an active political commentator through various media. He specializes in the Japanese electoral system and contemporary Japanese politics, and is the author of the *Kokkai giin hakusho* (White Paper on Diet Members, https://kokkai.sugawarataku.net), a collection of data on the activities of successive generations of Diet members.

Takenaka Harukata is professor at the National Graduate Institute for Policy Studies (GRIPS), Tokyo, and the chair of the Editorial Planning Committee at Nippon.com. He graduated from the University of Tokyo's Faculty of Law and received his PhD in political science from Stanford University. He has previously taught as associate professor at GRIPS. His publications include *Korona kiki no seiji* [Politics of the Covid-19 Crisis] (Chūōkōron Shinsha, 2020), *Failed Democratization in Prewar Japan* (Stanford University Press, 2014), and *Sangiin to wa nani ka* [What Is the House of Councillors?] (Chūōkōron Shinsha, 2010), winner of the Osaragi Jirō Rondan Prize.

Tanaka Aiji is professor of political science and president of Waseda University. He also serves as president of the Japan Association of Private Universities and Colleges (JAPUC). He received his BA in political science from the School of Political Science and Economics, Waseda University, and his MA and PhD in political science from Ohio State University. He has previously held positions as president of the Japanese Association of Electoral Studies, executive board member of the Japanese Political Science Association (JPSA), and president of the International Political Science Association (IPSA), and has taught at Seisa Dohto University, Tōyō Eiwa University, and Aoyama Gakuin University.

Tanaka Naoki is president of the Center for International Public Policy Studies (CIPPS). He graduated from the University of Tokyo's Faculty of Law and received his PhD from the same institution. He helped to create and was previously president of the 21st Century Public Policy Institute, established by Nippon Keidanren (Japan Business Federation), and has been a senior analyst at the Research Institute on the National Economy. He was also a special economic advisor to former prime minister Koizumi Junichirō. He has published numerous books and is the recipient of the Yoshino Sakuzō Prize and Ishibashi Tanzan Prize.

Taniguchi Masaki is professor of political science at the Graduate Schools for Law and Politics, University of Tokyo, and president of the Nippon Institute for Research Advancement (NIRA). He was commissioner of the National Commission for the Management of Political Funds (three terms), nominated by the Japanese Diet, and is currently on the board of directors for the Japan Productivity Center (JPC). He received his LLB from the University of Tokyo's Faculty of Law and PhD in political science from the same institution. He has previously served as a board member on the Japanese Political Science Association (JPSA).

Uenohara Hideaki is associate professor in the Faculty of Human Sciences at Bunkyō University. He graduated from the University of Tokyo and received his MA in law from the same university. He has previously worked as a project research fellow in the Graduate Schools for Law and Politics at the University of Tokyo and as a research fellow in the Research Center for Japanese General Social Surveys (JGSS), Osaka University of Commerce. His research interests include internet campaigning, political communication, media politics, money politics, and voting behavior.

Yamaguchi Jirō is professor of political science at Hosei University and a board member for the New Diplomacy Initiative (ND). He graduated from the University of Tokyo's Faculty of Law and was subsequently an assistant at the same institution. He attended Cornell University as a Fulbright scholar and worked as a visiting fellow at Oxford University's St. Anthony College and at Warwick University. He has also taught as professor in the School of Law at Hokkaido University. His primary research interests are public administration and contemporary politics.

Yayama Tarō is a political commentator and chairman of the Japan Forum for Strategic Studies (JFSS). He graduated from Tōhoku University with a BA in French literature. He worked as a political and overseas correspondent in Rome and Geneva at Jiji Press, going on to become a member of the editorial board. He previously served as representative director of the Association to Revise Textbooks.

（英文版) 論文集 平成日本を振り返る　第二巻 政治
Examining Heisei Japan, Vol. II: Politics

2023 年 11 月 30 日　第 1 刷発行

監　　　修	北岡伸一
責任編集・著者	飯尾 潤
著　　　者	猪口 孝、上ノ原秀晃、蒲島郁夫、上川龍之進、境家史郎、佐々木 毅、佐々淳行、信田智人、篠原 一、新川敏光、菅原 琢、竹中治堅、田中愛治、田中直毅、谷口将紀、中北浩爾、中野 実、野中尚人、牧原 出、待鳥聡史、御厨 貴、山口二郎、屋山太郎（五十音順）
企　　　画	公益財団法人日本国際問題研究所
発　行　所	一般財団法人出版文化産業振興財団
	〒101-0051 東京都千代田区神田神保町2-2-30
	電話　03-5211-7283
	ホームページ　https://www.jpic.or.jp/
印 刷・製 本 所	大日本印刷株式会社

定価はカバーに表示してあります。
本書の無断複写（コピー）、転載は著作権法の例外を除き、禁じられています。

Printed in Japan
hardcover ISBN 978-4-86658-247-4
ebook (ePub) ISBN 978-4-86658-171-2